Dis…Miss gender?

Dis...Miss gender?

Edited by Anne Bray

The MIT Press
Cambridge, Massachusetts
London, England

The MIT Press would like to thank the anonymous peer reviewers
who provided comments on drafts of this book. The generous
work of academic experts is essential for establishing the authority
and quality of our publications. We acknowledge with gratitude
the contributions of these otherwise uncredited readers.

This book was set in Lust designed by DesNeil Summerour
from Positype and Lato text designed by Łukasz Dziedzic.
Printed and bound in Italy.

Library of Congress Cataloging-in-Publication Data

Names: Bray, Anne, 1949- editor.
Title: Dis...miss gender? / edited by Anne Bray.
Description: Cambridge, Massachusetts : The MIT Press, [2023]
Identifiers: LCCN 2022045219 (print) | LCCN 2022045220 (ebook) | ISBN
   9780262546447 (paperback) | ISBN 9780262376129 (epub) | ISBN
   9780262376112 (pdf)
Subjects: LCSH: Gender identity. | Feminist theory. | Queer theory.
Classification: LCC HQ18.55 .D57 2023 (print) | LCC HQ18.55 (ebook) | DDC
   305.3--dc23/eng/20221227
LC record available at https://lccn.loc.gov/2022045219
LC ebook record available at https://lccn.loc.gov/2022045220

10 9 8 7 6 5 4 3 2 1

We dedicate this book to all those who justly
embrace the vast potential of gender.

contents

0   introduction   1

1   ain't i a womxn?   7

2   how does gender perform you?   37

3   what is the problem? my body? or socety's perception of my body?   55

4   sister, are you psyco?   71

5   what is your myth and fact about rape?   91

6   how can feminism support equality?   109

7   who decided your gender?   133

8   what makes you bang your head?   151

9   who do you worship?   171

10 what are they singing?   189

11 what were you born for?   205

12 love &/or fear   223

13 change the narrative   245

14 acknowledgments & contributors   250

introduction

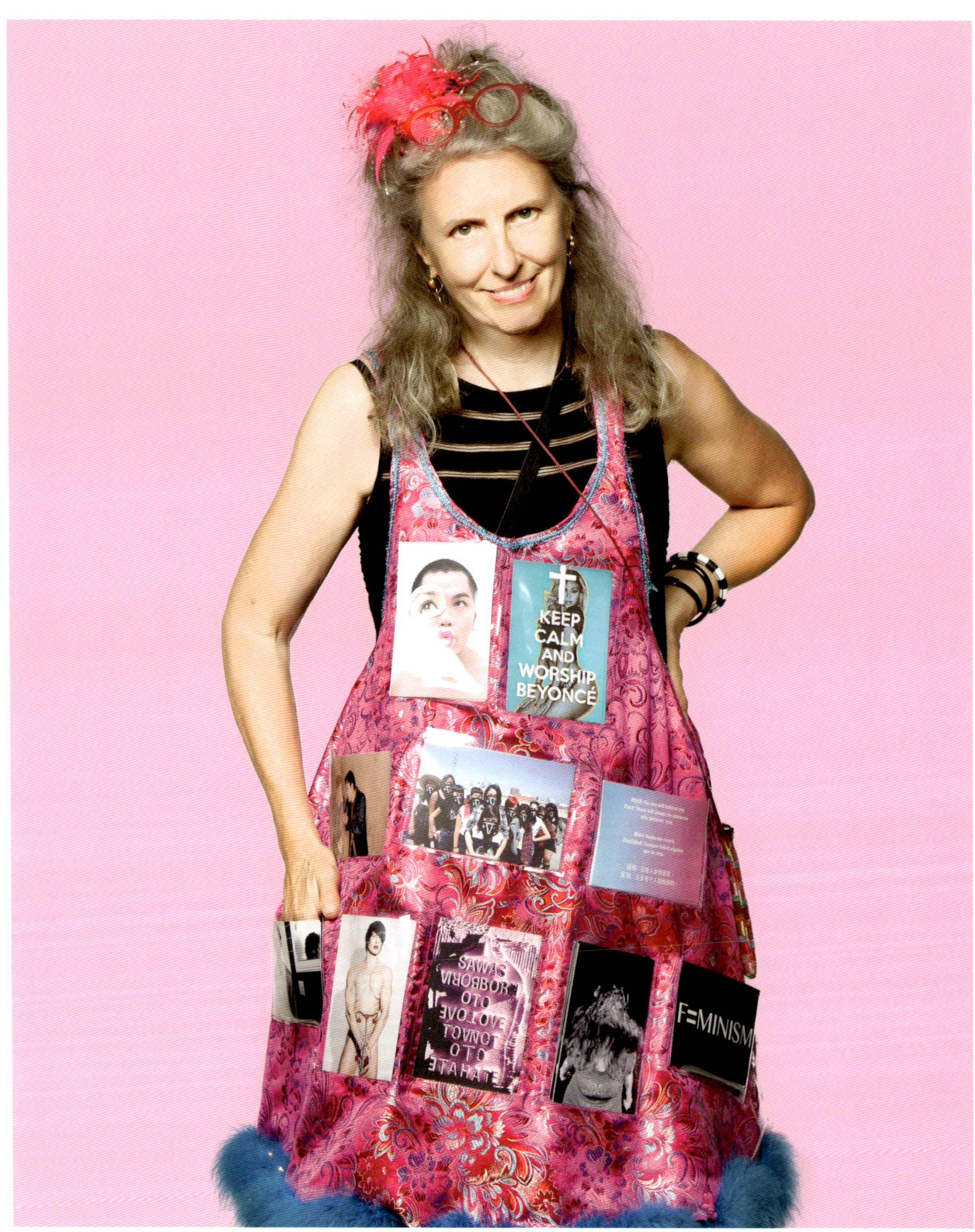

Anne Bray. Photo: Austin Young.

Dis...Miss

Anne Bray

The title *Dis...Miss* came from the words *discuss*, *discover*, *disrupt*, *display*, *discourse*, *dismantle*, *distribute*, *dissent*, and *disrespect*. We *dis* a lot in English, particularly about why women and queer people live in disrepute, still too often marginalized and disbelieved. The mystery needed some consideration: artistic exploration, audience feedback, analysis, and scholarship. The title evolved—at the start of this project, it referred to disrespect for women and then came to reference the possible demise of the word *gender*.

Dis...Miss Gender? We share the images and provocations in this book to ask questions of you, our readers, and ourselves: Are we approaching the end of gender as a restrictive identifier or its celebratory rebirth as something more open and redefined? As intersectionality and queer thought updated feminism, so too have trans, nonbinary, and BIPOC (Black, Indigenous, people of color) artists and writers revised feminism's tenets and vocabularies. Recently, the word *queer* stretched past the gay-lesbian spectrum to include many more people. This book will help all of us more deeply assess our present stages and resolve the potential paradoxical tugs between feminisms and LGBTQ genders. The visual and textual interplay here is as imprecise and nuanced as possible, just as public opinion itself is evolving in real time. Because I openly expect continuous change, as the instigator of this project I avoid defining terms. (For those curious about terms related to gender, the Feminist Center for Creative Work offers ever-updated definitions.)

To address omissions in the feminist past, we at LA Freewaves realized we needed to hear from the many perspectives, to add the voluminous voices of the previously excluded, to create a more complex tapestry to represent the emerging majority, and to learn from the new coalescing gestalt. More than 100 artists and writers brought their views of gender to this project, highlighting trans, nonbinary, lesbian, gay, and heterosexual perspectives. The ethnic demographics of Los Angeles represent a microcosm of the world, and I wanted to reflect these demographics so that the project would resonate globally. Once we incorporated the

views of audience members, we began to understand even better the complexity of perspectives on gender.

I conceived of this book while riding a city bus down Hollywood Boulevard among the LGBT Center, porn stores, Disney tchotchkes sellers, lingerie shops, and military-supply shops. The princess gowns and superheroes portray irreconcilable differences between stereotypical male and female, and these hyperbinary supplies deeply infect all our stories of self, no matter which city or screen we live in/on. In contrast, artists prefer gender as an idea, habit, identity, construct, and illusion.

The five-year evolution of *Dis...Miss* began during Hillary Clinton's presidential campaign in 2016, when I believed she would be the next president. I wanted women-identified artists to rise with her. Then during the Trump troubles, we found ourselves skirmishing constantly on many fronts against backlash toward and assaults of the very participants in our project.

Dis...Miss Gender? took shape amid a growing awareness around declaring pronouns, countermansplaining, preventing campus sexual assault, exclaiming #MeToo, and honoring trans visibility. Yet even as certain people and communities were evolving in these exciting ways, other elements of society were reluctant to change. Some institutions and those who ran them resisted addressing sexual assault on and off campus, restricted abortion access, balked at demands for equal pay, and restrained women from holding positions of power of all kinds (in corporations, churches, media, politics, museums, the military, and so on). Through *Dis...Miss Gender?*, we wanted to explore what artists were thinking about these subjects and how we could invite the public to contemplate these issues and attitudes with us.

With feminist processes in mind, we designed *Dis... Miss* around asking and listening rather than assuming and endeavored to engage general audiences through public art. We had taken this approach through our video screenings on public buses for years. After each art video screened on a bus, a very subjective question appeared on the screen, alongside requests for riders to text us their responses. Our audiences' willingness to go personal thrilled us. With each medium thereafter, we purposefully aimed to engage audiences ever more deeply.

The multievent public visual experience *Dis…Miss* officially launched at Los Angeles Contemporary Exhibitions (LACE) in 2016, with video projections covering the walls and performers offering velvety postcards that featured images by artists. These images were made through photography, drawing, painting, sculpture, collage, and graphic design and were meant to be immediately comprehensible. At events, we asked people to choose a postcard that spoke to them; sensitivity to activism, nudity, nonbinary gender, and critique played a part in people's choices. It felt to me that people lusted after the cards.

Each of the tactile *Dis…Miss* postcards included a question on the back that was related to the image on the front and chosen by the artists to clarify their intentions (and that are here used as chapter titles). At events, I served as a human postcard rack, wearing an apron with a different transparent pocket for each card. We invited viewers to choose a postcard and then anonymously answer the question on the back. We gathered answers via audio, handwriting, and online surveys. Queer urban-planning scholar Marisa Turesky analyzed these answers, and user-experience designer Catherine Bell then visualized this analysis through inconclusive graphics. (In this book, the analysis and graphics appear at the end of each chapter and as animation at freewaves.org/dismiss-analysis.)

Art crowds responded to these postcards most creatively and receptively, many already somewhat familiar with interactive experiments, while the Hollywood Boulevard public assumed we were trying to sell them goods. Hollywood studio executives were the only ones to refuse the postcards altogether, though families often did back away from the nudes, while young boys came up close. Students responded most openly as their identities are still solidifying. Elders often needed to hear the questions before they were jolted out of their binary perceptions.

From 2016 to 2018, *Dis…Miss* engaged audiences through 33 screenings, the postcard giveaways, workshops, discussions, and exhibitions across greater Los Angeles and far beyond.

In 2018, we went big, outdoors, and live. The exhibition *Ain't I a Womxn?* occurred on July 28 at Los Angeles State Historic Park. The event's title refers to freed slave Sojourner Truth's "Ain't I a Woman" speech at a feminist convocation in 1851. She compared the disregard (that prefix again) afforded Black women versus the regard afforded Black men and white women. We wanted to acknowledge the long history of the intersectionality we strove to advance. For this participatory event, thirty LGBTQI+ and feminist artists and groups came together under a full moon to explore queer and intersectional art and activism in public space. They stretched gender expressions in new directions for an audience of 2,000. We tested whether these disparate activists and artists with their diversity of styles, ideas, genres, and identities could come together and be appreciated under one sky. Audiences relaxed and enjoyed. At a party a month later, the artists' earlier trepidation about their differences melted away, turning the previously fragmented scene into one full of camaraderie, though the struggle toward an inclusive intersectional community continues.

A year later, *Dis…Miss* staged a second night of performances. *LOVE &/OR FEAR: A Celebration of Genders* welcomed everyone to fearlessly enjoy an evening in a public space without sexual aggression. Prevention of violence, the worst element of misogyny, had particularly motivated the project from the start. We wanted to invite artists to be vulnerable in a public space without any fear of facing the kind of retaliation or brutality that is at the core of so many other troubles. For this event, our community partner Peace Over Violence safely declared two city blocks of legendary Hollywood Boulevard a sexual-harassment-free zone, and 20 artists and 10 collectives sashayed, paraded, marched, and circulated along the street. Two thousand intentional and 2,000 inadvertent audience members came together without any aggravation. Nevertheless, to maintain this conflict-free zone, we had three layers of security: volunteers, neighborhood patrols, and cops on bikes in the vicinity.

Before COVID arrived and interrupted our plans, we had scheduled moderated, in-person Sunday dialogues that we titled *Dis…Miss Connecting the Dots* as a way to evaluate the project to date and move it forward. We adjusted and held these dialogues on Zoom, further

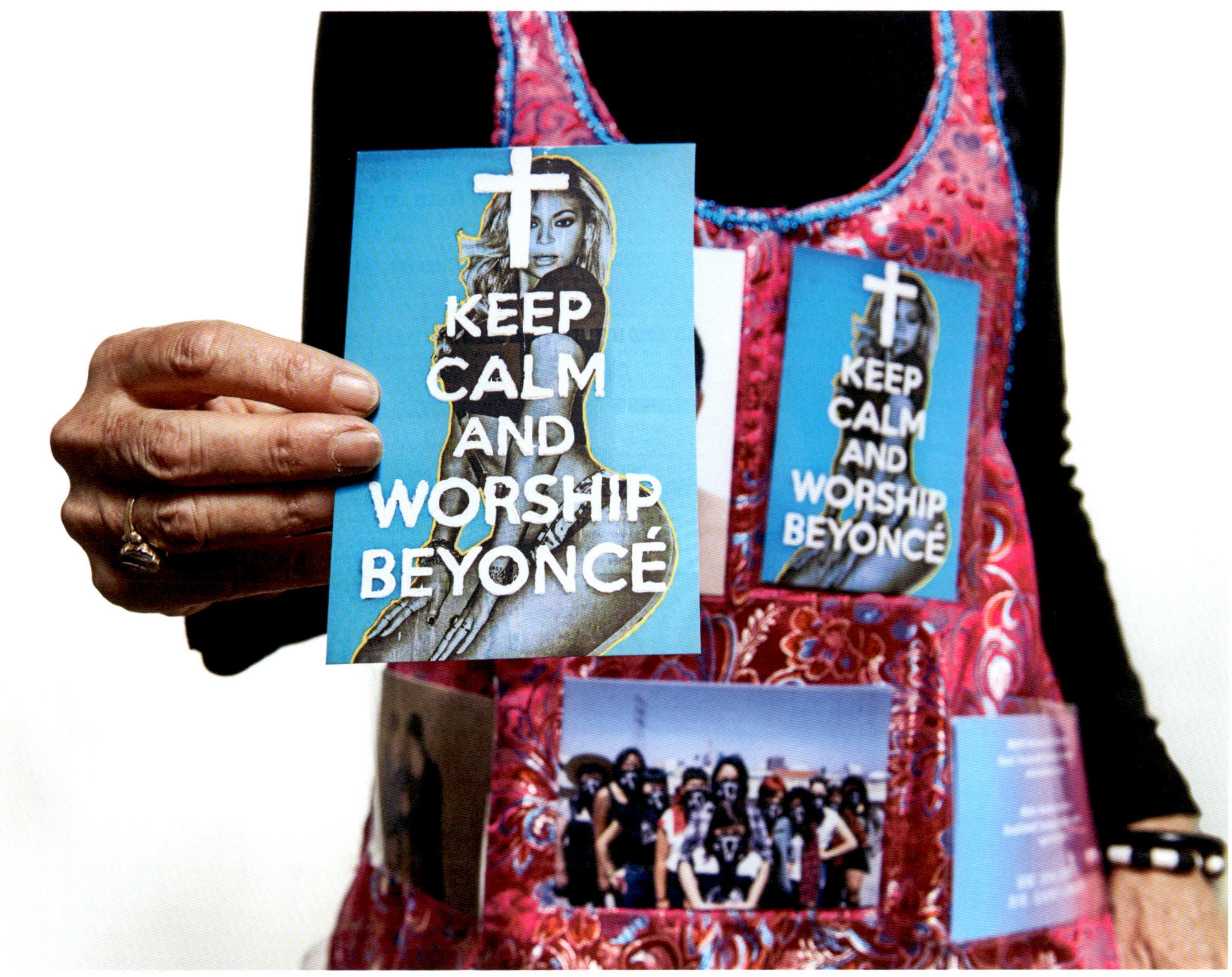

Anne Bray as a walking display of *Dis…Miss* postcards. Photo: Ken Marchionno.

exploring remaining uncertainties: Who decided your gender? Is nonbinary feminism possible? How do we enact intersectional power? How do you perform gender? How can artists use art to address sexual assault? Over three-hour conversations, we attempted to answer these questions but often brought up still more questions. We returned to these dangling questions via more group Zoom discussions, summary essays, and brief, two-person dialogues on Instagram Live (these dialogues are viewable at Instagram.com/lafreewaves/channel/). To propel us even farther forward, we included three more assists, commissioning essays about trans wishes now, Black gender justice, and gender-based violence-prevention efforts by artists.

Through these events, performances, conversations, and now this book, we aspire to end genderphobia or at least rape or, minimally, harassment and to find our way toward a safer, more inclusive future. Many more hours of interaction and conversation are needed to fully affect such change, and we wish to continue to engage a wide public, inviting them to join us as we move toward greater awareness and self-consciousness. Performance art in particular uses bodies to engage viewers' minds and to encourage them to think deeply and differently. Audiences undergo new experiences alongside artists, and spontaneous live mirroring results from the performances. This book aspires to nourish change, model diverse identities, question options, reduce judgments, and explore artists as originators of archetypes and destroyers of stereotypes.

1

ain't i a womxn?

PROMENADE PERFORMING GENDERS

AIN'T I A WOMXN?

public
celebration
performance art
spoken word
sound art
projections
zines
LGBTQ
feminist
outdoor
participation
intersections
full moon

LA STATE HISTORIC PARK

7/28/18 8–11PM

PERFORMANCES PROMENADING GENDERS

Ain't I A Womxn? Flyer by Soyun Cho.

PERFORMANCES
Christy Roberts Berkowitz
Nao Bustamante
Zackary Drucker
Rafa Esparaza
Rudy Bleu Garcia
Janice Gomez & Fatima Hoang
Raquel Gutiérrez
Jennifer Moon & KCHUNG
Amitis Motevalli
Thinh Nguyen
Reach LA
Snatch Power
Yozmit Walker
Kristina Wong
Xina Xurner (Marvin Astorga & Young Joon Kwak)

INSTALLATIONS
Bitchface
Martha Carrillo
Reanne Estrada & C. Ree
Feminist Library on Wheels
Las Fotos
Elana Mann
Ni Santas
Self Help Graphics
Austin Young

VIDEOS
Adebukola Bodunrin
Johanna Breiding
Deanna Erdman
Andre Keichian
Mail Order Brides
Gloria Morán
Meena Nanji
Caress Reeves

BRING FLASHLIGHTS, FIND CONNECTIONS

At LA State Historic Park (Not A Cornfield) 1245 N Spring St LA CA 90012

Saturday July 28, 2018, 8-11 pm

LA Freewaves Freewaves.org

FOOD TRUCKS

GROUP BIKE RIDE
Multicultural Communities for Mobility

ZINES
ArtworxLA, Daisy Noemi, Brenzy Solorzano

CURATORIAL ADVISORS
Toro Castaño
Evonne Gallardo
Dirty Looks
Daisy Noemi

PARTNERS
East LA Women's Center
Go Metro
LACE (Los Angeles Contemporary Exhibitions)
LA LGBT Center
L.A. State Historic Park
Peace Over Violence
Women's Creative Center for Work

SUPPORT PROVIDED BY
Mike Kelley Foundation for the Arts
City of Los Angeles Department of Cultural Affairs
Los Angeles County Arts Commission
Metabolic Studio
Pasadena Art Alliance

#dismiss   **#lafreewaves**   **#aintiawomxn**

Ain't I A Womxn? Flyer by Soyun Cho.

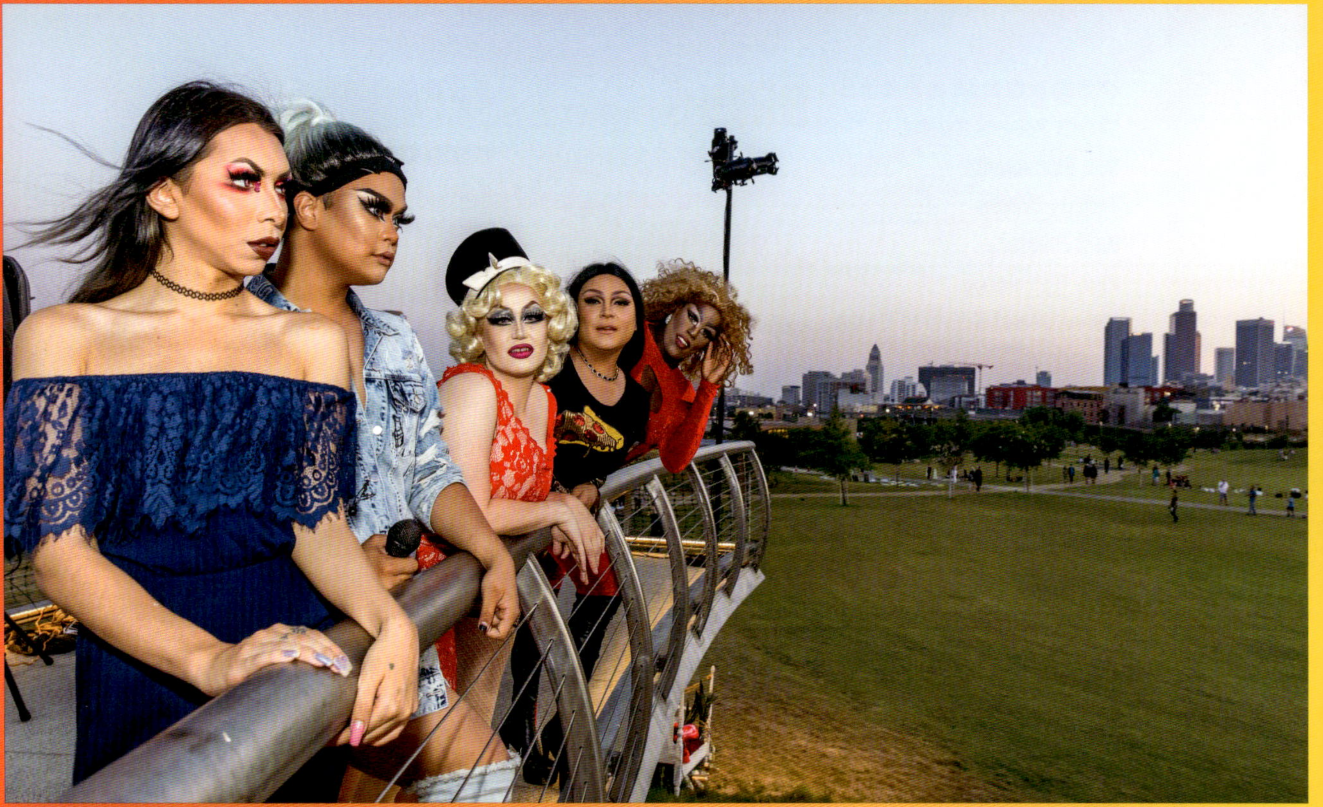

Exposure Drag. Photo: Monica Orozco.

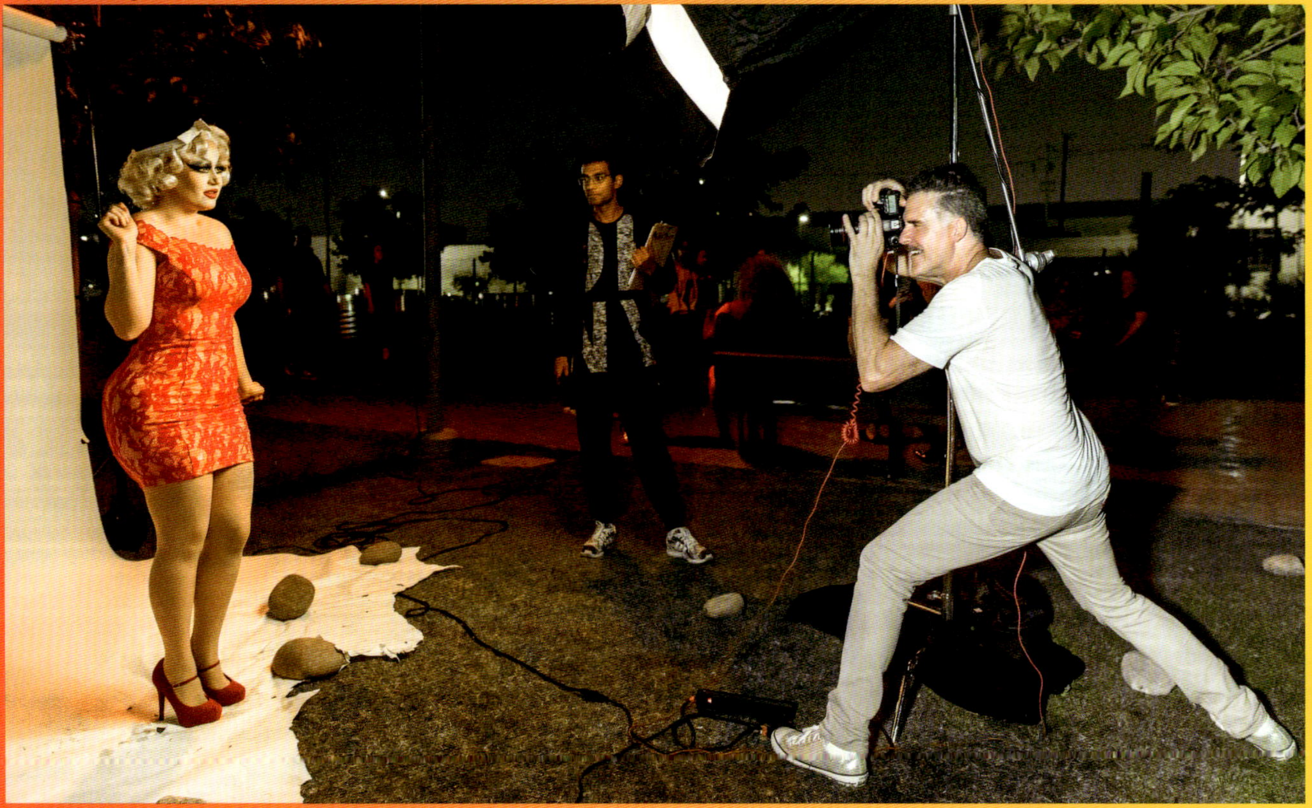

Austin Young at work. Photo: Monica Orozco.

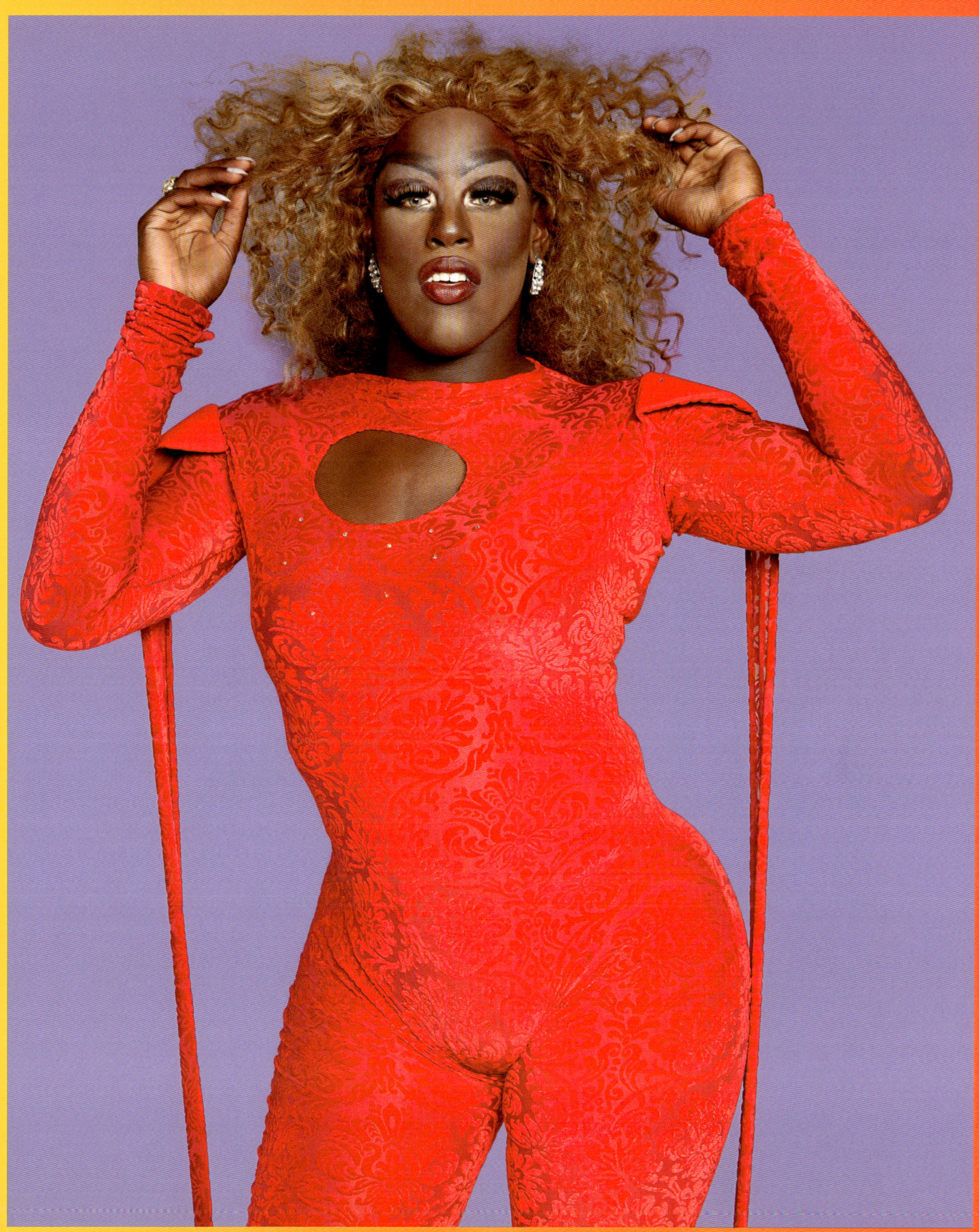

Essence of Exposure Drag. Photo: Austin Young.

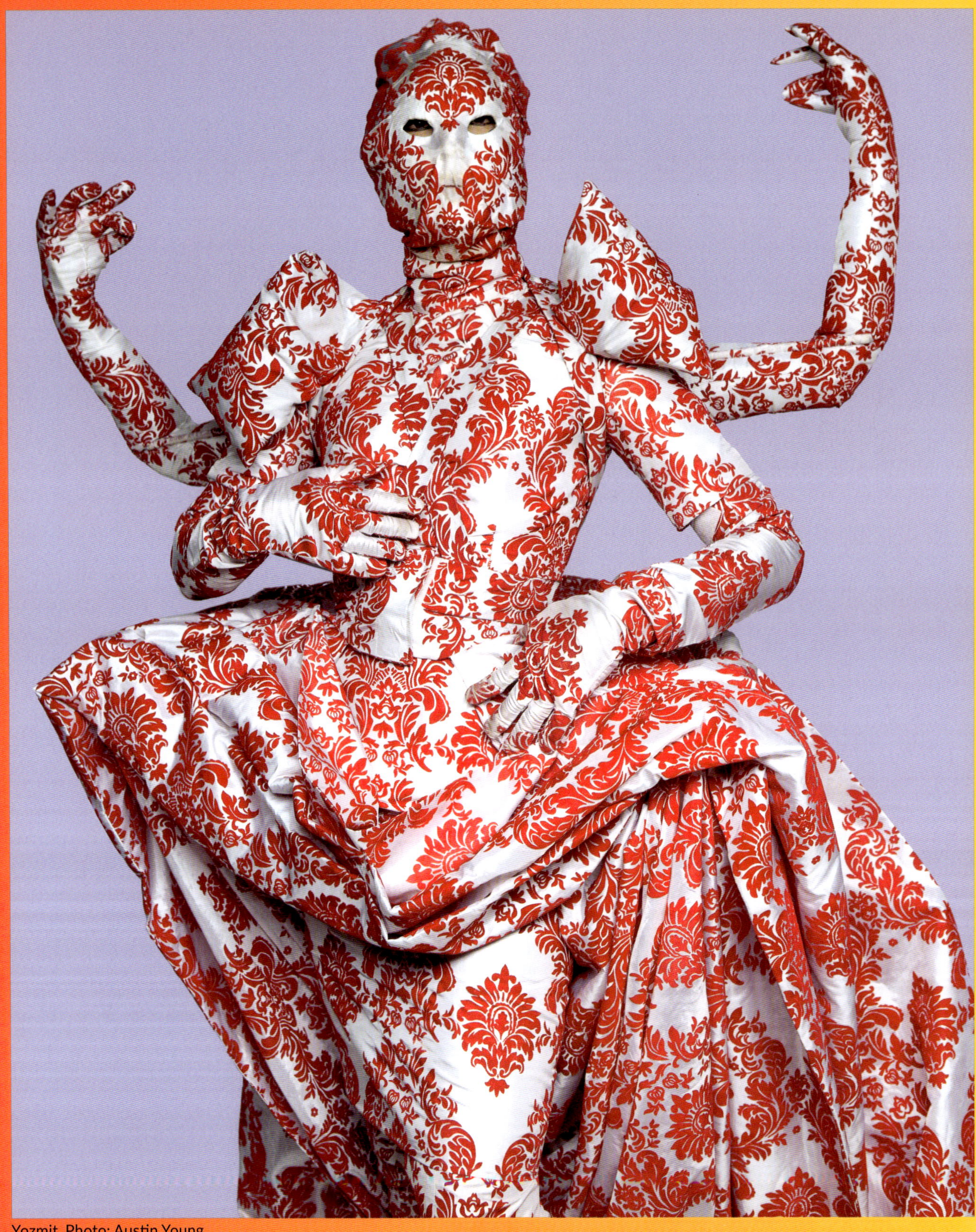

Yozmit. Photo: Austin Young.

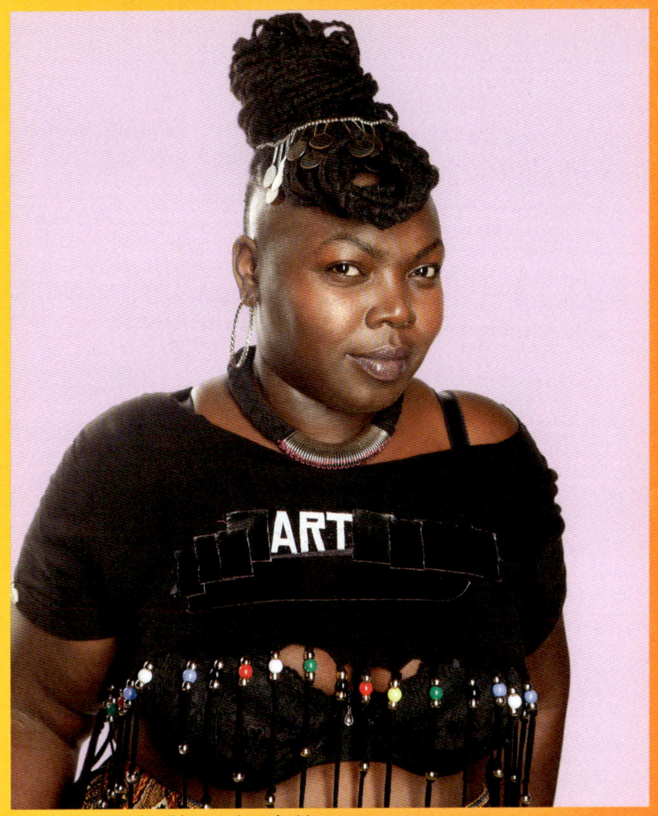

sondriaWRITES. Photo: Austin Young.

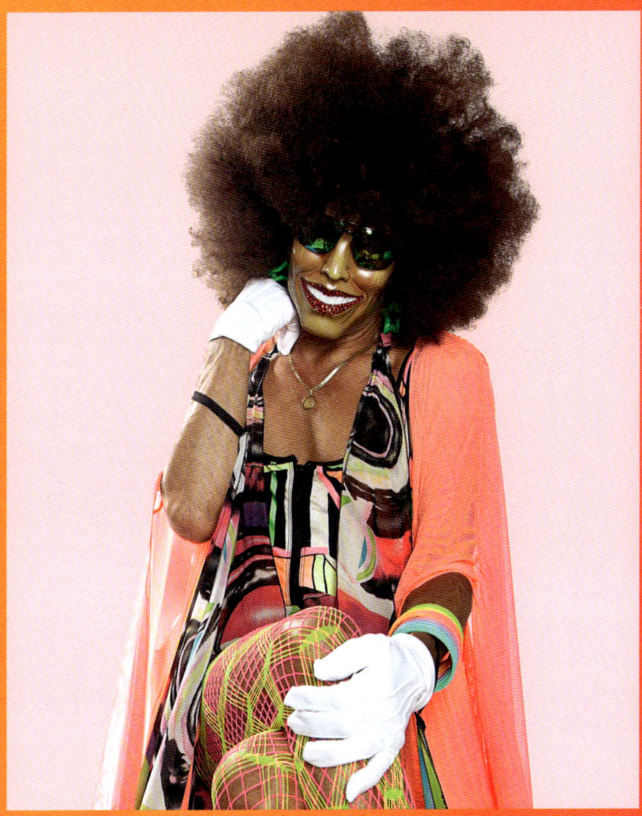

Kiki Xtravaganza. Photo: Austin Young.

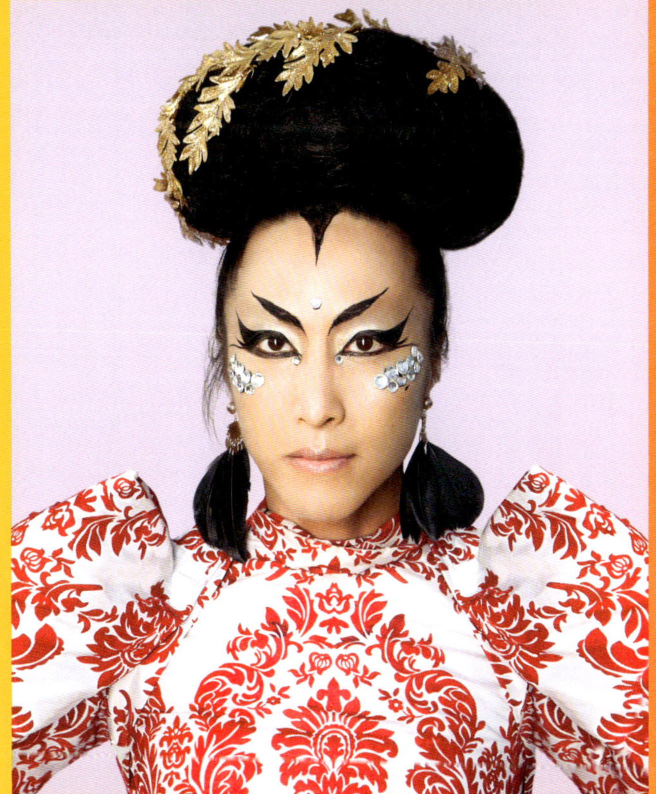

Yozmit. Photo: Austin Young.

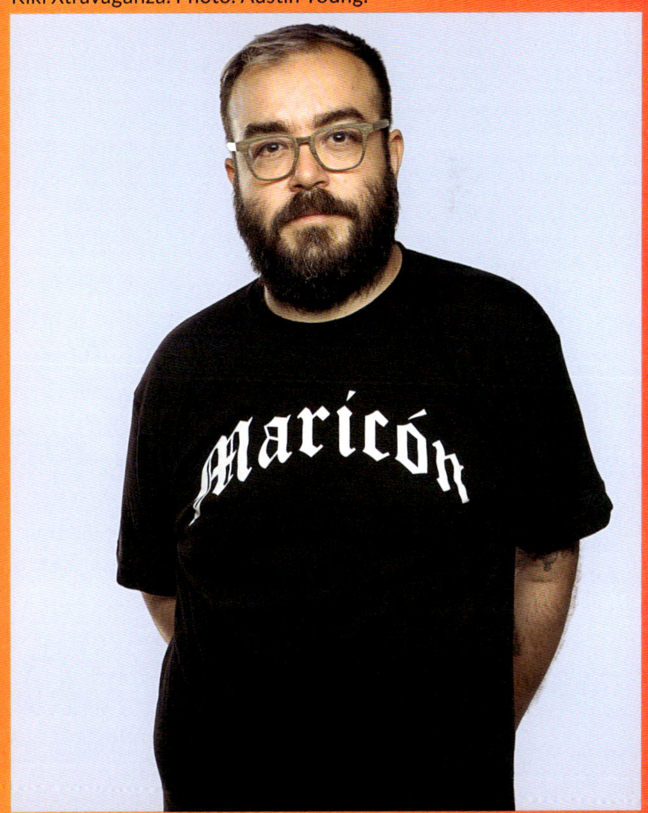

Rudy "Bleu" Garcia. Photo: Austin Young.

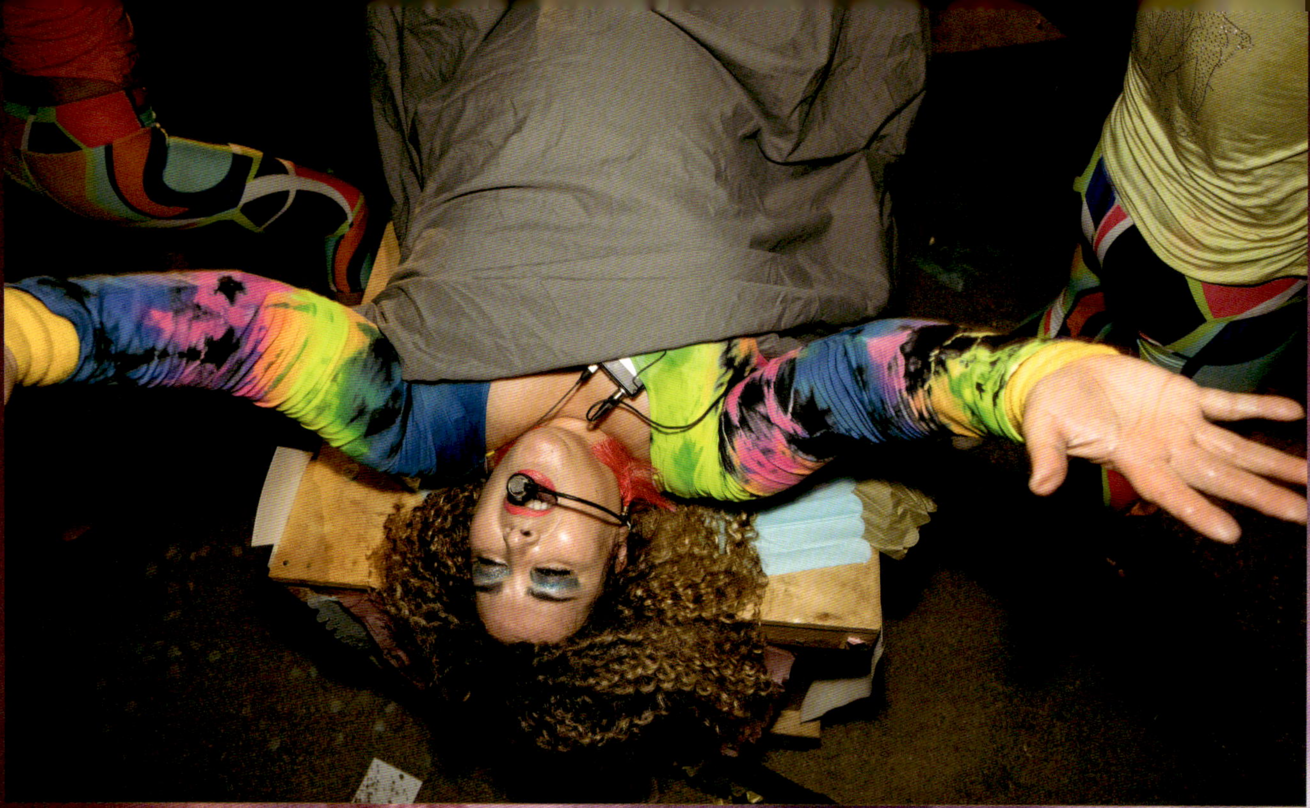

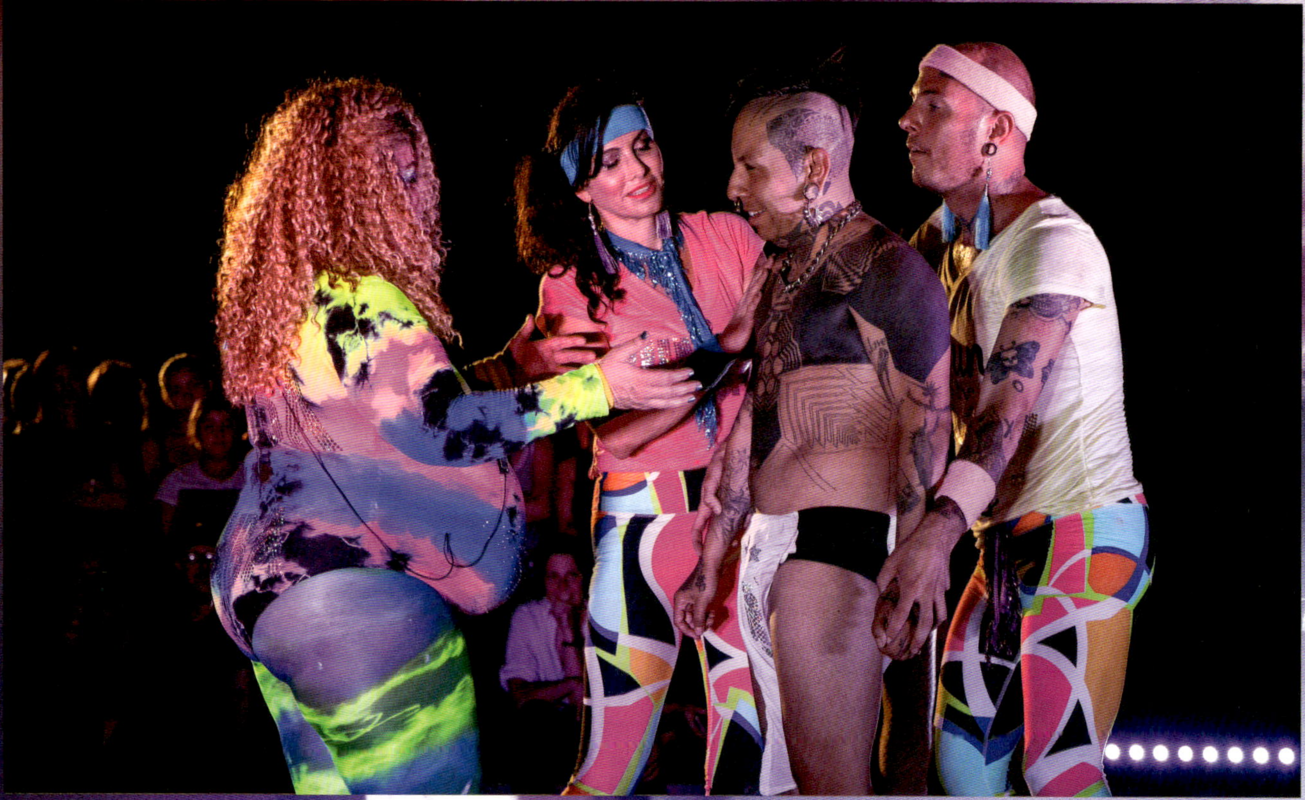

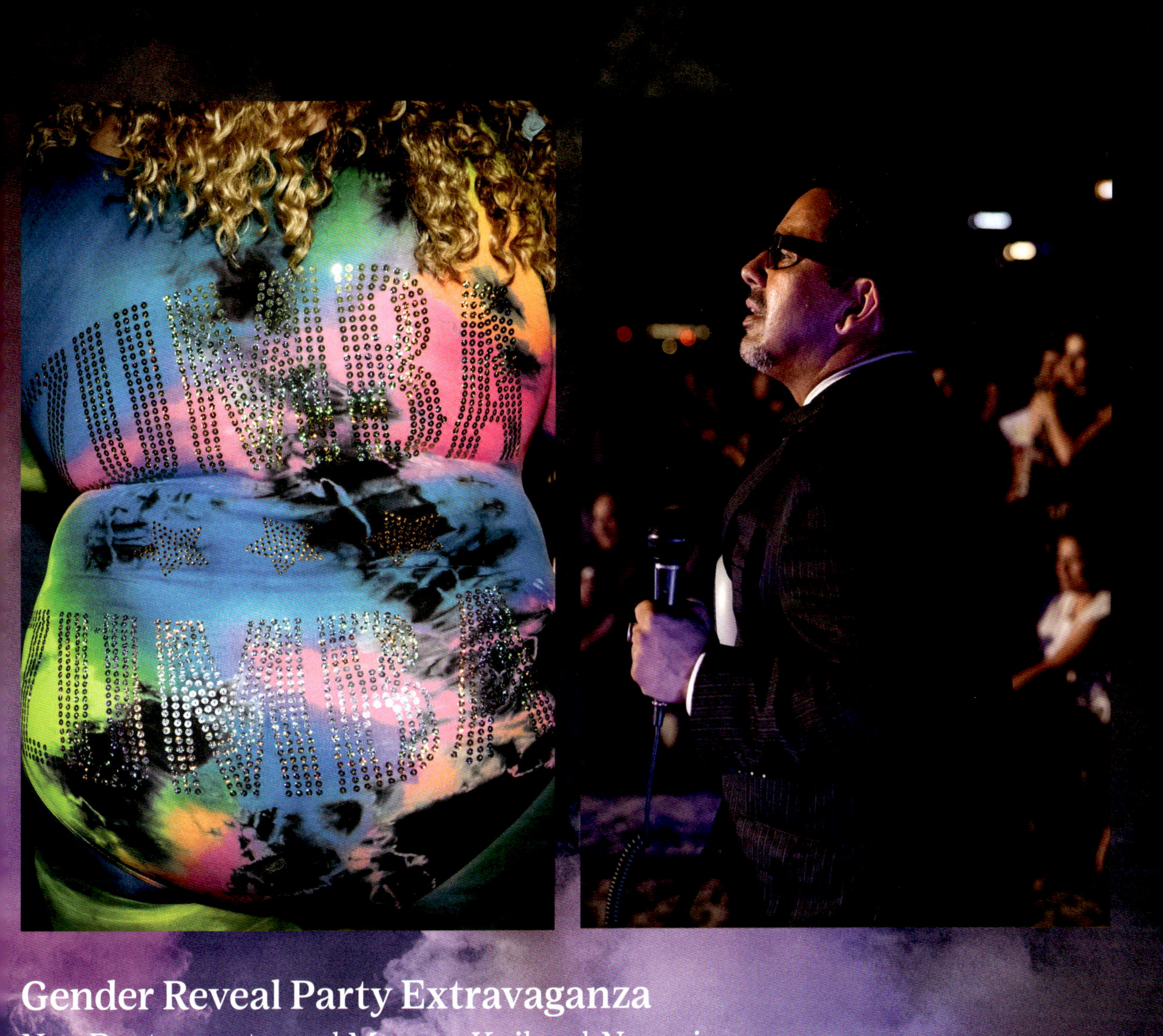

Gender Reveal Party Extravaganza
Nao Bustamante and Marcus Kuiland-Nazario

Gender Reveal Party Extravaganza, performance by Nao Bustamante and Marcus Kuiland-Nazario. Photos: Sah Alla Shabaik.

We Emerge from Zanja Madre:
Performing Genders in *Ain't I a Womxn?*

Sue Bell Yank

The park, formerly a cornfield and before that a rail yard where immigrants first landed in this city, was lit by hundreds of twinkling rope lights in the humid dark. A livid full moon hung over the landscape's benighted curves, and the park's lit pathways were punctuated by art installations, performances, and the murmuring of gathered groups. The heavy air seemed almost womblike—but maybe my perceptions were somewhat distorted.

This evening of performances, *Ain't I a Womxn?*, was my first big art event since I had my baby five weeks earlier, and I had spent much of that time getting used to the idea of navigating my own changed body in public space. Where is it acceptable to be with such a small baby, to feed her, to expose my extra rolls of baby fat that don't really fit into my clothes yet? How do I perform motherhood in public, and who is judging me and why? Anxiously, I wondered how I should navigate, hide, or reveal my status among those who may desire to procreate but cannot or who may not want to procreate but feel instantly judged by anyone who has, thanks to societal dictates about what life and family should look like. I left all that aside for a moment to enter the land that was mother, the motherland of the Tongva people. It was also the home of the Zanja Madre, or Mother Ditch, the first large aqueduct that funneled water to the Pueblo of Los Angeles, thought to be built with the forced labor of this land's Indigenous people.[1] Zanja Madre is now marked only by a red-brick structure completed in Spanish colonial times and rediscovered in the 2000s during the excavation for the LA Metro Gold Line.

Although *Ain't I a Womxn?* was billed as an event that explored gender, it was also inexorably bound up with its site and context. According to Anne Bray, the director of LA Freewaves, the original impetus of the event was a deep desire to question the viability of the feminism of the 1970s and 1980s in the face of today's fluid, intersectional identities. A media arts and video organization, Freewaves had often focused on issues of race and public space in Los Angeles while maintaining a through-line of feminist values. Spurred as many of us were by the misogynistic politics of 2016, the organization recently embarked on a participatory project called *Dis...Miss*, which interrogated gender identities head-on and attempted to learn more about the failures of identity politics while taking the pulse of how people think about gender fluidity today.[2] *Ain't I a Womxn?*, the first ambitious performance organized as part of *Dis...Miss*, took this conversation to the next level—addressing these inquiries in an embodied way that felt visceral and immediate because audience and performer could interact and negotiate their identities fluidly, in real space.

I already knew this enormous, tapered swath of land behind downtown, a massive acreage of flat, open space in the center of it all. Once called "LA's Ellis Island," the Tongva land that the Los Angeles State Historic Park now occupies was the site of a Southern Pacific Railroad railway station known as the River Station from the latter part of the nineteenth century into the early twentieth. It opened in 1876, and in the 20 years after that LA's population would explode from 6,000 to nearly 50,000 souls, both middle-class white midwesterners and working-class immigrants, many of them first glimpsing the city from this vantage. The Zanja Madre aqueduct coexisted with the passenger station throughout its operation on this land that was the lifeblood of the city's growth, but it was abandoned in 1904 as the city put into place more modern water systems.

In 1901, three years before the aqueduct's obsolescence, the site ceased to operate as a passenger interchange. After the interchange's closure, even though the land remained a hub for transporting industrial material, it became a contested site, where the desires of the moneyed clashed with the hopes of local communi-

---

1   The event began at sunset with a land-acknowledgment ceremony conducted by Olivia Chumacero to recognize the land's original people. Chumacero, an artist and gardener who was formerly in residence at the park, considers themselves a "First Nation Being" who does not believe in gender.

2   Anne Bray, interviewed by the author, July 2018.

ties. The last of the rails were removed in the 1990s, and in 1993 the City of Los Angeles's Downtown Strategic Plan recommended that 12,000 units of housing be built on the site. At the same time, the Los Angeles Unified School District proposed a new high school there. Ultimately, the land was acquired by Union Pacific Railroad in 1996, and in 1999 the railroad entered into a deal with Majestic Realty, which planned to build one million square feet of warehouses. In an unprecedented uprising in 2000, however, local neighborhood and community groups adjacent to the site lobbied for an open, public, green space; the Chinatown Yards Alliance formed and successfully blocked the Majestic deal. At the same time, historic buildings and the remains of the Spanish colonial aqueduct, the Zanja Madre, were excavated on the site, and the state legislature finally slated the site to become an historic park, on September 28 of 2001, approving a $36 million fund to purchase the land and turn it into a park. In 2005, the artist Lauren Bon planted a cornfield called "Not a Cornfield" on the site to help prepare and remediate the toxic soil, organizing many community-oriented public programs over the five years of Not a Cornfield's existence.[3] The LA State Historic Park finally opened to the public on Earth Day in 2017.

> Gender is not always constituted coherently or consistently in different historical contexts. As a result, it becomes impossible to separate out "gender" from the political and cultural intersections in which it is invariably produced and maintained.
>
> — Judith Butler, *Gender Trouble*

Navigating this already contested site during a performance event about feminism and intersectionality made it strikingly evident how the control and occupation of space relate to how we often define gender. Who is this city for? Or who may occupy this space, and how? In Los Angeles, as in many places across this globe, those in power largely determine what is normal for bodies in space, and that "mythical norm," as Audre Lord described it,[4] is youthful, thin, white, male, heterosexual, Christian, financially secure (in the United States at least), and, we might also add, cis. Those who do not fit into that category must constantly question the acceptability and reception of their bodies in space. When there is such a norm in place, then we are not acknowledging the glorious range of human difference and are forced to constantly whisper, "That is not me," while fearing the label *deviant*.[5]

LAND

A concave bowl in the rough middle of the park, embraced by a raised path and pedestrian bridge, served as the event's main stage. The audience gathered in the round on raised slopes, the performer lit up in the sunken center. Writer, poet, and performer Raquel Gutiérrez was the first act I encountered on this stage, and during their compelling reading of a work in progress (a draft version of an essay titled "Art in the Time of Art-Washing," later published on the San Francisco Museum of Modern Art's *Open Space* blog),[6] they spoke not just about their queer identity but also about race, displacement, land, and how they occupied contested space and acted upon it. They recalled stories of "a Brown life in the arts," of being called out by an affluent white trans man on Instagram as a "Whitina," complicit in the displacement of the low-income residents of East Los Angeles because of their participation in an art show. "The accuracies are what we lose in the constant, unrelenting discourse anchored in perception and optics," they read, "or what happens when nobody interfaces in person anymore." Their achingly honest essay also explored their own family history and the beginning of their performative career. They recalled with longing how they always wanted to

---

3   Timeline of the Cornfield site compiled by Janet Owen Driggs, in *Not a Cornfield: Timeline and Essays,* ed. Janet Owen Driggs (Los Angeles: Hemlock Printers, 2007), 156–183.

4   Audre Lorde, "Age, Race, Class and Sex: Women Redefining Difference," in *Sister Outsider: Essays and Speeches* (Freedom, CA: Crossing Press, 1984), 116.

5   Lorde, "Age, Race, Class and Sex," 116.

6   Raquel Gutiérrez, "Art in the Time of Art-Washing," *Open Space*, September 20, 2018, https://openspace.sfmoma.org/2018/09/art-in-the-time-of-art-washing.

show their work in the neighborhoods of their childhood, but they asked, "When it's your old neighborhood you have to stop and wonder how your complicity persists even when Brown bodies—our Brown bodies together—are more suspect in navigating the same sociopathic capitalist regime that others whose careers have arrived on the backs of those same Brown bodies they proclaim to fight for."[7] For Gutiérrez, there are no easy categories. There is no acceptable path on which to tread, so they must forge their own complicated way. It is clear that gender is tied up with race, class, and place. The complexities of growing up queer and Brown and as an artist in East LA influence how they perform their identity, how they are received by others, and how they grapple with navigating the demands of career when doing so may involve complicity in the mechanisms of power that (sometimes violently) reshape a neighborhood.

Another installation just to the north of the main stage likewise shed a bright and bitingly satirical light on how the performance of identity, gender, and our capitalist complicity is deeply tied to the violent histories of contested land—this time focusing on the park itself. This performance took place on the raised north wall of the park, where the LA Metro Gold Line slid by every 24 minutes or so. The enormous moving shadow of a four-bladed fan, lit by spotlights, beat inexorably against that wall, the lights illuminating those of us who stood in their path: our thrown shadows, dwarfed by the fan, were sharp enough that each curve, each haircut, stood in high relief and just large enough for all to see. It was a promenade of silhouettes. As I approached, one of two women dressed in white but for the black type on their shirts (the artists Reanne Estrada and C. Ree) handed me a printed fan that said "Zanja Madre Fan Club" and whispered conspiratorially, "She was a bad girl, a very bad girl." Her T-shirt had an agenda for the evening printed on it: "New Fan, Orientation," "Fanifesto Do-Over," and "Closing Fan Dance." A small metal cart covered in Dixie cups and pitchers offered "Free Water Pours." This tongue-in-cheek work referred to the Zanja Madre, or Mother Ditch, now marked only by the Spanish colonial red-brick cylindrical structure. The aqueduct and its accompanying structures destroyed one of the most important and populous Tongva villages, Yang-Na, and many enslaved Native people were thought to have performed forced labor on the project and perished during construction.

"Recognition of Un-Free Labor (RUFL) in ZM—let's NOT IGNORE!," read the sign Estrada and Ree held up. "Overthrow of Native nations—LET'S not ignore!" It all took place right here, they seemed to proclaim, and iterations of this historical oppression and subjugation are being produced again and again all around us, embedded in societal structures that dictate the performance of our identities in space.

EMBRACE

Several performances joyfully endeavored to dismantle these structures of oppressive power, manifesting as hopeful, celebratory imaginings of a world where mainstream conceptions of gender have been upended. These future-looking propositions imagined popular culture embracing what is now considered radical, playing out in the meme space of the gender-reveal party and the daytime talk show.

In one of the highlights of the evening, the performance artists Nao Bustamante and Marcus Kuiland-Nazario cleverly leveraged the concept of the gender-reveal party to call into question the stability of the terms *male* and *female*, *boy* and *girl*, *man* and *woman* as well as the societal power constructs and restrictions that support these terms.

You could argue that babies have no gender; they exist in a fungible and fluid mode. They cannot choose to perform gender in one way or another; they have not yet learned how the context of their birth shapes society's reception of their expression. Society, however, immediately begins to work on them, as parents who attempt to raise their children in a gender-neutral way quickly realize. Other parents overcompensate for their babies' genderlessness by adorning them in pink or blue, unicorns and princesses or trucks and baseballs, ruffles or bowties.

Dressed as a Zumba instructor and wearing an explosion of curls, Bustamante spoke with a heavy, affected accent as she gathered her fellow Zumba dancers, a joyous mix of performers and audience members, in a euphoric circle of gyrating bodies of all gender expressions. Kuiland-Nazario, who wore a suit and let loose a flow of high-velocity Spanish through a megaphone, recalled a macho Mexican performer in his demeanor. After protracted dancing and crowd warming, Busta-

---

7   Raquel Gutiérrez, work in progress, http://raquelgutierrez.net.

mante began to pull volunteers from the audience to have their gender revealed to them via a magic cupcake.

One volunteer bit in to reveal pink icing ("Rrrrrosa!," proclaimed Kuiland-Nazario), one revealed blue, and one white. Bustamante dipped her finger in to show the audience the glob of frosting and promenaded it around the circular stage. "Whiiiiite," she droned. "Wowwww. I guess you can choose your own gender!"

A sound piece by bitchface—an installation qua performance—also successfully combined wit, joy, and acceptance with a radical critique of categories of identity. Originally a podcast run by bitchface's Nicole Kelly and Phoebe Unter, the piece *Daytime Talk Show 2018/2028* edited together actual interviews of trans women on the *Oprah Winfrey Show* into an imaginary episode in which Winfrey interviews Black trans lesbian separatist scholar Yocheved Zenaida Cohen. *Daytime Talk Show* collaged audio clips of Cohen's voice from a panel for Intersectionality NOW in 2017 with audio from the interviews on the *Oprah Winfrey Show*, to paint an improbable and hopeful vision for the mainstream acceptance of radical ideas around gender. As bitchface proclaimed on a broadside accompanying the installation,

> Yocheved Zenaida Cohen is a gender prophet. And here we place her in conversation with America's talk show host and in a lineage of the scholars and radicals before her—Marsha P. Johnson, Audre Lorde, Angela Davis, Judith Butler. This is our canon, these are our gxds. These are the thoughts we fuck with. And this alternate reality is our collective future—the one just out of reach. A time when all trans women are safe & affirmed, especially Black trans women.

The installation itself mimicked daytime talk show aesthetics: two empty 1980s-era armchairs faced rows of white folding chairs, and above the armchairs a blinking pink neon sign read, "homoprah," collapsing the words *homo* and *Oprah*. *Homo* would light up when Cohen spoke, and *Oprah* would light up when Oprah commented, though of course Oprah's voice was recognizable even without the flashing neon. Yet despite Oprah's fame and familiarity, in the collaged-together interview Cohen always remained completely in

control, and an awestruck Oprah seemed to accept her ideas and personhood enthusiastically. The audience went wild for the radical critiques of Judith Butler and for Cohen's proposition of reparations. As the artist Nicole Kelly put it when I emailed her to ask about this performance's genesis, by the end of the conversation "Oprah is questioning her own sexuality—her biggest aha moment is when she finally realizes that the binary is dead. You could think of Oprah as mainstream cis culture, queering. And Yocheved as part of a lineage of radical scholars, the queer vanguard."[8]

There is an exhaustion in educating the oppressor, and as Audre Lorde points out, that is exactly what the oppressed (i.e., those who do not fit the mythical white, cis male, young, affluent, hetero, Christian norm) are expected to do in American society. "There is a constant drain of energy," Lorde writes, "which might be better used in redefining ourselves and devising realistic scenarios for altering the present and constructing the future."[9] When *Ain't I a Womxn?* was at its best, all of these artists' energy and wit were poured into a nuanced redefinition of self, a cultivation of empathy and engagement, and the reimagination of present and future possibilities—rather than being flat, didactic efforts to explain and "settle" categories of identity.

A WARNING

The unsettling of identity can also manifest quite violently, and several performances unveiled the complexities of contested space and gender. Referencing the interconnected mechanisms of power exerted on both bodies and land, the performances by rafa esparza and Amitis Motevalli involved a symbolic sacrifice in some way. The violence of forcing false coherence out of complex identities, the literal violence on queer bodies, and the violence done to the land itself nonetheless manifested in a hopeful catharsis—a glimpse of a different possibility, a new paradigm, and a warning if we fail.

Around 9:00 p.m., a lowrider car edged slowly through the park, dragging artist rafa esparza behind it on the ground in a performance titled *Xipe Totec: the flaying of man*. An inch-thick rope was wrapped nearly 20 times around his thighs and attached to the back of the car. The artist was seated and wearing a cap,

8   Nicole Kelly, email to the author, August 1, 2018.
9   Lorde, "Age, Race, Class and Sex," 115.

workman's boots, thick jeans, and a dusty, dark, button-up shirt. It was hard to tell if he had a board under him to shield his legs from the decomposed gravel of the path, but I guessed probably not. He, in turn, was dragging another dummy that read as male, dressed in very similar clothes, stuffed and with a brown cardboard face and appendages. The performance looked painful and was chilling in its effect, especially since a loud and happy crowd followed behind the dragged esparza. The artist was pulled along at a slow speed, tense and struggling to maintain a seated posture; the dummy looked like a corpse. The lowrider, a dark 1980s-era car and a defiant symbol of LA Chicano culture countering the domination of whiteness, was lit up and bouncing on its hydraulics, music blaring from its interior. The performance was torture as spectacle, but it also spoke to the uncomfortable necessity of violence and sacrifice in birthing a new power paradigm. In Aztec mythology, Xipe Totec is a god of nature, agriculture, and war. He is known as the "flayed" god, said to have flayed himself (similar to the way the maize seed sheds its skin upon germination) to provide food to humanity.[10] The artist embodied the flayed god in this performance, painfully connected to the land once known as "the Cornfield," and reflecting the way this center of agriculture and site of life-giving irrigation was violently industrialized and poisoned, then birthed anew as a park.

The park is a significant swath of land, and the huge effort it must have taken to pull off this event nevertheless resulted in a fairly dispersed, quietly activated landscape, small groups wandering from one performance to another without ever gathering in very large numbers. I felt a bit swallowed up by the acreage and the darkness at first, but in retrospect I realized that *Ain't I a Womxn?* succeeded because of the overwhelming presence of the land, not in spite of it. Race, class, ethnicity, histories, politics, and culture are inevitably implicated in any conversation around gender. And all of these modalities are bound up with place, how our places are made, colonized, decolonized, seized, bought, owned, fought for, and organized. Place produces culture, which produces identity, and any thoughtful unpacking of any one element of identity must interrogate the production of place. In this place, these artists could manifest and navigate the complexities of multivalent modalities, urging us to imagine a reconstituted land and a future beyond binaries.

---

10   Tuby Evans and David Webster, *Archaeology of Ancient Mexico and Central American Encyclopedia* (New York: Garland, 2001).

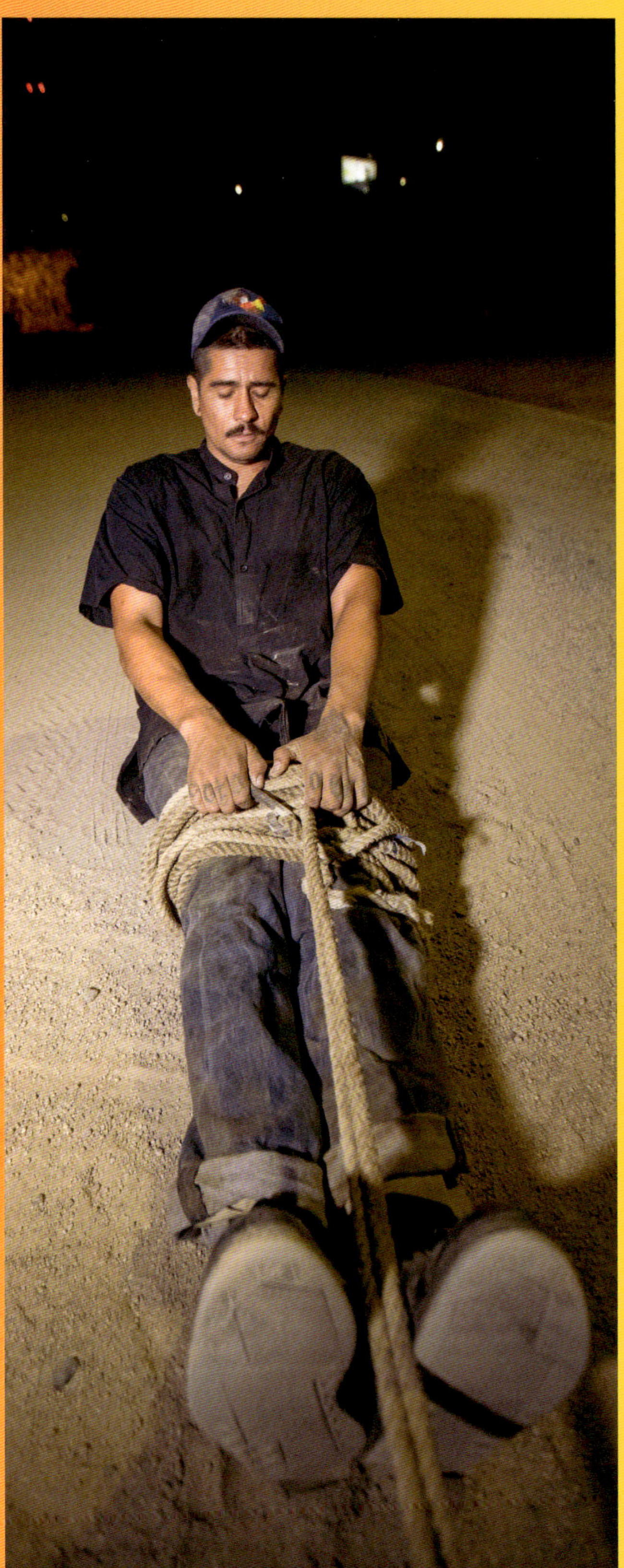

Xipe Totec: the flaying of man, performance by rafa esparza. Photo: Monica Orozco.

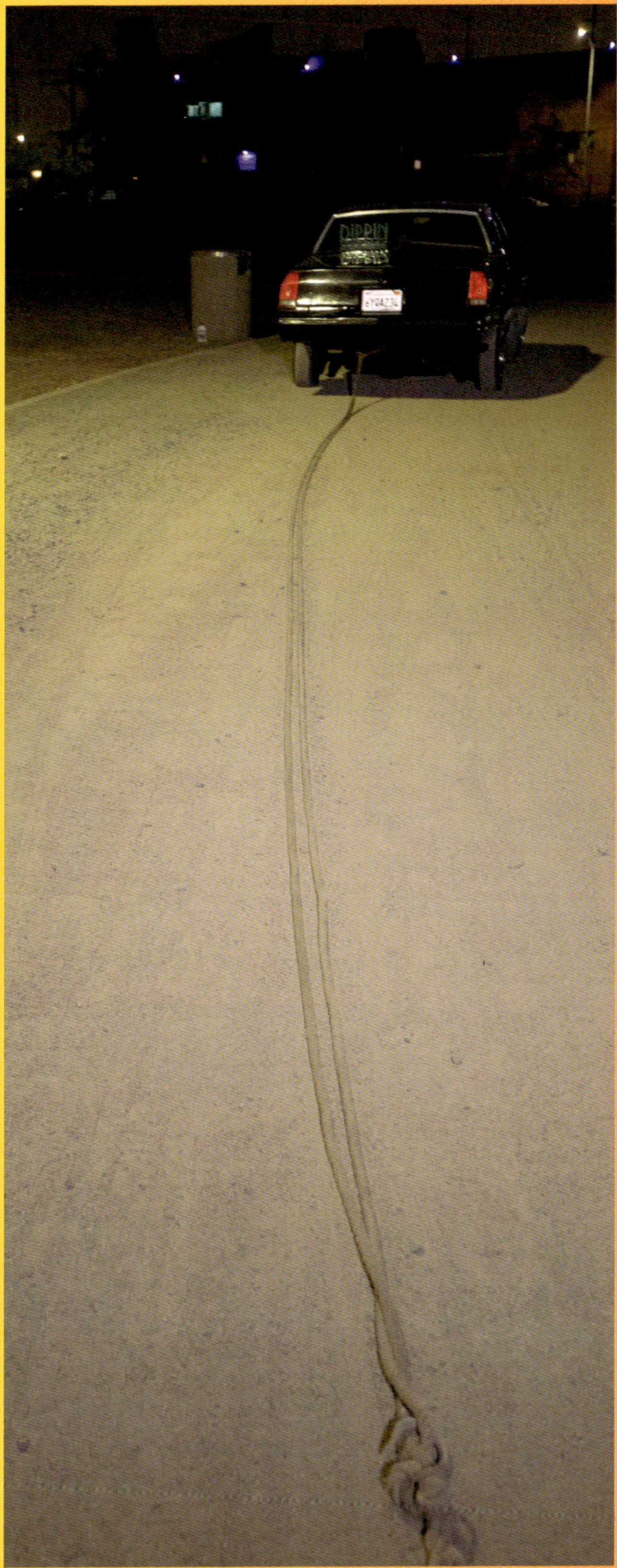

Xipe Totec: the flaying of man, performance by rafa esparza.
Photo: Monica Orozco.

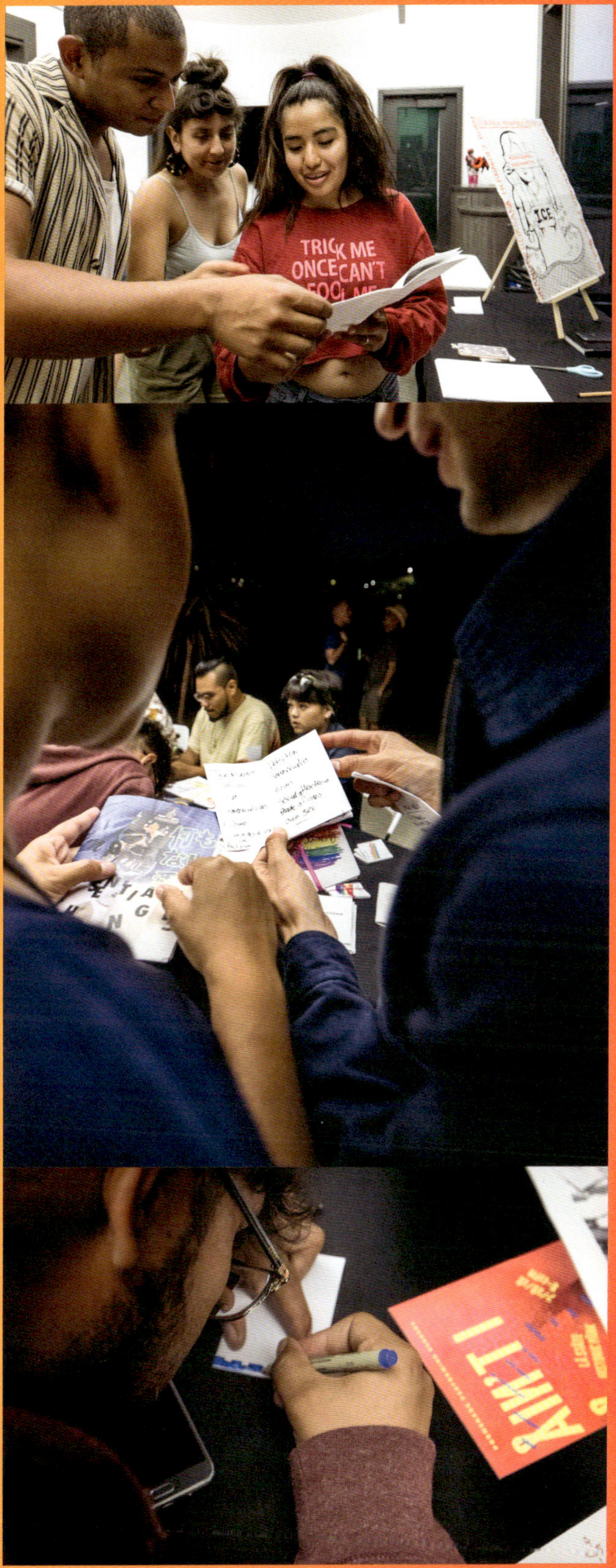

Zine display by Daisy Noemi. Photos: Monica Orozco.

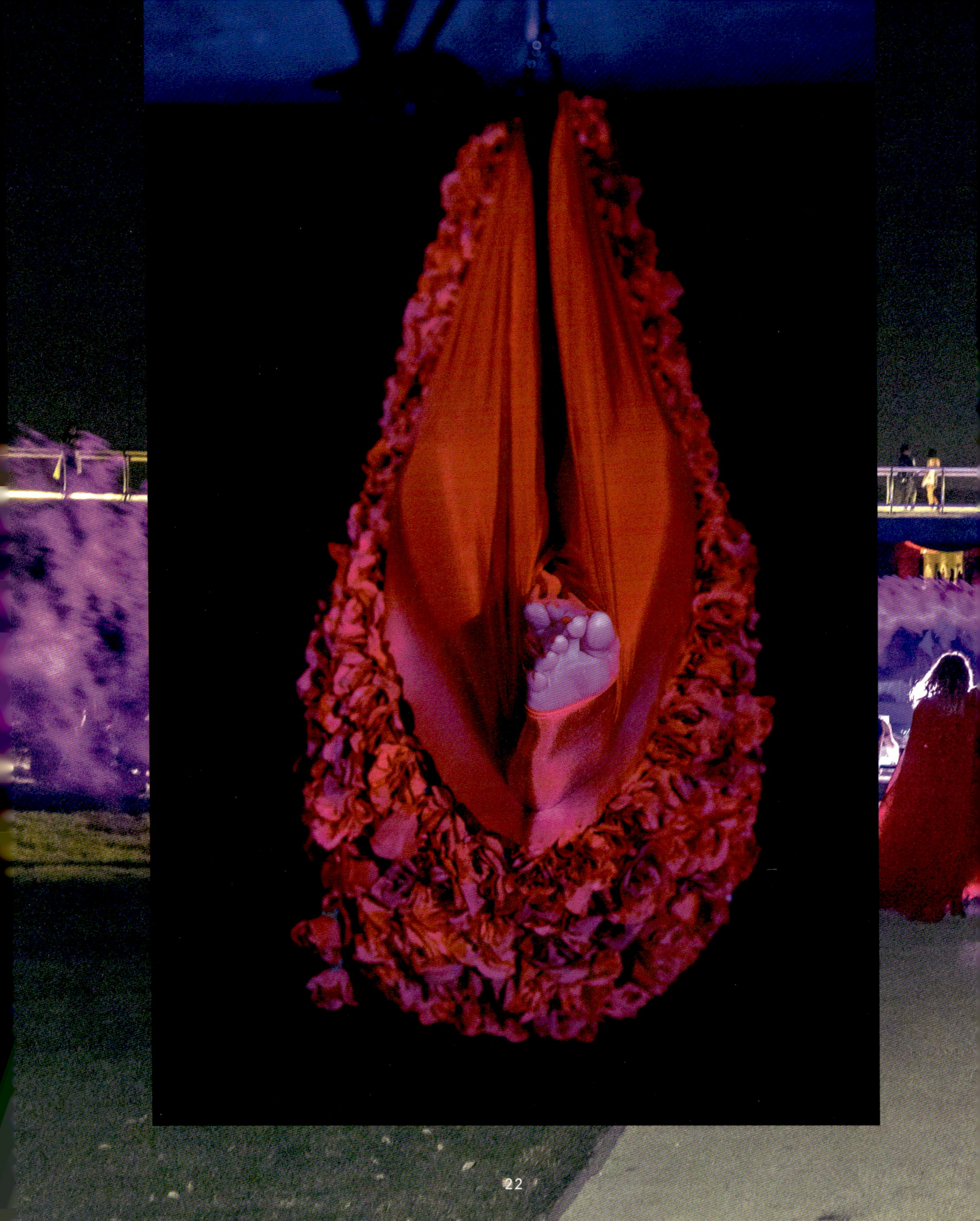

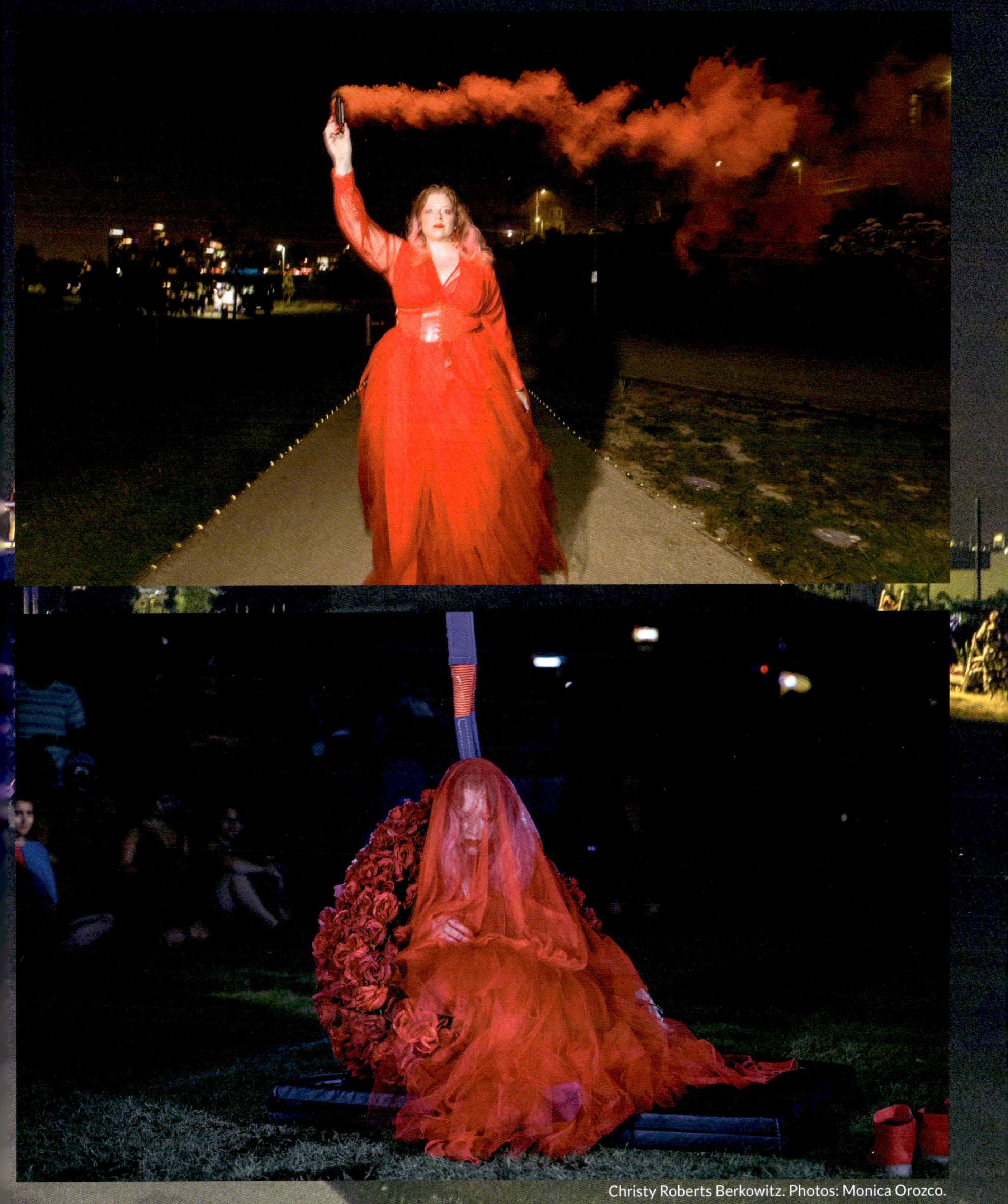

Christy Roberts Berkowitz. Photos: Monica Orozco.

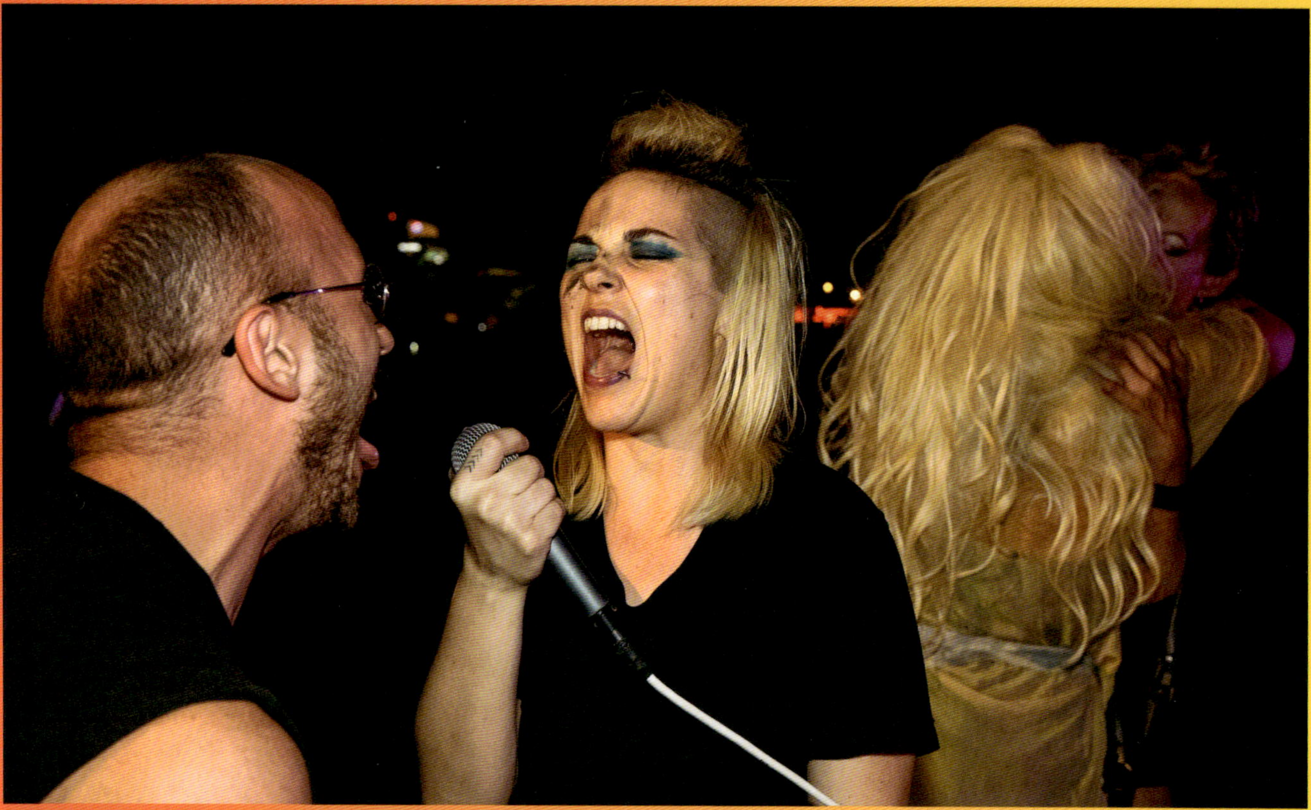

Patty Schemel and Object as Subject. Photos: Safi Alia Shabaik.

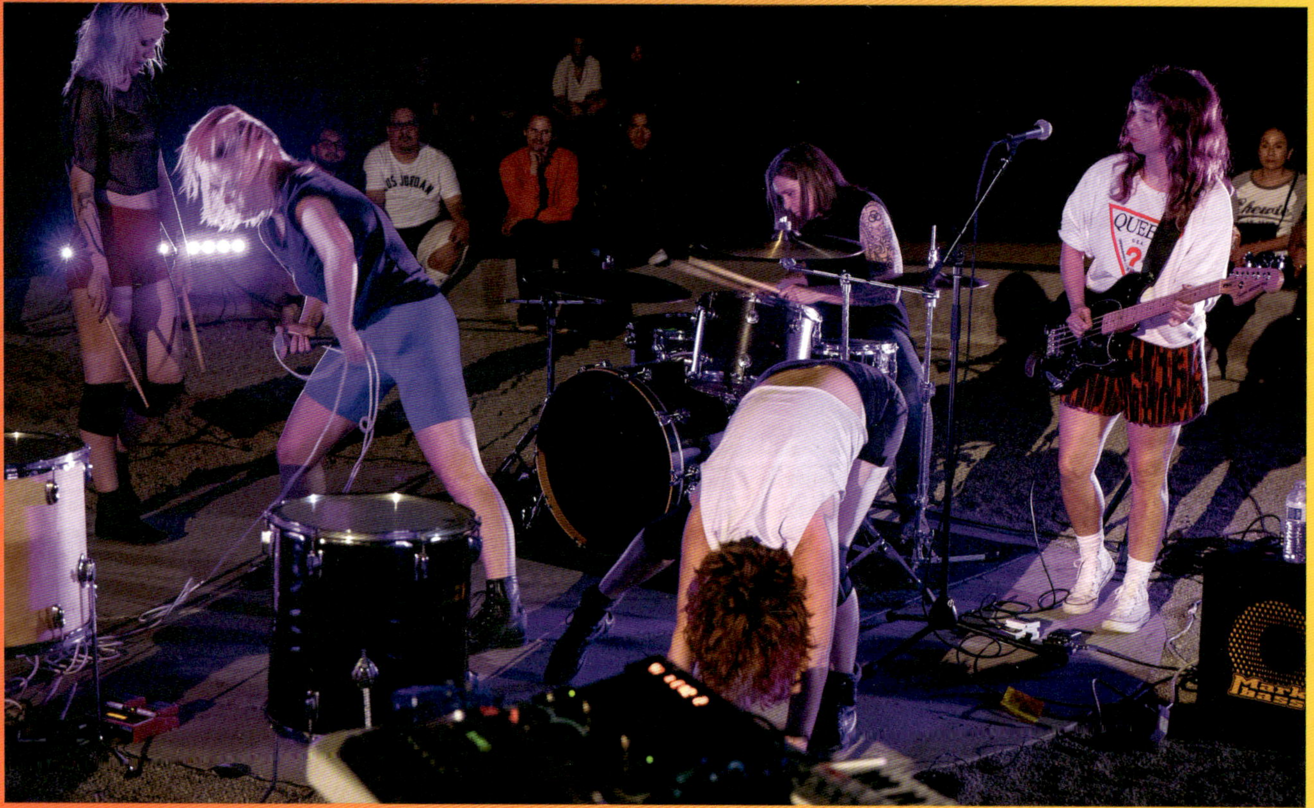

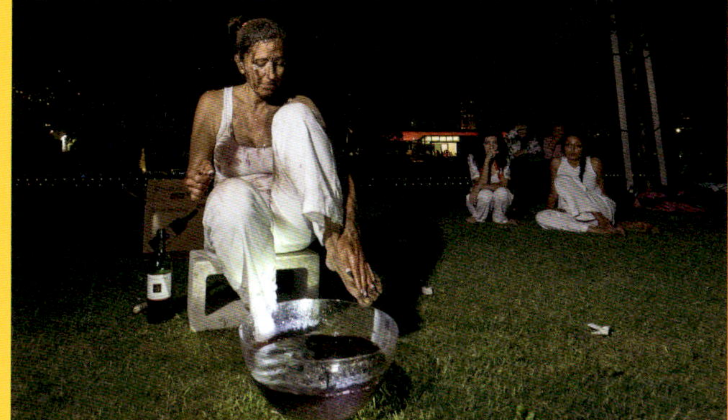

Amitis Motevalli. Photo: Monica Orozco.

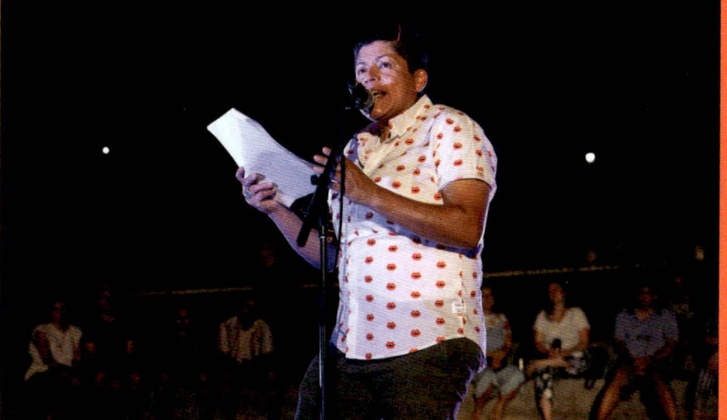

Raquel Gutiérrez. Photo: Safi Alia Shabaik.

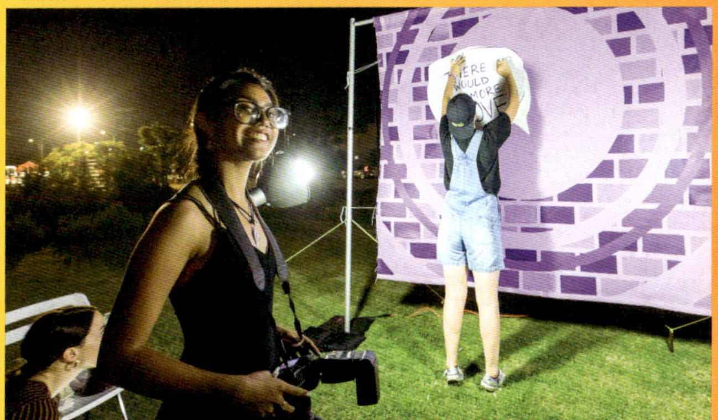

Elana Mann and Las Fotos Project. Photo: Monica Orozco.

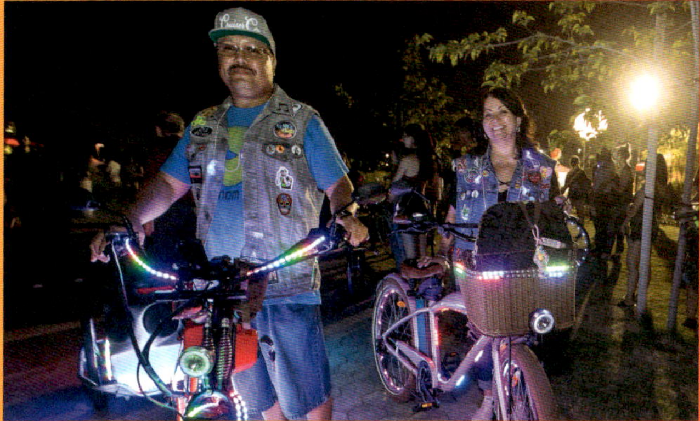

People for Mobility Justice. Photo: Monica Orozco.

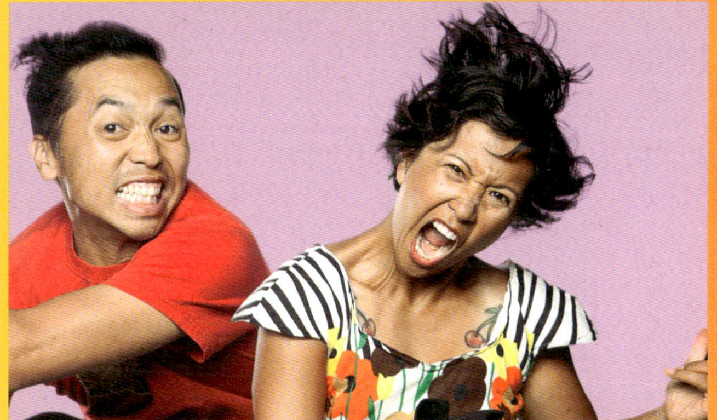

Janice Gomez and Fatima Hoang. Photo: Austin Young.

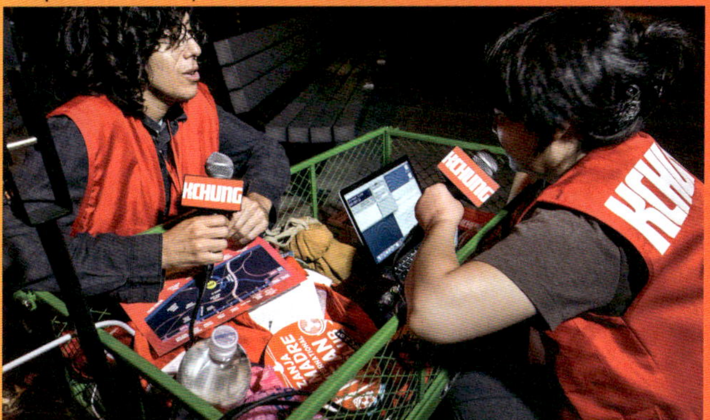

Jennifer Moon and KCHUNG. Photo: Monica Orozco.

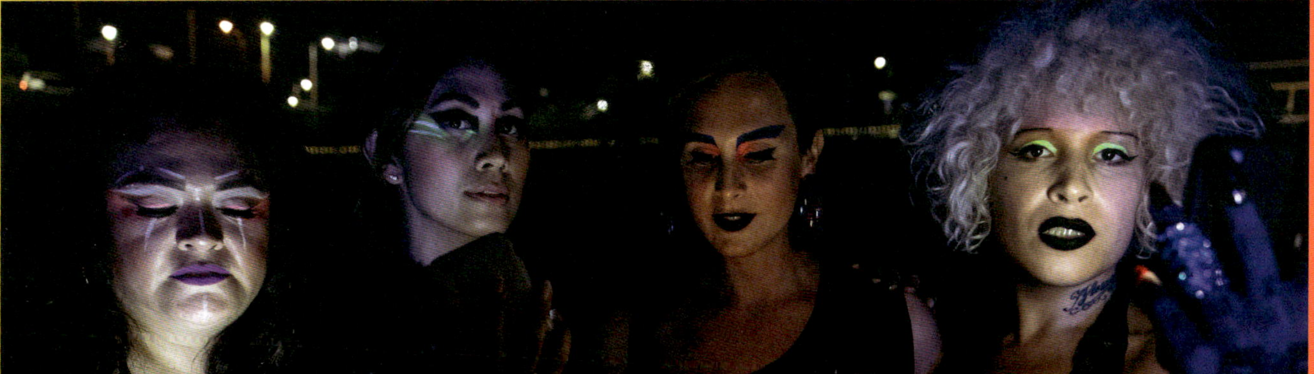

Mariana Marroquin, Rain Valdez, Zackary Drucker, and Mz Neon. Photo: Safi Alia Shabaik.

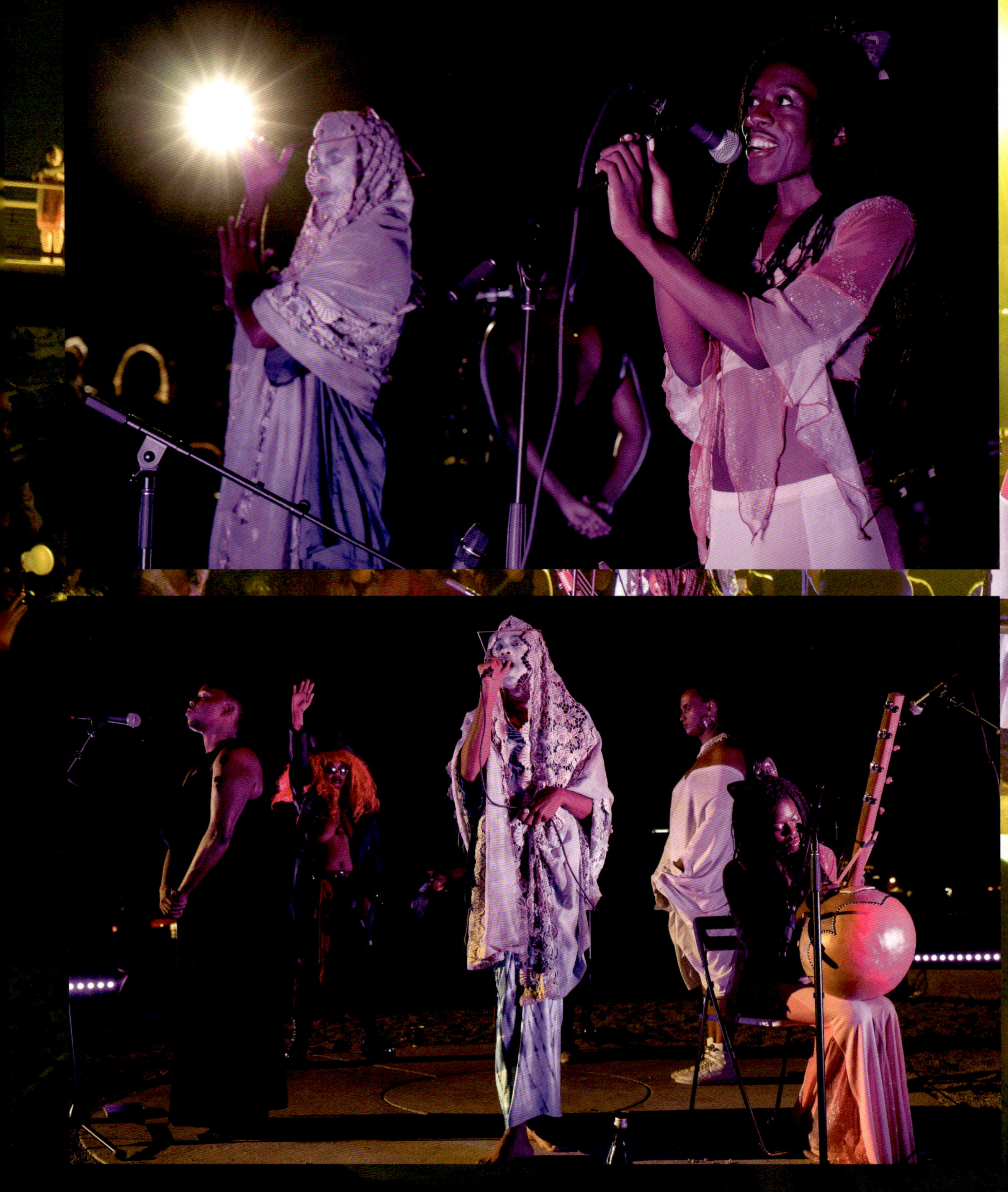

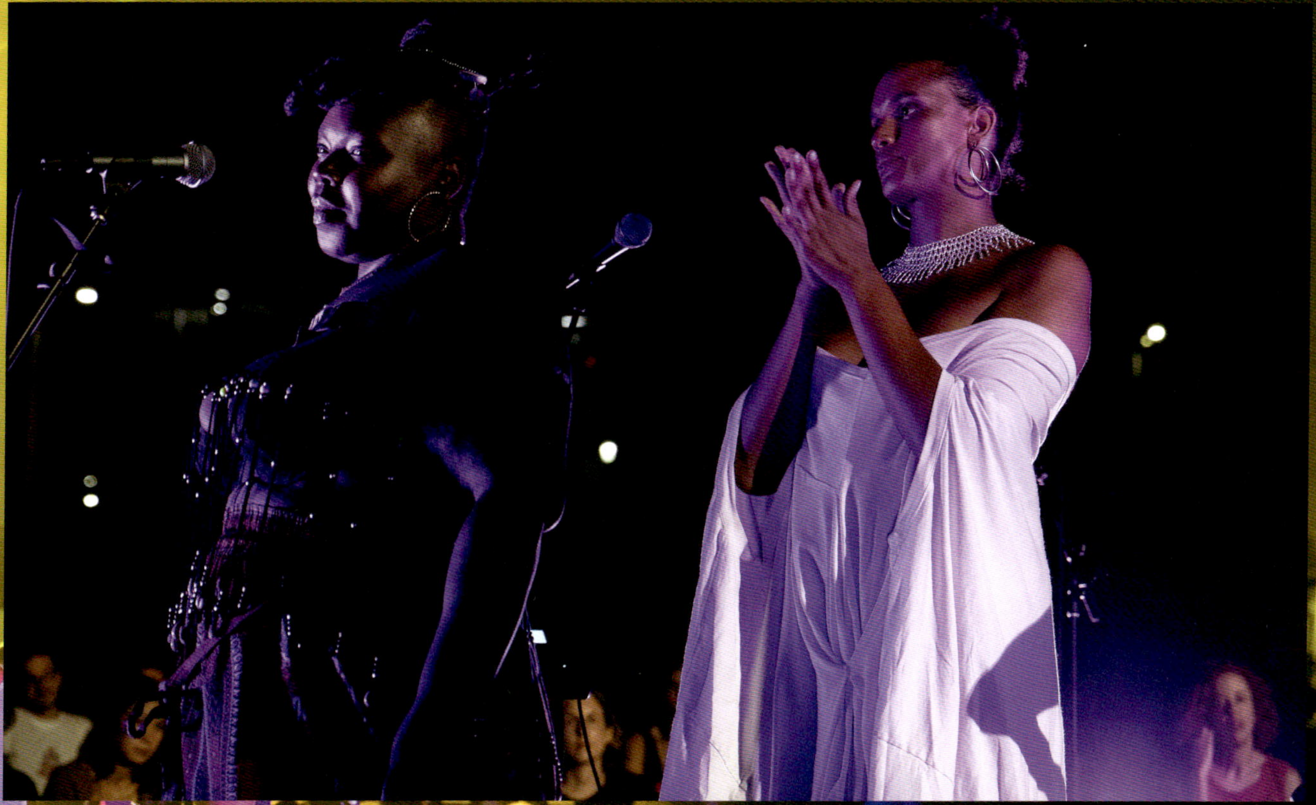

#SNATCHPOWER

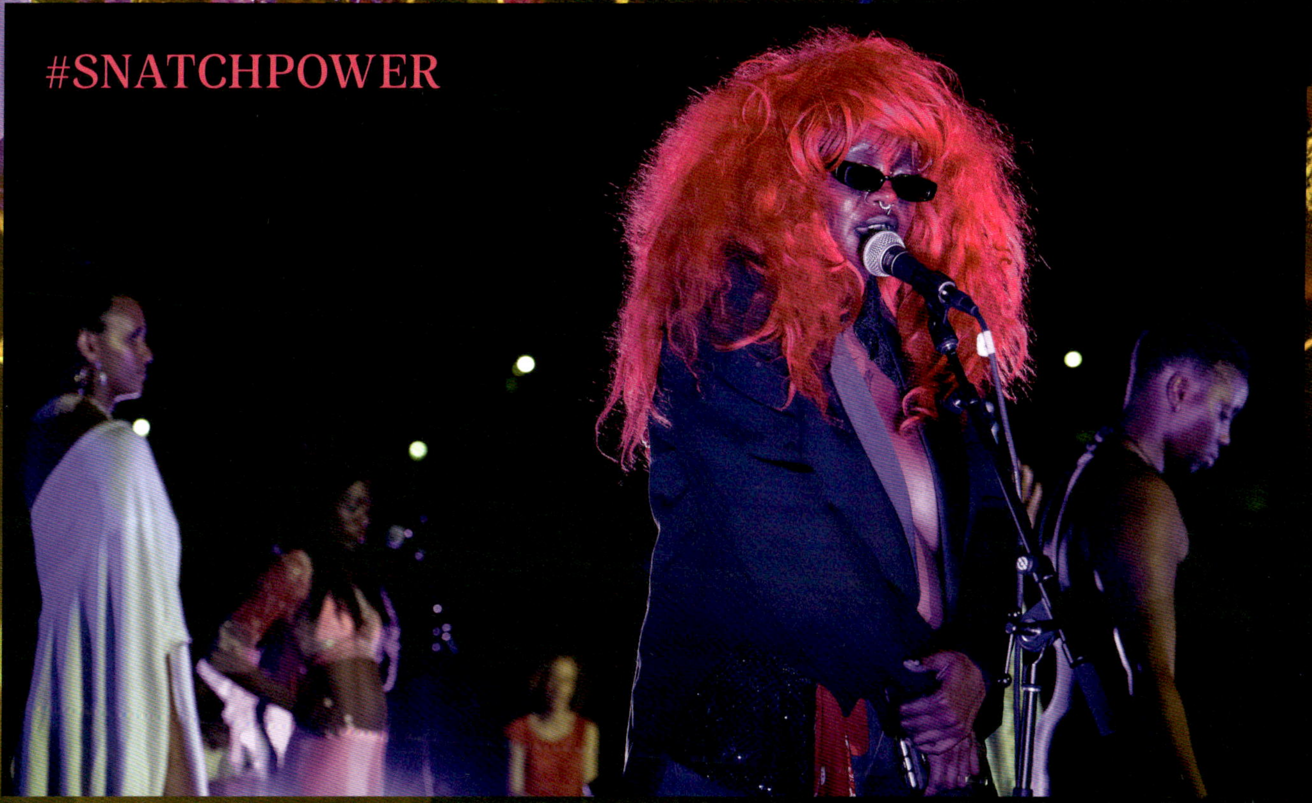

#SNATCHPOWER: The Uhuruverse, Earth to Jordi, Sarah Gail, Davia Spain, Ayotunde Osareme, sondriaWRITES. Photos: Safi Alia Shabaik

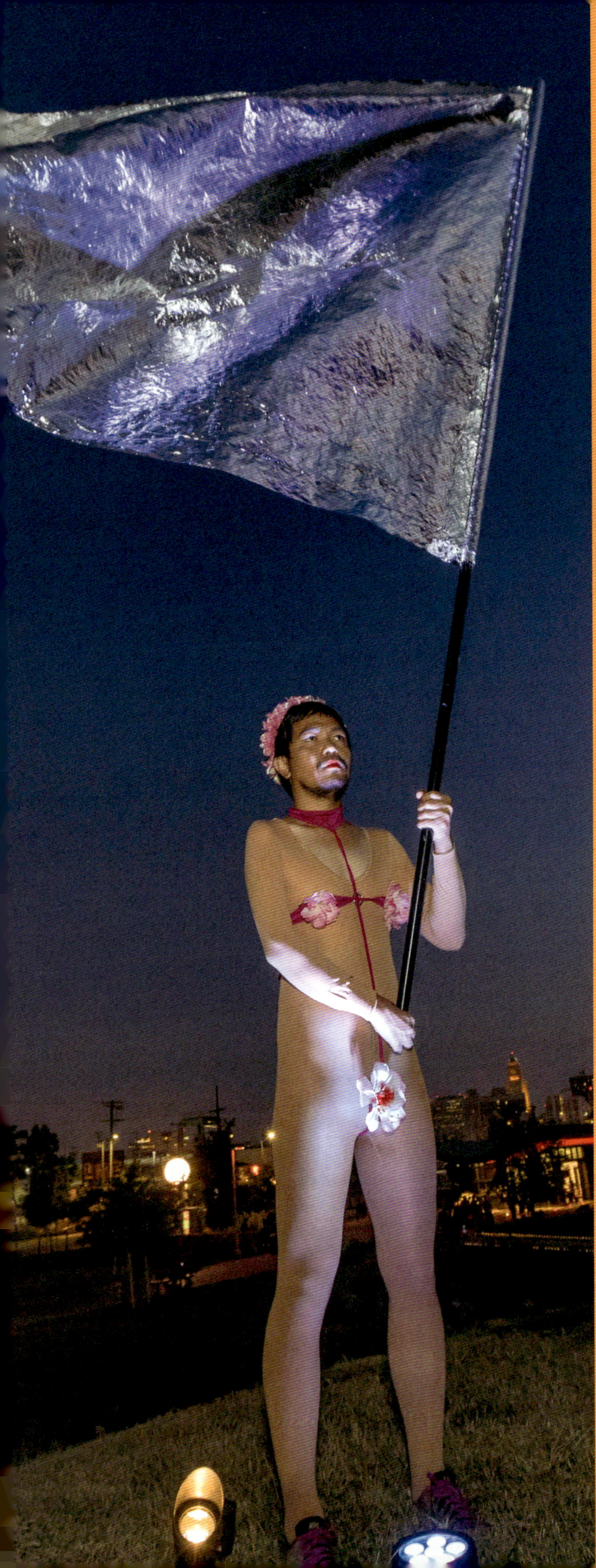

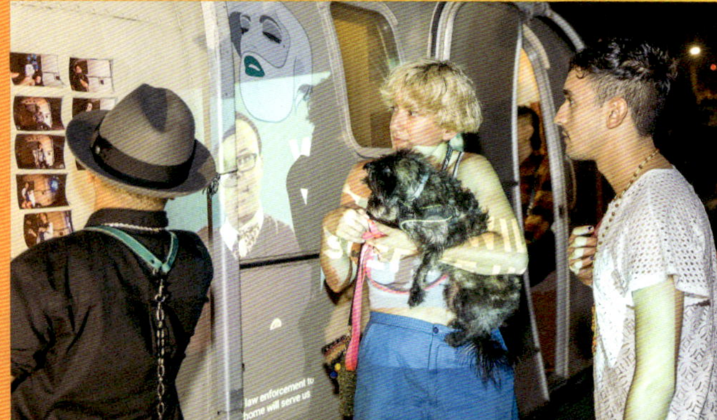

Gender Justice LA. Photo: Monica Orozco.

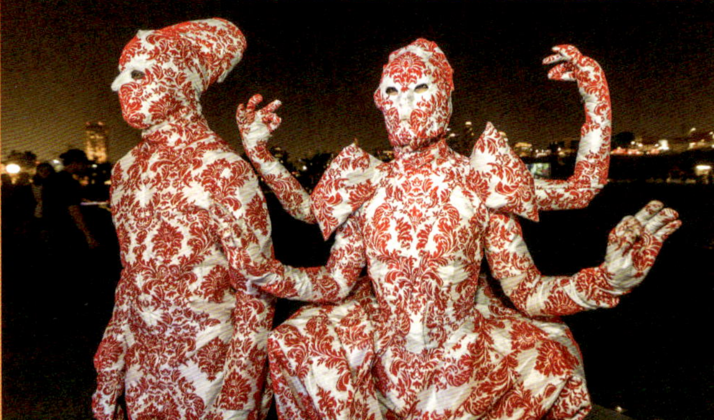

Yozmit. Photo: Monica Orozco.

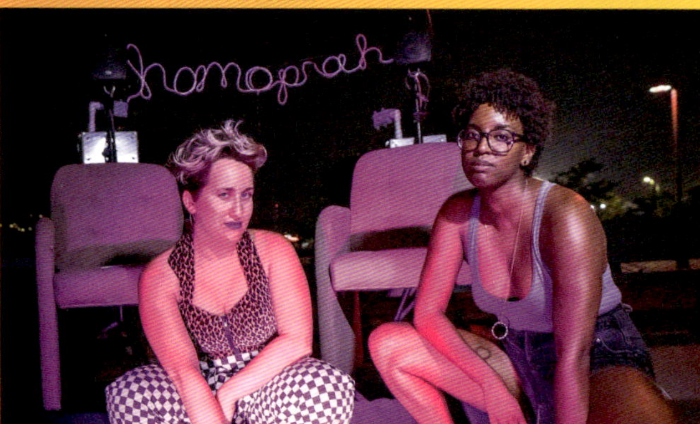

bitchface. Photo: Monica Orozco.

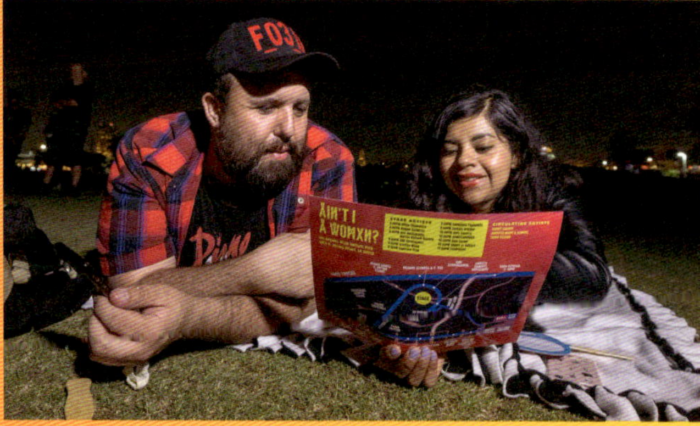

Audience member. Photo: Monica Orozco.
Left: Thinh Nguyen. Photo: Monica Orozco.

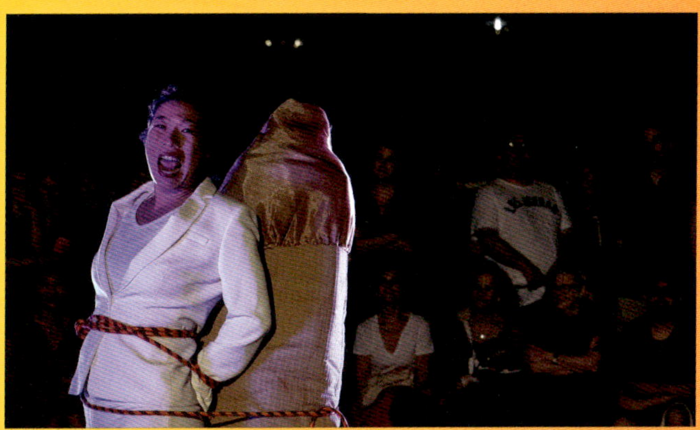

Kristina Wong. Photo: Safi Alia Shabaik.

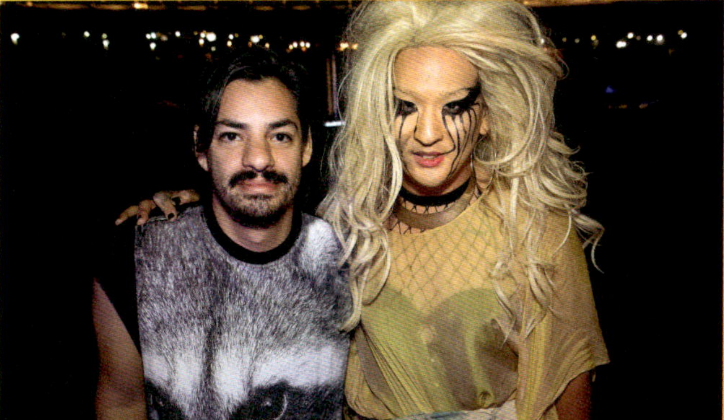

Xina Xurner. Photo: Safi Alia Shabaik.

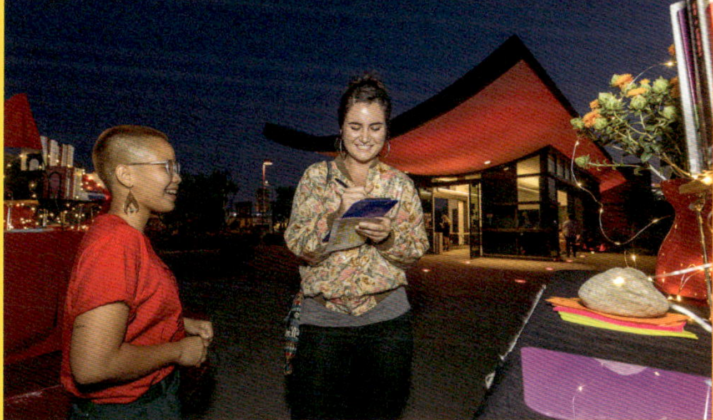

Feminist Library on Wheels. Photo: Monica Orozco.

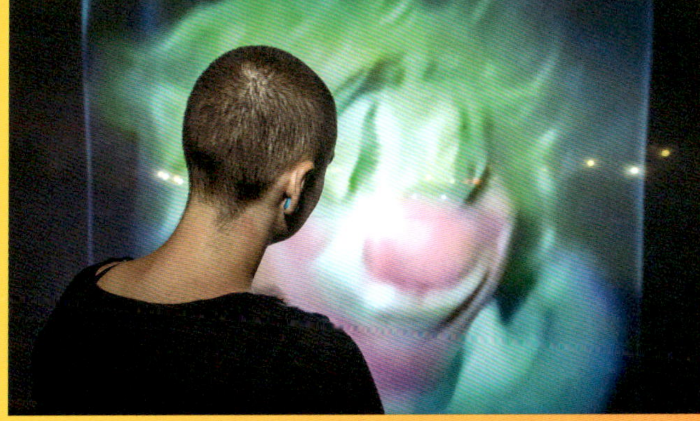

Audience member. Photo: Monica Orozco.
Right: Sculpture by Martha Carrillo. Photo: Monica Orozco.

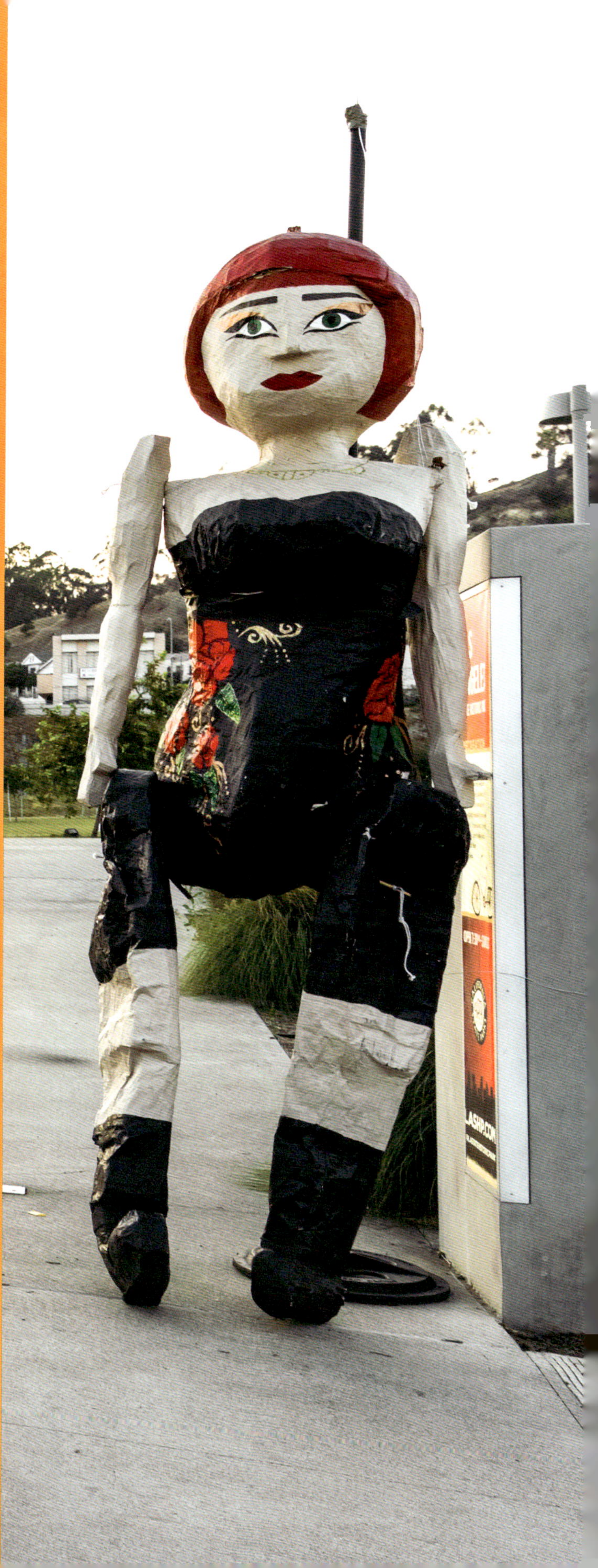

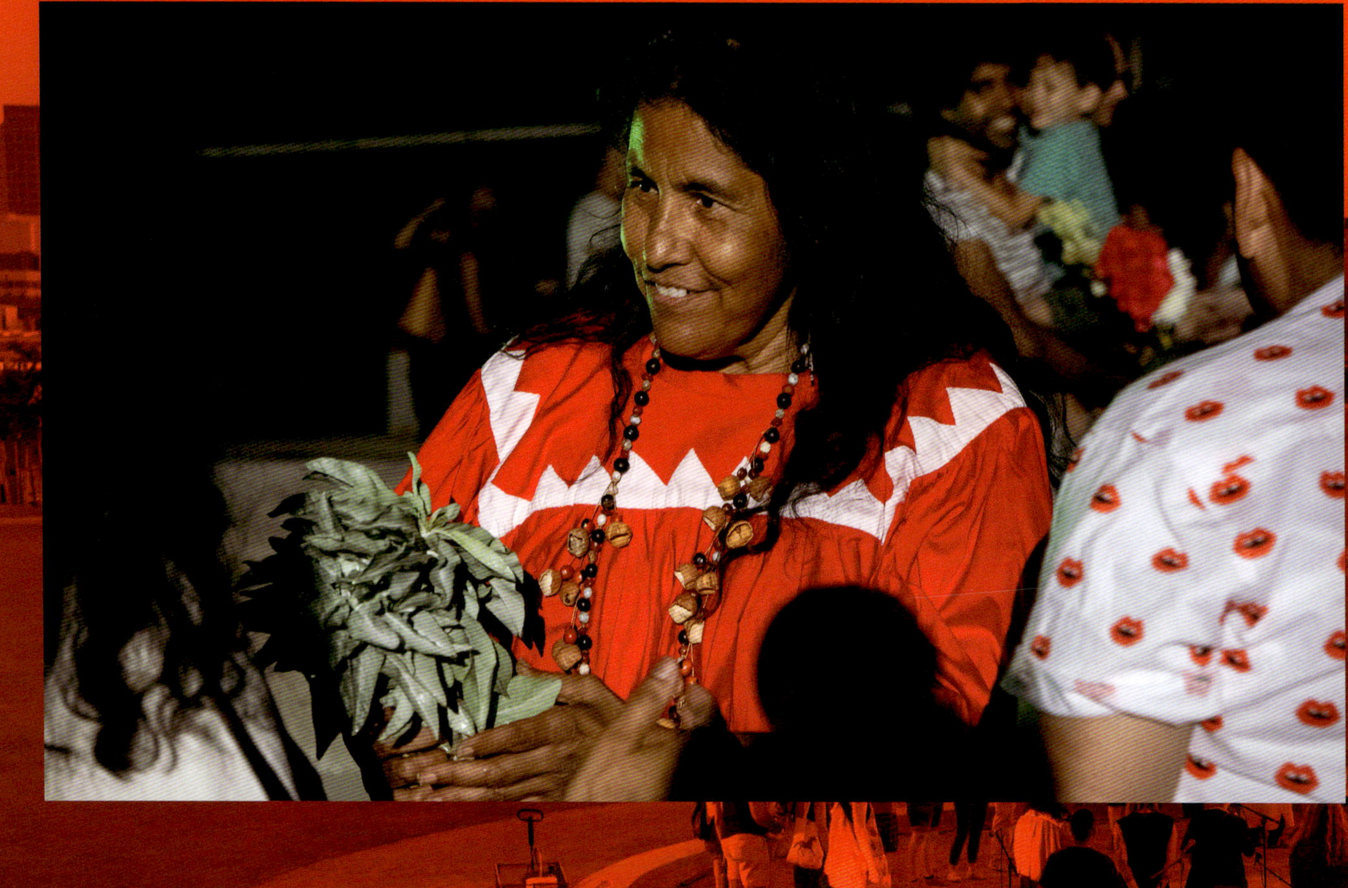

Everything Is Medicine/e.i.m.

Olivia Chumacero

Art is a tool. Science is a tool. These two principal tools are continually evolving from the collective knowledge of the humxyn species. EVERY existing culture on our mother planet holds some aspect of this collective knowledge in its blood memory. Personally, I draw from my Indigenous legacy.

I weave oral traditions, coyote stories, anecdotes, ceremonies, spirit runs and observe the unspoken, the unwritten, the intangible. Armed with these tools, I maneuver a path that we call life.

www.EverythingIsMedicine.wordpress.com

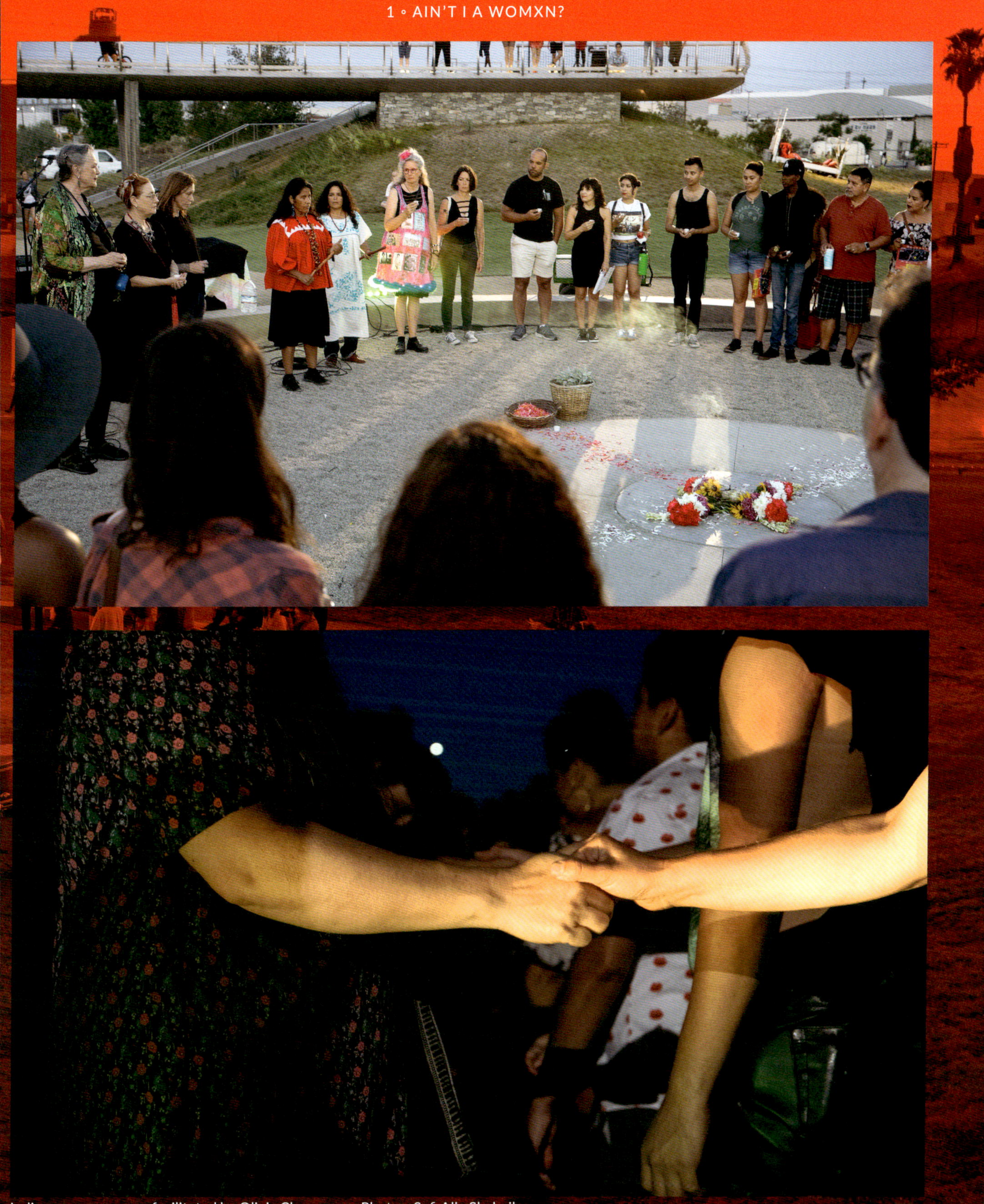

Indigenous ceremony facilitated by Olivia Chumacero. Photos: Safi Alia Shabaik.

Under A Dark Sky amidst Strangers, Not so Unfamiliar
Eva Recinos

You might mistake the glittering holes in the sky for stars, but they're helicopters lazily hanging over us, high above the city's smog. But while some parts of the Los Angeles State Historic Park are bright tonight, you have to feel your way around the dark in other parts, trusting your legs to get you there. Martha Carrillo's larger-than-life dolls—papier-mâché giants with impressive sartorial taste, one wearing an all-black get-up—greet you, and you realize, then, that this must be the place.

The entrance is one of the brightest spots, energized by students showcasing their zines on tables. The zines tackle issues of social justices in ways far wiser than most adults would expect. They talk about safe spaces, about transgender discrimination, and about ICE. On the other side, Daisy Noemi of LA Zine Fest greets you, and you flip through gorgeous pages of creatives' work—some glossy, some photocopied, others hand drawn. Some are uplifting, some funny, some sexy, and some raw. Teens made a group of these zines, too, after participating in an ArtworxLA workshop with artist Brenzy Solorzano and reflecting on gender. You're impressed by the creativity of these students. You pick up the carefully made publications one by one, treasuring the vision that went into each, then head into the park because you know that performances are about to begin.

You're used to seeing art in an institutional setting or reading about it inside a bookstore or a bar. But this is the dry outdoors of the city, and you know the sun will set soon. You know the helicopters are watching. Something about the whole thing feels risky, being out so late,

being so open to creative expression in a space that the next day will go back to being a park. You feel exposed, but you're ultimately OK with it.

On your way to the makeshift main stage, set up near a footbridge in the middle of the park, you see the performance trio Ni Santas setting up: they've covered a bed with dark-red sheets and pillows screen printed with words that read "never again." Soon, fake blood gushes down the middle of the mattress. The piece reflects on the relationship that femme-identified people often have to beds, to pain, and on the way that pain is often ignored. Even then, the piece also refers to "sisterhood" and a shared trauma.

The main stage is a circle, so that you can see others in the audience laugh or cry or nod along. You can watch people snap enthusiastically or drape their arms around the bodies next to them. Writer and artist Raquel Gutiérrez takes their place in the middle of the circle and talks about so many things that you have struggled to put into words—so many art world controversies that seem to be cut and dry but are anything but. About how Latinx artists want more spaces to be creative in their neighborhoods; about what it means to "endure the professionalization that comes with higher educational institutions." You nod along with so many others in the crowd, hearing words that lay a certain truth to your own narrative.

As Gutiérrez reads, a drone flies nearby, and the couple near you flips it off. It's recording the event as part of the official documentation team, but the couple doesn't

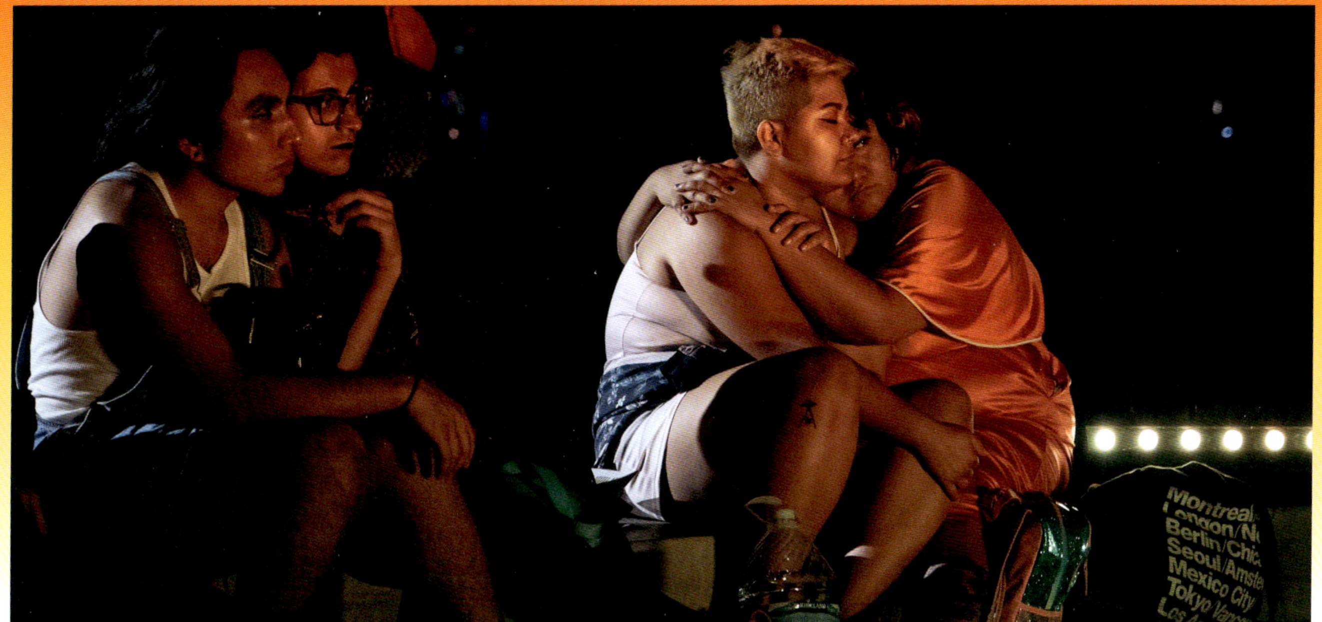

know that, and neither do you. You feel as if in this city someone or something is always watching.

You keep walking the grounds, your eyes flitting from one performance to another. Soon, Christy Roberts Berkowitz hangs from the nearby bridge enshrouded in a silky womblike cocoon made of bright-red fabric adorned with matching fabric roses. She has been hoisted up by collaborators, her cocoon held by a harness attached to the bridge, and her body swings slowly at first, then more quickly. She shifts her weight occasionally to make herself more comfortable. The sight is gorgeous yet eerie, like a slant of light coming through a slightly open door.

Later, on top of that same bridge, you watch Kiki Xtravaganza turn the concrete sidewalk into a runway. Kiki wears a mask with a permanent smile and a dark visor with just a little bling. Her outfits unfurls in a cacophony of patterns, topped off with a cape and white gloves. She shimmies and vogues and struts her way across the length of the bridge: each step deliberate, each turn razor sharp. This is her stage; you're just lucky to be near it.

Later still, you strike up conversations with strangers. This is not something you often feel safe doing either because you usually get leered at on the streets this late at night or because you feel shy, unsure of yourself, incomplete. Here, the conversation seems to flow easily.

You turn just in time to see the artist rafa esparza being dragged by a lowrider, a crowd following in the dust of its wheels. Then back at the main stage, a man with a portable speaker and microphone exclaims, "No tengan miedo de la reina." Volunteers push through the crowd, which sways slightly as it makes room for them. Nao Bustamante is at the center, dressed as a Zumba instructor who is many, many months pregnant. This is a gender-reveal party, but not for the unborn child the Zumba instructor carries—instead, the instructor reveals audience members' genders with the help of cupcakes she and her helpers hand out.

Even a dog joins the party, picking a cupcake of its own as the hype man with the microphone—artist Marcus Kuiland-Nazario—yells, "¡Perra, perra, pinche perra!" Soon, a full-grown, tattooed adult emerges from the Zumba instructor. Pony Lee Musgrave runs around in a diaper, and Bustamante starts to chase her quasi-newborn. Rainbow-colored smoke breaks up the inky black of the night, like drops of paint on a canvas.

It seems the night might never end, even after the sky can't get any darker. You want to head home, but it takes a while to find a spot where an Uber can pick you up, and in the darkness you feel vulnerable yet powerful. You walk with the certainty of someone who feels validated, even if for that one night. The rest of the city seems so distant. You get in the car and close the door, but the feeling is still there.

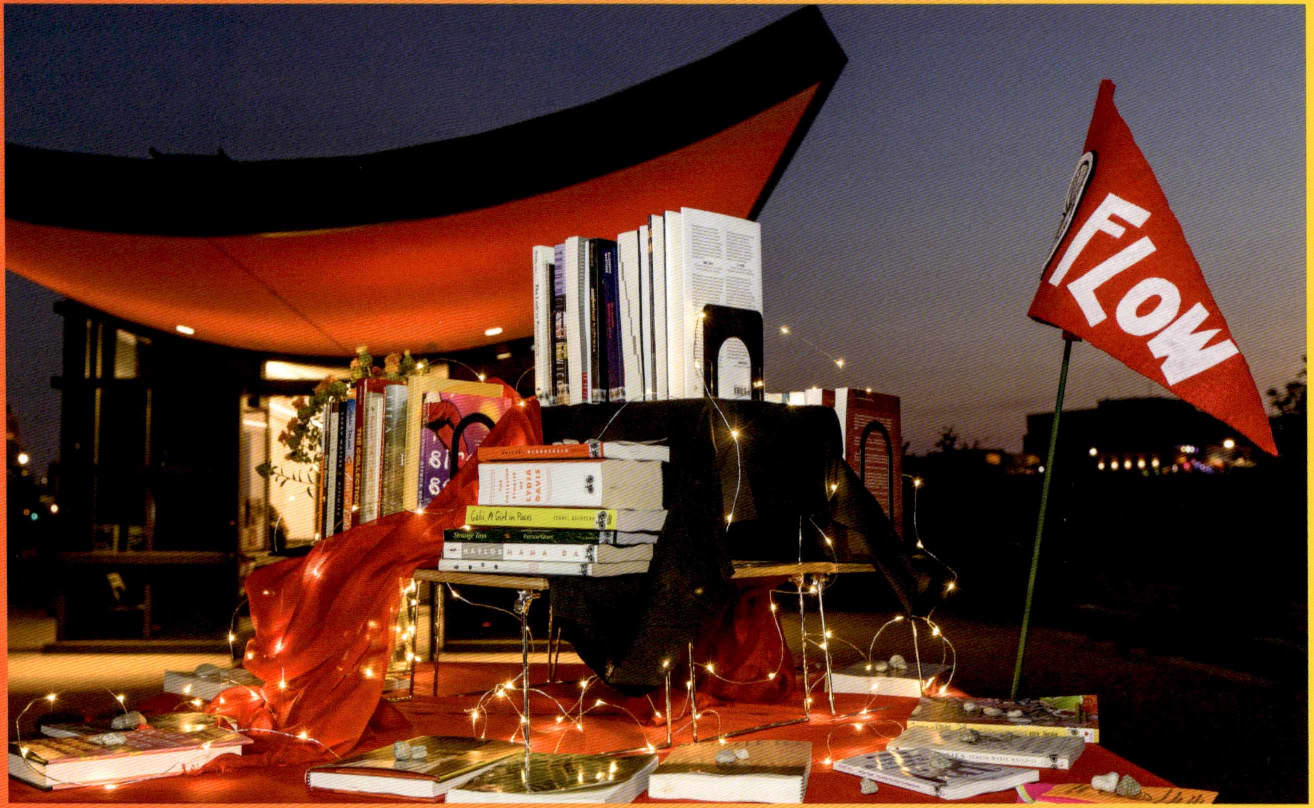

Feminist Library on Wheels. Photos: Monica Orozco.

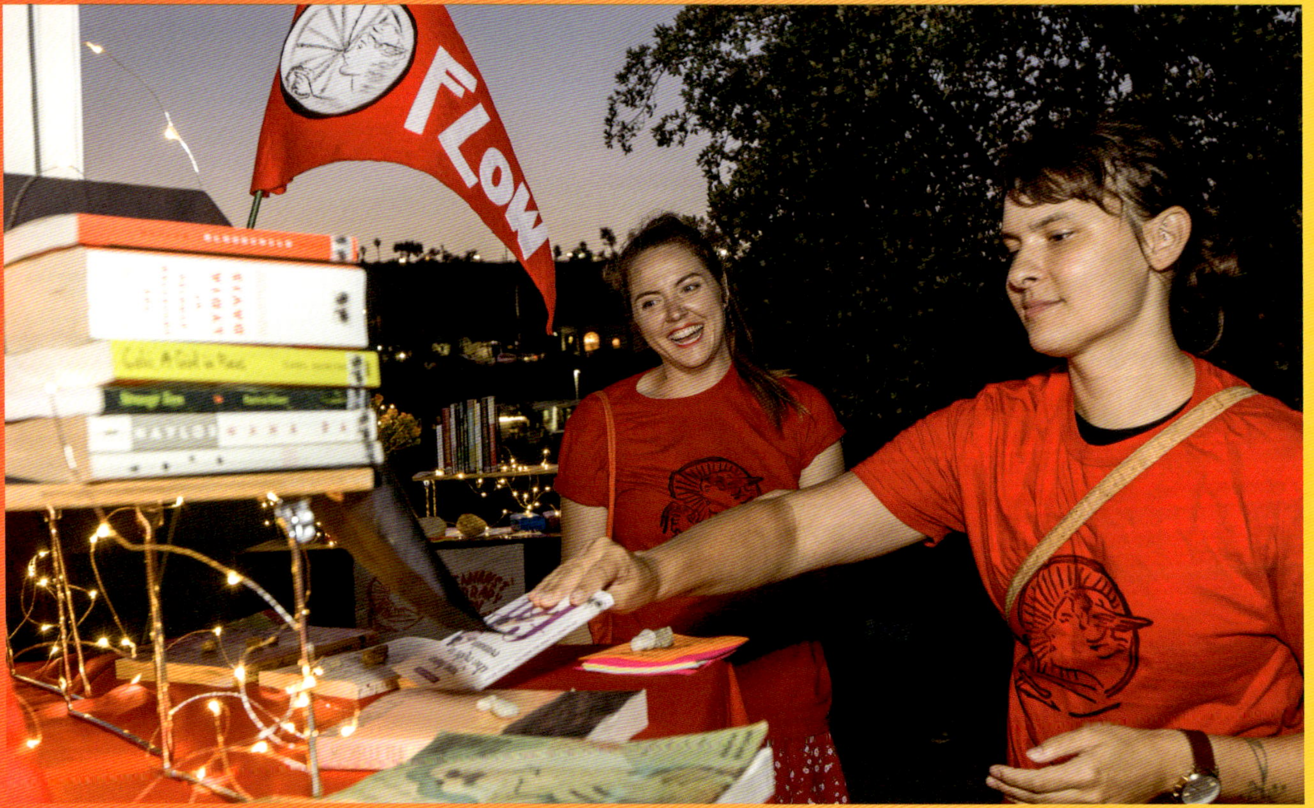

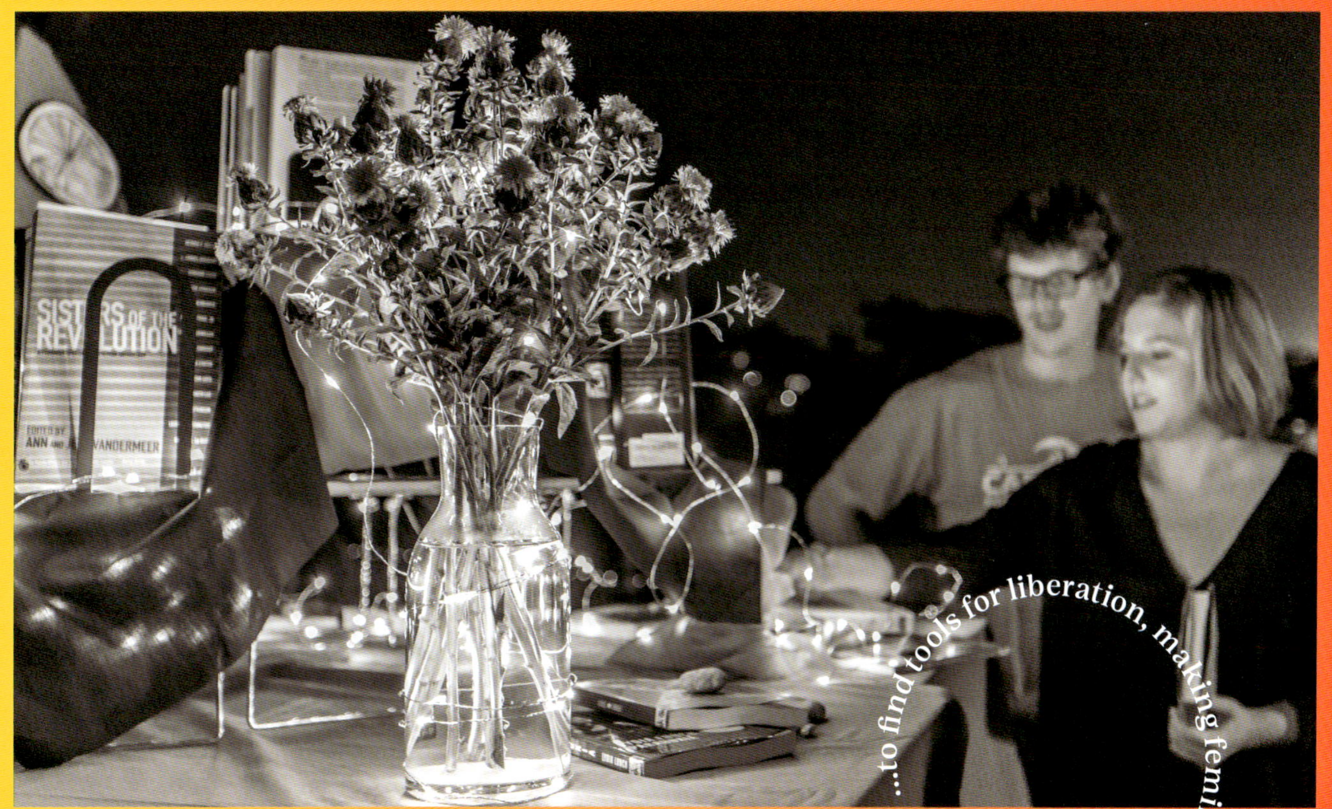

The Feminist Library On Wheels (FLOW)

The Feminist Library on Wheels (FLOW) is a free mobile lending library of donated books, founded in July 2014. Anyone can sign up for a free library card with us and check out as many books as they want, for as long as they want. Our main branch is located at the Feminist Center for Creative Work, and we have drop-off locations and attend events all over the Los Angeles area. Our mission is to celebrate and promote feminist works and move them among communities to center marginalized voices and experiences. FLOW joyfully empowers people to find tools for liberation, making feminism accessible to all. We're nonhierarchical, collaborative, and antioppressive; we strive to be anticapitalist and aantiracist through our sharing of material resources and knowledge as well as through the programming we do and events we attend. FLOW makes feminism, books, and human-powered transportation more accessible and visible. All three can be tools for self-determination, greater mobility, and welcoming community.

2

how does gender
perform you?

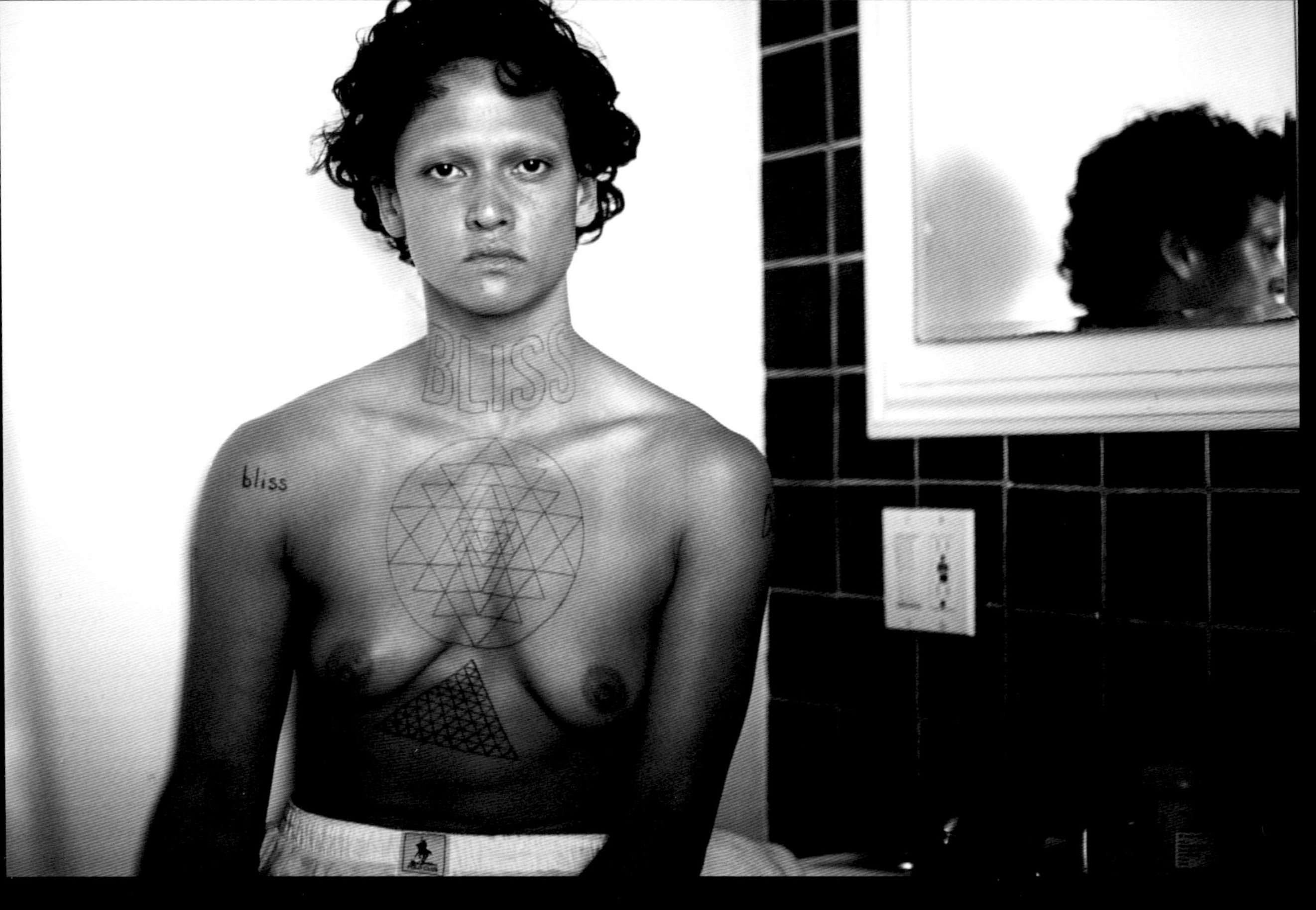

Untitled Self Portrait by boychild, 2015.

Portrait of Bliss
Allison Noelle Conner

boychild perches on the edge of a sink, topless and bare-faced. Her gaze is direct and unwavering, as if she is looking past your exterior appearance and into the murky depths of your soul. Because she is in the bathroom, framed by a white wall to the left and black tile to the right, the photo feels diaristic and unfussy. We could be glimpsing a quiet moment before the glitchy glam and strobe lights.

No matter how many times I view the black-and-white self-portrait, my eyes always seek out boychild's tattoos. *BLISS* is written out in big block letters across her neck. Underneath that are two large geometrical designs spanning her chest and abdomen. And *bliss* appears again, a small scrawl in lowercase handwriting, in the space connecting the shoulder to the upper arm. I repeat the words while staring at the triangular designs. *Bliss, bliss.* Isn't that what we're all after? A taste of euphoria? It feels like a spell, silently chanting as my eyes wander the hexagonal mazes.

If you're familiar with the artist's bizarro-maximalist costumes and performances, then the photo could read as an anomaly. There are no incandescent white contact lenses in her eyes. Volcanic paint isn't oozing from the top of her shaved head. Her figure, usually pliant as a canvas, isn't covered in intricate cipheresque patterns or a thick armor of gold glitter. Her mouth is shut tight, so we're unable to see if her teeth are flashing neon or metallic or corralled by thin threads, as in her performance *BODY|SELF* in 2013.[1]

The performance alias of artist, dancer, and photographer Tosh Basco, boychild, is known for mixing improvisatory movement with queer-nightlife aesthetics. The character blossomed from research Basco conducted on the healing role of clowns and shamans in non-Western cultures. Inspired by and incubated within the drag scenes in San Francisco during the 2010s

---

1   Jack Halberstam, "Unbuilding Gender," *Places*, October 2018, https://placesjournal.org/article/unbuilding-gender/?cn-reloaded=1.

(performer Dia Dear was an early influence), boychild's agitated physicality teeters on the thresholds of presence and transformation, confession and fantasy. These early performances, which she has referred to as "freak shows," attracted many admirers, including Shayne Oliver, the visionary behind the radical streetwear label Hood By Air, who cast her as a model in their runway shows.[2] From there, boychild has brought her visceral energy exchanges to museums, festivals, fashion events, and more.

Unlike the self-portrait, these works fuse the physical body with the virtual body, translating the vast malleability engendered by the internet to life outside of the screen. Within this fusion and the bewilderment it may cause is the celebration of bodily forms divorced from our binaristic definitions. One of my favorite performance clips is from the OFF Festival in Poland in 2013. Taken on a shaky cell phone camera while boychild was on tour with the musician Mykki Blanco, the clip shows the artist lip-syncing to a house remix of the nervy Destiny's Child anthem "Say My Name."[3] Bathed in streaks of dark-blue light, mouth and hands glowing, boychild looks like a wayward glitch that has escaped its system. Writhing and flexing, every inch of her contorted body summons up a combustible emotion, pushing us beyond the limits of language. The song transforms from a take-down of foolish men into a frenzied horror tale of recognition and longing, becoming a prescient plea and warning from the very digital images we think we control.

In contrast, the self-portrait—part of Freewaves' *Dis...Miss* postcard series—seems rather straightforward. Are we seeing the *real* boychild? At first glance, it would appear so. boychild seems to be presenting her rawest self: casual, zero adornments, vulnerable pose. It's tempting to think we're being shown Oz behind the curtain or, in other words, the singular and comprehensible self beneath all the makeup and masks. Reading the portrait this way not only assumes there's a clear demarcation between *person* and *persona* but also suggests the difference can and should be easily spotted. It implies that the more fanciful images are fantasy, in no way consequential to

<hr>

2   Rachel Small, "Boychild," *Interview Magazine*, December 10, 2014, www
    .interviewmagazine.com/art/boychild.
3   Agata Rakotny, *Mykki Blanco / boychild's performance* (Off Festival, 2013), 2013, YouTube,
    https://www.youtube.com/watch?v=DQw_kHoGKic.

"real" life. The person is the one who stays the same, while the persona is the social facade, subject to external societal pressures. The more a person adheres to our idea of conventionality, the more "true" we find them to be.

While viewing the photo, I wanted to believe I was seeing an unfiltered version of boychild, one turned away from the flamboyant theatrics. It can be comforting to know there's a solid, unyielding form guiding us through the ebbs and flows of existence—to confirm that selfhood is a fixed state. My comfort was short-lived, however, disrupted by the question appearing on the back of the postcard:

How does gender perform you?

Suddenly, I was no longer a passive viewer. The question scrambled my thoughts around person/a. We've been told gender is an inherent truth, but we all know it's another construction, a mask we're forced to wear for legibility. To that end, where does that performance end and your essence begin?

Like a trickster imp, boychild teases us with beguiling riddles, daring us to activate the unspoken energy between image and audience. The question slows us down, facilitating a deeper engagement than our knee-jerk reactions. The rush to define what or who we're seeing can inadvertently reveal more about our desires for simplistic narratives of identity and self-expression. We balk at depictions glorifying the precarity of self and reject them as unnatural or unrealistic. We parrot the ruling political class, who demand a selfhood that is easily identifiable and co-optable. As the curator and writer Legacy Russell states, "The body is a text: every time we define ourselves, we choose definitions—names—that reduce the ways our bodies can be read."[4]

boychild disregards all that desire for clarity, torquing our expectations of self-portraiture along the way. Her work, according to her own bio, strives to communicate "what remains impenetrable through images and through language."[5]

---

4   Legacy Russell, "Glitch Is Error," in *Glitch Feminism: A Manifesto* (New York: Verso, 2020), 73.

5   "Tosh Basco," *Schauspielhaus Zürich*, 2010, www.schauspielhaus.ch/en/personen/205/tosh-basco.

As I scroll through her Instagram feed, it's hard not to think of that impenetrability. Since 2012, boychild has intertwined the app with her process, utilizing it as a sketchbook, behind-the-scenes diary, and digital gallery. No two images are the same—like a subversive riff on #OOTD (Outfit of the Day) accounts, her selfies treat followers to a hallucinogenic trip of galactic avatars and mystical personas. Instead of cycling through an assortment of clothes, boychild presents new identities, stretching selfhood past its breaking point. She continually recedes from viewers—one day she's a reptilian charmer, wearing yellow contact lenses and slathered in green paint; the next day she's a burst of brilliant stardust; on other days, she looks like a feral spirit beamed down for a ritualistic ceremony.

Her selfies subvert the idea of the knowable face. Social media rewards parasocial relationships, where users develop a one-sided bond with media personalities based on highly subjective interpretations of appearance, gesture, and more. Instead of presenting us with a repeatable brand, boychild shares drafts and fantasies, mirroring emotional and spiritual evolutions not easily tracked by likes and retweets. Each selfie is a confrontation that defies the vocabulary we have for concepts such as "body" and "gender." Words such as *otherworldly* and *surreal* do not fully capture boychild's twisting of form and presentation. The drag performer James St. James once described boychild's movement work as an "unraveling of digital images,"[6] and her Instagram selfies certainly extend this unraveling project. Like the artists Claude Cahun and Cindy Sherman, who use self-portraiture to critique and rewrite gender roles, boychild proliferates the self in ways that make us question the stability of identity and intimacy.

The black-and-white self-portrait slyly gestures to this accumulation of selves. While boychild stares directly at us, the mirror to the right captures her blurring reflection. The subtle doubling creates an uncanny effect as the reflection seems to be rapt by something beyond the frame. The tattoos also unsettle our image of the body. At first, the geometric designs reminded me of ancient symbols. Now they also look like technological codes, a figure transformed by the generative merg-

---

6   WOWPresents, *James St. James and boychild: Transformations*, 2013, YouTube, https://www.youtube.com/watch?v=YZpYUNr9eH8.

ing of human and machine. Though shorn of her outré digital aesthetics, boychild's identity cannot keep still.

Meanings continually shift and multiply, but that roving quality does not cancel out the confessional tone. Intimacy should not be understood as the ability to define and name. The impulse to categorize is an oppressive, slippery slope. By refusing to settle upon one text or one definition, boychild enacts an intimacy based on nuance and reciprocity. *How does gender perform you?* Her question flips the camera toward the audience, forcing us to acknowledge the ways in which we mindlessly perform coercion. If we are to make room for our infinite possibilities, we must approach identity as a conversation, a hypertext linking to infinite sources and experiments.

For boychild, the portrait is porous enough to hold multiple subjects. As a viewer, I am implicated by the question, drawn into an improvisatory performance by boychild's beckoning look. Our encounter is less about knowing boychild and more about contemplating our modes of connection. While the question transforms us, the audience, into the subject, the portrait disrupts our unilateral approach to knowledge.

Bliss is found in the fluidity of the self, in the blurred collaboration between person and personas. Stripped of abstractions, the portrait becomes a site of slippery exchange, no longer a static opportunity to categorize and project. In that way, although presenting a tamer side of the boychild persona, the self-portrait still works through similar issues of (re)creation and embodiment. Rawness and construction aren't mutually exclusive. They're all a negotiation, part of a continual dance between exposure and refusal.

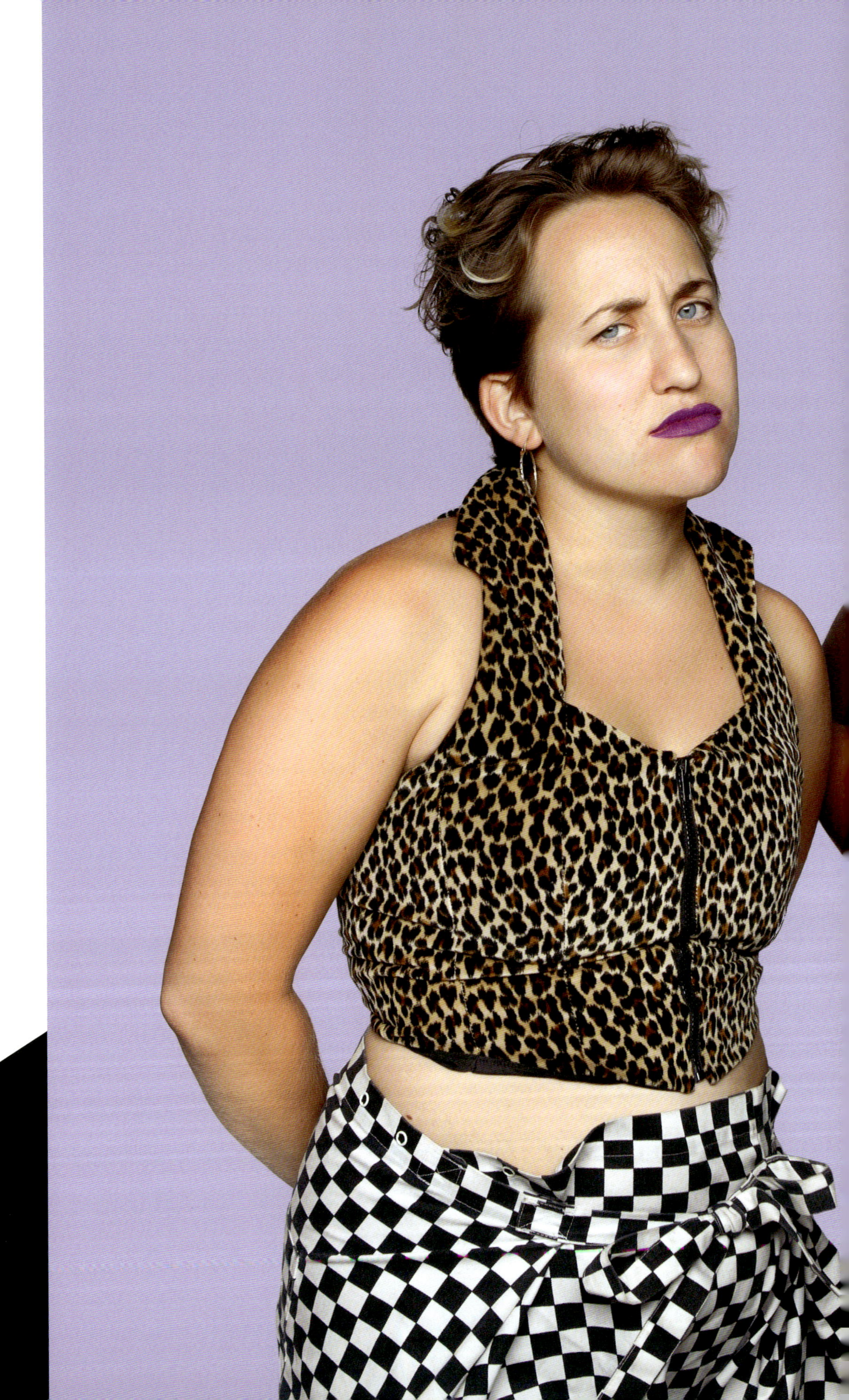

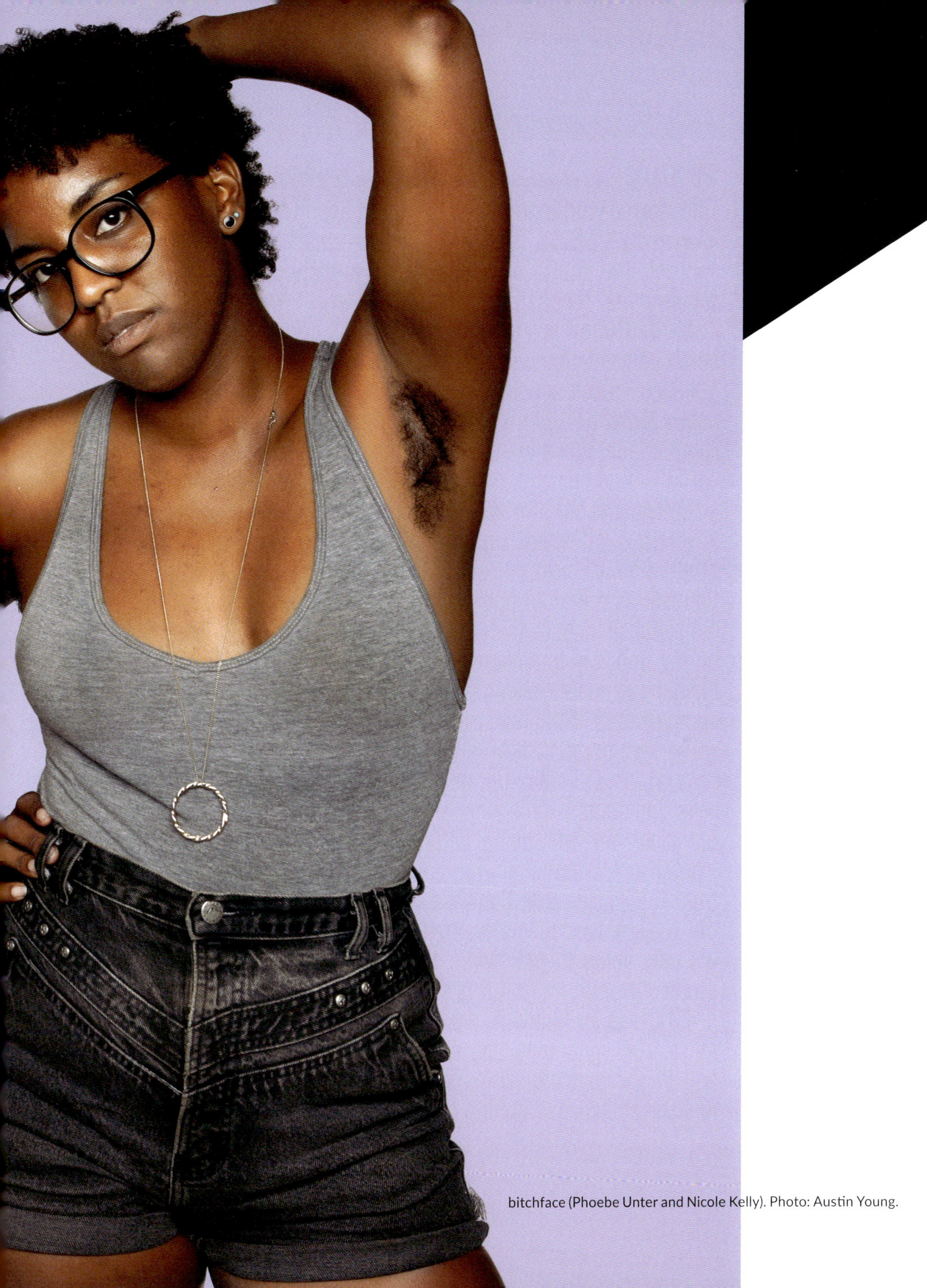

bitchface (Phoebe Unter and Nicole Kelly). Photo: Austin Young.

Whose imagination are you living in?

This started with a dream about Oprah and **Yocheved Zenaida Cohen.** We love Oprah – the woman, the survivor, the journalist – and we love Yocheved – the scholar, the theorist, the *"woman etc."* **Yocheved Zenaida Cohen** is a gender prophet. And here we place her in conversation with America's talk show host and in a lineage of the scholars and radicals before her – bell hooks, Marsha P. Johnson, Audre Lorde, Angela Davis. This is our canon, these are our gxds. These are the thoughts we f*ck with. And this alternate reality **is** our collective future – the one just out of reach. A time when all trans women are safe & affirmed, especially Black trans women. A time when **all womxn** see positive representations of themselves reflected back at them in the culture. When we seriously debate the usefulness of the gender binary, and not of feminism. When it's a given that Black & Indigenous people in this country are long overdue to be compensated. When we are at work dismantling prisons, along with borders. A time when all women are lesbians, finally. Oprah's **most** Tweetable, most a-ha moments: Trans women have always existed in feminism. Try *not* saying *heterosexual* for 365 days. All women are intentional women, on purpose. We suffer from the illusion that there's a great gap that separates the experiences of cis women and trans women. And it's only going to get worse the longer it goes on. We prefer utopic visions to dystopian nightmares. If **Oprah** builds it, we will **come**. We too can move from ignorance and wade through our confusion and in the end emerge smarter and gayer than ever. And the audience watching from home will be **ecstatic.**

of activism.

DAYTIME TALK SHOW (1992 /2028)

ACT I: We long to understand, we want to think ourselves tolerant, yet we still have so many dumb lingering questions
ACT II: But I think it's also evolving, isn't it?
ACT III: First of all what the fuck does a woman look like
ACT IV: You know the binary doesn't relate to feminism for me
ACT V: Our activism means nothing without reparations!

DAYTIME TALK SHOW (1992/2028) includes the voices of Marsha P. Johnson, Jill Johnston, Angela Davis, Judith Butler, bell hooks, Reina Gossett, and Audrey Lorde. In that order. Yocheved Zenaida Cohen was recorded at Pieter Performance Space in 2017.

Our Activism Means Nothing Without Reparations!

STOP USING THE WORD HETERO SEXUAL

YOU DON'T HAVE AN OPPOSITE SEX

Yocheved Zenaida Cohen

is a Black trans lesbian separatist who writes a lot about the intersections of people of color, separatist space, and intentional, womxn's separatist space. She lives in a coven of lesbian separatists who write theory. She was compensated for contributing her voice & ideas to bitchface.

If you heard this, you have been transformed.

Contribute to Yocheved Zenaida Cohen's School & Health & Survival Fund:

www.gofundme.com/yocheveds-survival-and-medical-fund

bitchface

is a podcast hosted, written, recorded & produced by Nicole Kelly and Phoebe Unter, usually taking the form of experimental audiodocs about art, gender and power. NK & Phoebe also collaborate on performances, host events, & publish zines.

Subscribe on iTunes, Stitcher, SoundCloud, wherever. Call 406-28-BITCH and say whatever you want.
Follow: @bitchfacepodcast & @bitchfacepod
www.bitchfacepodcast.com

also have the right to code their genitals the way they want. A lot of people have left feminism. Butchness is not man lite but a subversion of masculinity and a form

Trans women feel underrepresented in feminism because of vaginocentrism. You can be transgender and still have body parts of another sex. All women are intenti

onal women, not because someone told them. All women have the right to a sex designation. People

Daytime Talk Show (1992/2028) by bitchface.

We long to understand, we want to think ourselves tolerant, yet we still have so many lingering questions.

We're on the verge of a new way of thinking about sexuality and gender.

So all these years of doing the *Oprah Show* and now on OWN and in all my conversations, I consider myself open-minded and understanding that homosexuality or sexuality sexuality, heterosexuality, is a spectrum. I was really proud of myself for figuring that out many years ago.

So when you're a lesbian ...

I am a trans lesbian separatist who writes a lot about the intersections of people of color, separatist space, and intentional women's separatists sp@ce. And I am so honored to be here. Now would be a good time to mention that I am a nonbinary trans woman, which I'd like to write as a "woman, etc." It's racialized and specific, and I don't have 20 minutes to explain.

I know some of you have grown up in smaller communities, who have gone on and married and done the thing that society said that you should do and are leading really miserable lives now because you didn't have the courage to say, "This isn't who I am."

I heard a lot of critiques from trans women friends about feeling underrepresented in feminism because of vaginocentrism.

AF3IRM

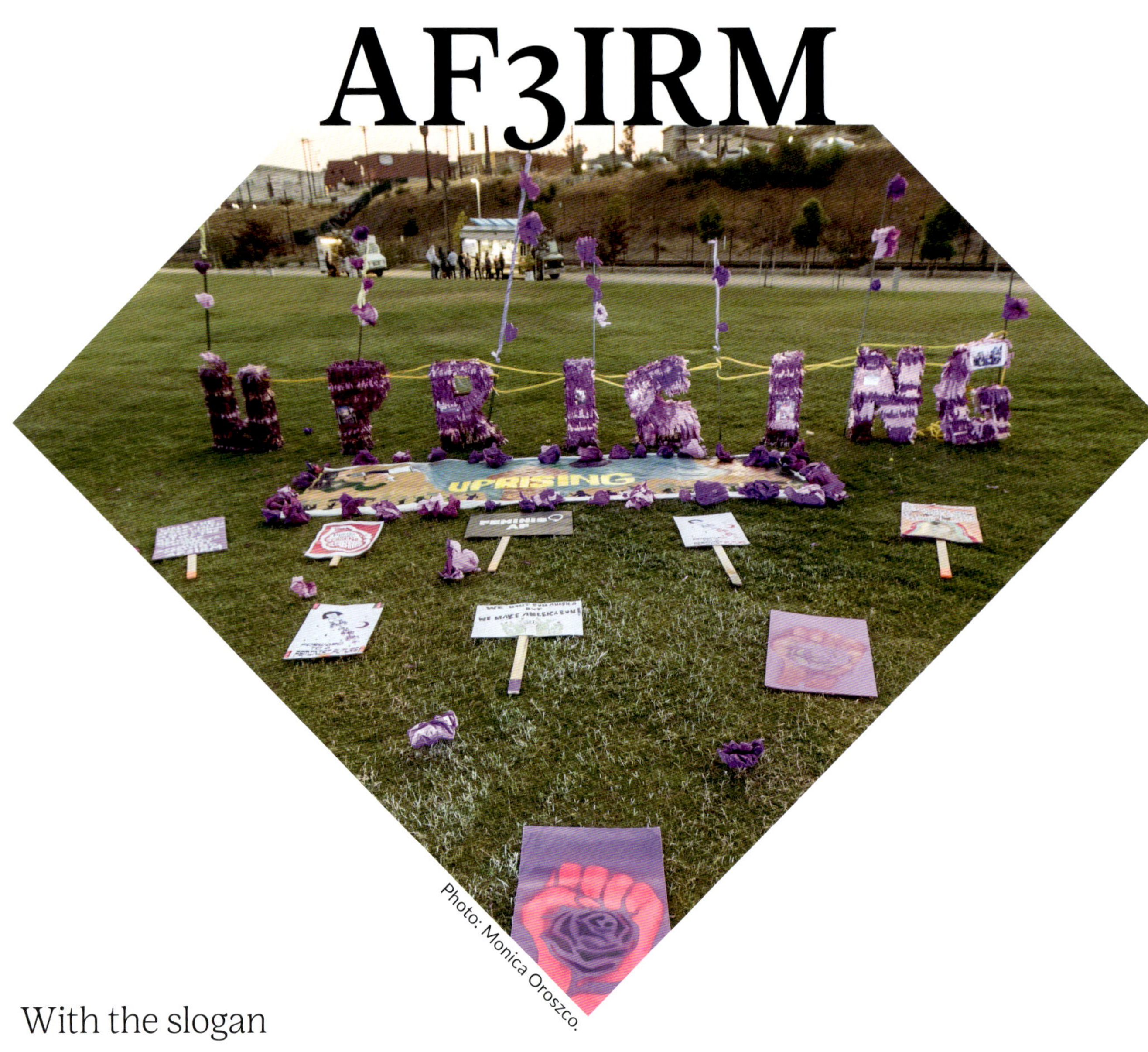

Photo: Monica Oroszco.

With the slogan

"A woman's place is at the head of the struggle"...

AF3IRM is a national organization of women engaged in transnational feminist, anti-imperialist activism and dedicated to the fight against oppression in all its forms..

AF3IRM's diverse, multiethnic membership is committed to militant movement building from the United States and effects change through grassroots organizing, transethnic alliance building, education, advocacy, and direct action.

AF3IRM is an all-volunteer, grassroots organization whose members recognize the intersectionality of their struggles and the absolute necessity of women's revolutionary resistance.

AF3IRM has chapters around the United States:

Hawaii
Los Angeles
New York
San Diego
San Francisco Bay Area
South Bay of Los Angeles
Las Vegas
Seattle/Pacific Northwest
Twin Cities, MN

Organizing committees are also actively building new chapters in other areas.

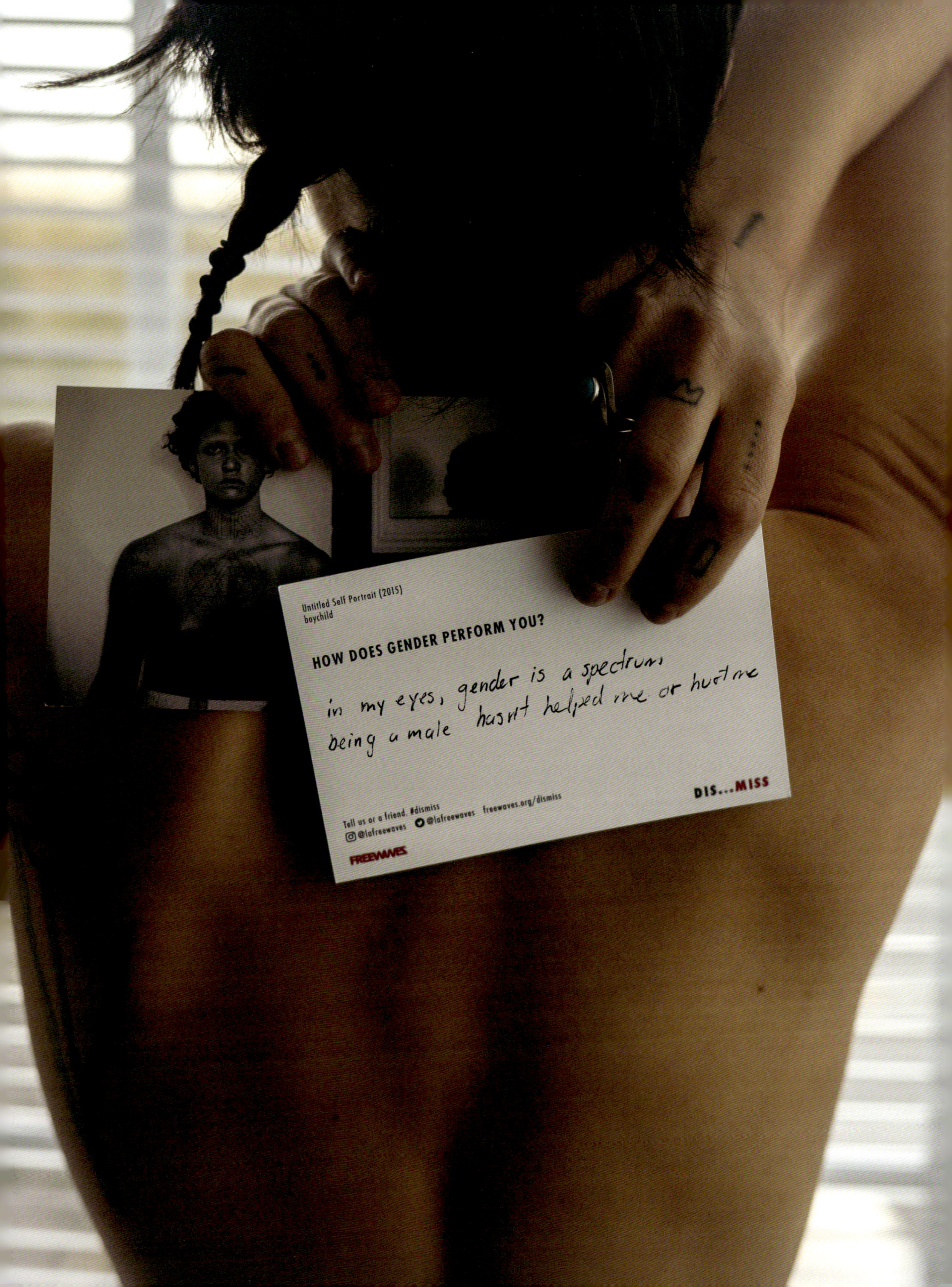
Untitled Self Portrait (2015)
boychild

HOW DOES GENDER PERFORM YOU?

in my eyes, gender is a spectrum,
being a male hasn't helped me or hurt me

Tell us or a friend. #dismiss
@lafreewaves @lafreewaves freewaves.org/dismiss

FREEWAVES

DIS...MISS

how does gender perform you?

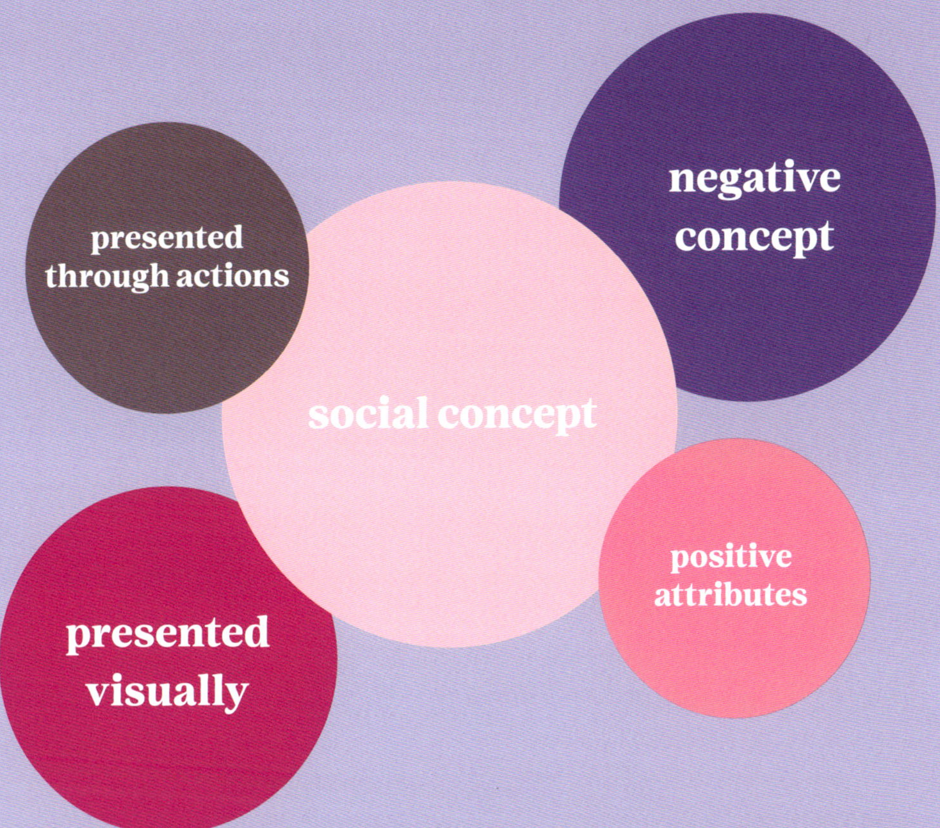

Gender plays me like a violin: sometimes it can be melancholy, sometimes celebratory; it's quick, fragile, subjective. Gender plays me with nimble fingers, appealing differently to every listener that it encounters.

ANALYSIS

Gender is seen as problematic yet important to observe. Respondents see it as something to question, as they understand it to be a social concept acted out by everyone.

"DIS…MISS, Inconclusive Infographic Animation." Analyzed by Marisa Turesky. Animation designed by Catherine Bell, 2019. Left: Postcard portrait by Alejandra Sone.

3

what is the
problem?
my body?
or society's
perception of
my body?

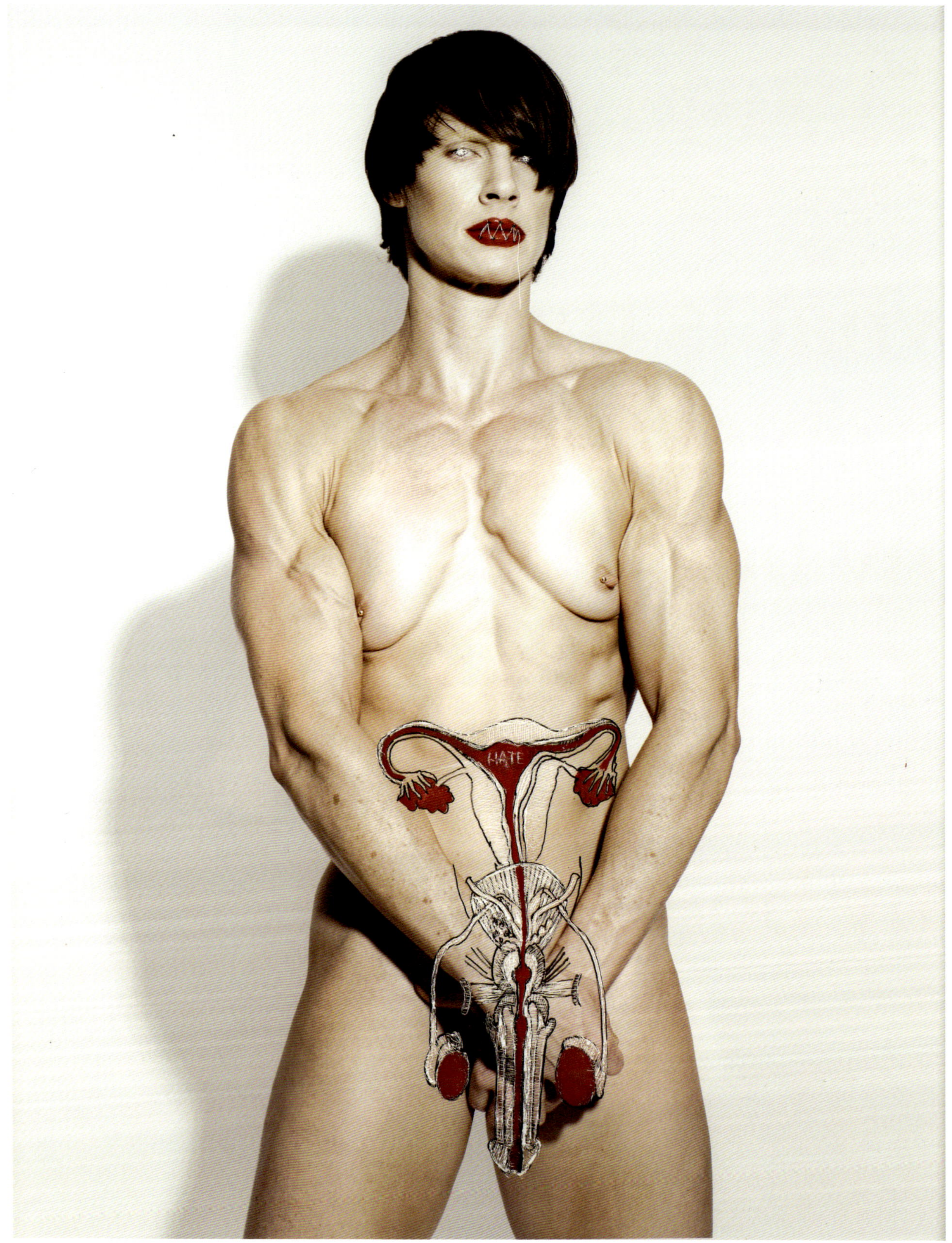HATE

Anatomically Correct:
Cassils Performs Gender
Amelia Jones

I'm looking and seeing gender and the biologically sexed body being performed in a color photograph (as John Berger put it in 1972, "Seeing comes before words"[1]). I will first attempt to describe (in words) what I see and then more deeply analyze how this described image is working (on me and perhaps on you, my reader). This exercise, I hope, will lead to a greater understanding of how this image *works* specifically in relation to Cassils's larger body of performances, which, I argue, amplifies in different ways how bodies perform gender and gender performs bodies in social spaces.

Disfigured Image: Anatomically Correct (2013). Collage: photo paper, marker, gouache, razor etching by Cassils, Photo: Cassils with Robin Black.

Entitled *Anatomically Correct* (2013), Cassils's self-portrait image is in color. Their body is naked, cropped at the thighs. The eyes hold an eerie, vacant expression as they stare off to the distance. This body is clearly white, statuesque, heroically muscular, buff, and masculinized but with breasts: it is thus both gendered in heightened ways and yet not clearly "male" or "female." The effect of gender confusion is increased by drawings on the photographic "skin" of the image (not on the body itself): a diagram of both male and female reproductive organs—with red gonads and ovaries—hovers over the body's abdomen and pelvis. The gaudily red-lipsticked mouth appears to be sewn shut with sutures drawn over the red of the lips. The short dark hair frames the porcelain-white face with its blood-red lips (this is Snow White and her prince merged into one hybrid, gender-complex body).

The image is a highly charged picture of a white body that is, in terms of Western norms, confusingly gendered and literally inscribed with the signs of female and male sexual organs. In their larger body of work, Cassils unhinges the expected connection between perceived bodily attributes (which may seem "real" and "immutable") and a fixed and inherent

---

1   *Ways of Seeing*, produced by Mike Dibbs, written by John Berger, BBC Four, aired January 1972.

gender/sex identity—paradoxically by deploying the most realist art mediums, photography and performance. It is the very expected "realism" of these mediums (our assumption that the appearance of the body in the photograph or performance aligns with or "is" an actual body) that jolts us into thinking about gender and sex differently because we can *see* with our own *eyes* that our expectations of what a female or male body *looks like* are here thwarted apparently "in real life." By performing their body live and in photographic media in a state of in-betweenness, finding creative ways to inscribe and portray the body, Cassils troubles conventional codes of sexed/gendered being. In fact, their insistent portrayal of their mostly naked body proves that gender is not inherent (lodged in the body) but performed.

The most startling effect of *Anatomically Correct* is thus that it plays with extreme binaries (the clearly male and clearly female internal sexual organs; the clearly masculine musculature and clearly feminine red lips), only to result in constructing the image of a person who resides on a gender/sex continuum rather than at either end. The picture seems to demonstrate that bodies perform gender in fluid and sometimes indeterminate ways (even given the seeming "realness" of the live or photographed body).

Cassils clearly "performs gender" in this and other works, aligning in complex ways with the structures of gender performance central to much feminist queer theory of the 1990s. Born around 1980 in Toronto and raised in Montréal, Cassils came of age in the heyday of the idea of gender performance or queer performativity as articulated in the work of theorists such as Judith Butler and Eve Sedgwick. Drawing on the linguistic phenomenologist J. L. Austin's concept of the performative in language, Butler famously argued in 1988 that "gender is in no way a stable identity or locus of agency from which various acts proceed; rather, it is an identity tenuously constituted in time—an identity instituted through a *stylized repetition of acts*."[2] In a revised version of this argument, she asked in 1990: "What kind of gender performance will enact and reveal the performativity of gender itself in a way that destabilizes the naturalized cate-

---

2   Judith Butler, "Performative Acts and Gender Constitution: An Essay in Phenomenology and Feminist Theory," *Theatre Journal* 40, no. 4 (December 1988): 519.

gories of identity and desire?"[3] Already by 1993, in a follow-up book called *Bodies That Matter*, Butler struggled to correct the tendency to misread her complex theory, with many in the arts and humanities flinging the idea of gender performance around as if individuals could simply "choose" to perform in any way they like, following or "subverting" gender fashions willfully.[4]

It is tempting to continue along these simplistic lines and to define Cassils's image as perfectly fulfilling Butler's call for a "performativity of gender" that is destabilizing. But, as Butler herself pointed out, this reading would be far too simple: gender performs us even as we perform it. Bodies (and images of bodies) take on gendered significance through the reiteration of established codes that take place in particular contexts and are received and interpreted by others. In this way, we can see that Cassils's work is hardly just an illustration of Butler's theoretical arguments, which derive just as much from a long history of self-imaging practices in Western art (from the gender-bending, performative self-portrait photographs of Claude Cahun in the 1920s and 1930s to the gender-critical performances and photographs of feminist artists such as Yoko Ono, Lynn Hershman, and Martha Wilson in the 1960s and 1970s) as from any of the images or performances that "illustrate" Butler's ideas. It is more useful to understand Butler's work as situated in parallel to larger cultural understandings of selfhood and identifications—with artistic practices also situated in the shifting social terrain after 1960, wherein philosophers, social scientists, artists, and activists in North America and beyond began to articulate the subject as multiple, decentered, performative, or "postmodern."[5] In this picture, gender and sexuality are simply one axis among many axes of interrelated identifications (including race and class) along which the subject multiplies, destabilizing previous modernist beliefs about gender as anatomically fixed in male or female bodies, with sexual orientation aligning as "normal" (straight) or "deviant" (lesbian/gay/queer).

---

3 Judith Butler, *Gender Trouble: Feminism and the Subversion of Identity* (New York: Routledge, 1990), 139.
4 See Judith Butler, *Bodies That Matter: On the Discursive Limits of "Sex"* (New York: Routledge, 1993).
5 See my book *In Between Subjects: A Critical Genealogy of Queer Performance* (New York: Routledge, 2021).

Cassils is performing Cassils, and *Anatomically Correct*, like all of the images from their performances (very, very carefully orchestrated, usually involving professional photographers for documentation), pushes both the concept of gender performativity and our relationship to their body in new directions. With its title, *Anatomically Correct* in fact promises exactly what it refuses to deliver: a simple alignment of a recognizably "male" or "female" body with a "correct" internal identification and sexual-object choice confirming the heteronormative matrix. This body is anything but "correct" and revels in telling us so. On the one hand, the picture is direct in its refusal to confirm the heteronormative matrix, and, on the other, it implies infinitely complex and subtle nuances of a gender continuum.

Cassils's larger performance project in fact points to the more complex trajectory relating to this gender performance in *Anatomically Correct*. For example, for example, when known as Heather Cassils, the artist began their career by producing boundary-breaking performances with two queer/lesbian partners-in-crime (Clover Leary and Julia Steinmetz) in the collaborative Toxic Titties. One of their works, *Toxic Union* (2002), involved obtaining a license to legally bind the three of them in a semblance of a queer/lesbian "toxic union," both rejecting marriage as the only means of legally sanctioning queer relationships and questioning the whole concept of intimate relations or marriage as necessitating a heteronormative dyad (rather than a queer lesbian triad). In more recent years, Cassils has produced internationally influential solo performances deploying their own increasingly gender-indeterminate body in a range of extreme-endurance actions—from having their body lit on fire (in *Inextinguishable Fire*, 2015) to pummeling a massive hunk of dense clay in a dark room (*Becoming an Image*, 2012–2020) to having their body frozen in an ice sculpture that melts very slowly (*Tiresias*, 2011–2019) to beating up their own body (*The Powers That Be*, 2016) to grappling with a massive pane of glass (*Cyclic*, 2018). All of these performances present a mostly unadorned, mostly naked body, sweating and straining with physical effort or shivering with cold or trembling with extreme heat—a body whose gender has shifted over the decades, becoming more buff and sinewy, more physically powerful as Cassils expanded their career as a personal trainer as well. All are beautifully documented, often by iconic images of Cassils's body performing gender through various modes of endurance that draw us in or repel us.

All of these rigorous works performed over the past two decades (many of which I have had the privilege of witnessing live, others of which I have seen in documentation[6]) have expanded Cassils's performance of gender into real time and space, each complicating the ways in which their body *reads* in relation to gender/sex norms. Does Cassils perform gender, or does gender perform Cassils in these works, including *Anatomically Correct?* Their practice allows us to see that this question is not as simple as Butler's gender theory seemed to imply for those reading it superficially.

Whereas Butler's gender theory dwelled primarily on the mechanisms of how individuals perform gender (without implicating herself in determinations of how such performances come to mean), perhaps lending itself to these oversimplistic readings, Eve Sedgwick opened up these questions by formulating a theory that involves her and all subsequent witnesses in any gender performative. In her work on gender performance in the 1990s, or what she preferred to call "queer performativity," Sedgwick articulated the way in which any self-performance is relational, calling on and interrelating with those who witness and engage it. What this interpretation allows us to comprehend about *Anatomically Correct* is that we all engage its rendering of gender/sex identification through our own desires, fears, and self-identifications.

Sedgwick asserts *shame* as the basis of queer identifications in a homophobic society, specifically because shame indicates the role of interpretation and relations with others in our sense of self. Queer shame, in this model, takes place because of homophobia—and thus queer bodily identifications are relational, taking place between and among subjects in social situations. Sedgwick's model of queer performativity points to the contingency of any concept of self or meaning on *later*

---

6   See my review of Cassils's performance *The Powers That Be*, 2016: "Hurting and Hurling the Body in Feminist Performance: A Review of 'Tip of Her Tongue,' a Performance Series at the Broad Museum, Los Angeles, 2016–17 [curated by Jennifer Doyle]," in "Contemporary Feminist Theatre and Performance," special issue of *Contemporary Theatre Review* 28, no. 3(2018): 424–427; and my essay "Breathing New Life into the Biosphere 2 Lung," in *Cyclic*, exhibition catalogue, ed. Ginger Shulick Porcella (Tucson: Museum of Contemporary Art, 2019).

engagements, and this insistence on temporality is key to the term *shame*'s mobilization of antiessentialist notions of identity. Sedgwick thus concludes, "Shame interests me politically, then, because it generates and legitimates the place of identity—the *question* of identity—at the origin of the impulse to the performative, but does so without giving that identity-space the standing of an essence."[7]

Whether we now imagine shame to be motivating Cassils's gender performance as documented in *Anatomically Correct* or not (I certainly do not), Sedgwick's model insists upon interpretation itself as key to how any identifications function. *Anatomically Correct*, then, can be seen as more of an invitation to spark interpreters' or viewers' own feelings and awareness of our own identifications. If we contextualize this picture within Cassils's performances in real time and space, which assert their body in physical spaces with spectators who hear and feel as well as see their intensely unfixable gendered/sexed body, then we see that gender performance is both tied to actual bodies and *performs us*. We are determined by Cassils's deliberate confusion of gender codes even as we give the picture meaning.

---

7 Eve Kosofsky Sedgwick, "Queer Performativity: Henry James's *The Art of the Novel*," *GLQ* 1 (1993): 12–13.

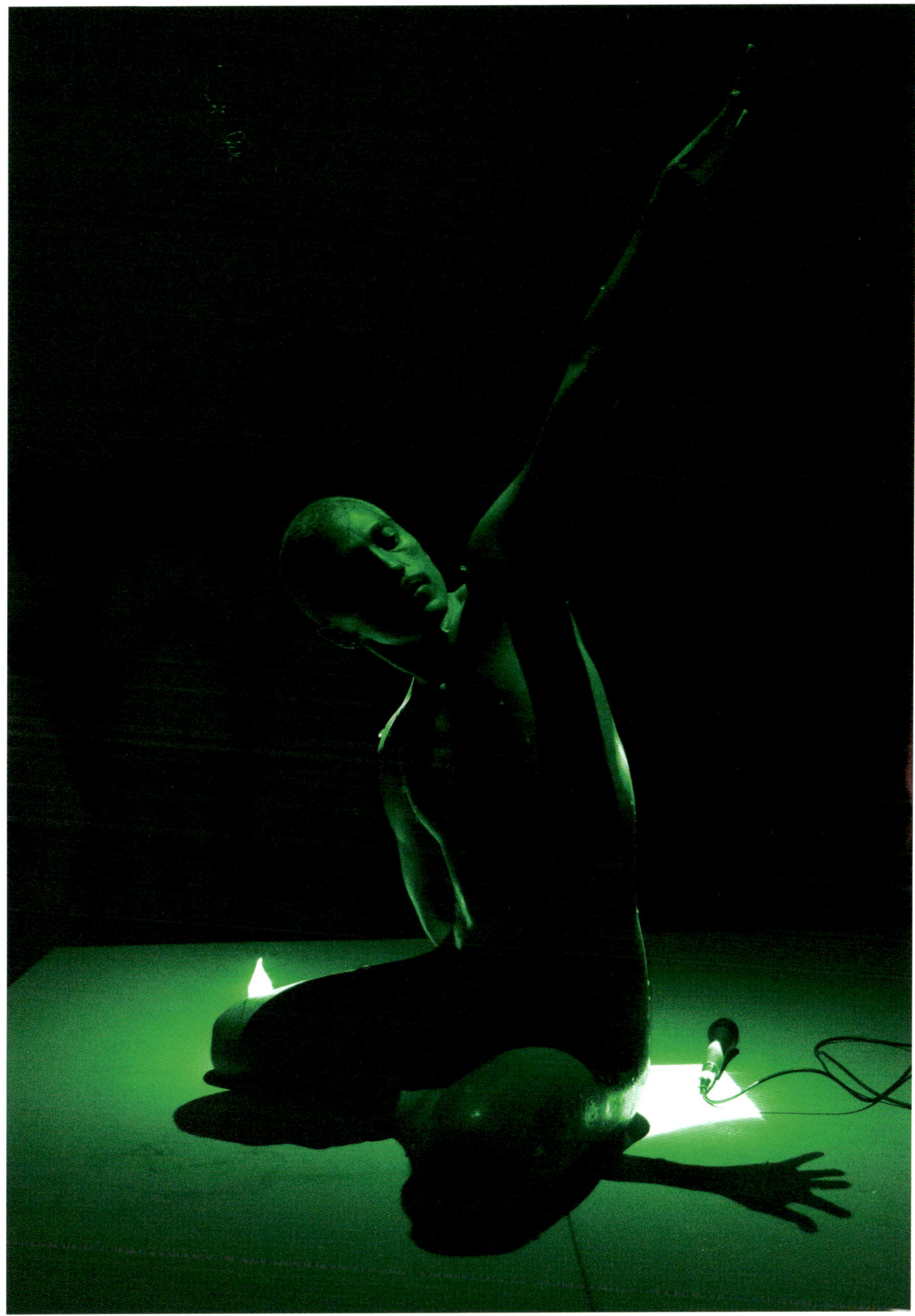

Performance by Sebastian Hernández. Photo: Safi Alia Shabaik.

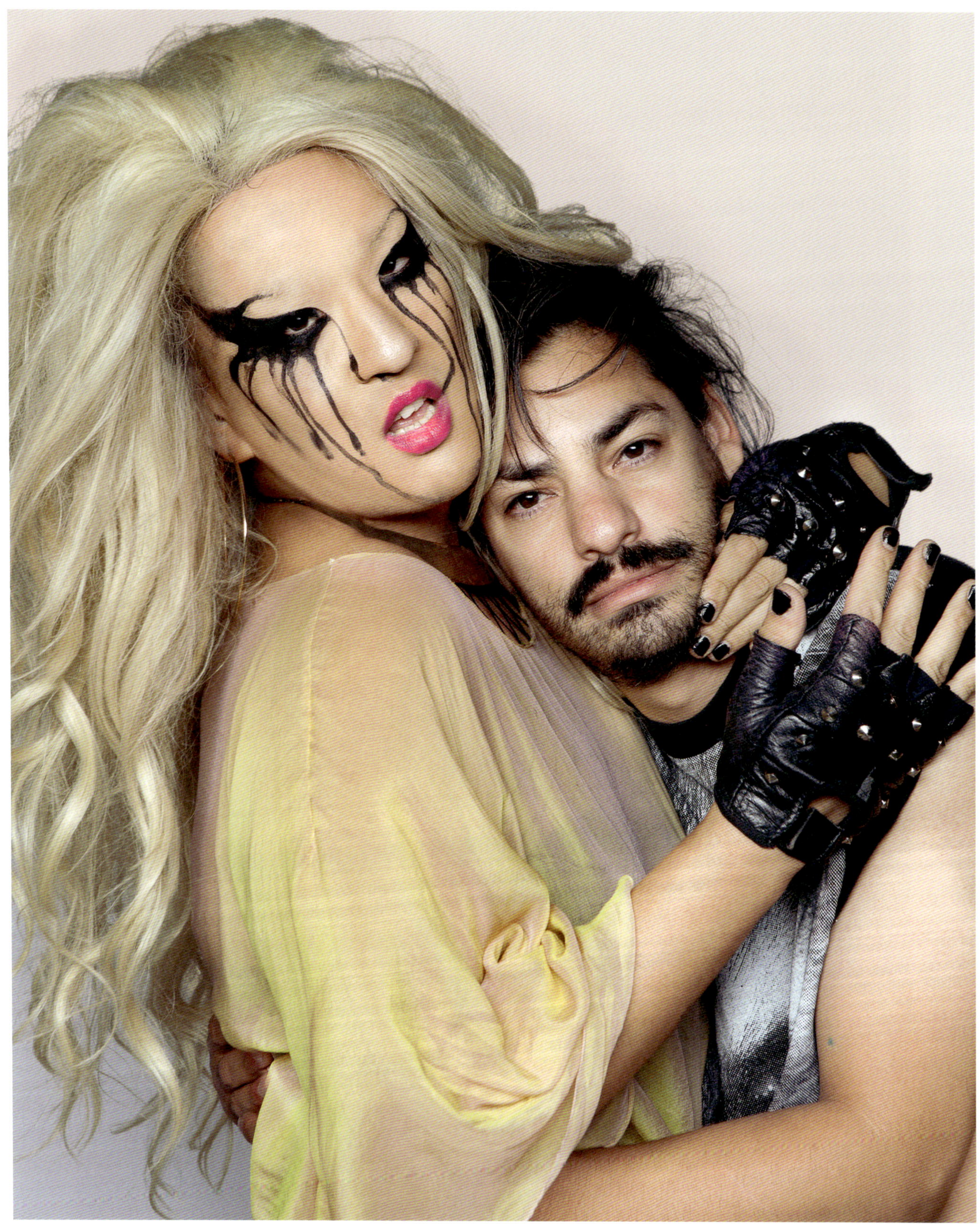

Xina Xurner (Young Joon Kwak and Marvin Astorga). Photo: Austin Young.

Am I Pretty?

Young Joon Kwak and Lily Robert-Foley

No.
Your worst fears about yourself are true.
So then, the ideal truth is beauty
but the truth about me is ugly.
Our project is to turn the monster.
Turn into, turn out, turn around.
And attack the grid
with the incalculability of muck, ooze, fluids.
Monstrous monstrosity,
monster, monsterate, demonsterate, remonsterate.
We are not born monsters, one becomes it.
The becoming monster is awakening,
growling, drooling, purring, howling,
calling to face the ideologies and affects that frame them
carve us.
It's the call to recognize
who are worth our love
those with the capacity to recognize that we
our worth
our weight in love.

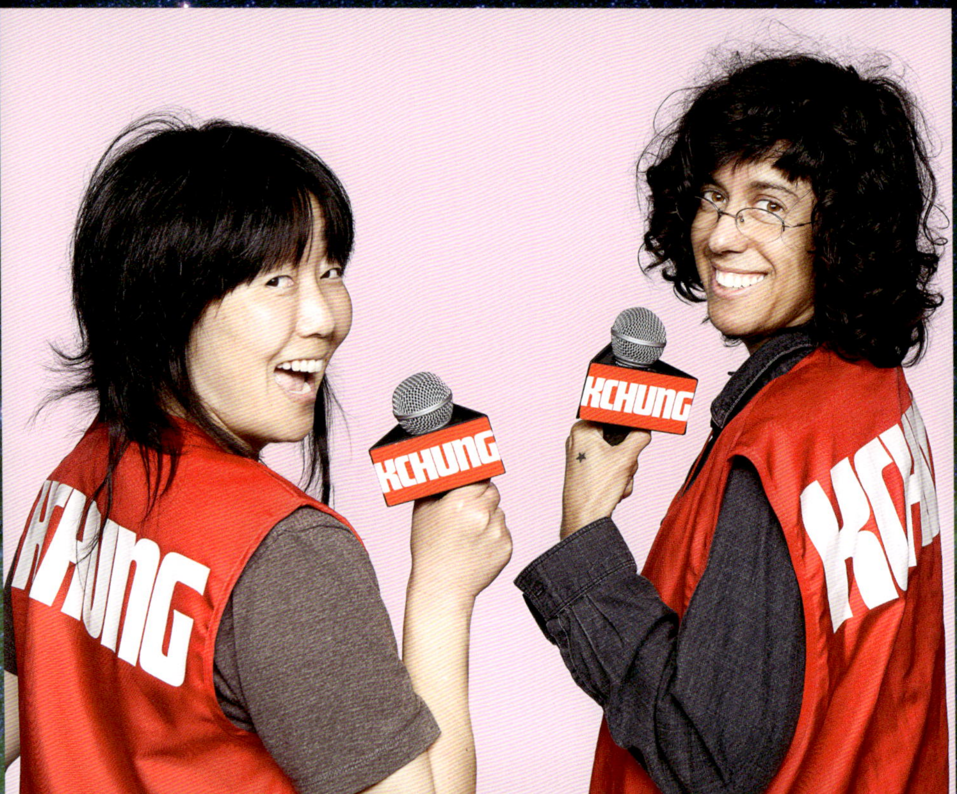

Left: Jennifer Moon and Dan Bustillo of KCHUNG Radio. Photo: Austin Young.

Below: Jennifer Moon and Dan Bustillo of KCHUNG interview Anna Ialeggio. Photo: Monica Orozco.

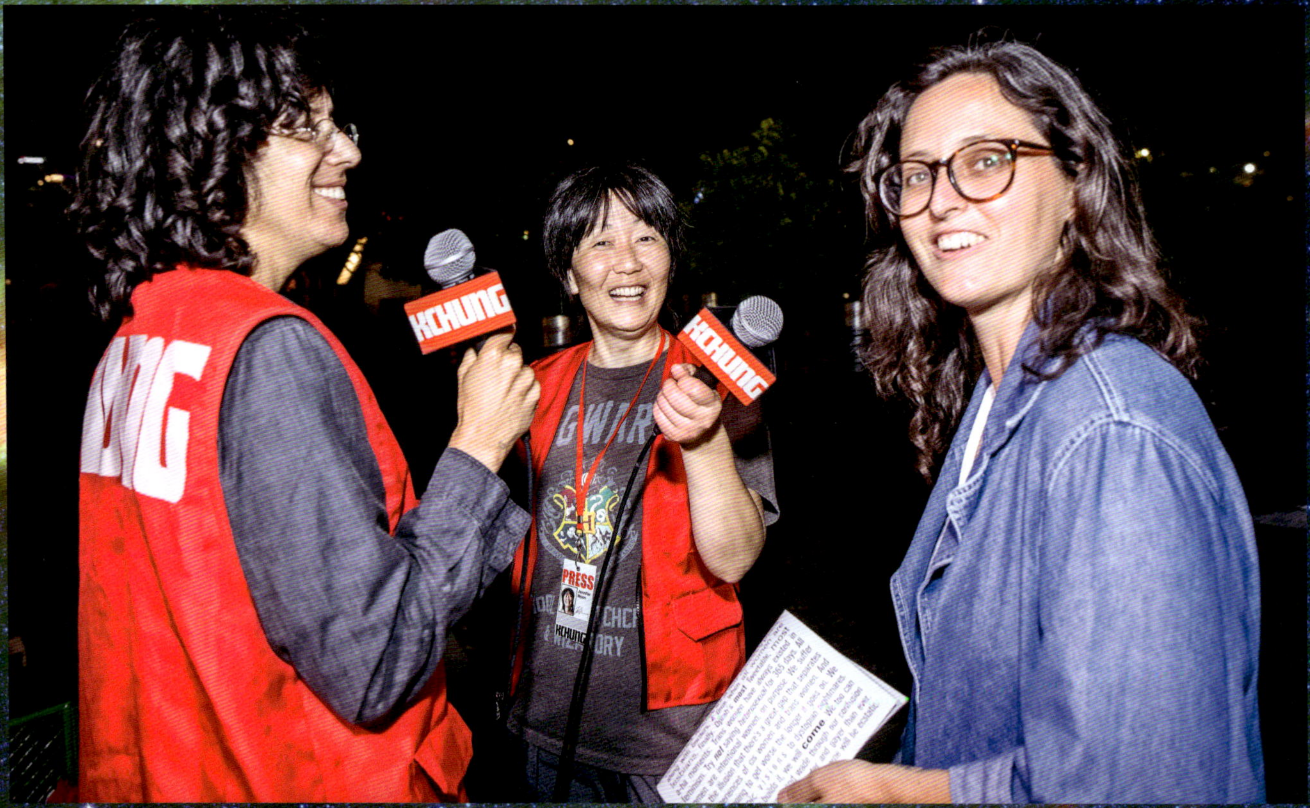

Background: PIA24579: Godzilla Nebula Imaged by Spitzer. Photo: NASA/JPL-Caltech.

At the Edge of Space and Time: Expanding Beyond Our 5% Universe
Jennifer Moon

Binaries are ever present in the natural world, to the point where they have been accepted as truths in many cultures. Perhaps you don't believe in gender binaries or any binary dichotomy that perpetuates and legitimizes colonial, white-supremacist, patriarchal power structures, but certainly yin and yang provide a necessary balance to the world: we must balance work with play and our mathematical equations. How about hierarchies? Hierarchies create marginalized, oppressed communities. Yet the animal kingdom, nature, functions in a hierarchical manner, so that must be a fact of the cosmos. Well, of course it does because it's all part of the Matrix, ALL OF IT, even the so-called natural world and our conception of the forces of the universe. Let's see how the universe behaves when we enter the quantum world of subatomic particles. In this extraordinary microuniverse, commonly known as "quantum mechanics," particles, such as protons, neutrons, and electrons, which bundle together into atoms—the stuff you and I and the entire visible universe are made of—behave in radically different ways than we do in the macroworld. In this queer world, particles hover in a state of uncertainty, seemingly being partly here and partly there, occupying all known positions simultaneously. The orientation devices we use to ground ourselves in our 5 percent universe, namely binaries and hierarchies, fall away. There is no such grounding in this world where particles exist in several states and several realities at the same time and spin in multiple angular rotations at once.

The incredible thing about all of this is that it is happening inside of us as we speak; all of this fantastic queering and disrupting of time and space is happening RIGHT NOW in the subatomic particles that make up our bodies and all the observable matter in the universe! So how does all this radical queering wash away into a system that converges into a single reality, this 5 percent rendering of our macroworld? By our acts of measurement.

The uncertainty principle in quantum mechanics states that the more precisely the position of a particle is determined, the less precisely its momentum can be known, and vice versa. Essentially, we can't measure the position and the momentum of a particle at the same time. In their unobserved state, particles exist as a fuzzy jumble of possibilities. However, once they are measured, the act of measurement forces a particle to relinquish all of the possible places it could have been and to select one definite location where we find it. When a particle is forced to choose a position, we lose its momentum.

Our singular, 5 percent reality is realized and sustained by our constant measuring. It is our endless acts of measurement, placing everything and everyone, every event, every phenomenon within a binary-bound, hierarchical spectrum that washes away the possibilities of us and our world existing in multiple states and multiple realities at the same time. Our incessant measuring of ourselves and others and the world around us forces us into a position, an orientation, an identity, a behavior, a way of being. And when we are forced to choose a position, we lose our momentum. And without momentum, we can never expand beyond our 5 percent universe.[1]

---

1   Excerpt from Jennifer Moon and Laub, "At the Edge of Space and Time: Expanding beyond Our 4% Universe," by originally performed for the exhibition *In Real Life: 100 Days of Film and Performance*, Hammer Museum, Los Angeles, 2016.

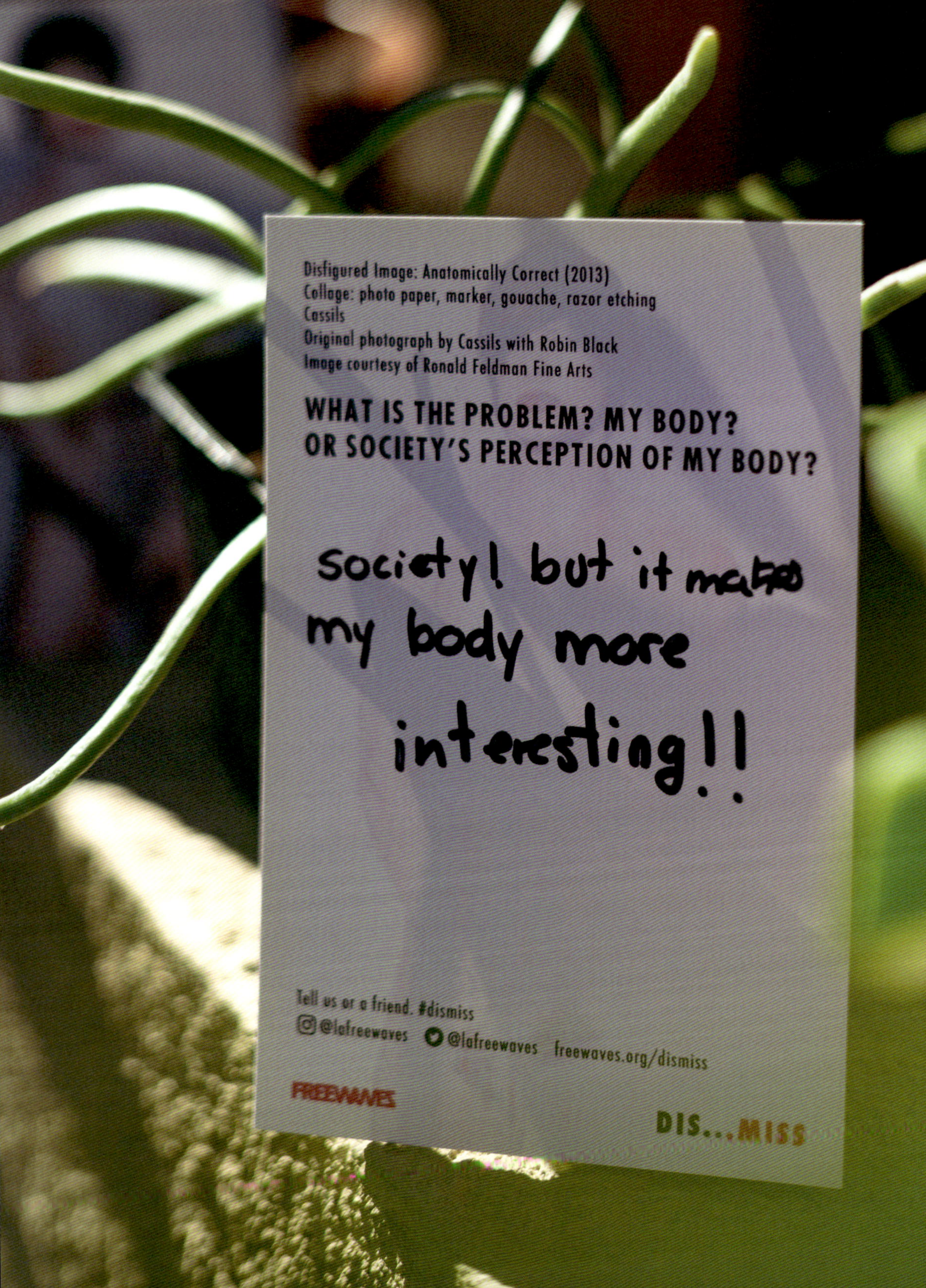

Disfigured Image: Anatomically Correct (2013)
Collage: photo paper, marker, gouache, razor etching
Cassils
Original photograph by Cassils with Robin Black
Image courtesy of Ronald Feldman Fine Arts

WHAT IS THE PROBLEM? MY BODY?
OR SOCIETY'S PERCEPTION OF MY BODY?

Society! but it makes
my body more
interesting!!

Tell us or a friend. #dismiss
@lafreewaves   @lafreewaves   freewaves.org/dismiss

FREEWAVES

DIS...MISS

what is the problem? my body?
or society's perception of my body?

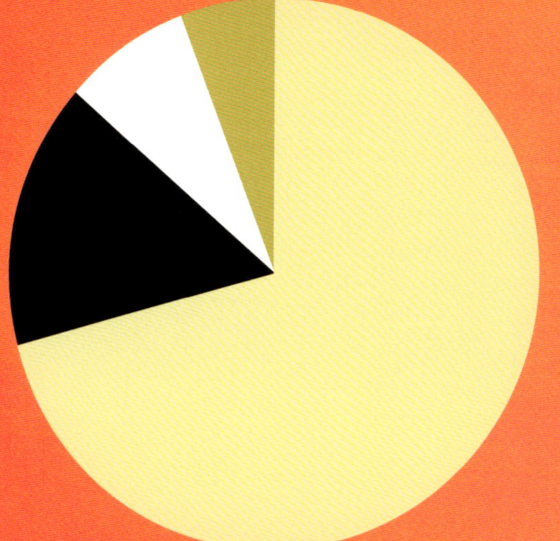

SOURCE OF PROBLEM

73% Society

16% No Problem

8% Self + Society

6% Self

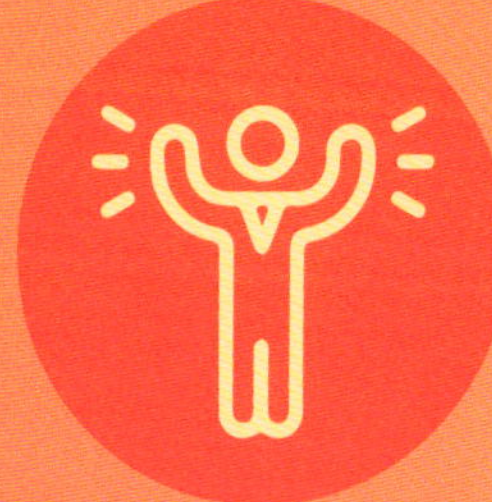

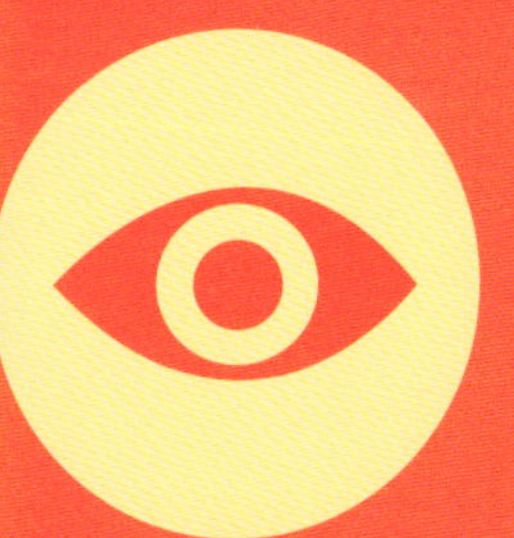

ANALYSIS

A lucky segment (16%) felt there is no problem at all. A few respondents characterized with: "mind your own business!"

"DIS…MISS, Inconclusive Infographic Animation." Analyzed by Marisa Turesky. Animation designed by Catherine Bell, 2019.
Left: Postcard portrait by Alejandra Sone.

4

sister,
are you psyco?

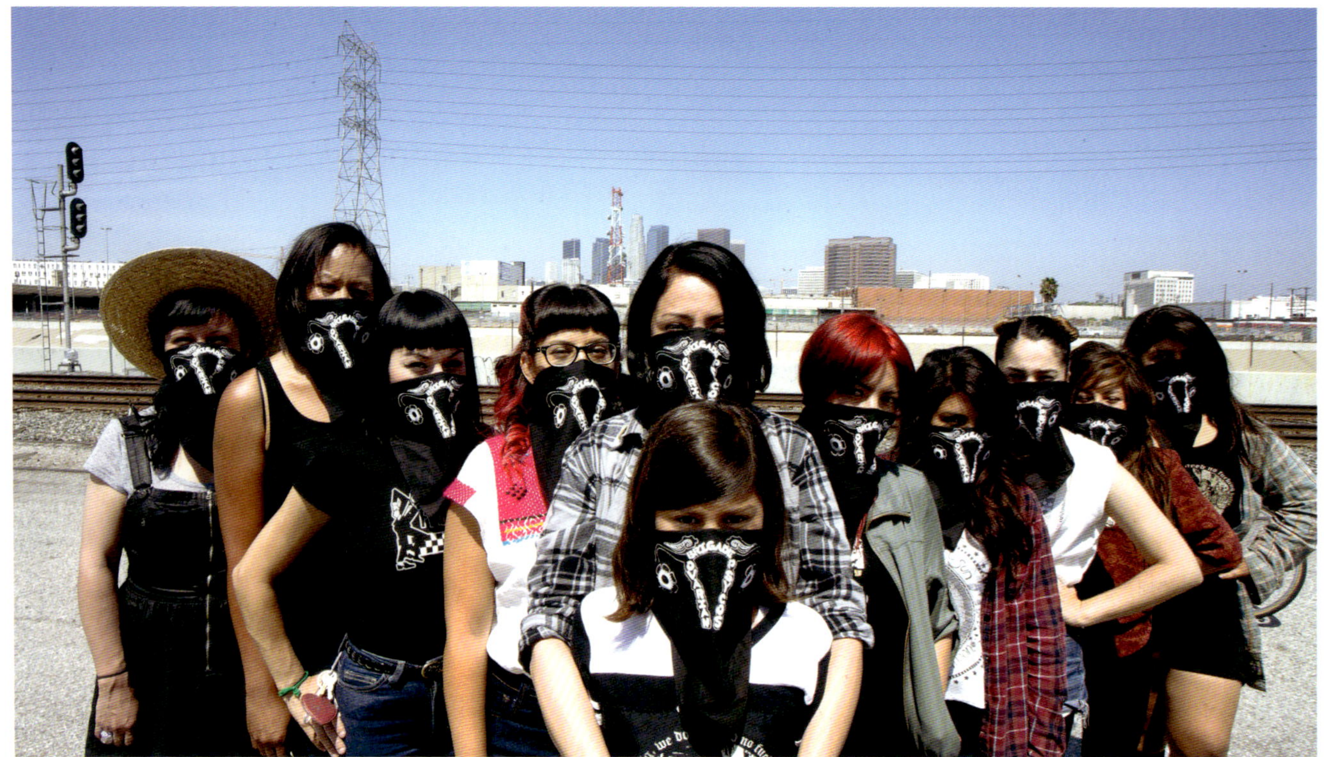

Publicity still for the documentary *Ovarian Psycos* (2017) directed by Joanna Sokolowski and Kate Trumball-LaValle. Photo: Michael Raines.

Xister, Are You "Psyco"?

Raquel Gutiérrez

I scan my body for an honest answer to a question I have been waiting my whole life to be asked. A question that is a hailing, that is a recognition, that is a promise pregnant with radical reciprocity.

Xister, I am.

I have awakened and arrived at this spiritual crossroads. And this time I'm not alone.

But, xister, who is she? And where is she from? And her and them and her and them and her? They are familiar.

From their mouths you'll learn that the members of the Ovarian Psyco-Cycles brigade (OPC) are "womxn of color, xisters, mothers, overgrown knuckleheads, riders, writers, students, wage slaves, hustlers, artists, MCs, poets, intellectuals, radical scholars, passionate womxn, environmentalists, urban farmers, medicine womxn, militants, feminists, renaissance womxn,

fearless *fierro* riders, and modern-day *charras* on steel horses!"

Do you see yourself in that mix? I do.

For I was an angry girl who turned that anger inward. I was an angry girl who was often heard but never seen, an acidic tongue, a whiplash of hurtful words strung together through joke and punchline. I was an angry girl who turned blue with dissociative wanderlust—I wanted to be anywhere except in my own body. I was an angry girl whose anger had no place to live in the world, so I housed it in my throat.

My memory expelled, a cavalcade of girlpain turned renegade. Some triggers bring forth a bile ready to expel, to necessitate a purging in your psychic space, to make room for the healing power of anger turned outward even and especially as a silent gesture of resistance. This is what I am reminded of as I lay my eyes upon this powerful image. The Ovarian Psyco-Cycles stand in a V-formation, a coven of the preternaturally bad ass—arms akimbo, hair dyed to conjure magic, shoulders back in fierce defiance—a feminist social sculpture who covers mouths and throats behind black bandanas, protecting chakras, the keepers of truths. How might you be granted entrance to the transitory houses where these truths reside? Where do you go to commit to protect the traveling xisterhood of liberation and revolution?

A gesture of resistance repeats across ten faces ranging in age, one young Psyco in the center whose eyes summon a future that the others behind her are ensuring happens on her terms. Honoring the Indigenous traditions of resistance inherited and activated by a Zapatista revolutionary bloodline, the *pasamontañas* of Chiapas become the *pasapuentes* of Boyle Heights. The black bandana eschews the familiar white filigree paisley implicative of cowboy wear. In its place we are gifted an insurgent rendering of the female reproductive system turned bicycle cyborg, where in lieu of ovaries we see bicycle-chain rings holding us together, keeping our gears from grinding, our chains from breaking. The individual becomes the collective. We see eyes from the left to the right and back again, staring back at us staring at them—the question of who is spectating whom in the wavering bridge between viewer and subject. Wavering bridges like what used to sit along the Sixth Street bridge, a carrier between worlds, where the world entered and exited Boyle Heights with maybe too much facility.

You can be the bad bitch behind the black bandana. Who doesn't want to be the bad bitch behind the black bandana? A hero's cape, it can strike fear in the hearts of heartless menfolk who have terrorized their wives and daughters and intimates with an uninterrogated machismo. A black bandana, an anarchist's veil, projects a powerful sentience that a scared girl can divine herself into, a future where she prevails.

Or do they cover their faces because the city behind them is looking to sell them out? A black bandana denies access to a girlhood gone rogue from a world that hasn't learned how to come correct, how to learn the names of their favorite bands or their maternal ancestral predilections. These are the girls who defy the world's questions. These are the girls who squat against an economic downturn, who shame a slumlord until he's shaking in his boots, and who spit on a hipster taking what he knows he is unable to give back.

While Los Angeles paves the concrete roads that allow for the convergence of the Psycos matrilineal lines to energetically charge the city, it still hasn't come correct and paid its due to claim the xisterhood. Boyle Heights, whose current identity has been Siamese twinning with gentrification for the past decade, isn't digging in its heels against the Panda Express taking Carnitas Michoacan No. 3 to an early grave, while the Psycos have been vocal in the calling out toxic Trump-supporting businesses encroaching on their turf. Biking through the streets that change every day with the stock market, the Psycos are witnessing the story slowly—and then quickly—unfold in all of its gray, intimate areas of the city.

Swearing 'hood loyalty was what you did as soon as you could walk and talk. But what happens when the 'hood stops being loyal to you? What if the 'hood never kept its word for its girls—homegirls and rockers and *ponqueras* alike? What happens when Boyle Heights stops being that familiar site where family comes first, and the violence becomes a ghost that haunts more than just houses? What happens when you see the people around get their labor stolen and exploited, fruit carts turned over by self-hating chipster bros?

Where in your body do you store rage?

I was an angry girl who could have benefited from a Brown-girl bike gang. I was she who needed strong girl arms around my ten-year-old shoulders. I was an angry girl who turned her anger into sarcasm, passing barbs to make up for the voids I would tend toward later in life. I was she who, riding a bicycle, could have burned off anger like sweat, opting for a body's exhaustion instead of the adrenaline familiar to fight or flight. Ten speeds to swiftly glide alongside a moving panorama of concrete and river, to soar into the night chasing a full moon rising like rage. A girl bike gang to swarm a city and compel anyone who's ever harmed a Brown girl to think twice, live in fear even if that fear is temporary. I am coming for you. We are coming for you. We, a girl bike gang. We, a girl bike gang, take the phrase "girl bike gang" back from a world that assigns meanings meant to control and indict Brown girls who gather, show up for one another, and fight back.

Before I drove a car, I was sedentary, the radio my escape. Nobody walked in LA, and that was my calling card toward a disconnected sense of belonging. Car culture was freedom. However, my mother held

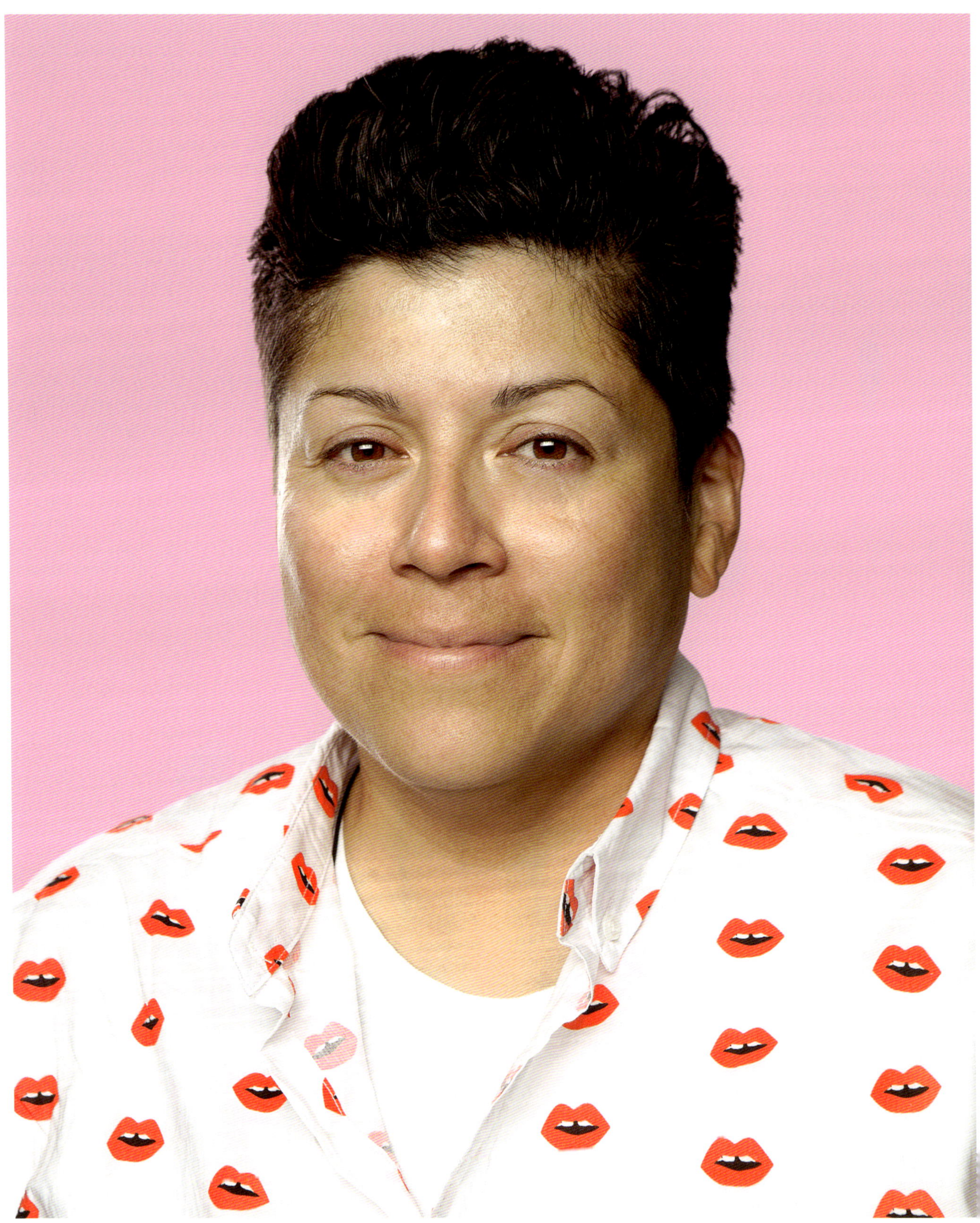

Raquel Gutiérrez. Photo: Austin Young.

a damning vigil, dictating where I could go and with whom. She, a Salvadoran immigrant who left her country to escape a violent husband, kept a watchful eye over my every move, hoping to control my environment. While her control produced a chorus of disapproval in my mind, in her absence I can look back in hindsight and see that it was an attempt at keeping me safe. But her control chipped away at me, instilling me with self-doubt, even as I did my best to understand. Doing my best often consumed me, racked me with the guilt prevalent among many children of immigrants who know full well the sacrifices their parents endured to provide a better life for their offspring. In my mother's absence, I took my instincts for granted, listening only to the voice she drilled into my mind—I would be injured if I let my curiosities lead me to worlds beyond the prison of my bedroom.

But my mother didn't realize it was already too late; transgressions happen so quickly against girl children every day, a mother can't ensure ubiquitous safety for her child. We are sullied and abandoned into our silent devices. We turn anger inward instead of toward their rightful monsters. Mothers wonder why the estrangement deepens the chasm between them and their daughters, whose English-dominant tongues reinforce that distance—a chasm made visible in the ways we inhabit understanding of the bodies we are blessed with or are trapped by, depending on the violences, lessons, and dysphorias we are dealt.

Our mothers could have used a Brown-girl bike gang.

I have never ridden with the Ovarian Psyco-Cycles, but my body knows the importance of a full-moon call to xisterhood. Xisterhood needs release. Xisterhood knows release is nigh, and release is signaled with each and every full moon. Feel the fullness of Coyoxauqui rise. Through her summons, we reach clitoral mass, an organized riot. My clit heats the metal of a steed that I built myself, xister blood smeared on my face, a semaphore of the many fucks that incite the bravery needed to enter the battlefield of an LA intersection, an MTA bus, the dragon to outsmart.

Raquel Gutiérrez at *Ain't I a Womxn?* Photo: Safi Alia Shabaik.

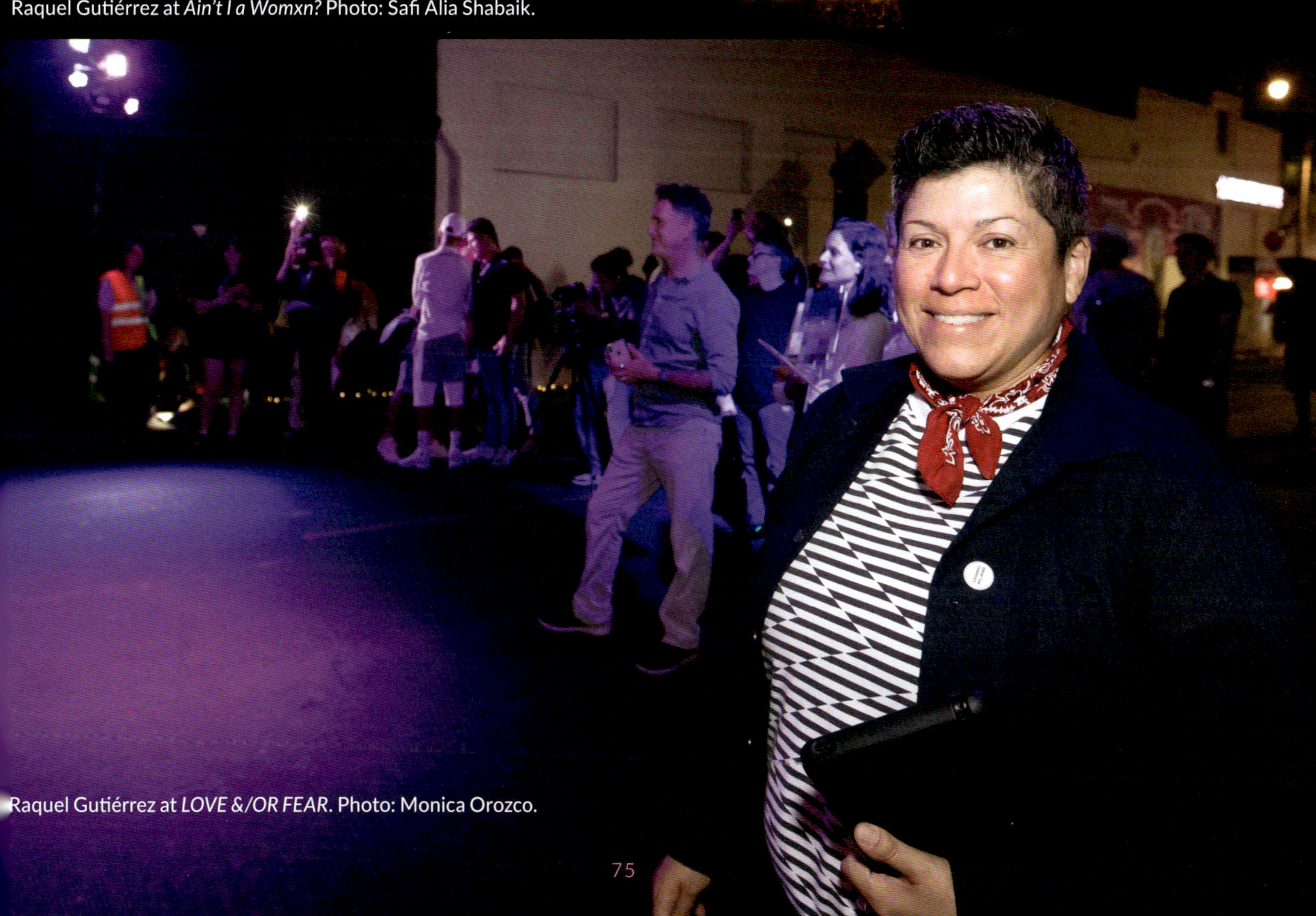

Raquel Gutiérrez at *LOVE &/OR FEAR*. Photo: Monica Orozco.

Ovarian

Before the initial invasion of the European colonizers, Indigenous people throughout Anahuac and Turtle Island were largely matriarchal societies in which womyn and our Earth Mother were respected not only as caregivers, leaders, warriors, and comrades but also, most importantly, as the foundation of a thriving, balanced, and holistically healthy nation.

We of Ovarian Psyco-Cycles (OPC) firmly believe that womyn of color and the land are now and always have been interchangeable. We both continue to be simultaneously exploited, occupied, and raped within patriarchal societies, specifically by the foreign power structures of white supremacy.

We view government and the agencies acting on their behalf as actively engaging in strategies to annihilate, displace, and enslave people of color while progressively harming our people and Mother Earth in the process.

OPC was established in the summer of 2011 because of a lack of sisterhood within our communities. The legacy of oppression dating back 500 years has created conditions in which many of us come from broken homes and are survivors of abuse.

We choose the bicycle not only because it allows us to exercise our bodies, while trying to reverse the cultural shift from a profoundly respectful relationship with Tonantzin, Mother Earth, to life in a concrete,

Psycos-Cycles

barren urban jungle, but also because we are broke inner-city oppressed peoples and cycling is our only means of transportation. For these and many other reasons, we recognize how vulnerable we are on bicycles and work to empower womyn to take back the streets with an understanding that sisters have our back.

OPC exists in Los Angeles because LA is dominated by car culture and bike culture is dominated by middle- and upper-class white men. We believe that it is dangerous to live in a society that doesn't cultivate community, sisterhood, brotherhood, and compañerism@.

OPC is womyn of color, sisters, mothers, overgrown knuckleheads, riders, writers, students, wage slaves, hustlers, artists, MCs, poets, intellectuals, radical scholars, passionate womyn, environmentalists, urban farmers, medicine womyn, militants, feminists, renaissance womyn, fearless *fierro* riders, and modern-day *charras* on steel horses!

Outside of working with OPC, we work with youth and the community. We do so because it heals and fuels us. We were raised under cultural norms that told us that Brown is not beautiful, that womyn of color are to be meek and subservient and that we should be afraid of freedom. We work daily to break these norms. We know that another world IS possible and that it is our duty and responsibility to pass that knowledge on to other young womyn of color.

Ovarian Psycos Instagram Statement

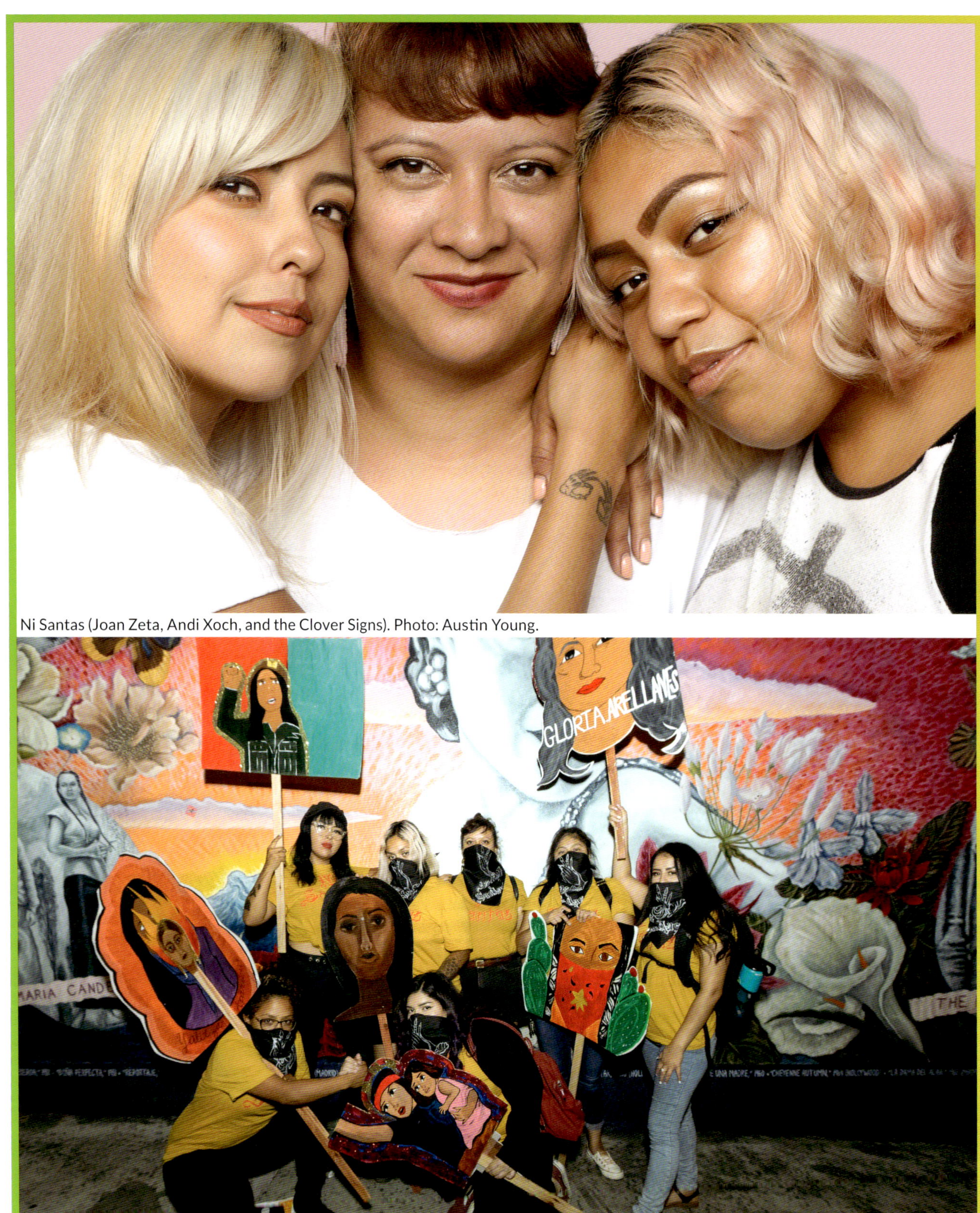

Ni Santas (Joan Zeta, Andi Xoch, and the Clover Signs). Photo: Austin Young.

Ni Santas, chanting, "Ni Santas, Ni Putas, Solo Muxeres" at *LOVE &/OR FEAR*. Photo: Monica Orozco.

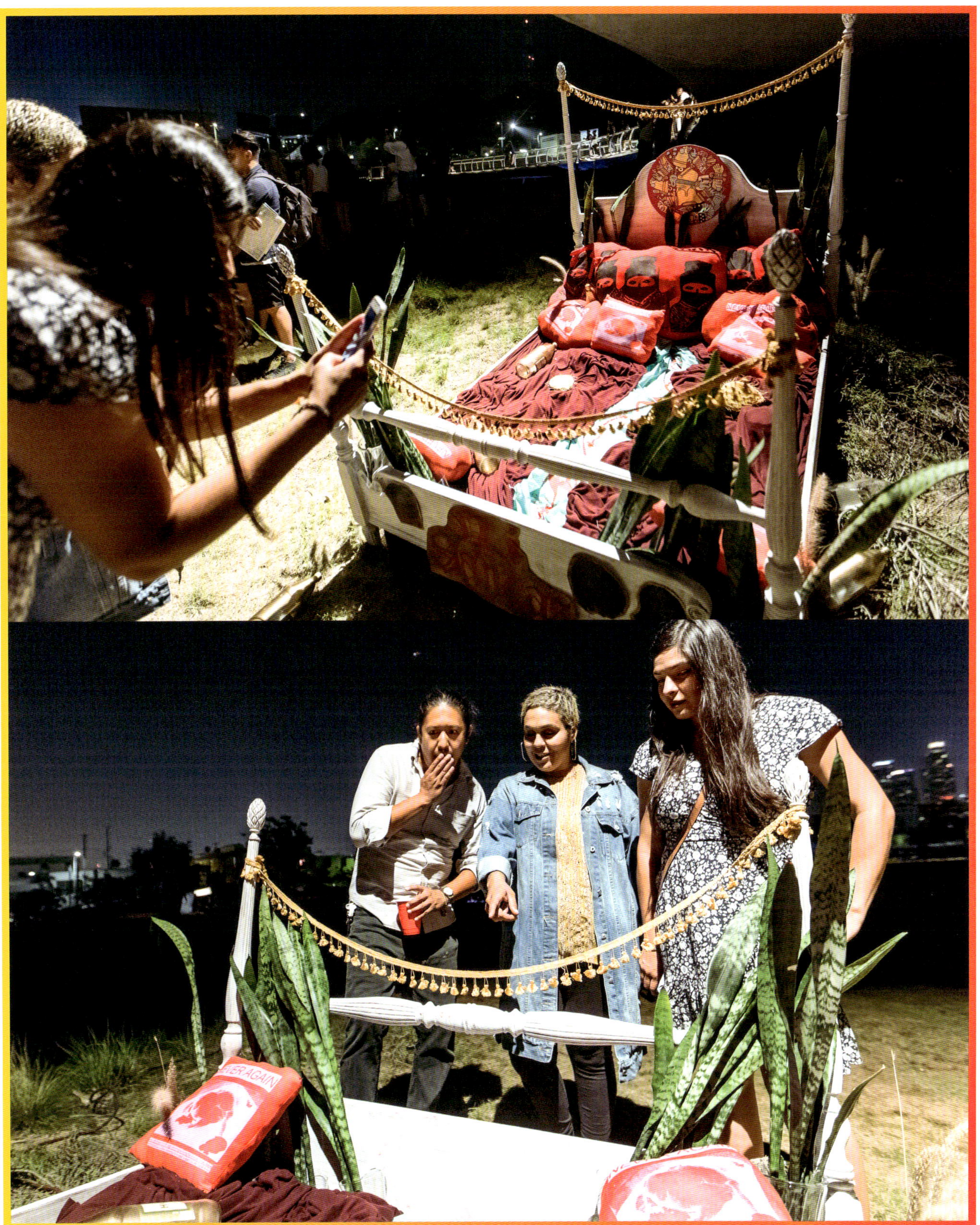

NI Santas Installation and viewers at *Ain't I A Womxn?* Photos. Monica Orozco.

The Three Visits
Olga Koumoundouros

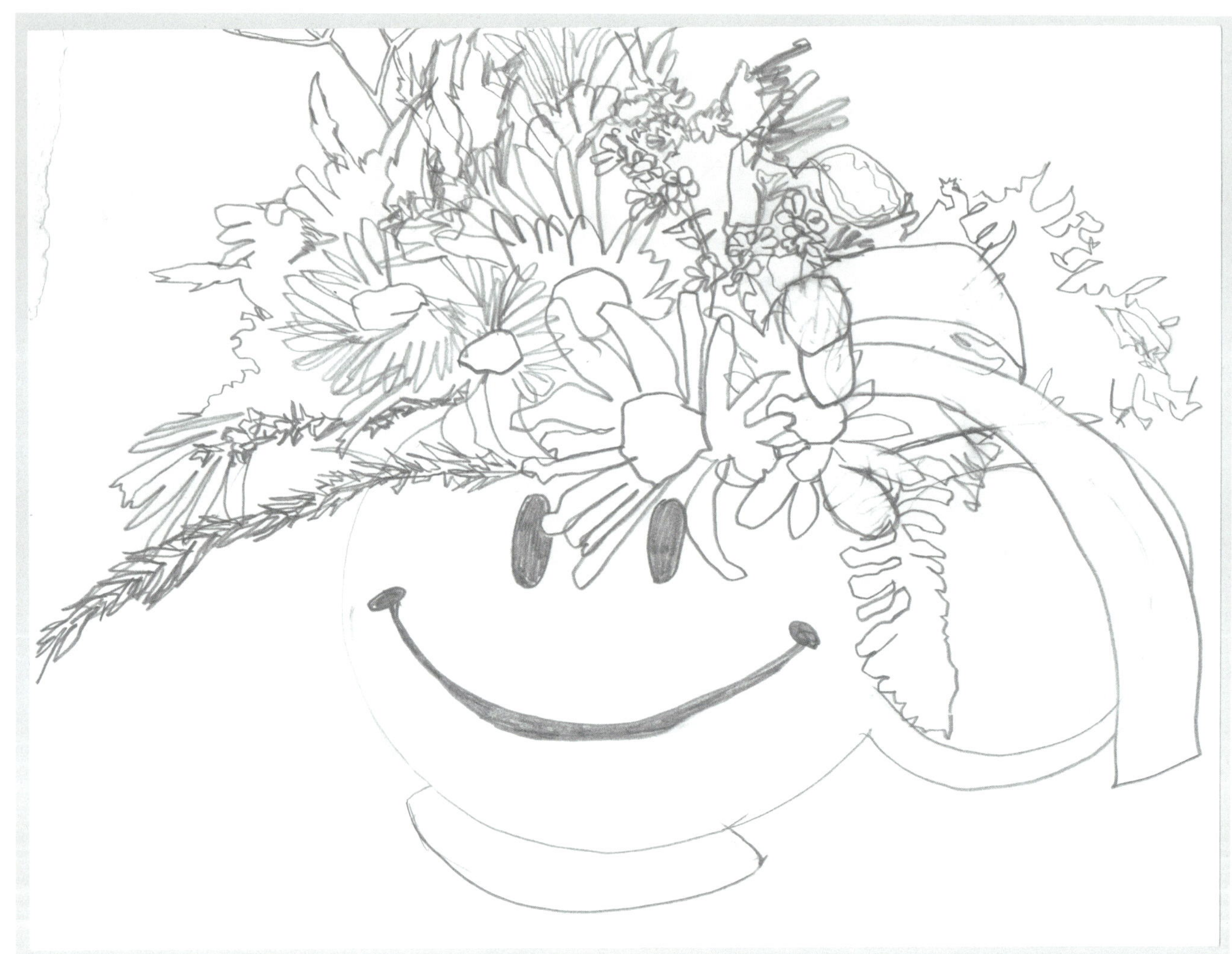

Drawing by Olga Koumoundouros.

VISIT TWO

Doctors at Morristown Memorial Medical Hospital informed me that they admitted him to the hospital with organ failure and that he was likely to die any day, so we made a second visit within the span of a year and a half to see Michael, my father, after about 30 years of almost no contact. Disoriented from our long flight from Los Angeles, my son, Niko, and I stood next to each other as I let the senior volunteer in the hospital flower shop sell me flowers. She suggested that the bouquet, snug in a yellow smiley face mug, was cheerful yet masculine. I thought her sexist analysis might resonate with Michael. He always had problems with the feminine in all its manifestations. He spoke ill of my mother and believed he had been her victim because she left him. I found out later that he had violently attacked her, even tried to kill her, which prompted her to initiate divorce. She told me about this violence between them only after he had murdered Eve, my stepmother. My mother still refuses to talk about this violence. The shame of being abused is complicated.

"Mmbullshit," he said when I offered the flowers, snug in their smiley mug, to him.

"Come onnnnn, Michael … ," sang the attendant from Greystone Park Forensic Psychiatric Hospital under her breath. During his trial, he received a sentence of "innocent of murder by reason of insanity," which ordered him to a life sentence at Greystone Park Forensic Psychiatric Hospital for the criminally insane. A Krol Order was attached to this sentence, forever keeping him out of society. It applies to patients acquitted of violent crimes due to mental illness and mandates that there must always be a trained eye watching him 24/7, sort of like a human ankle bracelet. Just because he was acquitted of charges by reason of insanity didn't make him free; instead, he embarked on a life of court monitoring, reporting, and living according to conditions, including institutional commitment. A qualified attendant watched him at all times, making sure he didn't slip into the extremes of his illness, where he could be a danger to others again. This legal designation didn't acknowledge the fact that when he became unhinged, the casualties were always women. This inherent sexism was based in deep misogyny; this irrefutable bias was among his heaviest baggage.

VISIT ONE

We had visited Michael for the first time in July 2018. Back then, Niko and I went to see him at Greystone along with my sister, Susan, her husband, and their two kids. The protocol there was to leave our phones in lockers before entering, so we have no photos from this visit. Later, I learned that Greystone was being fined and sued for mistreatment of its patients. It seems that this no-photos policy was as much about protecting management of the locked-down facility from exposure and liability as about protecting the anonymity of patients forced into public care. The tears that flooded my eyes upon seeing my father for the first time in nearly three decades stopped just as quickly as they began. With an attendant present—the law prevented us from being alone with him—we shared information as if we were in a go-round at our jobs, giving detached but detailed descriptions of our family and work lives, eager to catch him up while simultaneously avoiding any reminders of the circumstances that kept us from seeing him for so long. We prepared to leave after about 40 minutes. It was all too much to digest, and we ran out of things to say. We just kept standing there as a group, silently looking at him in his recliner. He was largely paralyzed from advanced stages of Parkinson's disease and was unable to move. Privately, I considered whether I wanted to touch his hand.

I'm aware of the damage those hands have done to us. He murdered Eve, my stepmother and ally in life, in 1988 when I was 22. She was 40 years old. I was finishing up my junior year of college in Vermont at the time. We were left with no home and no money. Not even a stuffed animal or family photos could be charmed from the grips of predatory debt collectors. As the eldest of the five kids, I ended up making decisions for my two underage siblings with the help of my other two sisters, college roommates, and a handful of well-intentioned social workers at public agencies.

All our sets of godparents, whom my parents chose to serve as some kind of ballast of support in times of emergency, ran away in horror after what happened. They said they had no capacity to advise us, let alone take in more kids. Longtime family friends and whatever extended family we had left were so upset that they wouldn't even try to help us. As if murder were contagious, we were instantly looked on as marked and as burdens by the very people we were taught to look up to and lean on. We all were clinically in shock as we turned to a neighbor, someone relatively new in our lives. My brother, Roger, then just eight years old, remained unable to speak for weeks after being forced to witness our dad's murderous actions, as if he were being invited to join some patriarchal club within this household of women. Not knowing where else to go, we all moved to camp out in our neighbor's multistory house for weeks as we registered for victims' rights funds, attended therapy, tried to help Roger recover, and made funeral arrangements. Relative strangers, new to most of us, were startling in their short-lived generosity. I don't even remember their names.

Due to the combination of our own psychological overwhelm, gaps in response, and the ineffectuality of the New Jersey public child-welfare system, Roger and our thirteen-year-old sister Patricia were taken in by the supposedly well-meaning parents of a classmate of Patricia. "You can't raise these kids; you are a kid yourself," these parents, definitely 20-plus years my seniors, said to me. We took Roger to a children's therapist, but no bonds were made. The therapist advised us that immersion in the "normalcy" of a stable household and its routines would help Roger. I don't know if county services would have been better, but in a stupor I nodded in agreement, relieved by the removal of some weight from me. Looking back, I realize we all suffered from a dearth of information about trauma and trauma therapies compared to what is available now.

So Patricia and Roger lived together in this neighboring family's home. Somehow, all of us were trying to hold onto any modicum of privilege our family had managed to achieve for themselves, and we blindly presumed the kindness of middle-class strangers would be better than sending our siblings into the world of governmental intervention and care. At that time, we thought the child-welfare system served people more disadvantaged than ourselves, and so we still couldn't see how deeply affected our family was. To this day, I don't know which would have been better—well-meaning strangers or the government. Meanwhile, after three months Patricia didn't get along with her classmate anymore, and the mother called. She asked me to pick Patricia up by September 1 and find another place for her to live for the school year because she needed to protect her own daughter. Yet she assured me that young Roger was doing great in her home. "How can we separate the kids?," I asked. I was bewildered when she told me Roger was too young to move into our college household. She parroted back that he needed the "normalcy"

of a suburban household with heteronormative parents and a male role model. So Patricia moved into my small, collectively run home during her ninth grade of high school. After about six months and a run-in with the law for shoplifting cosmetics, she said she didn't like living with me anymore. This lifestyle change to living with college-going roommates on food stamps and the occasional Hamburger Helper from the corner store was too much for her.

I searched for other options for her tenth-grade year of school and came across the generous Casey Family Services, a privately funded foster agency. It was a part of the Anne E. Casey Foundation, which can be heard advertising on local NPR stations. Patricia met their program requirements for having no labeled disabilities and minimal special needs and was moved into the large house of an upper-middle-class, white, Protestant family in Hanover, New Hampshire. Patricia, unlike her older siblings, had few memories of living in Flushing, New York. She was accustomed to and longed for the suburban life in New Jersey that she had lost. The Casey Foundation sponsored her through the tenth grade and on. This family, who still includes Patricia in their lives, embraced her as a beautiful, exotic project, a new quasi-family member for a mother with empty-nest syndrome. With two kids in tow, Patricia is currently in the process of a complicated divorce from an abusive, volatile husband. All of us siblings are trying to lend our hands in any ways we can to save her life, to get her out, to break the cycle without unraveling ourselves too much by diving into our own flashbacks.

Meanwhile, every time I visited Roger, his nonverbal acting out, from trauma and anger he could not articulate, escalated. What was going on here? It was clear he was not well. Why weren't they taking him to his therapist? Evidently, he was struggling to make bonds. The murder that my father had forced Roger to witness had such a large psychological impact on him that he was unable to tell me what was happening in this new household. Eventually, through repeated questioning, I pieced together that he was being sexually molested by the father of the family. I should have pressed charges, but I was so traumatized by the idea of the police that taking him far away from there was my only concern. I only knew the police as the bringers of bad news that caused irreparable upheaval over which I was powerless. When I was nine years old, they were the ones who had knocked on our door at 6:00 a.m. to tell us my stepfather had been found dead on the side of the road

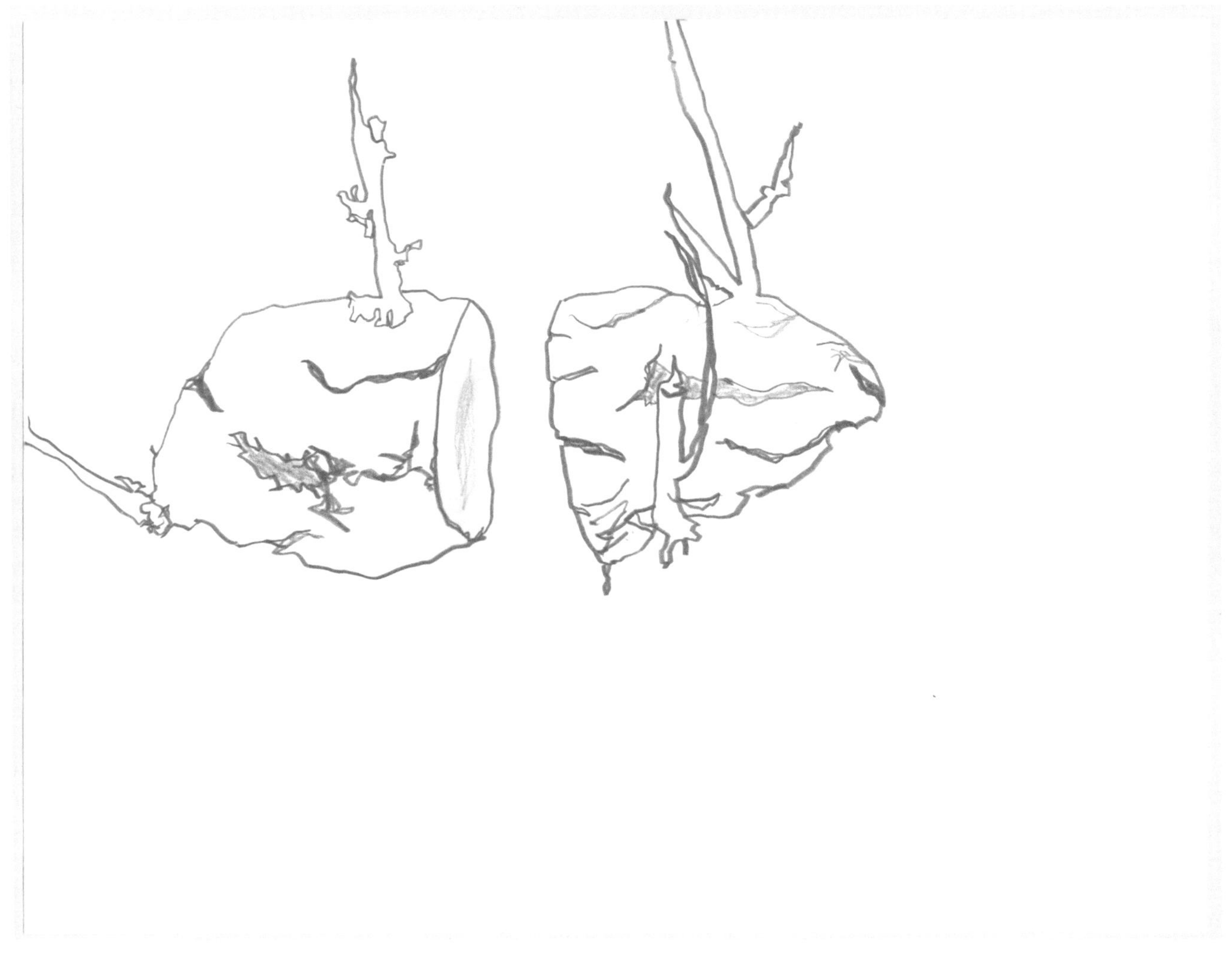

Drawing by Olga Koumoundouros.

and then years later called again at 6:00 a.m. to tell me about Eve's murder.

On the day I learned of Eve's murder, the call from the New Jersey police woke me from sleep. The call began with a volley of terse questions meant to verify that I was the appropriate recipient of this news. I had to prove I was the oldest by giving my birthdate and the names of my siblings and then explaining that grandparents weren't around, that there were no others wiser, more responsible, or capable present to take the call. After this hostile scrutiny, they determined that there was nobody else to take charge. They told me of Eve's death and that my father had been taken into police custody. They then told me to go pick up my trembling brother from the neighbor's house in New Jersey, where he had run in the night, fleeing for his life. For the caller, going through all of this amounted to checking a cold, hard box, but for me it dropped a forever life-changing bomb of violence. So when I discovered later what was happening to Roger, it didn't even occur to me that the police would ever listen to us about anything, let alone about a child being sexually abused.

As soon as I told Casey Family Services what was happening, though, they pulled Roger out and found him a new family to live with in Woodstock, Vermont, so he could be close to Patricia, Tracy, Susan, and me. These new people were well intentioned and kind, and Roger lived there for a few years, but the symptoms of his trauma kept creeping in and taking over. Therapies were not effective, and he began to self-medicate by smoking weed in the sixth grade. The family said they feared his behavior was destructive to the well-being of their own children, so he moved again, this time in with me and my partner just in time for middle school— his "last chance," Casey Family Services called it at the time. At this point, Roger was medicating himself extensively, and we utilized all the therapy and drug-rehabilitation services available to us. My partner, now a trans man, had talent with boys in trouble, and he made some headway in connecting with Roger. Incidentally, my partner founded and is the director of a school for system-impacted boys, a vocational choice highly influenced by this experience. However, for Roger, drugs worked better than what any of us could provide, and he disappeared into the intoxicated universe of touring misfits that followed the band Phish for years. This was a very painful part of my life. I worked at a community-action agency, where I advocated for people's rights to get the various public benefits they deserved, from Aid to Needy Families with Children to Medicaid and food stamps. Through this work, I learned the ins and outs of these programs and helped people fill out the intimidating required forms. I regularly argued with the rigid welfare workers who acted as gatekeepers and behaved as though they believed everyone who applied was a criminal. I strongly believed in a social contract: a web of support should be there to help all members of our society thrive, and nonprofit and public-sector systems are obligated to help people in need. Of course, now I know how so many people slip through these ill-funded and precarious safety nets.

I began to search for my father's whereabouts when my son asked to meet his grandfather. There were newspaper articles available online because the murder had been well publicized, which is relatively uncommon in cases of homicide of women by their partners. I was able to track down my father's former attorney, and I made a cold call. The attorney knew my name and referred me to my father's social worker. I had the idea that this was the right thing to do as a parent—that it would help my son to clearly see an aspect of his heritage in full light, including the legacy of violence we had escaped and that had affected his whole family in so many ways. I thought that perhaps my son could also see that a life of punishment wasn't useful to survivors or offenders. I didn't think I was ready to forgive my father, but perhaps I could begin a process of cultivating the capacity within myself to hold space for Michael's humanity while knowing he took away someone else's life. So I proceeded.

As that first visit with Michael at Greystone Park came to its close, I tried to ground my body in the present and remind myself that I was no longer in the past. Even though I did that exercise, I still found myself fixating on his spotted, cold hands, tracking the erratic movements they made due to the Parkinson's, and wondering if they were safe. I saw their mushy impotence and decided they were, so I reached for one. His round brown eyes looked at me meekly. In a flash, I recalled my protracted efforts as a child to please this berating man: singing songs that he'd rank, concocting plays with fabulous props, turning elaborate untrained dance routines into visual spectacles—all as an excuse to ask him for costume or plot suggestions and, ultimately, to ask for his approval. Those batting eyelashes of his were selfish back then, but I decided not to read this look he was giving me now as icky or manipulative.

I wondered if he was afraid of rejection. He should have been, my rage told me. The murder was not a lone error. He had held the family captive on and off in a reign of thunderous quakes that alternated with moments of calm, paranoia, surveillance, and scrutiny. Yeah, he was charming and handsome, and he could turn on an entertaining gregariousness at will with acquaintances and strangers alike—the life of the party fueled by a brooding insecurity. I know he had a hard life; he himself was psychologically wounded because of his own father's suicide, which left his older sister and single mom to raise him. But when he was unbalanced, whatever problems he had in the past or encountered in the present were always women's fault.

OK, I thought, one squeeze to say I see you and I'm not afraid of you anymore, and then it is time to go. Niko and I walked away from my father's rolling chaise lounge. The guard held the door open, and we stood in the hallway waiting for my other family members to finish their goodbyes so that we all could leave. I thought I would never go back—I had faced my demons—and that this was the final closure. It wasn't.

VISIT ONE

A year and a half later, the hospital called me with the news that Michael was dying. Niko really wanted to say goodbye. I felt so unsure about this; I had thought Michael and I were done. I had visited him in prison only once. He'd been arraigned, but his trial hadn't happened yet, and he was out of his mind, asking me to call him "Gemino," his new tough-guy name as he barked orders in a doubly thick New York accent. He continued to make calls to me from jail with aggressive, bossy demands, acting as if I owed him something. The New Jersey State prosecutor was seeking the death penalty, and I was so confused as I tried to hold everything together. At the end of these phone calls, I would feel both bereft and full of rage. With the help of a therapist and the support of my friends, I stopped taking the calls and doing tasks for him. I had to focus on making decisions for the kids left behind. His attorney kept in contact with me until Michael was sentenced and moved to the psychiatric facility, where he was psychologically stabilized with medication. It was puzzling to me that he never reached out to any of his other kids and sought me out only when he thought he could push me around—once I refused to do his bidding, all I got was total silence.

By comparison, sitting by the bedside of a dying parent to say goodbye seemed like what "normal" people do. I wanted to enact the kind of scene from television dramas or to mimic other dished-out, socially acceptable cultural norms. People dying in hospitals of progressing, age-related conditions seemed closer to a marker of stability than what I had experienced in my own past. Also, Niko told me that after the first visit he had been under the impression that we were going to visit Michael again. I decided I should give my son this chance to grieve over time and to experience the closure that might follow. It would be better than letting Niko's last images of his grandfather be of that horrible Greystone.

So we made our second visit to Michael, who now was at Morristown Memorial Hospital for medical treatment. Michael had been so meek and apologetic at Greystone during our first time seeing him that we were startled to hear his rancid shouts as we approached his bed, which was surrounded by machines and tubes. We stood there in a stupor, holding the flowers in the smiley-face mug. With resolve, I put down the flowers, which he didn't like, and tried to interrupt his verbal vulgarity to show him some photos from his past that I framed—of himself with his children and some of his grandkids—thinking this would make him happy. He managed to hold his eyes only on the images of his grandchildren. I showed him pictures of his mother and my siblings, too. He just shook his head, muttering "horneee" or "mmbullshit" repeatedly. Without missing a beat, Niko pulled a blue fleece blanket out of his school daypack and began wrapping it around Michael's body, careful not to unplug the tubes and monitors. Michael softened at being tucked in by his grandson. I considered leaving soon to save Niko a good last memory, but Niko wanted to stay.

I was pissed off. I had thought Michael was going to be peaceful, calm, and somewhat remorseful, as he had been on our first visit. I learned from the attendant that he became vulgar when agitated. He tried to grab breasts and harassed anyone who passed near, including the doctors and nurses who treated him. He would tell them that he didn't trust them, making it challenging for them to come up with treatment plans he approved. His kidneys were failing, and the doctors said general organ failure was imminent. He had a peg in his gut to help him digest liquid food.

The attendant told me she had agreed to work with him because he could also be quite nice sometimes. He still had the keen, sharpened tools of a serial charmer of women. After he was first sentenced to life in a psychiatric hospital and began life at Greystone, he had entered into a romantic relationship with Mary, one of his nurses. According to newspaper articles I read, a court hearing over the relationship was held, and Mary's nursing license was revoked, but the judge agreed to release Michael to live with her under the conditions that she gave him the requisite care, made sure he took his meds and attended weekly AA meetings, and would notify the courts if his signs of paranoia arose again. She accepted these conditions, essentially a life sentence as his legally assigned personal aid, which meant following all sorts of protocols and filing reports. That is how he finagled getting out of his prison sentence: he seduced one of his nurses, and she decided to marry him. She returned him to Greystone once his Parkinson's condition became too much for her to handle, she said, and later we learned from Medicaid that she also did so just after she received a large cash settlement from a malpractice lawsuit she and Michael initiated together. The staff of Greystone were not fans of her. I didn't know her, but I'm sure she tolerated a lot living with Michael, and perhaps the settlement can be looked at as a kind of deal they made. It was as if he paid her to take on the burden of appeasing the court so he could secure this reprieve from his life sentence. Mary certainly received more from him than my mother or Eve had, let alone his children, all of whom were so drastically affected by his actions. Mary died shortly after receiving this settlement and bequeathed those funds to her grandchild, Justin.

The attendant and I intermittently chuckled and shuddered with repulsion at Michael's repeated profane outbursts. After a while, I stopped feeling angry and zoned out between the occasional emotional lurches, sitting there with everyone that afternoon and watching the movie *Hairspray*—Michael enjoyed controlling his own TV. He also sometimes conducted whispered business meetings on an invisible, imaginary phone. Occasionally, his coughing fits—loud, viscous, plumbing-like gurgles—made us jump.

Finally, I noticed Niko slumped in a chair, half asleep. Now it was really time to go. We gathered around Michael once again and let him know we were leaving. He didn't seem to mind. He turned to look directly at me with water-filled eyes and said, "Thank you for all you have done for me. I'll meet you on the other side!" He cheekily smiled.

Michael didn't die at Morristown Memorial Hospital that November 2019. He moved to a palliative-care home, where his aggressive verbal outbursts, which had occurred because doctors at the hospital had taken him off his psych meds, stopped once he began receiving both medical and psychiatric treatment again. This allowed him to flourish, and his rebound surprised everyone. After a brief period, he was moved back to Greystone. His positive experiences at Morristown Memorial Hospital and the palliative-care home made his social worker think that, given his responsiveness to medical treatment, he could maybe have a peaceful end of life.

We could get Medicaid to pay for long-term nursing home care if someone was willing to be his guardian. My ethics compelled me to take this on. I believed in rehabilitation and treatment for offenders. I felt that all incarcerated people, Michael included, deserved to die humanely and peacefully. I did not believe punishment led to a just society. Michael, now completely immobile, clearly no longer posed a threat to others, so what would be gained from keeping him locked up in that brutal place surrounded by guards?

In February 2020, I walked out of Morris County Courthouse with my sister Tracy, who had come down from Vermont to join me as I gained guardianship of our father. I raised my hand and swore to a judge so that I would have the power to work with the social worker to initiate the changes that would allow our father to pass away more comfortably. Michael's ravings indicated he did not understand the state of his health well enough to advocate for his best medical interests, and yet his health improvements did prove that he would do better in a nursing home environment with round-the-clock medical and psychiatric treatments. After the legal proceedings, Tracy and I headed over to Greystone to visit Dad.

VISIT THREE

This time he was wearing a new polo shirt and jeans. They wrapped around his skinny body like a bag, yet he still looked dapper. He spoke to us in Greek, and I spoke back in Greek, but Tracy had forgotten hers. He needed to tell us about how close he was to his third wife, Mary, whom we never knew personally. I felt that maybe he needed us to know that he had moved on and had created a life with emotional attachments that we were not a part of. I felt stung but wasn't surprised, while Tracy was just totally flabbergasted. She had no idea that he really had moved on. We talked about how I was arranging to get him into a nursing home so he could get more well-rounded, supportive health care. He nodded and mumbled his agreement with this change. I signed a bunch of papers, and a few nurses came to meet us, curious because he had lived there for so many years without visitors. The social worker told us she wanted us to meet the people who cared for my dad, but I think it was more that she wanted to show us off to the disbelieving staff and caregivers. Before we left, I gave Michael a hug and kissed his forehead.

A month and half later, he was again moved to Morristown Memorial Hospital. He had tested positive for COVID-19. His tenacious fear of death gave him enough energy to fight this illness for a week, but within a day of the virus moving to his lungs he died, on April 9, 2020.

I believe participating in this slow process of physical death alongside our father helped initiate another level of healing for our family. This process was never about regaining a loving father. We all were certain of that. In many ways, our father was dead to us already. Years ago, he closed that door when he didn't reach out to us from Greystone. It was always up to us to search out the latest info on him, usually prompted after someone contacted us about an article that had run in the newspaper after a hearing. At the very least, he could have let us know he was thinking of us half as often as the triggers from our trauma plagued us. This process of being somewhat part of his dying helped us shift some baggage that wouldn't have moved on its own. All of us siblings are now talking among ourselves more often, even though we lived far apart geographically. Those visits with Michael held space wide open for us to see our wounds a bit more fully before the closure that came with his passing. Some of these wounds had been too painful to touch in all these years since the loss of Eve. But as our lines of communication reopened, we shared our stories of those days, stuff we hadn't been able to talk about ever before. As we began to see the past from each other's vantage point, the information that each of us had carried alone has now become part of our collective understanding as family. As the story became externalized, each of us became better able to handle it. His death prompted us to feel and process more about the murder of our stepmother and the brutal ending of our family as we knew it. We are beginning to see how much each of us suffered over the years and are able to witness with more compassion the ripple effects this violence continues to have in our lives. The barbs and hard edges, formed through the idiosyncratic techniques each of us cultivated to cope and survive, are softening.

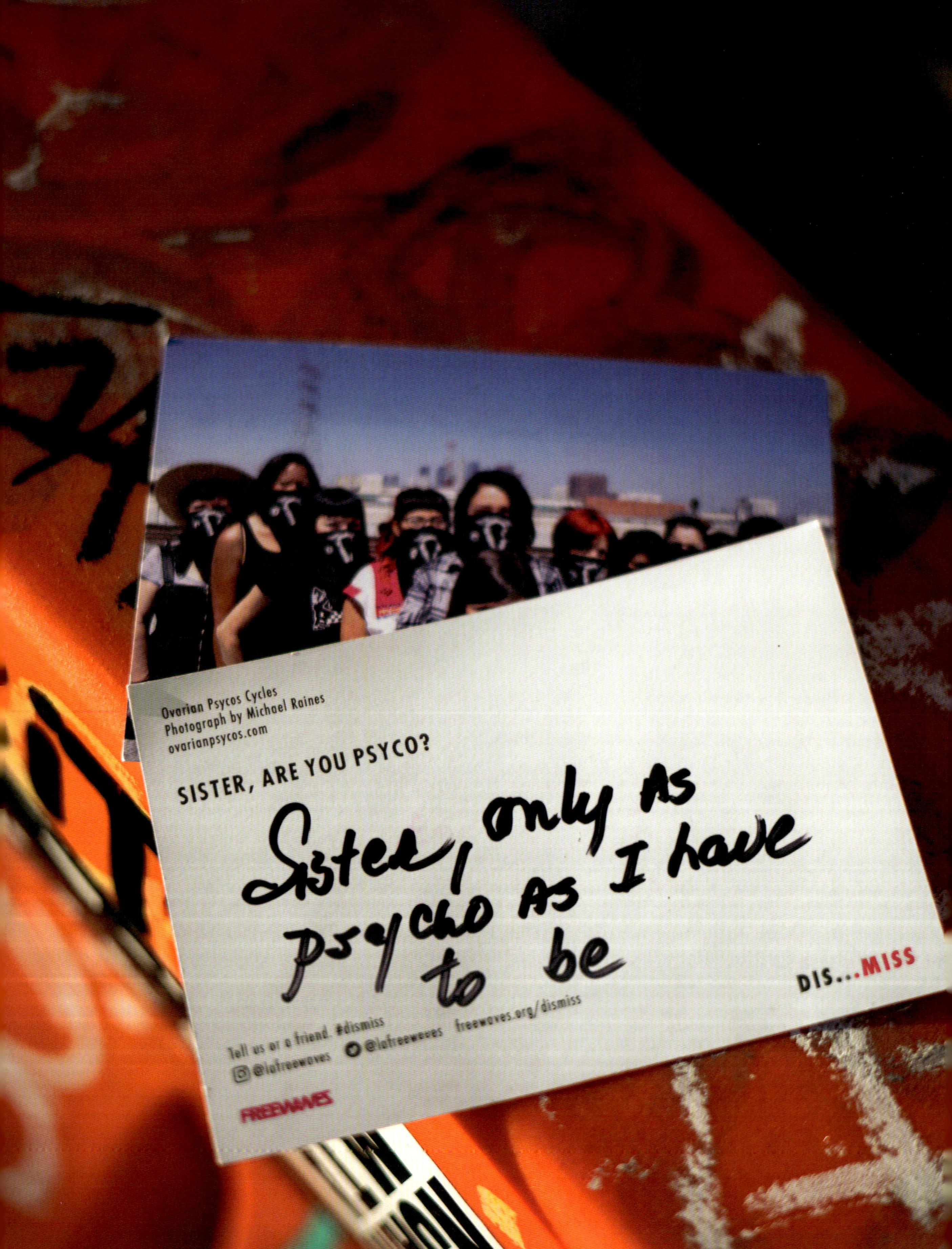
Ovarian Psycos Cycles
Photograph by Michael Raines
ovarianpsycos.com

SISTER, ARE YOU PSYCO?

Sister, only As
Psycho As I have
to be

Tell us or a friend. #dismiss
@lafreewaves   @lafreewaves   freewaves.org/dismiss

FREEWAVES

DIS...MISS

sister, are you psyco?

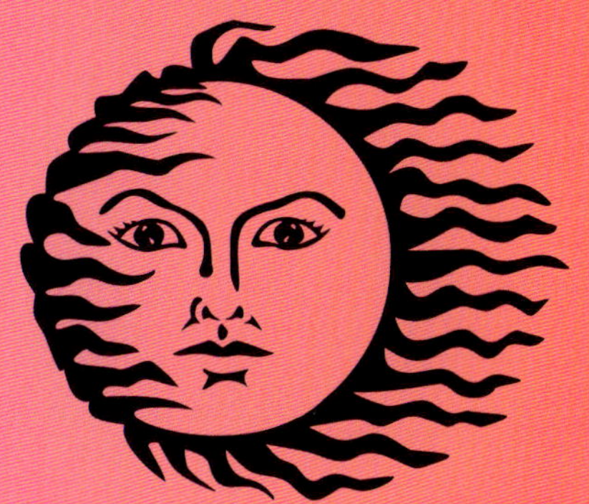

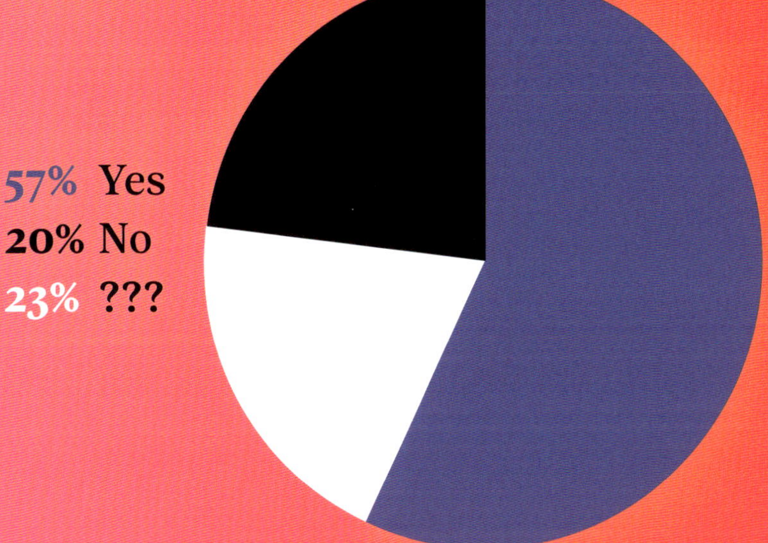

"DIS...MISS, Inconclusive Infographic Animation." Analyzed by Marisa Turesky. Animation designed by Catherine Bell, 2019.
Left: Postcard portrait by Alejandra Sone.

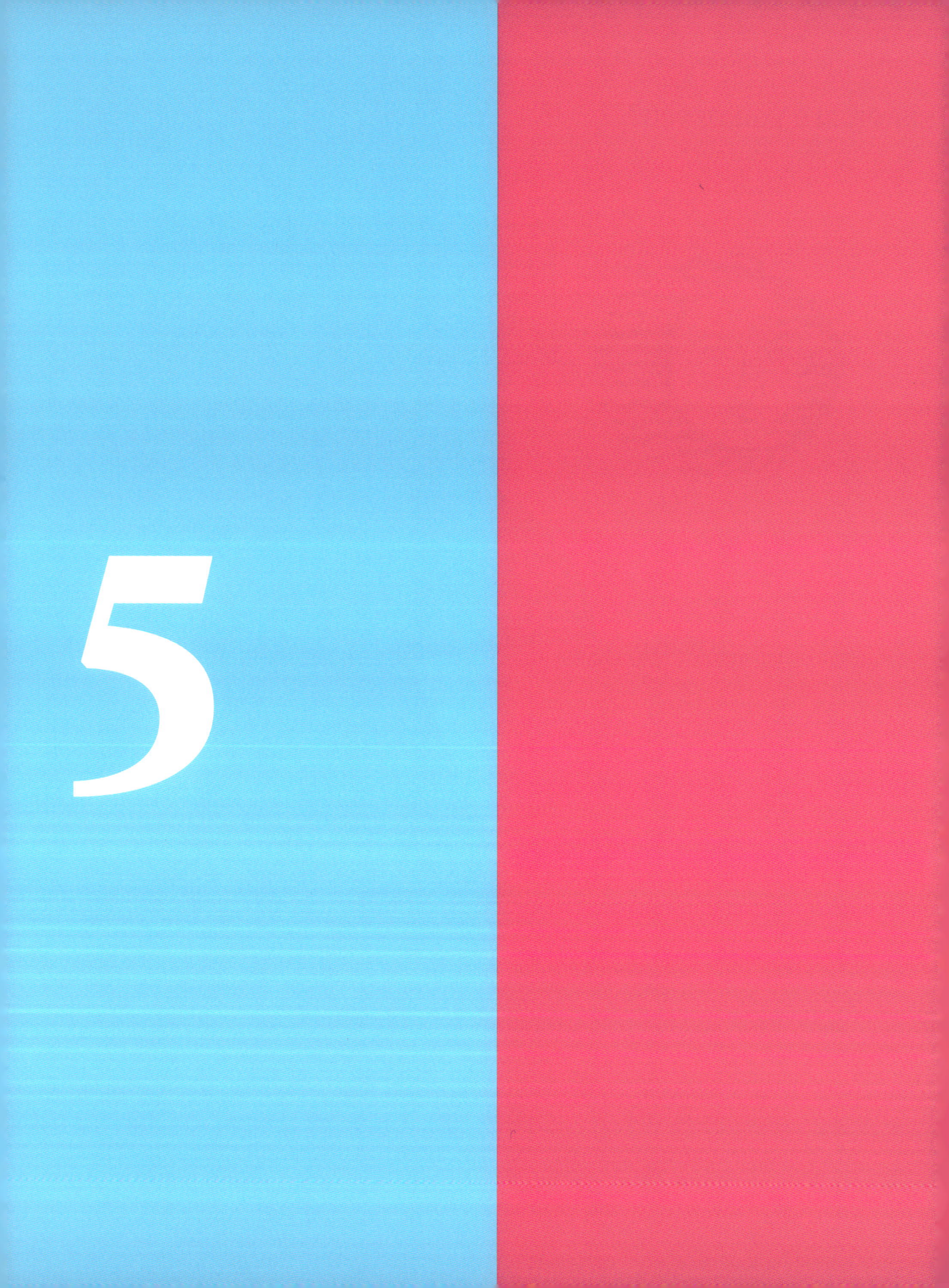

what is your myth
and fact about rape?

Myths of Rape (2016) by Audrey Chan and Elana Mann Reinterpretation of Leslie Labowitz-Starus's *Myths of Rape* (1977), Part of Suzanne Lacy's *Three Weeks in May*

Anuradha Vikram

Myths of Rape by Elana Mann and Audrey Chan.

The postcard that Audrey Chan and Elana Mann produced for *Dis...Miss* invokes the artists' reenactment in 2012 of an artwork that Leslie Labowitz-Starus originated in 1977 as part of Suzanne Lacy's watershed artwork-as-protest performance project *Three Weeks in May*. Chan and Mann's reenactment, produced as part of the Getty-led Pacific Standard Time performance festival, translated Labowitz-Starus's modular work of street theater into a reproducible artistic gesture within an art space, which Labowitz-Starus and the other artists of *Three Weeks in May* had deliberately avoided when mounting the project in 1977. Chan and Mann's reenactment maintained the collaborative dynamic and the assertive feminist politics of the original work. In a sense, the postcard of 2016 is a return to the street where the project originated.

Myth: No one will believe me.

Myths of Rape (1977) began as a four-act durational performance work performed at the City Mall Shopping Center in downtown LA by eight members of the Woman's Building community of feminist artists. Each woman was dressed in white or black, blindfolded, and carried a large, hand-stenciled placard on which Labowitz-Starus had inscribed the titular myths. The four acts of the performance were titled "Myths about Rape," "All Men Are Potential Rapists," "The Rape," and "Fighting Back." The intrusion of language about a topic usually met with silence into a space of public gathering and commerce added potency to the work. The performers used the setting of the mall as a foil, identifying displays as contributing to rape culture and then appropriating these displays as the backdrops for their protest tableaux.

Three Weeks in May was addressed to the nearby Los Angeles City Hall and barbed with the accusation of inaction on the part of city leadership. It brought attention to and sought to end the deafening public silence around increasing rates of rape and sexual assault of women in the late 1970s, both in Los Angeles, where the original maps that grounded the project were oriented, and on a broader scale. For women in the era engaged in collective consciousness-raising, the magnitude of reports of sexual assault and rape being shared within feminist communities was as overwhelming as the public refusal to admit the problem's existence. During

the action, a rape occurred within steps of City Mall, a fact that Lacy referenced in her performative lecture on May 25, 1977. "It's not where you are," Lacy explained in her speech. "Two nights ago, a woman was raped right here in the mall." Of feminist art Lacy went on to say, "It does have a purpose … to provide information about women's experience, invite an exchange with its audience on the issues raised, and ultimately to transform culture."[1]

In contrast to the speech, Labowitz-Starus's performance was executed in silence, the blinded and muted performers mirroring the justice system's lack of perception.

The actions that Lacy and Labowitz-Starus organized in 1977 were equal parts street theater, activism, and group therapy. An element of *Three Weeks in May* included Lacy visiting the Los Angeles Police Department central office each day to obtain the locations of the previous day's reported rapes, which she would then stamp on a large city map hanging in the installation. Each stamp was surrounded by nine additional markings representing the much larger number of sexual-assault crimes assumed by researchers to go unreported. Factors in not reporting rape include the fear that authorities won't believe a victim's story or will inflict revictimization through repeated interrogations; the fear of bringing shame or social ostracization upon the victim or their family; and fear of prosecution for unrelated offenses (such as sex work, drug use, or immigration violations) brought to light through an investigation into a sexual assault.

Fact: There will always be someone who believes you.

Myths of Rape was intended to be reperformed, which it was first by Labowitz-Starus and Lacy in Las Vegas in 1978 and again in 2012 when artists Audrey Chan and Elana Mann restaged it at the LA Art Show, another downtown venue. Thirty performers of varied ages, races, and genders participated in the movements, created in collaboration with the choreographer Mecca Vazie Andrews. Though the setting had been transferred from a generic site of commerce to an art-specific site, the fair environment likewise offered performers a number of displays to engage as foils. While Chan

---

1 Suzanne Lacy, "'Three Weeks in May': Speaking Out on Rape, a Political Art Piece," *Frontiers: A Journal of Women Studies* 2, no. 1 (Spring 1977): 6/–/U.

and Mann's reperformance at the LA Art Show in 2012 brought *Myths of Rape* back to life as a work of art, the postcard *Myths of Rape* in 2016 brought the dialogue back into public space. Distributed through LA Freewaves' many public art events and actions, the postcard circulates as a consciousness-raising device that can connect simply with audiences outside the arts in multiple languages.

Mito: Nadie me creerá.

Chan and Mann took inspiration from "traditions of feminist agit-prop, the Occupy Wall Street movement, and the Arab Spring" in their re-creation of *Myths of Rape*.[2] The latter two movements had recently brought class consciousness to the political fore, temporarily casting aside rhetorical tribalisms as well as gender-specific policy positions. The confluence of historical and contemporary reference points in Chan and Mann's reenactment of *Myths of Rape* also opened a path to include more international perspectives in the work to reflect the multilingual and multicultural environment of contemporary Los Angeles. In the Los Angeles Convention Center, the sterility and commercialized architecture of the City Mall was preserved, but the audience for the performance was more tightly regulated, and the performance was less available to the general public. There was no direct target for the reenactment in the sense that the original performance had been directed toward LA's city hall. Fitting for the twenty-first century, the performance-protest's target seemed to have shifted from the state to the market.

Chan and Mann sought to reignite the urgency of 1970s feminism in younger generations through their ongoing collaboration and to revisit feminist performance histories, while bringing the political messages up to date. In the 1970s, the history of feminist art in Los Angeles, the epicenter of which was the Woman's Building at 1727 North Spring Street in downtown, was written by a majority-white, middle-class group of women. This group expanded to become more inclusive of women of color and working-class women by the 1980s. In the spirit of the radical inclusion that the earlier era aspired to, Chan and Mann's *Myths of Rape* in 2016 widened the circle of awareness and healing further to include immigrant and non-English-speaking survivors of sexual violence.

Realidad: Siempre habrá alguien que te crea.

By targeting Spanish and Chinese speakers with their iteration of *Myths of Rape*, Chan and Mann sought to focus outreach within marginalized communities in Los Angeles that have limited access to law enforcement, crisis centers, and other survivor resources. Women are further isolated by language in these immigrant communities. By printing and distributing postcards that translate the phrase "myths of rape" into two of Los Angeles County's most commonly spoken languages, the artists paralleled another element of *Three Weeks in May* (1977), which included a schedule of political organizing activities, such as self-defense demonstrations, presentations by law enforcement, private meetings for women and survivors, and informational presentations by advocacy groups. According to US census data from 2016, Spanish was the most commonly spoken language in the Los Angeles region, followed by English. People of Hispanic or Latinx descent made up 48.5 percent of the population. White European non-Hispanics made up 26.5 percent of the population. In 2017, the *Los Angeles Times* reported that fewer sexual-assault and domestic-violence charges were being filed by the city's Latinx residents amid fears that reporting these crimes to police would trigger punitive immigration actions against the victims' families.[3] Excluded from public amenities such as cultural institutions and social services as well as from the protection of law enforcement, these communities are often difficult for activists or artists to engage from the outside.

Since Chan and Mann moved their reenactment from a public site to an art context, we might consider data from the Los Angeles County Arts Commission's report *The Demographics of the Arts and Cultural Workforce in Los Angeles* (2017), which showed that 58 percent of the arts and cultural workforce identifies as white non-Hispanic, but only 9 percent identifies as Hispanic or Latinx.[4] No distinction was made regarding the rank-

---

2   Audrey Chan and Elana Mann, "*Myths of Rape* (1977/2012)," artists' statement, https://www.elanamann.com/project/myths-rape-19772012.

3   James Queally, "Fearing Deportation, Many Domestic Violence Victims Are Steering Clear of Police and Courts," *Los Angeles Times*, October 9, 2017, https://www.latimes.com/local/lanow/la-me-ln-undocumented-crime-reporting-20171009-story.html.

4   Los Angeles County Arts Commission, *The Demographics of the Arts and Cultural Workforce in Los Angeles* (Los Angeles: Los Angeles County Arts Commission, 2017), 14, https://www.lacountyarts.org/sites/default/files/pdfs/artsworkforcedemog2017.pdf.

ing of cultural workers of individual races within the institutional staff hierarchy. These statistics prompt the question whether an audience organized around art can relate to the topic of rape as concretely as the audience on the street.

神話：沒有人會相信我。

Los Angeles County residents identifying as Asian in the 2016 census made up 15.1 percent of the population. Foreign-born persons made up 34.5 percent. In the Los Angeles County Arts Commission report a year later, 10 percent of the cultural workforce identified as Asian.[5] No distinction was made between persons of Chinese, Japanese, Korean, Southeast Asian, South Asian, or Central Asian descent. The Asian Pacific Institute on Gender-Based Violence reported in 2014 that Chinese- and Japanese-descended Americans had the lowest reporting rates of intimate-partner violence (9.7 percent) among Asian immigrant groups surveyed,[6] a finding that, rather than suggesting low rates of violence, likely results from a combination of internal suppression due to the fear of family dishonor and the aforementioned precarity of non-English-speaking immigrant women, who fear deportation as retaliation for making a report. Like the "whisper networks" of professional women brought to light by the recent #MeToo and Time's Up movements in American public life, postcards can travel nearly undetected through extensive social chains.

事實：總會有人相信你。

Los Angeles is an international hub for human trafficking and sexual exploitation. The city's extreme wealth disparity, large immigrant population, and proximity to international borders contribute to this status. According to a report from the Pacific Council, the Coalition to Abolish Slavery & Trafficking (CAST) says the combination of these factors can work in favor of traffickers: the diversity of ethnic groups and communities in Los Angeles makes it "easier to hide and move victims from place to place, making it very difficult for law enforcement to locate potential survivors."[7] Increasing public awareness, specifically in non-English-speak-

ing communities with a high number of immigrants, is essential to addressing this problem. "Awareness building" through targeted marketing is a prime strategy for activists, as evidenced by the "Don't Be Silent" initiative, a collaborative effort between the county and LA Metro, which invested a quarter million dollars in advertising on public trains and buses in 2015.

For Leslie Labowitz-Starus, *Myths of Rape* was a work of art that lived foremost in the public realm, with recognition from art historians and venues somewhat slower to materialize. The Getty-led Pacific Standard Time performance festival, produced by LAXART in 2012, supported Los Angeles Contemporary Exhibitions in producing Chan and Mann's reenactment in 2012. Moving from public artwork-as-protest to institutional presentation, the work shifted from direct action to historicization. Although necessary and validating for the artwork's originators, reenactment is an ambivalent position for artists of the younger generation, who are as ready to make an aesthetic statement as a political one. The context for reperformance is too often an institutional one, whether a university, a museum, or a commercial setting. Even so, the support for and the visibility of the reperformance in 2012 enabled Chan and Mann to present the project internationally, traveling to China in 2014, while Labowitz-Starus worked with a group of students who reperformed the work in Allegheny, Pennsylvania, in 2015. These subsequent reperformances, which the presentation in 2012 brought about, are more in line with Labowitz-Starus's initial, viral action in the way they circumvent institutions of art and politics to bring an activist message about preventing sexual assault directly to the people.

---

5   Los Angeles County Arts Commission, *The Demographics of the Arts and Cultural Workforce in Los Angeles*, 14.

6   Asian Pacific Institute on Gender-Based Violence, graphic for Asian Pacific Institute on Gender-Based Violence, AAPIdata.com, 2014; data from C. Leung and C. Cheung, "A Prevalence Study on Partner Abuse in Six Asian American Ethnic Groups in the USA," *International Social Work* 51, no. 5 (2008): 635–649, https://www.api-gbv.org/about-gbv/statistics-violence-against-api-women.

7   Kaveh A. Farzad, "Human Trafficking in Los Angeles: A Global Crisis," Pacific Council on International Policy, July 2, 2015, https://www.pacificcouncil.org/newsroom/human-trafficking-los-angeles-global-crisis.

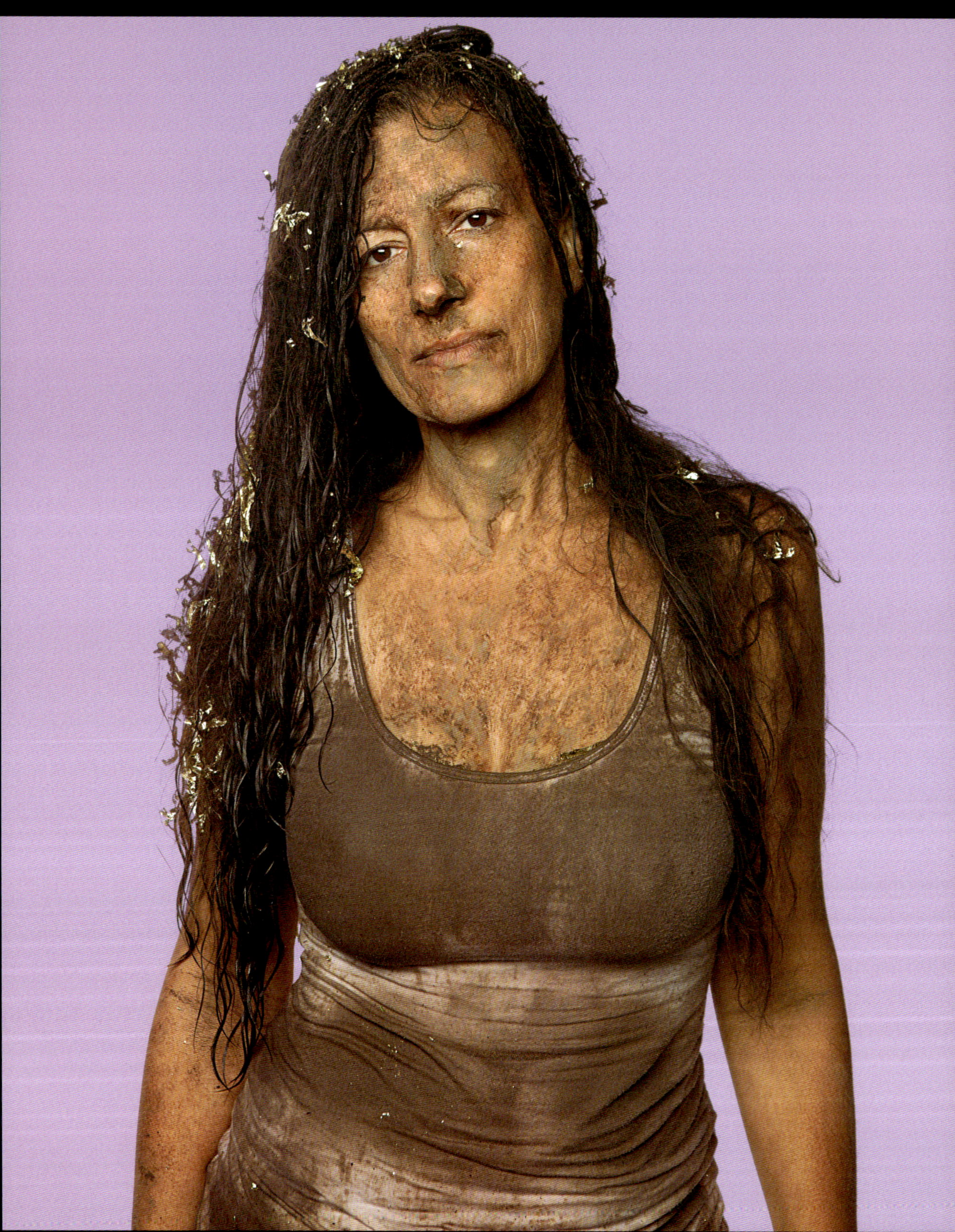

Amitis Motevalli. Photo: Austin Young.

Demystifying the Mystical for the Faranghi, Who May Or May Not Be Franks

Amitis Motevalli

Let me explain a *ghusl* to you to the best of my ability. …

It is a ritual cleansing, ablution, absolution, taking away dirt, physical, in action, in thought, in spirit.

I guess then I explain what a Zikr is to me. …

A performative Sufi ritual of meditation through repetition of movement or recitation. A Zikr is sometimes performed with music, in particular sa rhythm, the drum, to take the practitioners into a higher state of meditation. Sometimes this ritual is performed in public spaces.

On July 28, 2018, I invited two drummers, Hesam Abedani and Ariyan Khouroshi, to play Daf and zarb, with Iranian, in particular southern Iranian, Sufi rhythms. I also invited two dear friends, Arshia Fatima Haq and Asiya Farah Mir, to join me in the ritual cleanse. Arshia, Asiya, and I wore white. Hesam and Ariyan wore black.

Explaining *p'ak* …
P'ak means "clean" or "pure."

I placed five clear bowls in a circle, each one filled with a different material.

Bowls:

1. Water
2. Dirt
3. My favorite books torn up
4. Red wine
5. Gold confetti

I started by going around the circle and cleansing myself with the ingredients in each bowl. Slowly, Arshia and then Asiya joined in at their own pace. We repeated this process to help us enter into a spiritual conversation. For close to three hours, we stopped only to refill each bowl.

Even with the occasional disruption from the food truck calling out orders or stating "we ran out of steak" on its PA system, we left the park. Our bodies were present, but our spirits went into a space of discourse beyond earth. I didn't see my family come or go. We didn't see our friends, colleagues engage in small talk or networking. We didn't see Rafa get dragged by a low low.

Each of us spent the next few days washing the clean from our *p'ak* performance off of us.

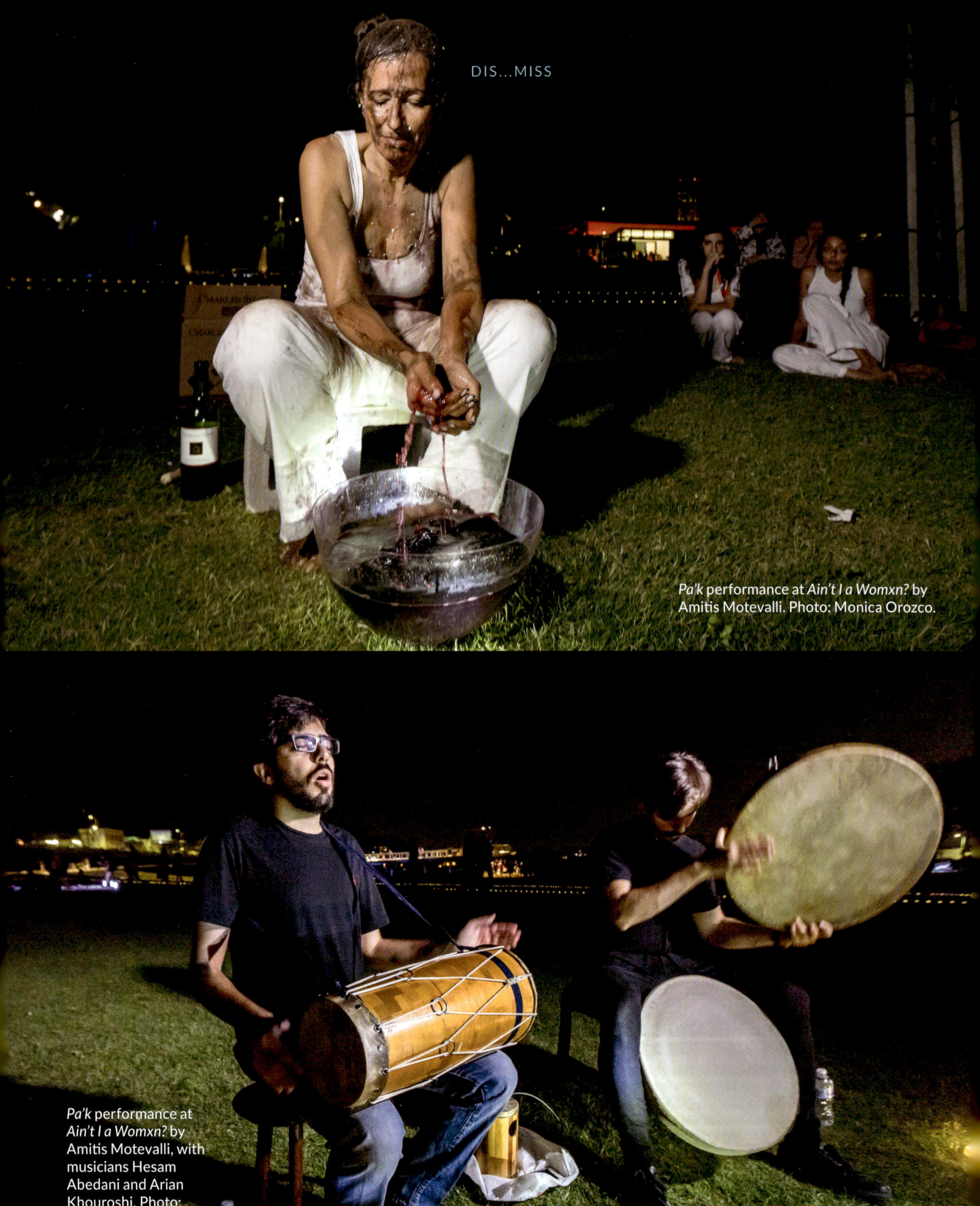

Pa'k performance at *Ain't I a Womxn?* by Amitis Motevalli. Photo: Monica Orozco.

Pa'k performance at *Ain't I a Womxn?* by Amitis Motevalli, with musicians Hesam Abedani and Arian Khouroshi. Photo: Monica Orozco.

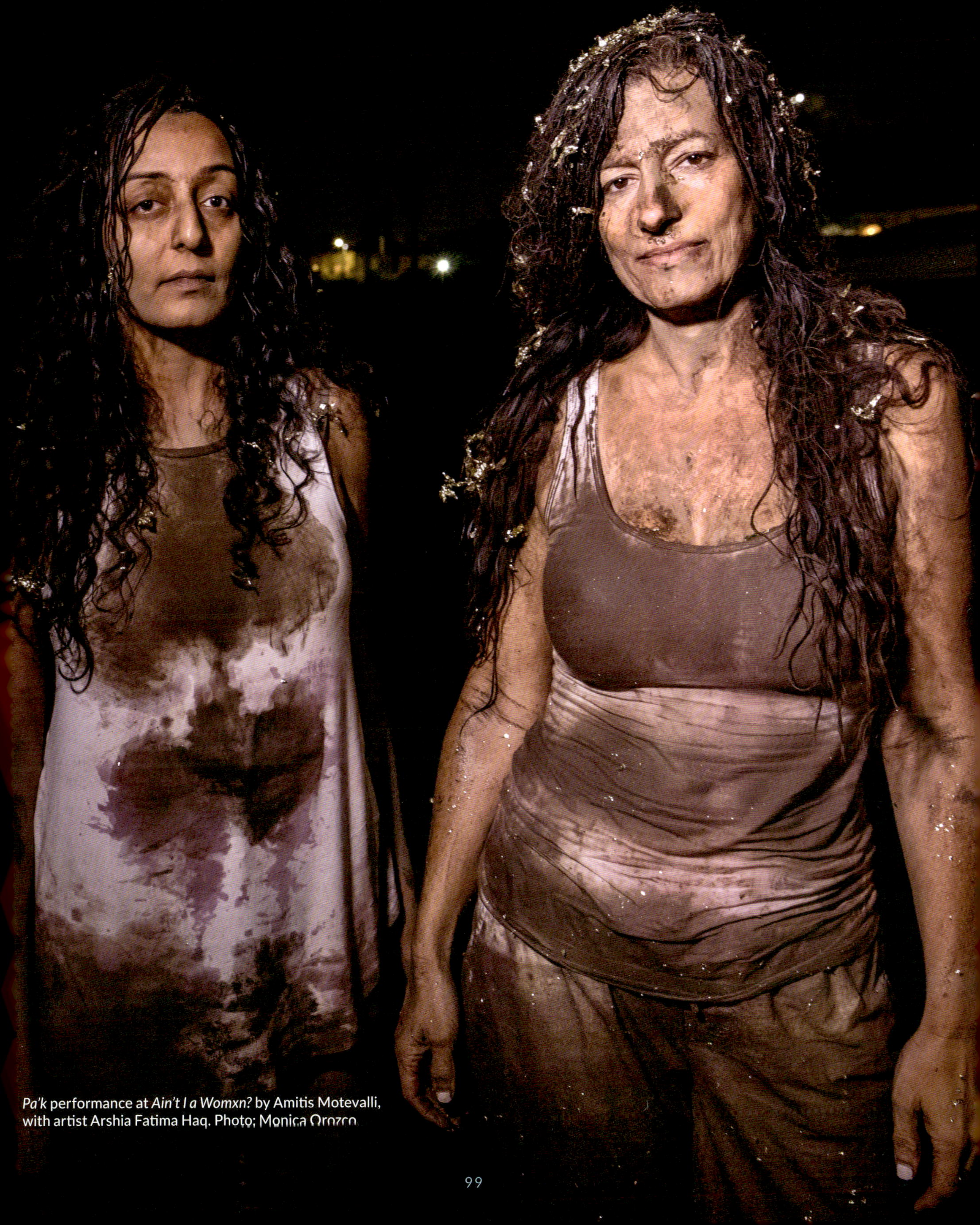

Pa'k performance at *Ain't I a Womxn?* by Amitis Motevalli, with artist Arshia Fatima Haq. Photo; Monica Orozco.

Unsettling Beliefs
Melissa Lo

In America, certain experiences are not supposed to be believed.

Rape was long one of them. Even among those who had lived the horror, the word could barely be uttered.[1] Up until the 1960s, state laws assumed survivors—if they were acknowledged at all—to be white women, most of whom had been violated by Black and white men. Should such a woman have sought her day in court, she would have been further saddled with extreme burdens of proof. Her testimony had to be validated by outside evidence. She had to be able to demonstrate she had put up a good fight against her assailant—that is, gave "earnest resistance." Her personal history had to make her out to be a Virgin Mary, chaste enough not to have invited sexual advances and honest enough to not lie about them. And if she wanted to bring rape charges against her husband? Forget about it. Marriage had yoked husband and wife as owner and property, respectively, permitting him to do whatever he wished to her.[2]

And what about any Black, Brown, Indigenous, or Asian women and queer people who sought justice? They need only have looked to the aftermath of the rape of the Black co-ed Betty Jean Owens in 1959, a case covered closely by the national press. When Owens brought all four of the armed, white men who had raped her to trial, they were convicted and sentenced to life in prison. But six years later, a darker coda to the story received much less media attention. One of Owens's rapists was paroled and went on to brutally take the life of a Black woman whom he thought was Owens but in fact was not.[3] If the burden of speaking out wasn't enough to deter all from seeking justice, surely white-supremacist vengeance would ensure the silence of women of color.[4]

Haunted by these perversions, artists of the late 1960s and 1970s began to address these concerns through their practices. But with sexual violence largely glorified by centuries of canonical white male artists—and aggressive, male sexuality soon amplified by the likes of Vito Acconci's performance piece *Seedbed* (1972)[5]—those who sought to grapple with the heightened risk to which female bodies were subject in the United States left the white cube and turned to performance in a range of public spaces. In March 1965, Yoko Ono performed her landmark *Cut Piece* at Carnegie Hall. As in her debut performance in Kyoto, she sat cross-legged and silent with a pair of scissors by her side, having instructed audience members to come snip away bits of her clothing. While Ono herself framed the work as a Buddhist giving and taking,[6] she couldn't help but notice that her initial Japanese audiences had shown more discretion as they cut away at her clothes.[7] Other stateside artists put their art in direct dialogue with examples of gender-based violence in the United States. In the month after learning of an Iowa nursing student's brutal rape and murder, Ana Mendieta, then a University of Iowa art student, invited fellow students to her apartment for *Untitled (Rape Scene)* (1973). There, they found her torso slack across the kitchen table, blood smeared across her buttocks, thighs, and calves, her ankles wrapped

1   Suzanne Lacy, "*Three Weeks in May* (1977)," suzannelacy.com, https://www.suzannelacy.com/three-weeks-in-may (accessed November 14, 2022).

2   Barbara Bradley Hagerty, "American Law Does Not Take Rape Seriously," *Atlantic*, January 28, 2020, https://www.theatlantic.com/ideas/archive/2020/01/american-law-rape/605620/. To this day, California still distinguishes between spousal rape and other forms of sexual assault, deeming the former a less serious crime than the latter. See Don Thompson, "California May End 'Spousal Rape' Distinction in Punishment," Associated Press, March 22, 2021, https://apnews.com/article/legislature-california-sexual-assault-962ff3592c5b86c35097de0e35d4c860.

3   "Convicted Rapist Is Sought," Bryan Times, February 11, 1969, https://news.google.com/newspapers?nid=799&dat=19690212&id=3pJPAAAAIBAJ&pg=4199,2608352.

4   For a rich history of Black women's refusal to remain silent about sexual violence, including in the case of Betty Jean Owens, see Danielle L. McGuire, "'It Was like All of Us Had Been Raped': Sexual Violence, Community Mobilization, and the African American Freedom Struggle," *Journal of American History* 91, no. 3 (December 2004): 906–931.

5   Nancy Princenthal, *Unspeakable Acts: Women, Art, and Sexual Violence in the 1970s* (New York: Thames & Hudson, 2019), 182–187, passim.

6   Julia Bryan Wilson, "Remembering Yoko Ono's 'Cut Piece,'" *Oxford Art Journal* 26, no. 1 (2003): 99–123.

7   Princenthal, *Unspeakable Acts*, 37.

in bloodied underpants. Mendieta stayed in situ for an hour as her audience talked about the work.[8] Her raw depiction of the crime scene gave unflinching form to that which US law refused to deem believable.

Throughout the 1970s, Suzanne Lacy was pivotal to turning Los Angeles—which she described as the nation's rape capitol in 1976[9]—into a crucial hub for creative consciousness-raising around sexual violence. This meant literally amplifying the audio of survivors telling their stories in Suzanne Lacy and Judy Chicago's *Ablutions* (1972)[10] or sharing each day's police reports, as Lacy would do in *One Woman Shows* (1975) at the Woman's Building.[11] The tragic accumulation of gender-based violence in Los Angeles was perhaps nowhere better enshrined than in the two 25-foot maps Lacy and Leslie Labowitz-Starus produced between May 7 and May 24, 1977. Installed at the City Mall Shopping Center as speeches, interviews, speak-outs, and self-defense classes populated the ambitious performance *Three Weeks in May* (1977),[12] Lacy and Labowitz-Starus stamped their maps with boxes of bold, red, capital letters to designate rapes that had been reported to the Los Angeles Police Department, while representing estimates of unreported rapes with clusters of ghostly, red-outlined letters.

That work echoed—and at times operated in tandem with—the drawn-out battles that civil rights attorneys, organizers, and community nonprofits were waging to change laws and public policy.[13] Survivors made gains. Rape-shield laws enacted in the 1970s ensured that defense attorneys couldn't probe a survivor's sexual history. By 1993, all 50 states had technically outlawed marital rape ("technically" because in practice this crime was rarely prosecuted).[14] And in 1994, Congress passed the Violence against Women Act, which notably maximized sentencing of repeat federal sex offenders, mandated restitution to survivors of certain federal sex crimes, and authorized moneys for more robust investigations of violent crimes against women.[15]

But all this progress came in the shadow of Anita Hill's testimony before Congress in 1991 and bundled with the Crime Bill of 1994.[16] Survivors wrestled with a promise of more justice predicated on the intensification of punishment based on racism and a status quo where survivors remained easy to ignore. Artists, meanwhile, had already begun to look to mediums apart from performance—painting, photography, and installations on white walls—to ironize the white patriarchal histories and collective memory through which gender-based violence had long been legislated and crafted into an artistic subject. Lorna Simpson's *Three Seated Figures* (1989) featured three Polaroids of the torso of a Black woman in a white, sleeveless dress, with the spare words *prints*, *signs of entry*, and *marks* above the pictures as well as the phrases "her story" and "each time they looked for proof" flanking either side. Simpson let her audience work through the inde-

8 Princenthal, *Unspeakable Acts*, 82, 89; Maggie Nelson, *The Art of Cruelty* (New York: Norton, 2011), 78–80.

9 Princenthal, *Unspeakable Acts*, 114.

10 Princenthal, *Unspeakable Acts*, 10, 76.

11 "*One Woman Shows* (1975)," suzannelacy.com, https://www.suzannelacy.com/one-woman-shows-1975/ (accessed November 14, 2022).

12 Vivian Green Fryd, "Suzanne Lacy's *Three Weeks in May*: Feminist Activist Performance Art as 'Expanded Public Pedagogy," *NWSA Journal* 19, no. 1 (Spring 2007): 23–38.

13 In 1971, Philadelphia-based sculptor Jody Pinto founded Women Organized against Rape, one of the nation's first rape crisis centers. See Martha Burt, Janet Gornick, Karen Pittman, and Tacie Dejanikus, "ANTI-RAPE PULLOUT: Ten Years After: RAPE CRISIS CENTERS," *Off Our Backs* 14, no. 8 (August–September 1982): 18; and Princenthal, *Unspeakable Acts*, 109.

14 Hagerty, "American Law Does Not Take Rape Seriously."

15 Congressional Research Service, *The Violence against Women Act (VAWA): Historical Overview, Funding, and Reauthorization*, April 23, 2019, https://fas.org/sgp/crs/misc/R45410.pdf.

16 German Lopez, "The Controversial 1994 Crime Law That Joe Biden Helped Write, Explained," *Vox*, September 20, 2019, https://www.vox.com/policy-and-politics/2019/6/20/18677998/joe-biden-1994-crime-bill-law-mass-incarceration; "How History Changed Anita Hill," New York Times, June 17, 2019, https://www.nytimes.com/2019/06/17/us/anita-hill-women-power.html.

terminacy of these combinations of word and text.[17] Throughout the 1990s, Kara Walker's installations applied the genteel "ladies' art" of the silhouette to antebellum and Jim Crow horror, with sobering passages of Black women being chased, forced to fellate, and hung upside down.[18] Sue Williams painted the comic idioms of *MAD Magazine* into a corner such that the cultural patterns perpetuating sexual assault became uncomfortably clear.[19]

*   *   *

Even as powerful perpetrators of gender-based violence are being called to account and intersectionality is no longer the province of academic journals, artists of the present are shaping public space to remind our communities that gender-based violence hasn't disappeared. The #MeToo movement has underscored the dynamics of power that made possible the behavior of assailants such as Harvey Weinstein, Bill Cosby, R. Kelly, and Larry Nassar. Kimberlé Crenshaw, who coined the term *intersectionality*, has drawn attention to the work in this area by taking over Selena Gomez's Instagram account.[20] There may even be something to celebrate in the recent statistic that here in Los Angeles reported rapes are down by 25 percent.[21] Still, we know that 80 percent of rapes and sexual assaults go unreported,[22] and these as well as other varieties of gender-based violence persist because power's default setting remains white and patriarchal.[23] Artists of this moment have responded with collaborations that center care and aim to eradicate the conventions that marginalize Black, Brown, Asian, trans, and gender-nonconforming bodies. Or, in the words of artist Elana Mann, "Artists

have the power of imagination and can work to foster the power of solidarity and community. Remembering and instrumentalizing these sites of power can push through fear."[24]

LA Freewaves has partnered with numerous Los Angeles-based artists to ensure that they are in community while carrying out that work. Alert to the ecumenical toolbox these artists have inherited, Anne Bray and her team make space for all manner of creative practices for combatting gender-based violence, whether performance, object making and installations, or social practice combined with printed ephemera. Though neat categories would fail to do justice to this wide variety, two currents especially animate the work now being produced in conjunction with Freewaves.

One current tenders reinterpretations of history. Take, for instance, the women-of-color collective Ni Santas's piece *Never Again* (2018). Installed at the Los Angeles State Historic Park for *Ain't I a Womxn* (2018), Freewaves's one-night "promenade" of feminism and intersectionality, this four-poster bed elegized intimacies compromised by violence—namely, the case of pregnant Gerri Twerdy Santoro in 1964, who was killed when the fetus's father performed a homespun abortion in a Norwich, Connecticut, motel room.[25] Ni Santas silkscreened the searing, notorious image of Santoro—her dead, naked body bent into child's pose as blood pooled beneath her—onto their bed's pillows.

As though in solidarity, they also made their bed bleed from head to foot, while pillows silkscreened with Zapatista women served as sentinels for bodies whose

---

17 For more on Simpson's body of work, see Huey Copeland, "'Bye, Bye Black Girl': Lorna Simpson's Figurative Retreat," *Art Journal* 64, no. 2 (2005): 62–77.

18 The go-to book on Kara Walker's body of work remains Gwendolyn DuBois Shaw, *Seeing the Unspeakable: The Art of Kara Walker* (Durham, NC: Duke University Press, 2004).

19 Dan Cameron, "Reserve Backlash: Sue Williams' Black Comedy of Manners," *Artforum*, November 1992, 71–73, https://www.artforum.com/print/199209/reserve-backlash-sue-williams-black-comedy-of-manners-33502.

20 "Please Meet Kimberlé Crenshaw," @selenagomez, June 7, 2020, https://www.instagram.com/p/CBI8210DDSy/?hl=en.

21 Kevin Rector, "A Year Like No Other for LA Crime: Homicides Surge, Robberies and Rapes Drop," *Los Angeles Times*, January 3, 2021, https://www.latimes.com/california/story/2021-01-03/pandemic-crime-trends-los-angeles; Claudia Boyd-Barrett, "The Pandemic Spurred a Domestic Violence Epidemic. It's Not Over Yet," *California Health Report*, July 29, 2021, https://www.calhealthreport.org/2021/07/29/the-pandemic-spurred-a-domestic-violence-epidemic-its-not-over-yet/.

22 Cameron Kimble and Inimai M. Chettiar, "Sexual Assault Remains Dramatically Underreported," Brennan Center for Justice, New York, October 4, 2018, https://www.brennancenter.org/our-work/analysis-opinion/sexual-assault-remains-dramatically-underreported.

23 Ezra Klein, "What's Really behind the 1619 Backlash?," *Ezra Klein Show*, podcast, produced by the *New York Times*, July 30, 2021, https://www.nytimes.com/2021/07/30/opinion/ezra-klein-podcast-ta-nehisi-coates-nikole-hannah-jones.html.

24 Elana Mann, facilitator, "DIS…MISS Digests, Connecting the Dots: Sexual Violence Prevention and the Arts," LA Freewaves panel discussion, April 19, 2020.

25 Amanda Arnold, "How a Harrowing Photo of One Woman's Death Became an Iconic Pro-Choice Symbol," *Vice*, October 26, 2016, https://www.vice.com/en/article/evgdpw/how-a-harrowing-photo-of-one-womans-death-became-an-iconic-pro-choice-symbol.

gender constantly put them at risk. As I learned from speaking with Joan Zeta, a member of Ni Santas, *Never Again* only unconsciously updated *Untitled (Bloody Mattresses)* (1973), in which Mendieta had outfitted an empty farmhouse as a crime scene, where mattresses were strewn with bruised evidence, all amounting to a crime without witnesses.[26] Both artworks remind us that sexual violence is all too frequently inflicted by people with whom survivors must share their homes, estranging survivors from the safe and familiar. But Ni Santas insist on reparative journeys that, with community support, undo disbelief. To this day, Zeta lays her head on the pillows silkscreened with Santoro's picture.[27] As reminders of a history that shapes the present, these objects compel her to fight against forgetting.

Similarly, Mann and her co-conspirator Audrey Chan, who collaborate as the duo Chan & Mann, have extended and multiplied the legacy of *Myths of Rape* (1977), a durational performance Labowitz-Starus produced for *Three Weeks in May* (1977). In her original *Myths*, Labowitz-Starus had directed eight women—some with blindfolds, others without—to carry large signs stenciled with misperceptions about rape and statistics that disproved them. In 2012, with Lacy and Labowitz-Starus's blessing and informed by Occupy Wall Street and the Arab Spring, Chan & Mann updated these myths for a large-scale performance on the floor of the LA Art Show. Each of 30 performers—no longer blindfolded, no longer only women, and no longer mostly white—walked up and down the art fair's thoroughfares, ultimately creating concentric call-and-response circles, where they would open and close posterboard triptychs, whose outer wings were stenciled with misconceptions about rape and whose central panels illuminated facts refuting the misconception. These facts ranged well beyond those from the performance in 1977 and included rape in prisons and the military, workplace assault, and domestic violence.[28]

Another cadre of creative practitioners offers glimpses into a world free from sexual violence—possible because Freewaves created the conditions that allow such world building, if only for an evening. In Septem-

ber 2019, Freewaves and numerous community partners produced the night of performances *LOVE &/OR FEAR* across the 6500–6600 block of the infamous Hollywood Boulevard. Collaborating with the rape crisis center Peace Over Violence, Freewaves designated these blocks—long home to lingerie purveyors and adult sex shops—a sexual-harassment-free zone, inviting artists to revel in the pleasure of their own skin. Here sondriaWRITES of #SNATCHPOWER performed a striptease, leaving behind a faux fur coat, pulling off a black spaghetti-strap dress, and, once near-naked, pulsing toward and away from the concrete curb on which dozens of viewers stood. At Los Angeles Contemporary Exhibitions, Sebastian Hernández invited visitors into a gallery bathed in emerald light, where they and their collaborators performed all manner of desire—a public invitation to a private space made possible because safety was ensured.

Having cut through the silence about gender-based violence, artists have turned to building community and setting conditions that may make possible a world free of gender-based violence. The risks that crackled in Ono's American performance of *Cut Piece* are not the same ones that enriched the work in *LOVE &/OR FEAR*. Instead of making their individual bodies vulnerable to shock an atmosphere thick with the denial of the white male gaze, today's artists must play Cassandra in a world prone to thinking the existence of rape crisis centers and gay marriage is enough progress. But artists such as Ni Santas, Chan & Mann, sondriaWRITES, and Hernández don't prophecy alone. They populate the landscape with what artist Shirley Alvarado describes as "art … truly based in community and about collective power." It's the kind of art "that is going to help activists reimagine what the future is going to look like."[29] Taking for granted that survivors ought to be believed, these artists foreground a self-possession derived from bodies that can be fully inhabited without shame—bodies that, whether recovering from harm or free from the threat of injury, imagine moving through the world according to their own desires. And because they imagine, they do.

---

26 Princenthal, *Unspeakable Acts*, 84.
27 Joan Zeta, interviewed by the author, Los Angeles, September 10, 2021.
28 See Anuradha Vikram's essay at the beginning of this chapter for a more comprehensive account of the history of Lacy and Labowitz-Starus's *Myths of Rape*, Chan & Mann's restaging of the piece, and the postcard collaboration with Freewaves that extended their reinterpretation.
29 Shirley Alvarado, in Mann, facilitator, "DIS…MISS Digests, Connecting the Dots."

PEACE OVER VIOLENCE

Mission

Building healthy relationships, families, and communities free from sexual, domestic, and interpersonal violence. "We know that violence is preventable."

We are a social service agency dedicated to the elimination of sexual and domestic violence and all forms of interpersonal violence. We provide crisis-intervention services and violence-prevention education. One on one, we listen, counsel, support, guide, and work to heal survivors of violence. One by one, we teach teens about healthy relationships, train girls in self-defense, instruct boys in conflict resolution, and advise on public policy.

Manifesto

Violence against women is the most pervasive yet least recognized human rights abuse in the world. For more than three decades, women's advocacy groups around the world have been working to draw attention to the physical, psychological, and sexual abuse of women and to stress the need for action. We have provided abused women with support and protection, lobbied for legal reforms, and challenged the pervasive culture of violence.

Peace Over Violence has a grassroots origin revolving around volunteer contributions. We are present in the streets, schools, hospitals, and courts, acting up, advocating against, and healing violence. Over the past 47 years, our call for action in pursuit of a world free of violence has garnered widespread respect, support, and dedicated allies among police, prosecutors, politicians, health-care providers, individual supporters, celebrities, and a growing list of sponsors from corporations and foundations.

"One on one, One by one."

We understand that violence in relationships, families, and communities is a root cause for violence in society. To address the problem at its core is to change how this problem manifests and magnifies itself in society at large. Changing an individual point of view toward sexual, domestic, and interpersonal violence will—one on one, one by one—cause social change, a transformation of society, a world without violence.

Our vision is a world without violence, where no child is abused, no wife battered, no friend raped. A world without terror, without threats, without wounds from intentional actions, where the strong provide for the vulnerable, where the vulnerable become empowered, where every kind of family is safe and secure, and where girls and boys and women and men have a fair and equal chance at the pursuit of happiness in a tolerant and talented society.

The agency's approach toward realizing this vision is to run crisis-intervention, violence-prevention, and education programs tailored toward women, youth and children, and, by natural extension, men. We listen, counsel, support, guide, and work to heal survivors of violence. We teach teens about healthy relationships, train girls in self-defense, advise politicians on public policy. We organize, we advocate. We not only believe but also know that violence is preventable. We stand at the center of a social movement that is advancing individuals, groups, and society to stand over violence.

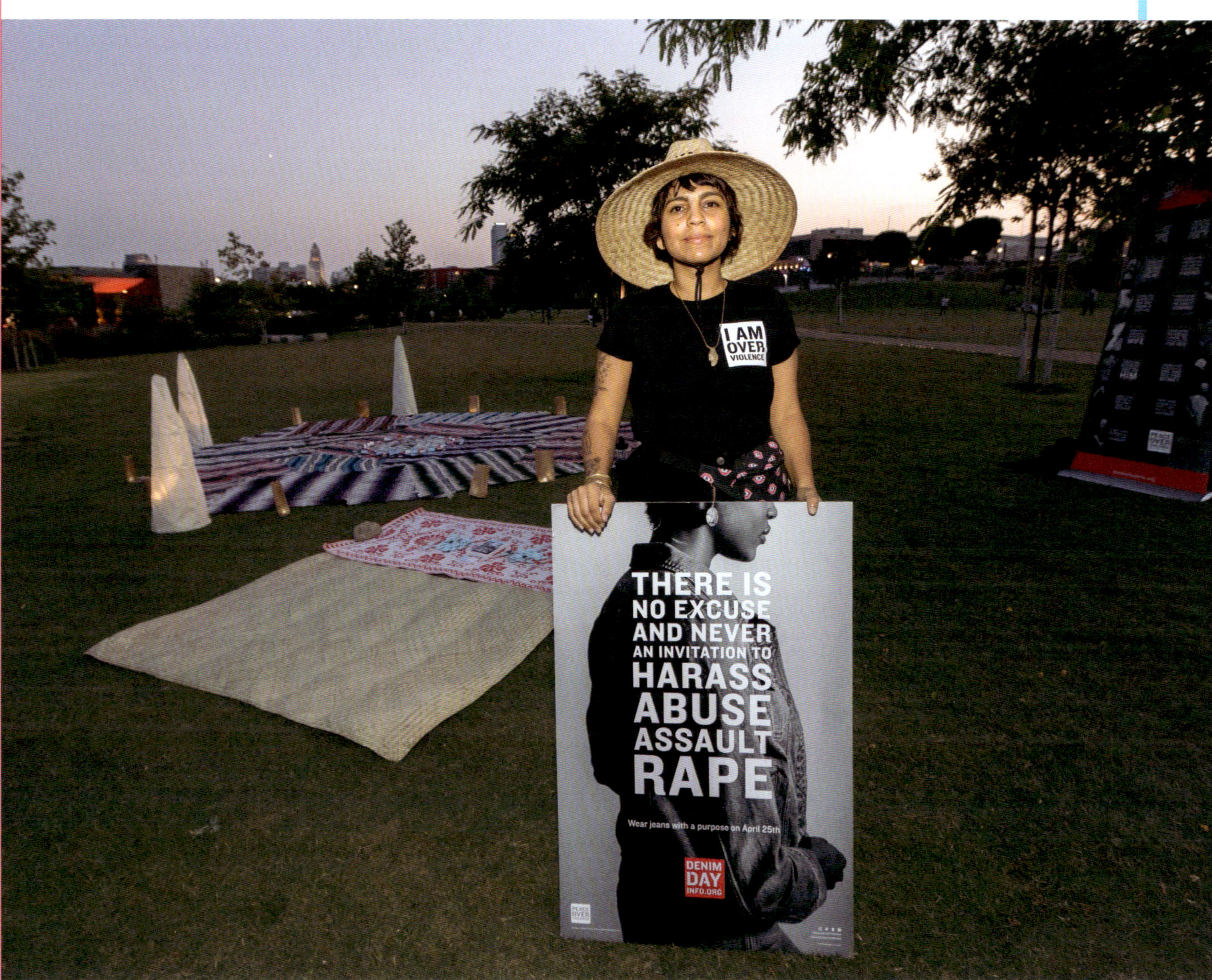

violence **is** preventable

Peace Over Violence mission. Photo: Monica Orozco.

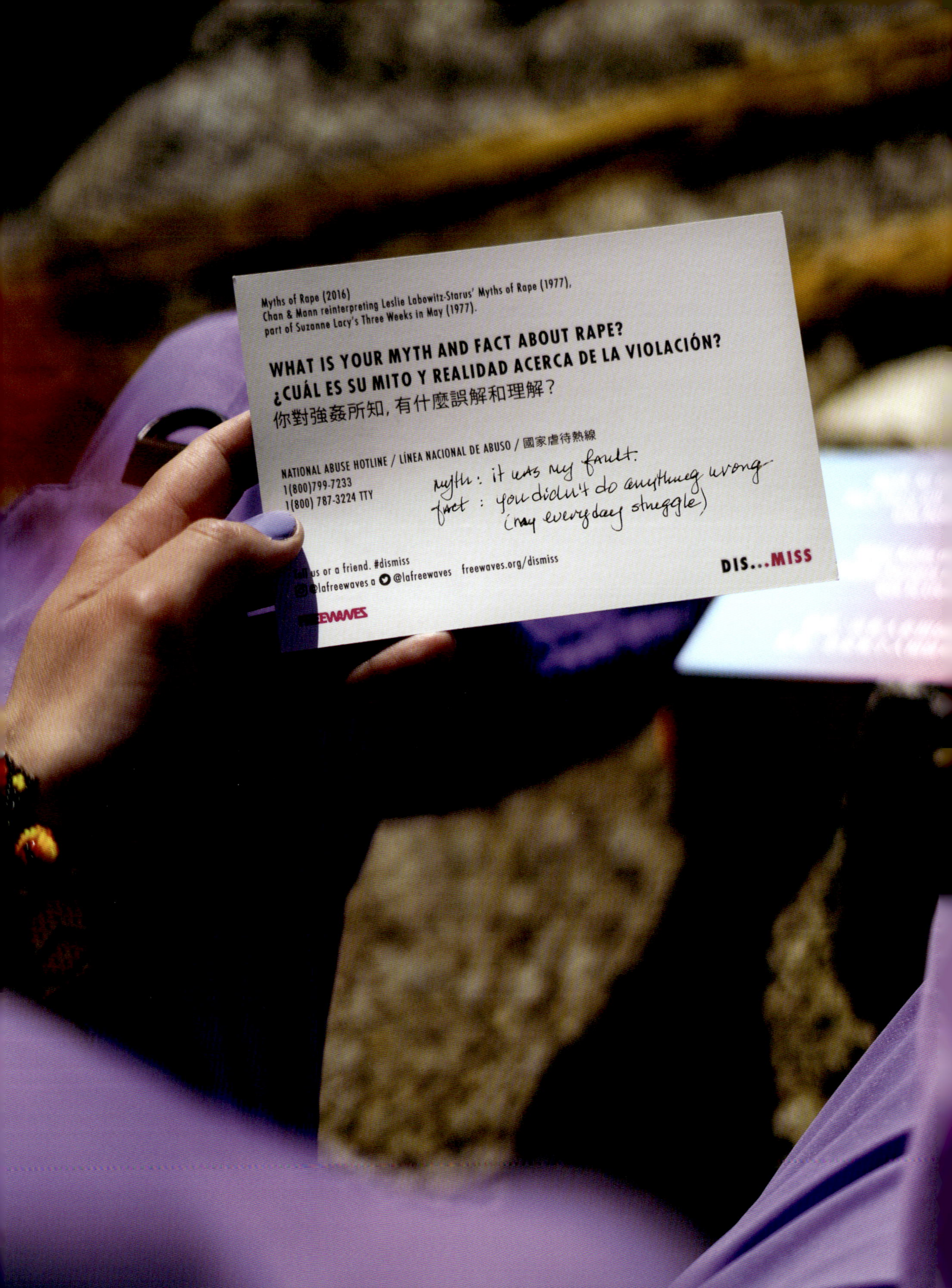

Myths of Rape (2016)
Chan & Mann reinterpreting Leslie Labowitz-Starus' Myths of Rape (1977),
part of Suzanne Lacy's Three Weeks in May (1977).

WHAT IS YOUR MYTH AND FACT ABOUT RAPE?
¿CUÁL ES SU MITO Y REALIDAD ACERCA DE LA VIOLACIÓN?
你對強姦所知, 有什麼誤解和理解?

NATIONAL ABUSE HOTLINE / LÍNEA NACIONAL DE ABUSO / 國家虐待熱線
1(800)799-7233
1(800) 787-3224 TTY

myth: it was my fault.
fact: you didn't do anything wrong.
(my everyday struggle)

us or a friend. #dismiss
@lafreewaves a @lafreewaves   freewaves.org/dismiss

FREEWAVES

DIS...MISS

Myth:
If I am raped, I will never recover.

Reality:
The consistent and unconditional love of my family and friends will always help me to persevere.

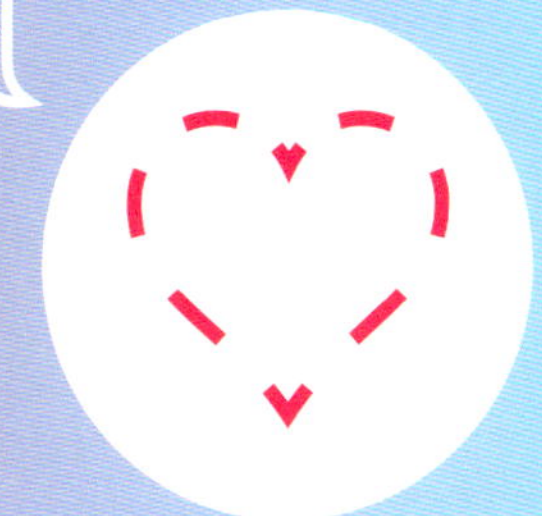

ANALYSIS

Concepts of **blame**, appeared as largest theme among responses (25%). In most instances the concept of blame was used to describe the myth that it is the victim's fault.

"DIS…MISS, Inconclusive Infographic Animation." Analyzed by Marisa Turesky. Animation designed by Catherine Bell, 2019. Left: Postcard portrait by Alejandra Sone.

6

how can feminism support equality?

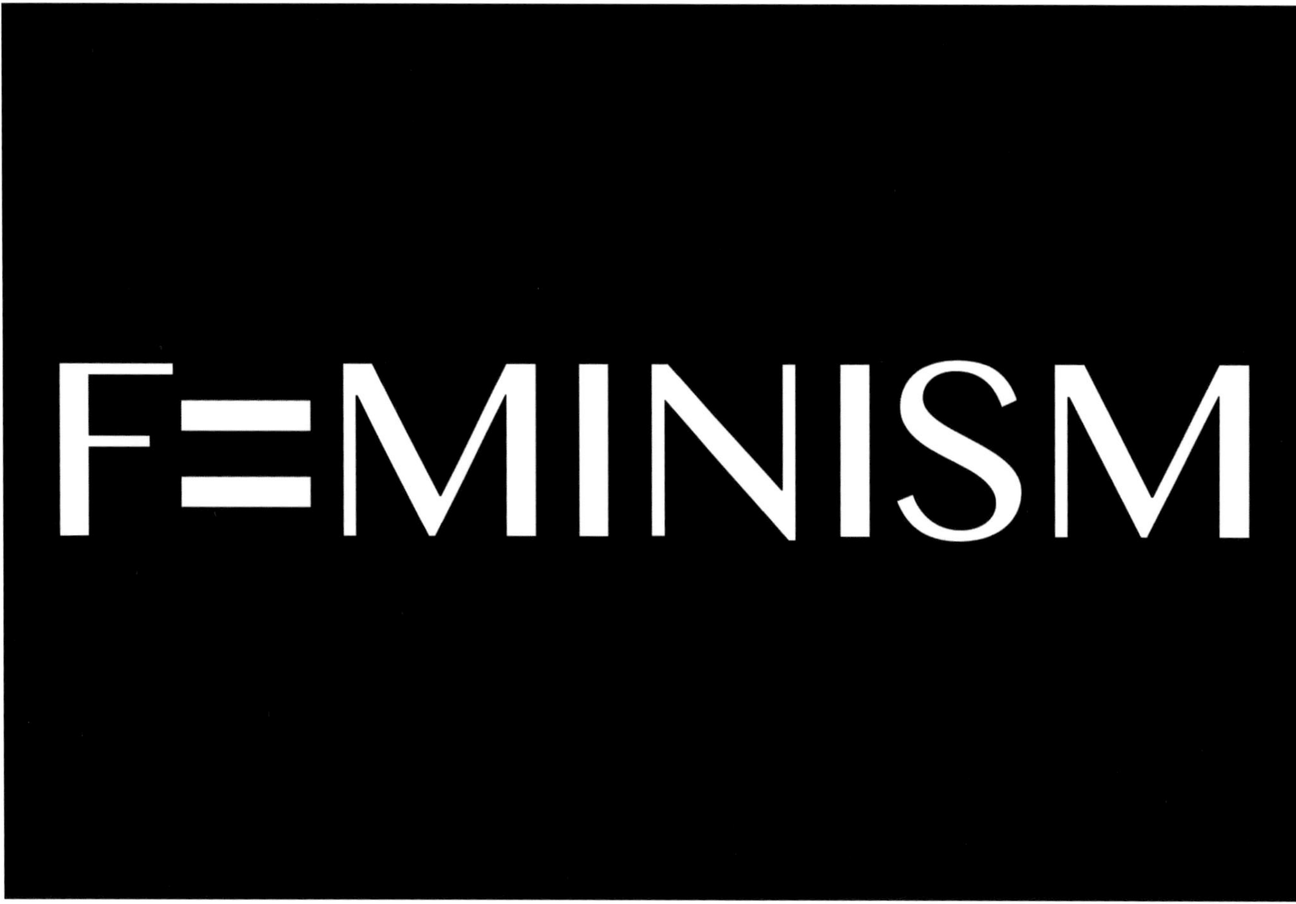

F=minism by Micol Hebron.

Dis...Missing Feminism
Tiffany E. Barber

At first glance, Micol Hebron's black-and-white post-card for *Dis...Miss* appears simple and familiar. Its rect-angular form, block text, and color scheme recall the visual culture of public announcements, from political posters to mail art to billboard advertisements. The arrangement of the text and the hard edges that result from the juxtaposition of black and white, however, make the postcard's visual schema more complex. In position and appearance, the word *feminism* intersects the rich, dense blackness that occupies the majority of the postcard's face, dramatically contrasting its surroundings. The bright-white letters seem to jump into the foreground as the boundaries between the text and the background vibrate, a visual effect that is simul-taneously energizing and unsettling to the eye. An equal sign replaces the E, an action that further punctuates the question Hebron poses on the back of the postcard: "How can feminism support equality?" These formal and linguistic turns catapult Hebron's gesture beyond the postcard into a broader discourse concerning the limits and possibilities of feminism, solidarity, and the color line in the twenty-first century.

Hebron's postcard began as a sticker. Akin to political posters, stickers affixed to telephone poles, laptops, the bumpers of cars, and other surfaces have played an important role in outlining urgent social issues and encouraging collective action. In essence and inten-tion, postcards are also public forms of ephemera that activate networks of exchange. The act of writing and sending notes that accompany the small-scale images on the front cultivates shorthand intimacy and dialogue between sender and receiver. Because of this, postcards became extremely popular at the turn of the twenti-eth century as an easy and quick way for individuals to communicate.

In the realm of avant-garde art practice, mail artists in the West have crafted postcards, stamps, photocopies, and pamphlets as transitory works on paper. Intended for a select few, mail art has historically been a prac-tice consisting of closed circuits and self-promotion—an ephemeral circle jerk. Though democratic in their aim to circumvent the commercial art market, mail artists such as Ray Johnson (who is considered to be the first mail artist in the United States), Chuck Welch (a.k.a. CrackerJackKid), Carlo Pittore, David Zack, and members of the collective N-tity have incidentally been predominantly white and male. The effects of this echo chamber are encapsulated in the negative reactions to *Mail Art Then and Now*, curator Ronny Cohen's exhi-bition of historical and contemporary works of corre-spondence art at Franklin Furnace in New York City in 1984. During the run of the exhibition, a coterie of white male mail artists organized two panel discussions to debate Cohen's selection process.[1] For Pittore and other mail artists, Cohen violated the sacrosanct practice of welcoming all artworks without judgment or fees. After these artists invited her to moderate and then eventu-ally demanded that she forfeit her role as moderator of the second panel, Cohen declined to participate in the talks altogether. Soon after that, Ray Johnson (who was not a panelist) penned a letter admonishing the mail artists' acts of reverse censorship and sexism.

---

1   For this infamous history, see "Mail Art from 1984 Franklin Furnace Exhibition," 1984, Franklin Furnace, Brooklyn, NY, http://www. franklinfurnace.org/research/projects/flow/mailart/mailart.html; Gary Azon and Dorothy Friedman, "The Mail Art Melee," *Village Voice* March 13, 1984; Faith Heisler, "International MailArt—Part II: The New Cultural Strategy," *Women Artists News* 9, no. 4 (1984): 18; John Held Jr., "A Living Thing in Flight: Contributions and Liabilities of Collecting and Preparing Contemporary Avant-Garde Materials for an Archive," *Archives of American Art Journal* 40, nos. 3–4 (2000): 10–16; Laura Dunkin-Hubby, "A Brief History of Mail Art's Engagement with Craft (c. 1950–2014)," *Journal of Modern Craft* 9, no. 1 (2016): 35–54; and the Spare Room's collection of mail art resources and writings at http://www.spareroom.org/mailart/mailart.html. The Franklin Furnace controversy of 1984 was the first attempt to discuss mail art with practicing artists in a public setting.

The collection of postcards commissioned and printed for *Dis...Miss* intervene in this history, highlighting the ways artists and administrators with racially diverse backgrounds and gender expressions remix and deploy ephemera to encourage social engagement in real time.

Like the alternative forms of participation that the artists and agitators of *Dis...Miss* aim to provoke, Hebron's design and her postcard's formal contrast in particular bear a relationship to public art and activism of the recent past—namely, the Silence = Death poster campaign of the late 1980s. A cohort of artists and designers intent on manipulating the ubiquity of printed matter in New York designed the poster to spur civic action concerning AIDS and its impact. At the time, New York City streets were papered with posters, meeting announcements, demonstration flyers, and advertisements comprising plain text and simple graphics; and the iconography of the Silence = Death poster campaign approximated the language of advertising. The equal sign in particular communicated with efficiency a political charge that was easily recognizable and had mass appeal. The phrase "Silence = Death," accompanied by a repurposed fuchsia triangle and articulated with white block letters and an equal sign— all pictured against a saturated black background— easily fit within the print landscape, effectively merging text and image with codes associated with gay liberation and the punchy visual vocabulary of US advertising in the 1980s.[2]

The black-and-white contrast of Hebron's postcard functions similarly, bridging the mass-appealing design strategy of Silence = Death with another, more recent pop-informed spectacle: the black-and-white backdrop that Beyoncé used for her closing performance at the MTV Video Music Awards (VMA) in 2014. The pop star's branding of present-day feminism, her embodiment of Black womanhood, and the publicness of her image make her performance an evocative interlocutor for Hebron's design. For her VMA appearance, Beyoncé performed singles from her self-titled visual album. Following *Beyoncé* (2013) and *Lemonade* (2016), the pop icon has become the embodiment of millennial feminism. Her song "Flawless," a feminist anthem of sorts, samples lines from the Nigerian writer Chimamanda Adichie's TEDxTalk of 2012, "We Should All Be Feminists"; at the VMAs, a gigantic black screen displayed Adichie's words and the word *feminist* in white capital block letters.

Queen Bey's larger-than-life display made feminism a trending topic for social media and news outlets. For a wider audience, it also visually and sonically mapped a genealogy of feminist thought for women of African descent in the twenty-first century. In full view of a generation reluctant to claim the words *feminism*

---

2   The triangle carried many connotations at the time. It was associated with the New Age religious movement; binary gender expression vis-à-vis the upward-facing triangle (masculine) versus the downward-facing one (feminine); and William Buckley's suggestion that LGBTQ people should be tattooed. The designers of the Silence = Death poster were wary of these connotations, but they ultimately included and repurposed the triangle for their image. See Avram Finkelstein, "SILENCE = DEATH: How an Iconic Protest Poster Came into Being," *Literary Hub*, December 1, 2017, https://lithub.com/silence-death-how-an-iconic-protest-poster-came-into-being.

and *feminist*, Beyoncé runs the world while nurturing her career, her marriage, her sexuality, and her role as a mother. For self-identified Black feminists, Beyoncé exemplifies intersectionality—the concept that mutually reinforcing vectors of race, gender, class, and sexuality constitute our subjectivities. Despite these endorsements, Beyoncé's revivification of feminism leaves much to be desired. In songs seemingly about independence and empowerment, her lyrics still largely center how men and their behaviors affect women. Alternately, her visual displays of accumulated wealth border on capitalist decadence. Fraught with cross-racial desires for freedom and recognition as well as upward mobility for Black and non-Black fans, Beyoncé's graphically compelling version of feminism is complex.

In its proximity to the visual culture of queer activism and mainstream feminism, Hebron's postcard for *Dis...Miss* likewise prompts multifaceted reflections about the potential for solidarity across racial and gender lines. How can feminism support equality now? For years, Hebron has been surveying and shifting the numbers concerning exclusion and gender equality in the art world. Founder of the LA Art Girls and the ongoing Gallery Tally project—which involves counting and broadcasting the disproportionate ratio of male-to-female artists whose work is exhibited at international galleries—she employs strategies of consciousness-raising, collaboration, generosity, play, and participation to support and foster feminist dialogues in art and life. Yet, on the whole, responses to the question on the back of Hebron's postcard, collected at early *Dis... Miss* events and archived on LA Freewaves' website, interpreted the prompt as theory, not activism. Many participants saw feminism as a concept and a method for identification. These responses aligned the term *feminism* with an outmoded binary, comparing and affirming women's equality relative to that of men without any regard for the spectrum of gender identifications that exist. This disregard applies to race as well. Only a few discuss and advocate for the role that feminism and intersectional perspectives play in communities of color. Others were reluctant to call themselves feminists at all. By design, then, the postcard and its circulation in the public sphere call up a critique not only of the uses and usefulness of feminism but also of feminism's core whiteness—a point that the postcard's lettering accentuates.

The conditions for the varying effects that the postcard produces—the vibrating edges, the intersectionality that comprises its center, how we consider the white text in proportion to the black background, and the critique of feminism that emerges—stem from color and its perception. This correspondence has social and political implications, especially in light of recurring cycles of racial and gender violence spurred by the current global pandemic and negligent politicians in the age of Black Lives Matter. Thus, the force of the artist's intervention attunes us to the intertwined histories of color theory, race, gender, representation, and the creative act. It models how the materiality of color shapes our collective imaginings of coalition, urging us to consider the limits and possibilities of solidarity in moments of social and political upheaval. In an era when calls for diversity and inclusion proliferate at every level, Hebron's postcard draws our attention not so much to the promise but to the faults of equality that are difficult for us to see.

what if women were in charge?
Elana Mann & Las Fotos Project

I am

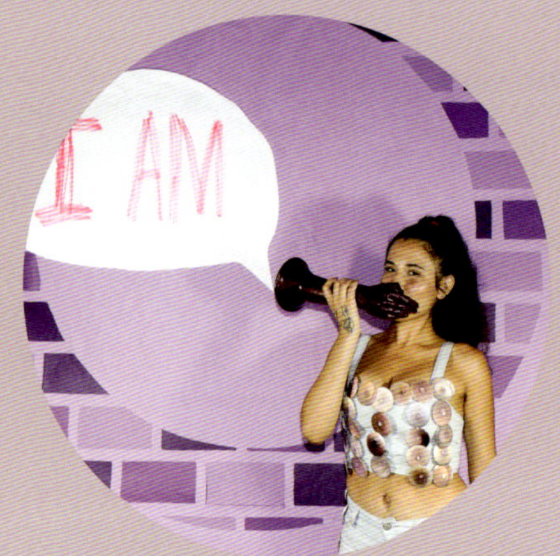

No war

It is pink

Hey we're gay

Woke realness

We'd all be *ni santas*

The world would rock

We will achieve utopia

Peace and Love Great

There would be no war

The ex will be in charge

Life would be less shitty

We'd be socialists by now

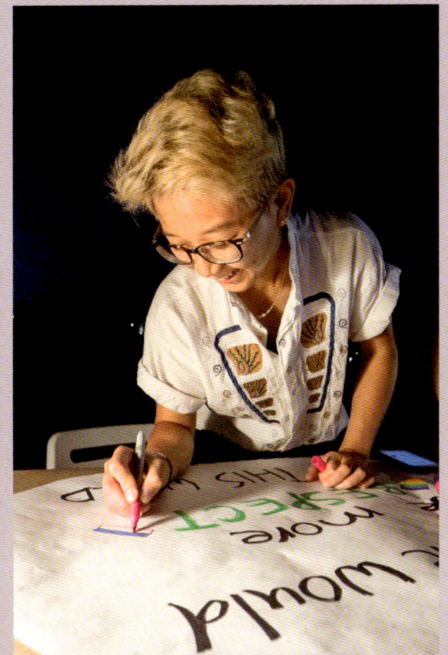

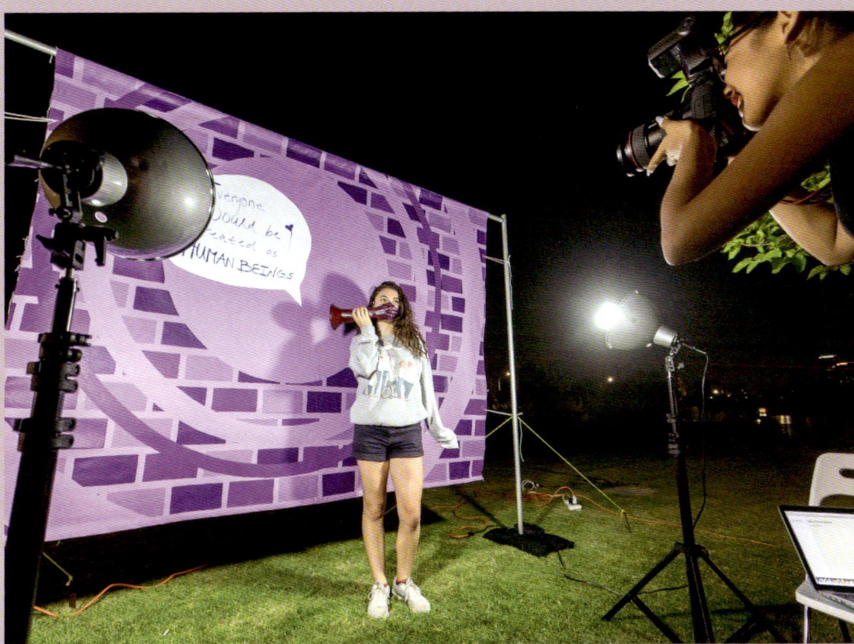
veryone
should be
treated as
HUMAN BEINGS

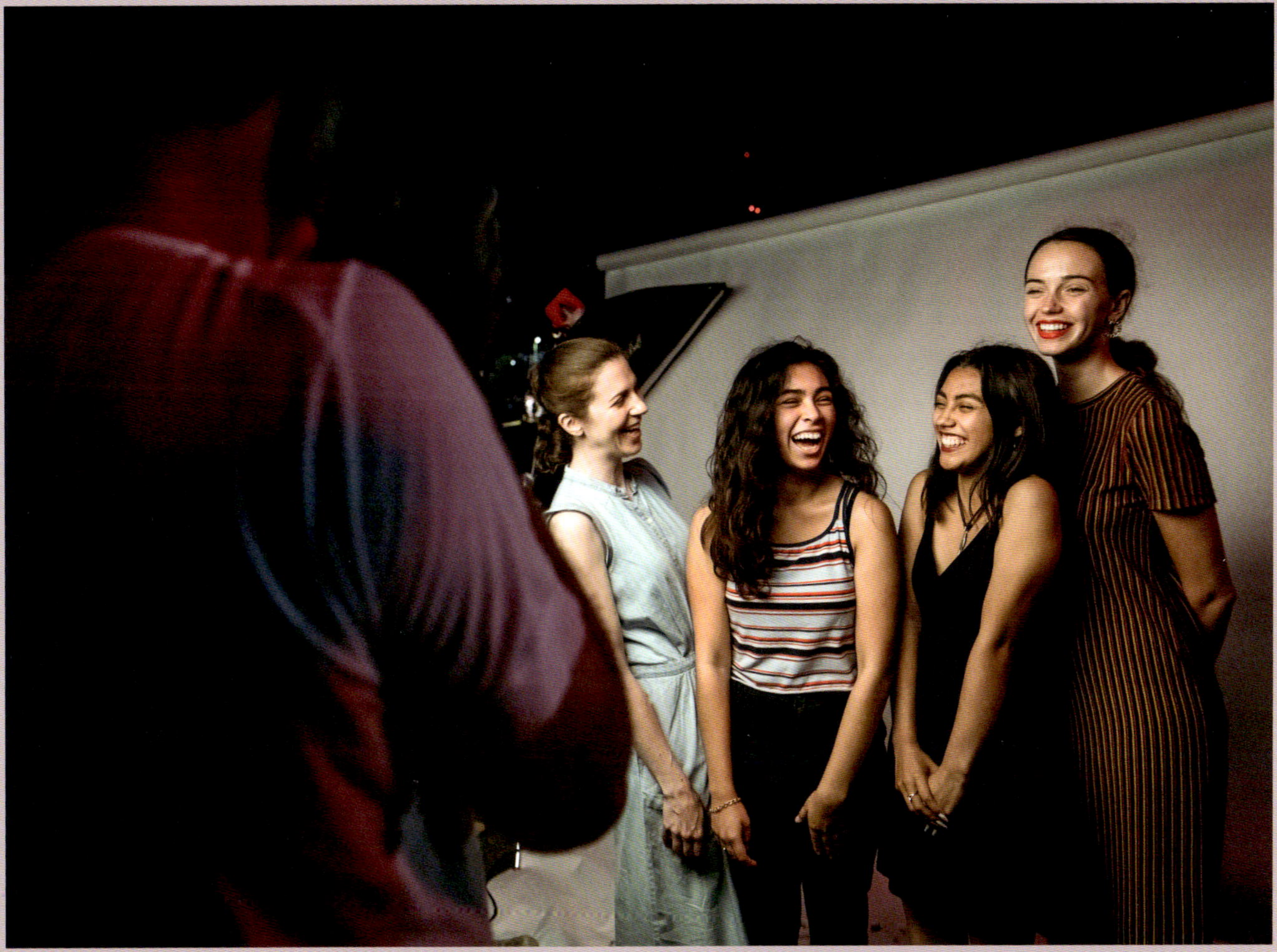

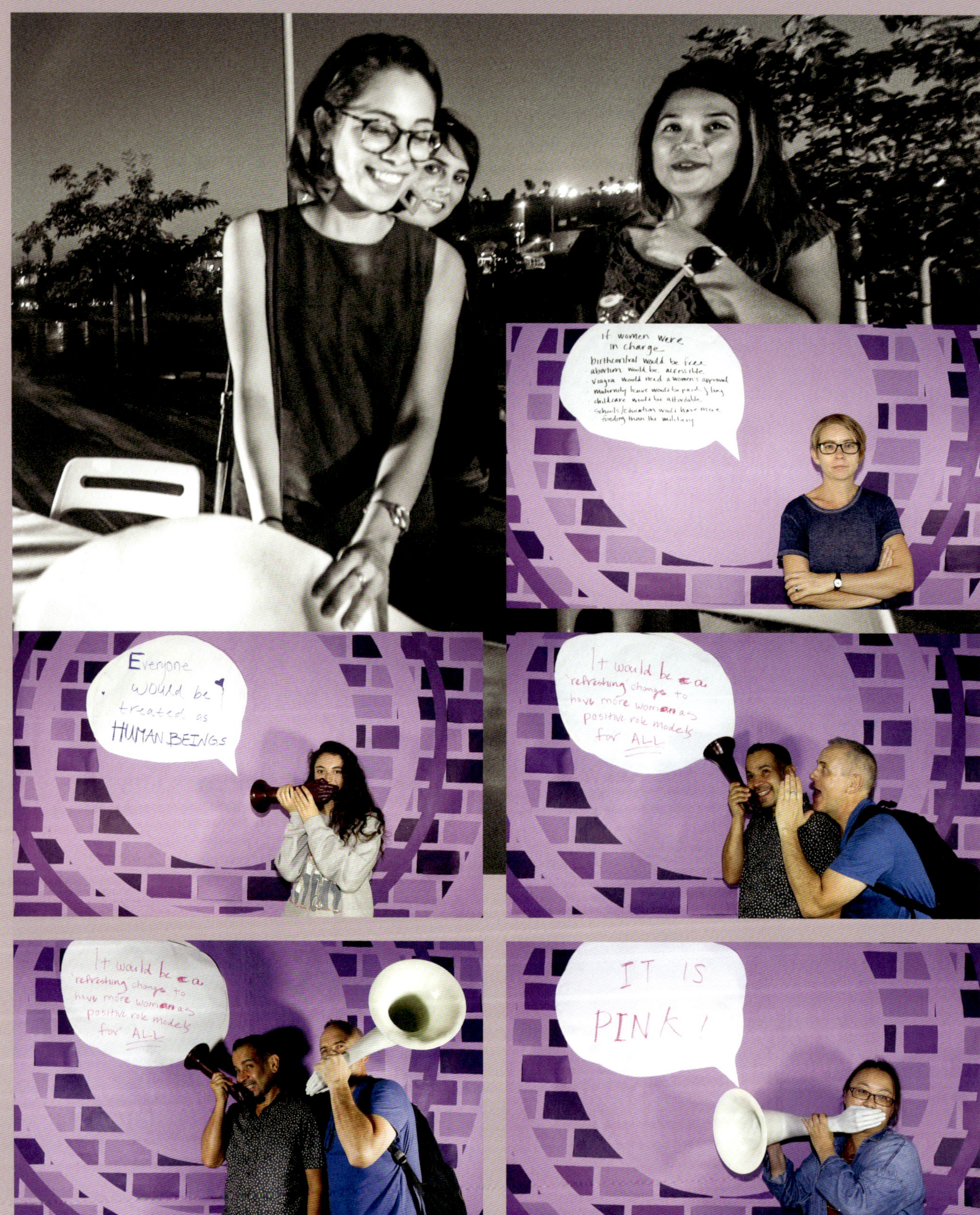
if women were in charge_
birthcontrol would be free
abortion would be accessible
viagra would need a women's approval
maternity leave would be paid & long
childcare would be affordable
schools/education would have more
funding than the military
Everyone would be treated as HUMAN BEINGS
It would be a refreshing change to have more women as positive role models for ALL
It would be a refreshing change to have more women as positive role models for ALL
IT IS PINK!

There would be more love

Everything would be great

Abortions would be a right

No more dominant genders

The world would feel more safe

The world would be more selfless

A person's body would belong to them

I'd feel more optimistic about the future

There would be more respect in this world

Everyone could wear whatever they wanted

Everyone would be treated as human beings

We would all have a deeper sense of self worth

We'll find a solution to everything thru dialogue

Cyclical accumulation not cumulative accumulation

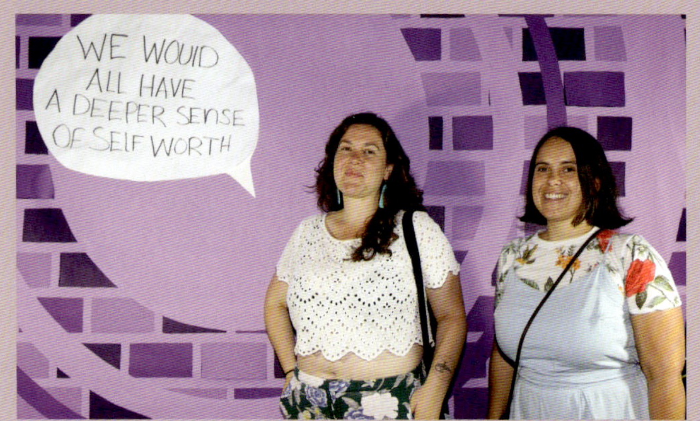
WE WOULD ALL HAVE A DEEPER SENSE OF SELF WORTH

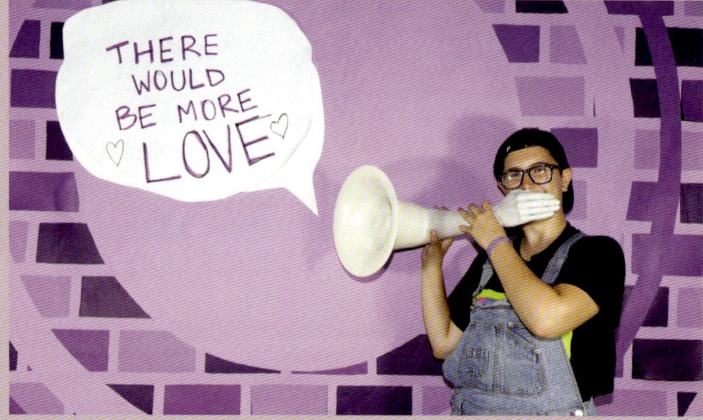
THERE WOULD BE MORE LOVE

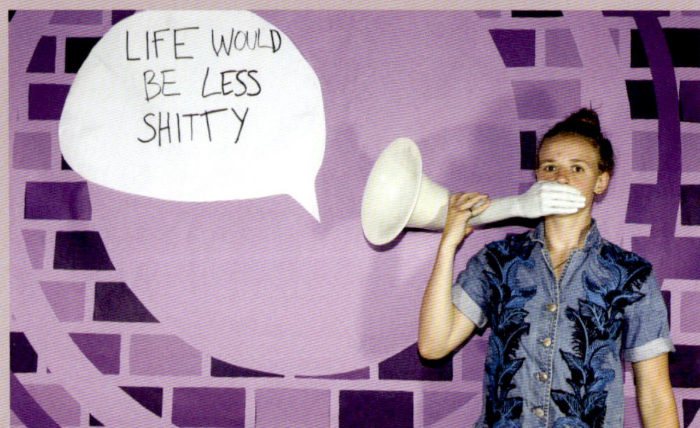
LIFE WOULD BE LESS SHITTY

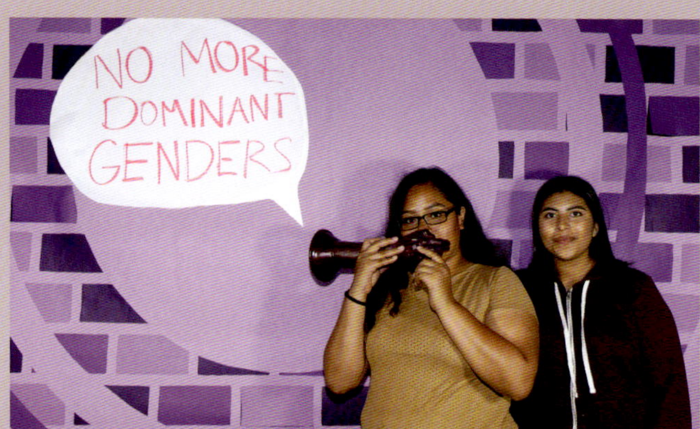
NO MORE DOMINANT GENDERS

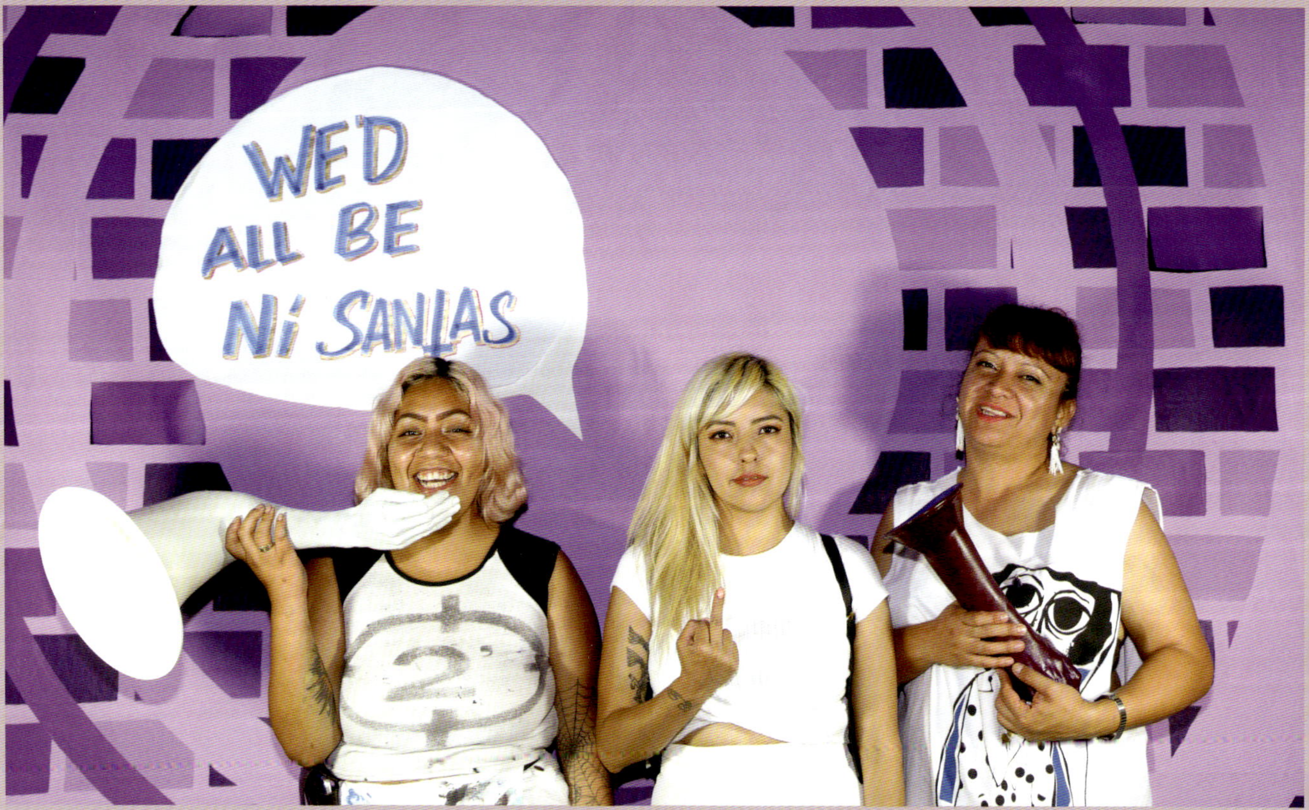

WE'D ALL BE NI SANLAS

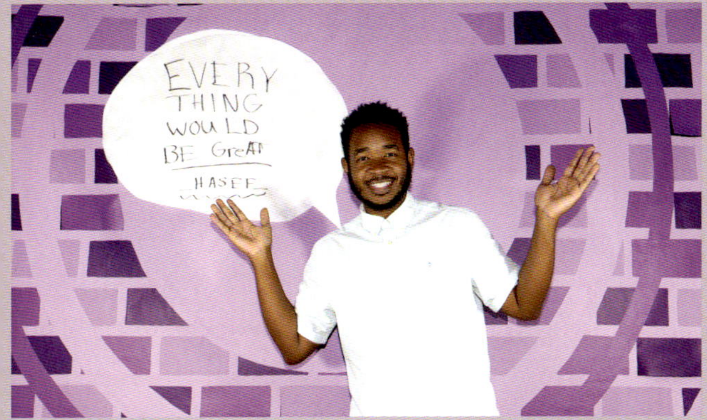
EVERY
THING
WOULD
BE GREAT

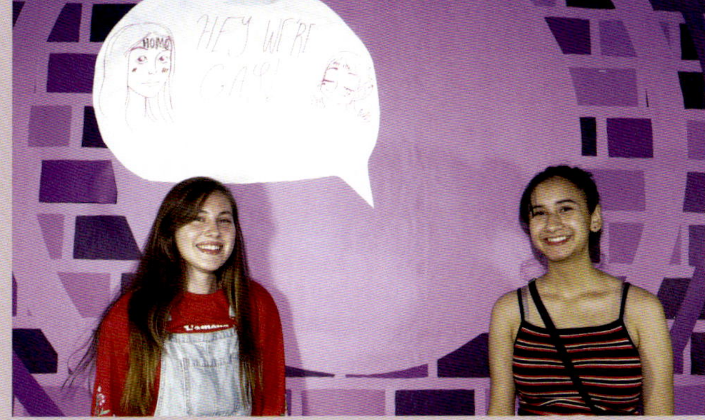

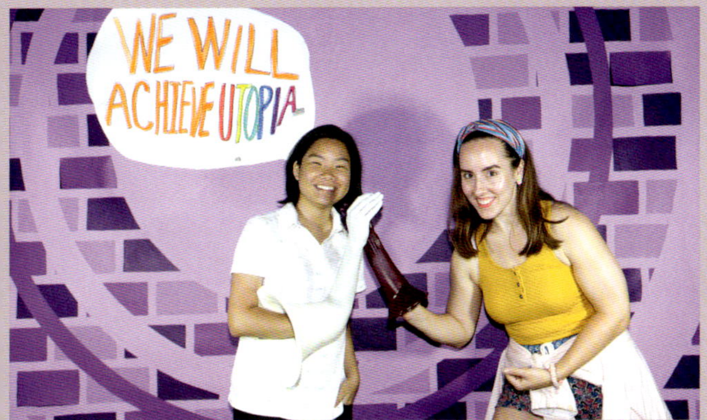
WE WILL
ACHIEVE UTOPIA

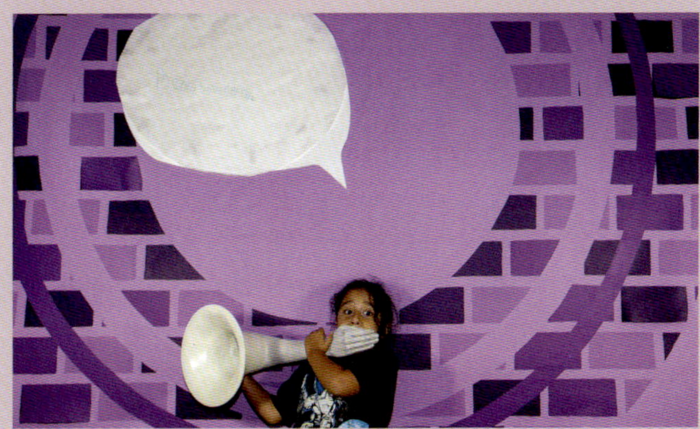

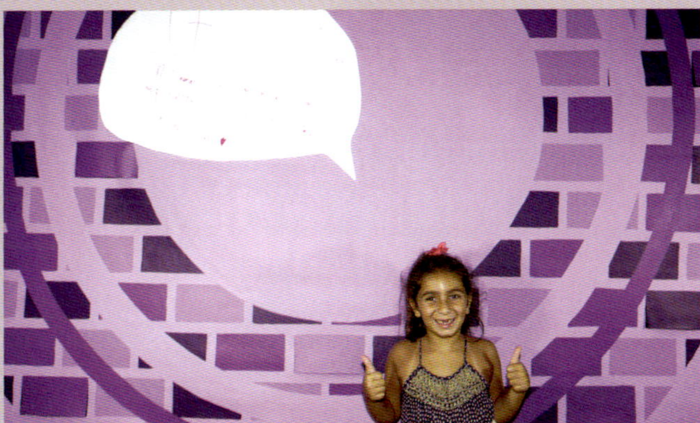

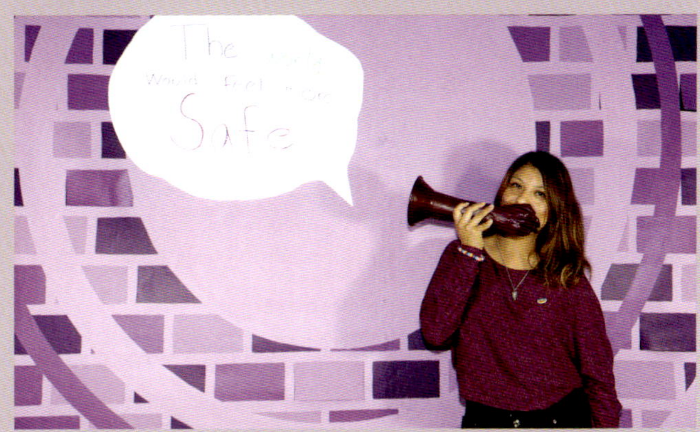
Safe

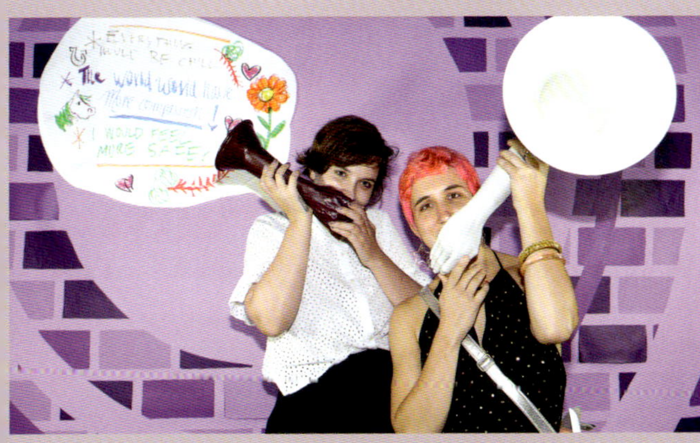

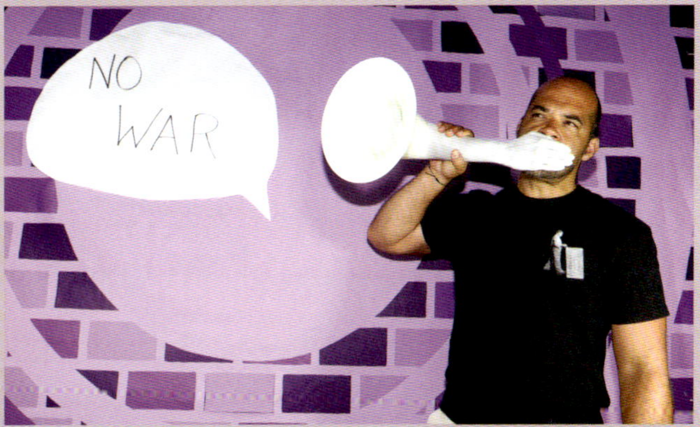
NO
WAR

We could walk down the street without being catcalled

Male or any senator would no longer wonder
if people still use diaper bags

Everything would be chill. The world would have
more compassion. I would feel more safe.

It would be a refreshing change to have more
women and positive role models for all

It would take some time to filter out all the misogyny,
but then it would be FUCKING AMAZING!

If I were in charge of the world I would help everyone sick or hurt

We would all be more connected to
ourselves and our surroundings

Women, men and children alike would have an
opportunity to have a more inclusive narrative
about what being "in charge" means

Birth control would be free, abortion would be accessible,
viagara would need a woman's approval, maternity leave
would be paid and long, childcare would be affordable,
schools would have more funding than the military

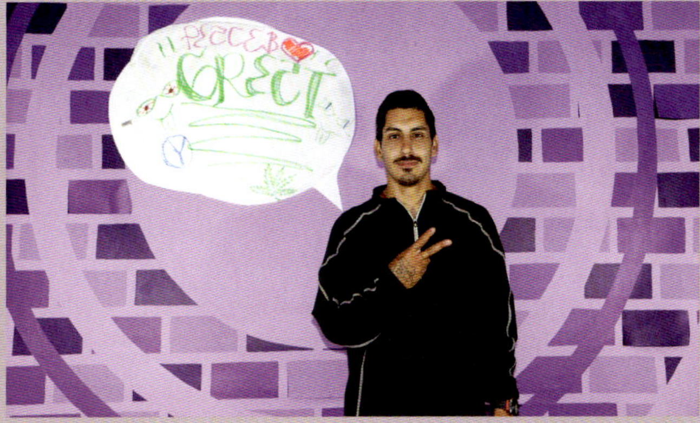

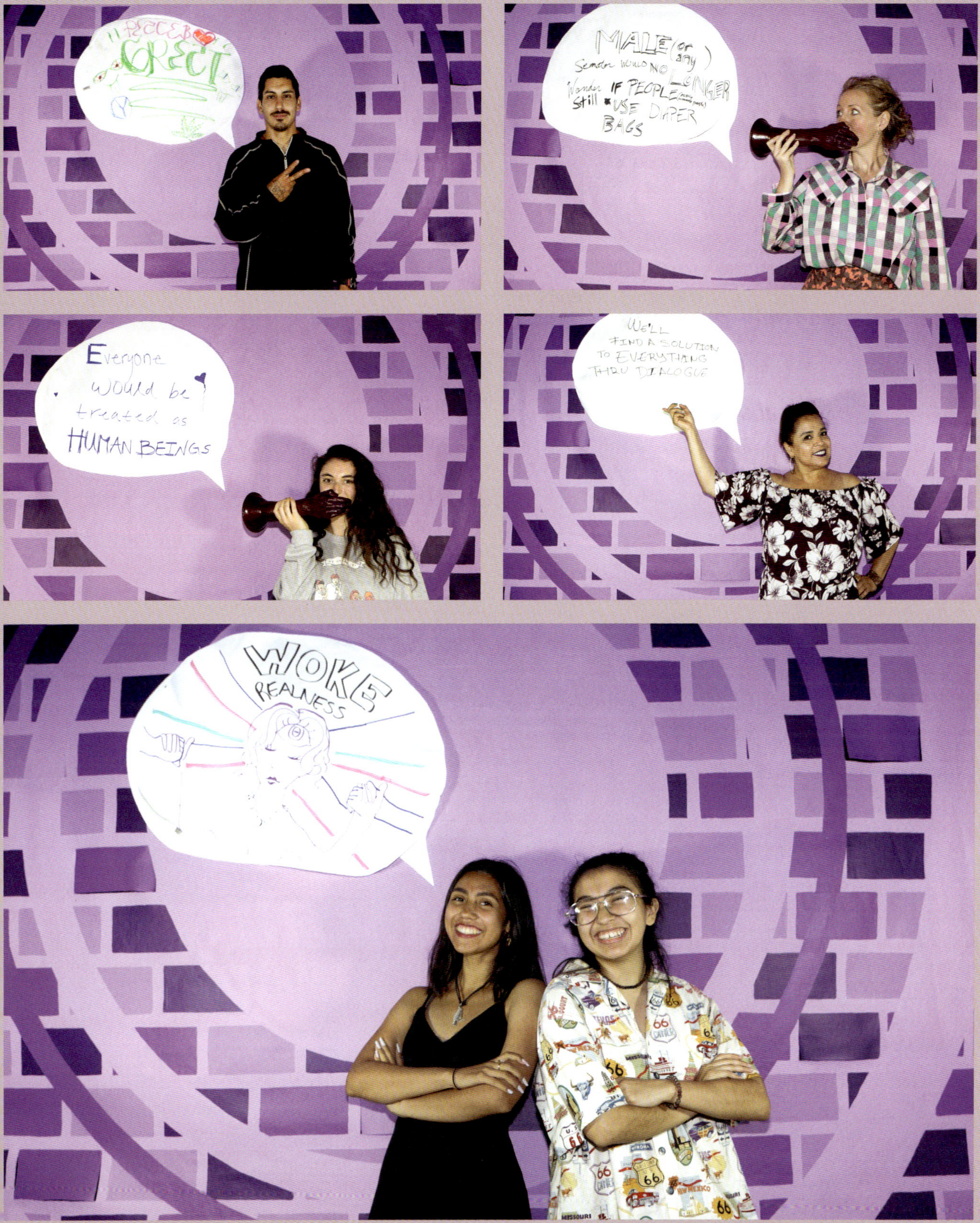

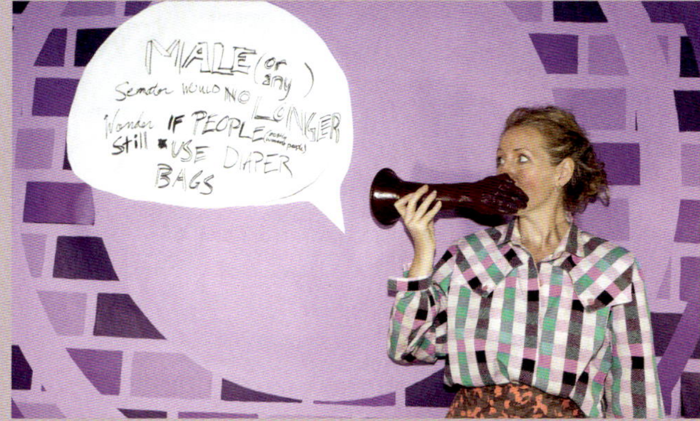

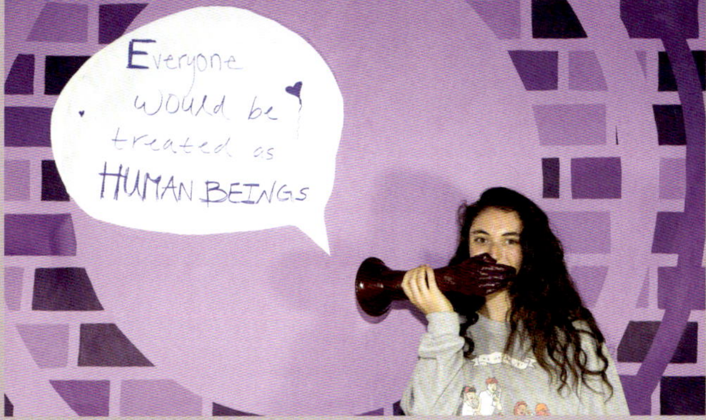

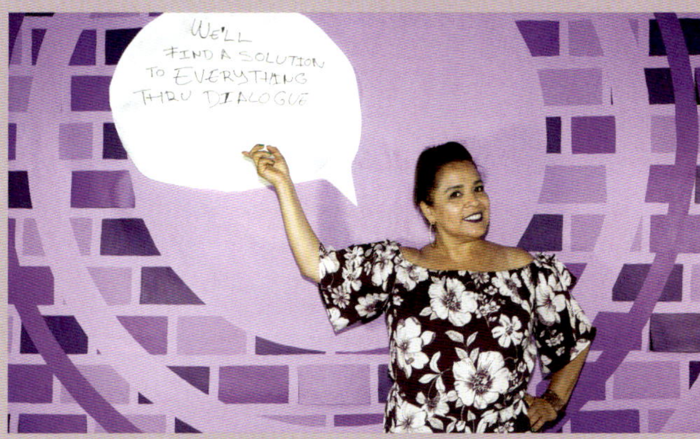

what if women were in charge? by Elana Mann and Las Fotos Project. Photos of audience members, Las Fotos, and artists at *Ain't I a Womxn?* Photos: Monica Orozco.

Reimagining Black Gender Justice

La Mikia Castillo

Black women in America have never owned the rights to our bodies. From the first beautiful Black woman stolen from Africa, stripped of her humanity and forced into slavery, to the newest, beautiful Black baby girl birthed through her mother's womb into this white-supremacist, anti-Black, antiwoman world and every Black woman, girl, and femme in between, our bodies have never been our own.

How can the body of someone who was deemed less than a person, someone whose being was equated with that of animals, someone who was considered chattel, personal property, and enslaved ever have ownership of anything, including a body, even one that is technically their own? How can a woman, a Black woman, who has never been truly free, whose personhood, existence, and value have never been elevated to that of the ever-precious status of white womanhood, have the right, the liberty, the freedom, the audacity to claim her body as her own?

Feminist cries of "my body, my choice" ring hollow for Black women. With years, decades, centuries, generations of violence and abuse enacted upon Black women's bodies, we have never been given a choice in how we carry, love, care for, use, or live in our bodies because in this country our bodies have never belonged to us.

Black gender justic

From slave masters and slave catchers who stole, sold, beat, whipped, and raped us to pimps and sex traffickers who steal, sell, beat, whip, and rape us to police and doctors who maim, rip apart, imprison, lynch, and murder us, our bodies have and continue to be a space for pain, pleasure, and experimentation at the hands of those who don't see our humanity and seek to control us like animals. They remind us that our bodies will never belong to us.

And yet we are given a false sense of ownership, being named promiscuous, deviant, and hypersexual, as if we truly have control over bodies; as if we have a choice in how we experience and enjoy our bodies; as if our bodies were our own. Even as our bodies are gunned down, raped, torn, ripped apart, maimed, and lynched, we are made to believe that we are unable to control ourselves or our bodies, which is why we must be controlled. We have no autonomy. We are not free.
So, what does Black gender justice look like in this white-supremacist, anti-Black, antiwoman world? What does it look like to reimagine gender justice for Black women, girls, and femmes in a world that continues to rob and deny us of our humanity, dignity, and the rights to our own bodies?

Freedom!

looks like freedom.

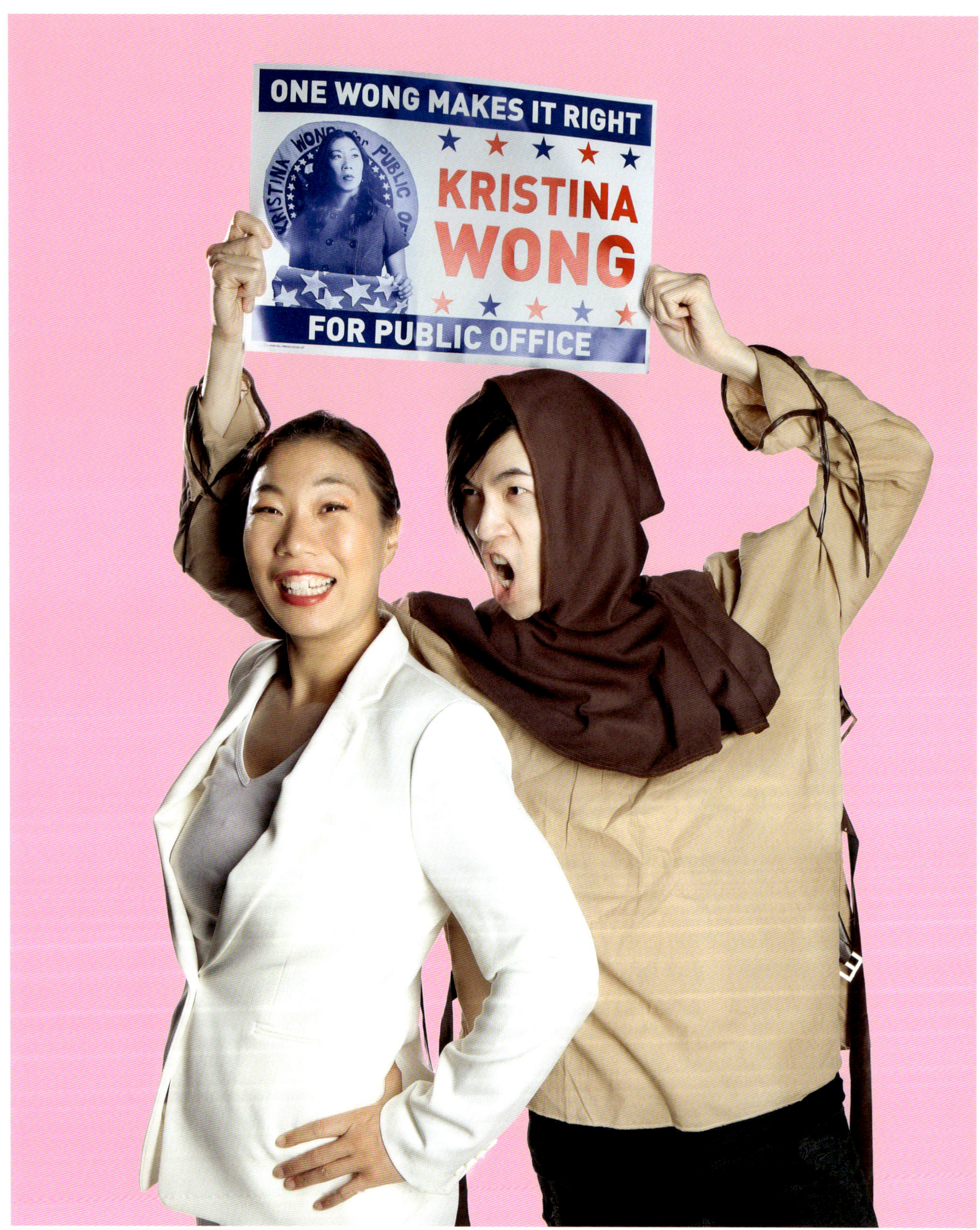

Kristina Wong and Asher Yap. Photo: Austin Young.

Script for a 2018 Witch Hunt
By Kristina Wong

"Throughout history, women who didn't do what they were told were seen as threats. As witches. If women were heard and not seen, that was reason enough to destroy them. But I am here today, campaigning for public office because of the rebellious witchy women before me. The women who refused to burn. The women who insisted on using their power to make change so that women like me could make change. I exist because of the witches before me."

—Kristina Wong's campaign speech
while being burned alive at the state in *Ain't I a Womxn?*

At some point in 2018, I couldn't figure out what the point of performance art was anymore when the 24-hour news cycle plays like a durational performance-art piece where none of us can figure out how to exit the gallery. Since I couldn't beat them, I decided to run for public office. For an entire year, I used my access to theater and art spaces to campaign for an office that I hadn't yet filed to run for.

Characters:
Ogre, Woman Running for Office

Setting:
Firepit with phallic stake (Is there
any other kind?) in the center.

General outline of action:

- Ogre drags a bound and gagged witch/woman candidate to the firepit. Calls upon townspeople to "Burn the Witch!"
- Ogre ties witch/woman candidate to a phallic stake.
- Ogre invites the Public to stone her.
- Witch/woman candidate insists on giving one last campaign speech before she dies.
- Woman candidate breaks out of the ropes binding her, topples the patriarchy, and finishes her speech.

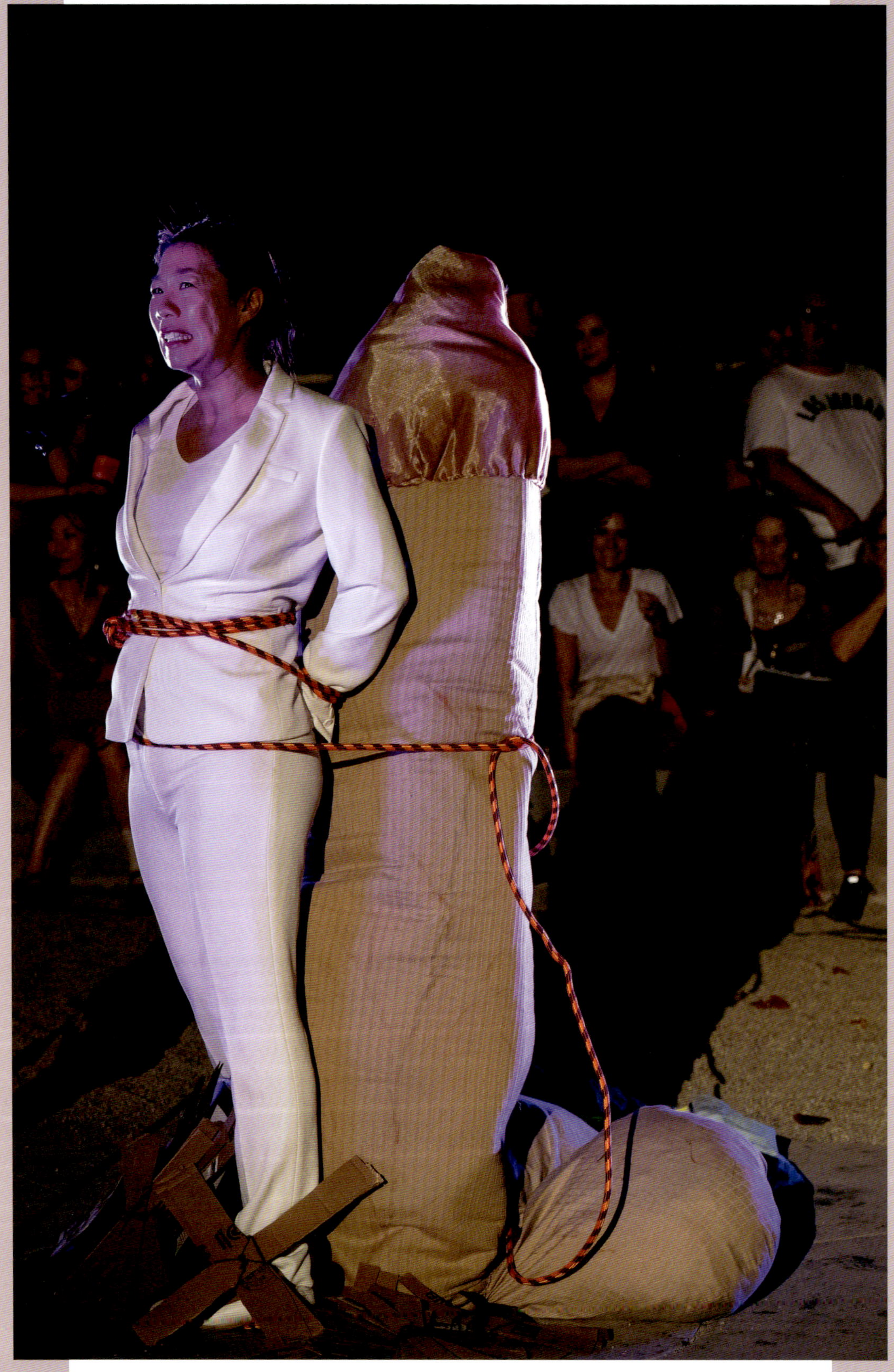

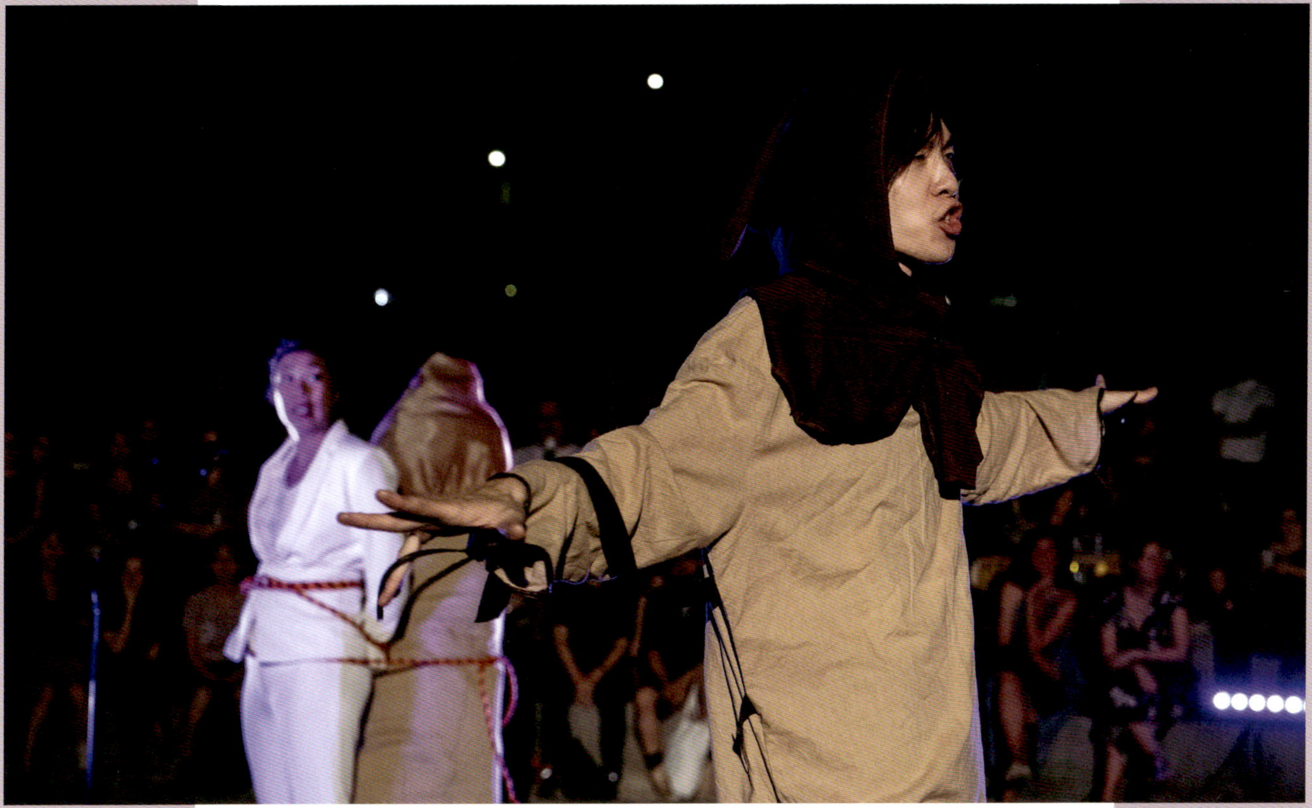

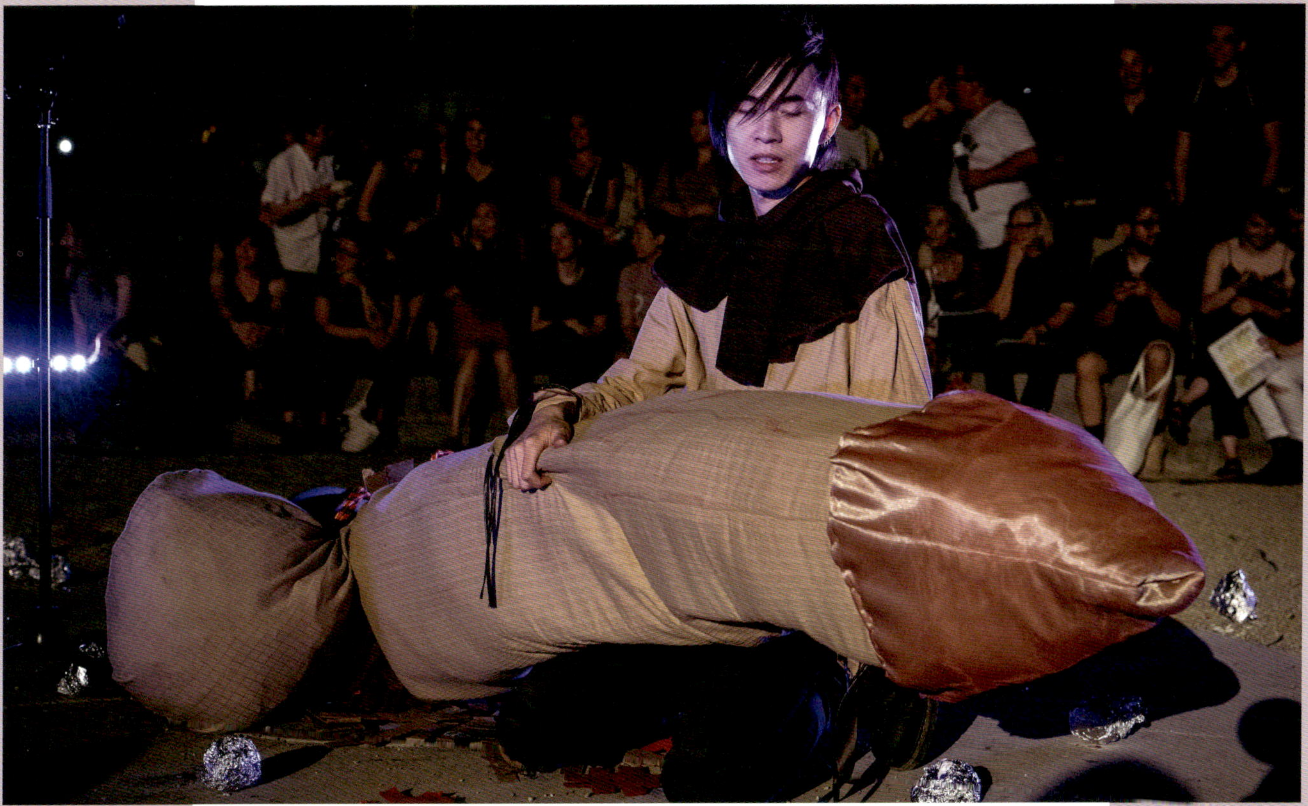

Script for 2018 Witch Hunt by Kristina
Wong. Performance at *Ain't I a Womxn?*
Kristina Wong and Asher Yap.
Photos: Safi Alia Shabaik.

People for Mobility

Mission

As a Black Indigenous people-of-color (BIPOC) collective, we seed critical consciousness about mobility justice across all communities.

Justice

Vision

People have the freedom and resources to move
in public spaces with love and dignity.

How We Make a Difference

As educators, we act as bridges that connect community expertise with urban planning and policy advocacy through professional-development activities with a range of audiences. As facilitators, we create safe learning environments where diverse, rooted communities can come together to build consciousness around mobility justice. As advocates, we build champions for mobility justice within transportation-equity policy and planning.

What Is Mobility Justice?

Mobility justice calls our attention to the fact that individuals face different challenges in transportation because the way we are socially controlled in public spaces manifests differently. To move toward more just mobility, we must end discrimination based on race, class, legal status, ability, gender, or age in how our travel is regulated and accommodated. People for Mobility Justice acknowledges the intersections between transportation and the other parts of people's lives, and we strive toward radical safety for all through multiracial organizing, self-determination, and economic empowerment.

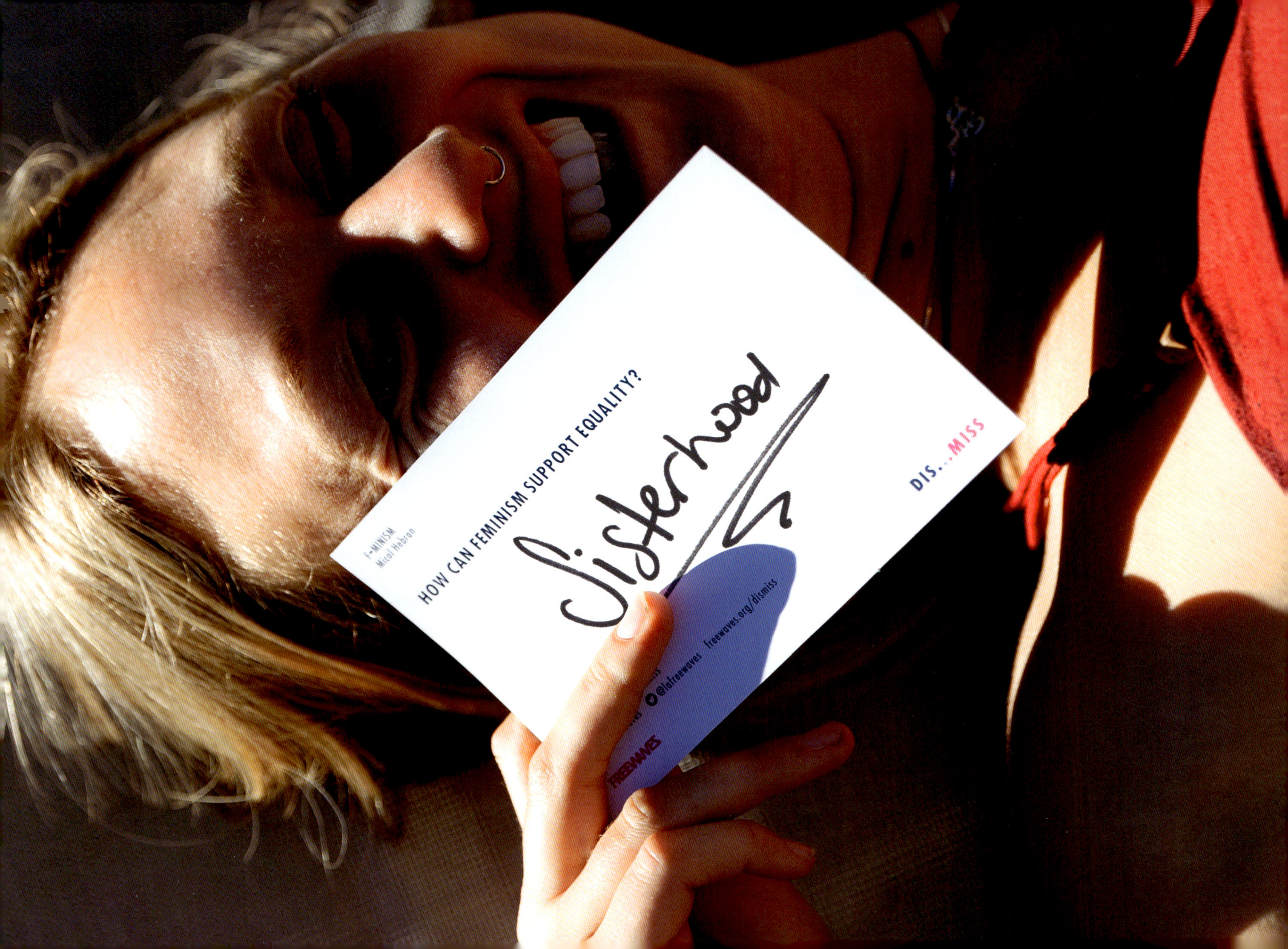
F-MINISM
Micol Hebron
HOW CAN FEMINISM SUPPORT EQUALITY?
Sisterhood
@lafreewaves freewaves.org/dismiss
FREEWAVES
DIS...MISS

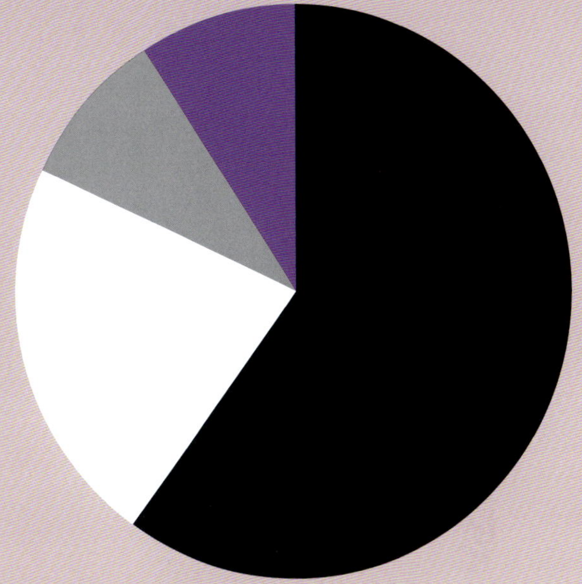

Show that
vulnerability
IS strength.

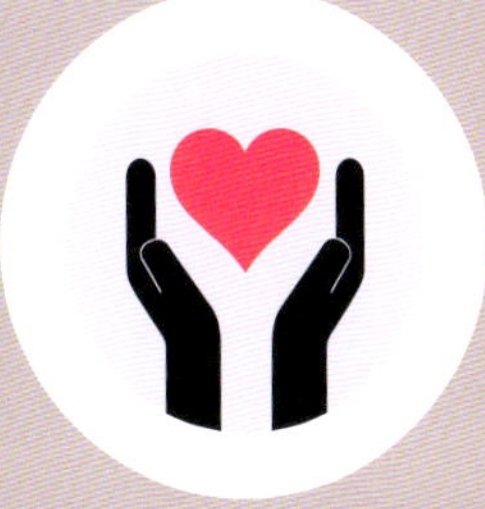

ANALYSIS

About 9% of respondents did not know how to answer. One noteworthy quote: "all the people who aren't feminists are sexists."

"DIS…MISS, Inconclusive Infographic Animation." Analyzed by Marisa Turesky. Animation designed by Catherine Bell, 2019. Left: Postcard portrait by Alejandra Sone.

7

who decided
your gender?

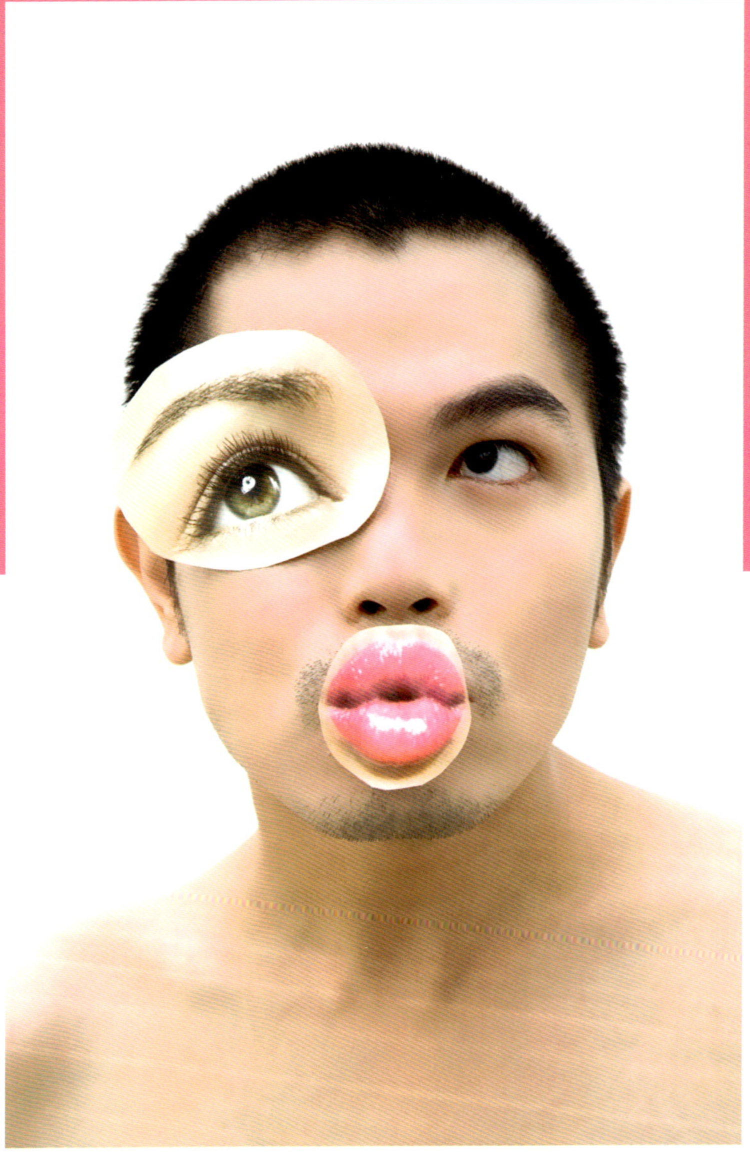

My, What Beautiful Eye You Have (2011). Photo: Thinh Nguyen.

My, What Beautiful Eye You Have, Thinh Nguyen

Eve Oishi

Thinh Nguyen's piece *My, What Beautiful Eye You Have* (2011), like the *Self Imposed* (2011-2017) series of self-portraits to which it belongs, asks viewers to confront the uncomfortable and unnatural experience of having dominant ideals of beauty imposed onto one's own body. This discomfort merges with a reflection on the experience of visually consuming self-portraits in the age of social media and the dominance of the selfie. In this piece, Nguyen, who prefers the gender nonbinary pronouns *xe* and *they*, cut out pictures of body parts from fashion magazines—gloss-shellacked pink lips puckered into a cartoonishly pillowy pout, a large green eye framed with mascara, and an artfully tweezed brow—and taped them onto xir own face. Nguyen then lightened xir skin via Photoshop to achieve the pale, poreless plasticity of the magazine fashion model.

My, What Beautiful Eye You Have, produced in the years immediately following the launch of Instagram in 2010, serves as a critical bridge between the rich history of photographic self-portraiture and the more recent art of the selfie. Looking at a photographic self-portrait is an intrinsically ambivalent and confusing experience. We are lured in by an artist's generous and vulnerable act of self-revelation as they offer their own body to the camera's aperture. Frontal self-portraits in particular invite viewers to explore the artist's interior emotional landscape. It is an act of almost tactile intimacy as our vision grazes the planes of their face, the textures of their hair, mouth, and eyes. At the same time, however, the staged and posed nature of the image—the choice of lighting, background, focus, and framing—erects a screen that reminds us of the impossibility of understanding with certainty anything about the person we are looking at.

There is a contradiction also built into photography's ability to render so effectively the three-dimensionality of objects. In some cases, an artist's use of key lighting or other methods to create a sense of depth can actually highlight the photograph's two-dimensionality. One of the pleasures of viewing self-portraits resides in these forms of ambivalence: the photograph's static two-dimensionality simultaneously stokes and frustrates our curiosity about the subject's elusive materiality, while the often ambiguous emotion we read in the artist's face both draws us in and keeps us at bay. The push and pull of these competing elements absorbe us in the image and ultimately pull forth an emotional response from within our own interior topography. Nguyen's photograph captures this tension, deliberately playing with several levels of flatness and depth. Setting the delicately contoured skin of xir face and shoulders against a washed-out background mimics the effect of fashion photography, which is designed to evoke pleasure, envy, and a sense of lack in the viewer. At the same time, the imposition of imagery from actual fashion photography introduces dissonant and literally sharp edges onto xir face, transforming the viewer's conditioned response into one of surprise, repulsion, and introspection.

Through this play, Nguyen's photographs serve as a critical reflection on the ubiquity of photographic self-portraits, or selfies, as forms of self-expression in the age of social media—forms that eliminate the pleasurable ambivalence of viewing self-portraits in favor of a glossy lacquered surface. Selfies are not meant to be lingered over and explored. They are a form specifically designed for widescale sharing within the massive public visual flow of social media. Selfies are meant to be quickly scanned, liked, and swiped in search of the next image, identically posed, framed, and shot. They are meant to stand out enough to arrest your attention (briefly) while blending in with the millions of other images. Instagram filters provide a deceptive sense of variety, allowing posters to instantly enhance their photos by choosing from among a narrowly prescribed range of choices. Filters such as Valencia, Nashville, and Gingham wash out the colors or add a yellowish tinge to simulate the look of Polaroids or faded family snapshots from decades past, creating a canned sense of nostalgia. Photo-editing apps allow you to erase blemishes and flaws and to shade and contour your face to mimic the retouched photos of fashion models.

The selfie phenomenon intersects deeply with feminist concerns about gender, beauty, and representation. A study done in 2011 found that people who perceive their self-worth largely through concepts of "appearance, approval, and competition" posted more photos online on sites such as Facebook. The study also found that "females [*sic*] tended to spend more time managing their profiles and shared more photos online" and that women also identified more strongly with the "contingency of self-worth" based on appearance.[1] In other words, for women in particular, there is a correlation between deriving one's sense of self-worth from others and participating in the selfie phenomenon. The visual culture of social media feeds the cultural imperatives for women to look outside of themselves for their value, a value that is disproportionately linked to physical features.

According to Nguyen, the photo series *Self Imposed* was inspired by a similar set of concerns about beauty and self-worth. After immigrating as a child to the United States from Vietnam, Nguyen dyed xir hair blond and wore blue contact lenses, believing these styles to be more beautiful than xir natural black hair and brown eyes. On a return trip to xir village in Vietnam, Nguyen was struck by the extreme measures that women were taking to keep their skin white, a new standard of beauty drawn from Western models. It wasn't until this trip that Nguyen finally connected xir own cosmetic practices to an understanding of the ways in which standards of beauty are linked to larger colonial and capitalist dynamics of power.

My, What Beautiful Eye You Have takes as its subject the intersecting demands of gender, race, and capitalism and their imposition on an individual's body and psyche. These impositions range from the use of lightening makeup and contact lenses to more invasive procedures, such as double eyelid surgery and breast augmentation, as well as coloring, covering, and cutting the body to fit into a shape dictated by dominant Western culture; they also range from slightly uncomfortable to extremely painful. Although Nguyen's photograph was produced using digital editing tools, this editorial intervention is no Instagram filter designed to elide the difference between real faces and magazine ideals. The artifice in the photograph is obvious, underscored not only by the mismatched skin tone and size of the cutouts but also by the dark razor stubble peeking out from under the glossy, feminized lips. The cut-out eye and lip could be from a model of any gender, but they are made up to conform to feminine standards of beauty, commenting on the ways in which Western beauty ideals intersect with and are mutually enforced by structures of heteronormativity.

All of the pieces in the *Self Imposed* series are inspired by advertising slogans from cosmetic and beauty companies. The other photographs in the series are titled *May Be She's Born with It, Kiss Your Thin Lips Goodbye*, and *High Drama for Every Lash*. The title *My, What Beautiful Eye* You Have also references the fairy tale of Little Red Riding Hood, in which the wolf masquerading as the heroine's grandmother responds to the young girl's questions by saying that his big eyes make it "all the better to see you with" and, ultimately, that his big mouth is "all the better to eat you with." By linking the menace of the fairy tale with the beauty campaign, Nguyen unmasks a seemingly benevolent set of representations to expose a carnivorous industry whose intent is not to adorn and improve you but to devour you. The title of the series, *Self Imposed*, reminds us that these unnatural ideals are enforced by the individuals who internalize them. Social media has become an efficient vehicle for the transmission of these ideals at little cost and great profit to global capitalism. In her book on cultural producers such as fashion bloggers engaged in gendered "aspirational work" in the beauty, fashion, and design industries, Brook Erin Duffy writes that "neoliberal ideologies of individuality and self-governance have instigated more self-conscious efforts to *brand the self*. Increasingly, many of these practices take place across a raft of social media networks: Facebook, Twitter, Instagram, and LinkedIn."[2] We learn to police, control, and exhibit our own bodies to the benefit of a multi-billion-dollar beauty industry.

Nguyen's concerns with the social framing of bodies and identity are ongoing in xir work and can be found in another form in xir project *I Am That I Am* (2018), a series of black T-shirts with simple "I Am" statements painted in white acrylic on the front in capital letters. The "identity" statements are drawn from the right-wing and xenophobic nationalist movements that have seen a resurgence in popularity and visibility in the United States and Europe in recent years, including "I AM WHITE POWER," "I AM A BIGOT," "I AM RACIST," and "I AM SEXIST." In contrast to the plenitude of jokey or hipster statement T-shirts currently available for sale, Nguyen's shirts are decidedly not ironic. The T-shirts function instead as both works of visual art and performance art because Nguyen wears them in daily

---

1   Michael A. Stefanone, Derek Lackaff, and Devan Rosen, "Contingencies of Self-Worth and Social-Networking-Site Behavior," *Cyberpsychology, Behavior, and Social Networking* 14, nos. 1–2 (2011): 41–49, doi:10.1089/cyber.2010.0049.

2   Brooke Erin Duffy, *(Not) Getting Paid to Do What You Love: Gender, Social Media, and Aspirational Work* (New Haven, CT: Yale University Press, 2017), 11.

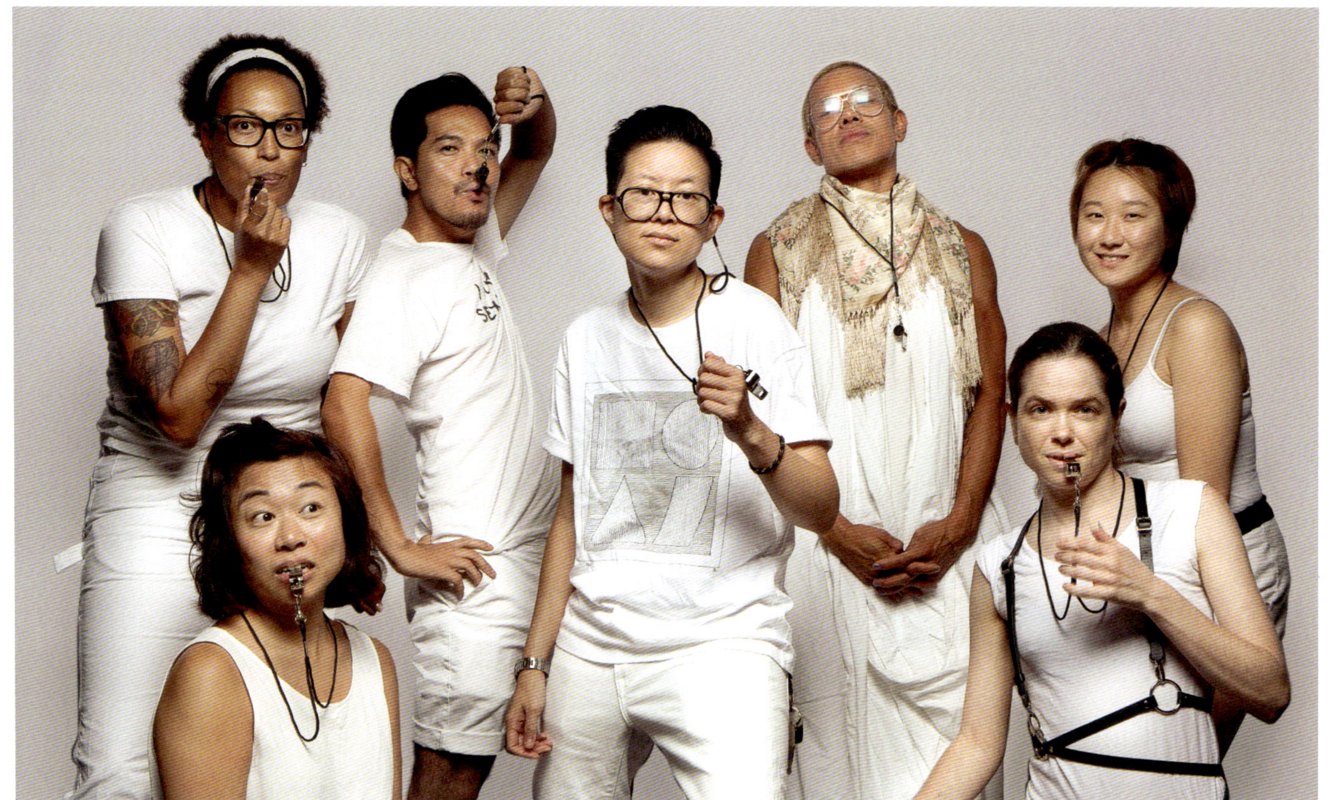

Thinh Nguyen and friends, performance group at *LOVE &/OR FEAR*.
Photo: Austin Young.

life. Moving through the quotidian spaces of Los Angeles, Nguyen compels people in grocery stores, public streets, and banks to encounter and attempt to make sense of a visibly Asian body wearing a T-shirt declaring "I AM WHITE POWER." Although most of us are familiar with principles and actions that are associated with the terms *white power*, *bigot*, *racist*, and *sexist*, when these beliefs are baldly stated and claimed, it is usually done online under cover of anonymity and rarely "IRL" (in real life) in a public space where the declaration is linked to a physical body. The visual and cognitive dissonance of this vision forces a reckoning with the viewer's own beliefs, assumptions, and identifications as well as with the codes and symbols with which we transmit these identities to the outside world.

Nguyen states that the power of xir art is not to be didactic but to "reflect and illuminate. ... How the work leads you to the truth, that is the power of art."[3] The confrontation with the incongruous vision of the artist wear-

ing one of these T shirts obliges me to consider what "I am," how I have come to inhabit, enforce, and communicate that identity, and how that identity connects or disconnects me from the bodies around me. Nguyen is interested in making people linger with the uncomfortable emotions that arise out of the questions "Who am I?" and "Who are you?" As xe states, "I need to reveal the illusion."[4] This project can be seen as part of a continuum that links back to *My, What Beautiful Eye You Have*, made in 2011. Although that photograph can assuredly be read as an indictment of Westernized heteronormative standards of beauty enforced by global capitalism, it is also an invitation to the viewer to tarry in the ambivalent emotional space that beauty culture evokes. We are simultaneously drawn in by the creamy and varnished surfaces and repelled by their distorted and plastic nature. The deconstruction of the illusion brings us to a new and necessarily awkward relationship with ourselves.

---

3   Personal conversation with the artist, May 16, 2018.
4   Personal conversation with the artist, May 16, 2018.

DGendering

I AM

Thinh Nguyen

You are more than your gender
It is not about being a man or a woman,
Rather it is the cultural meaning
attached to being masculine or feminine.

Binary gender identity is
a hierarchical construct of cultural values
privileging masculinity over femininity.
It serves to maintain the conflict between the sexes,
to reinforce gender roles and stereotypes
that uphold brutal patriarchy.

The greatest predictor of violence
is gender binary perpetuated
by toxic masculinity.
So why uphold a gender identity
that reduces your being
to a system of social injustice
based on discrimination, prejudice,
and gender inequity?

What are the values of your gender identity?
Does your gender expression reinforce cis-sexism?
Does it embrace the already existing
diverse gender identities and sexual complexities?

Can your gender be
both masculine and feminine?
free of oppressive social norms?
kind, loving, and compassionate?

Remember, you are
more than just your gender.
So de-gender yourself.

I am not a man or woman
I am not male or female
I am not straight or queer
I am not cis or trans
I am not a person of color

Who defines me as a man or a woman?
Who assigns me as male or female?
Who identifies me as straight or queer?
Who specifies me as cis or trans?
Who classifies me as a person of color?

I refuse to be labeled as such
I refuse to be less than
A man, male, straight, cis, white.
I am but flesh and bones

My gender is kindness
My sexuality is love
My identity is compassion

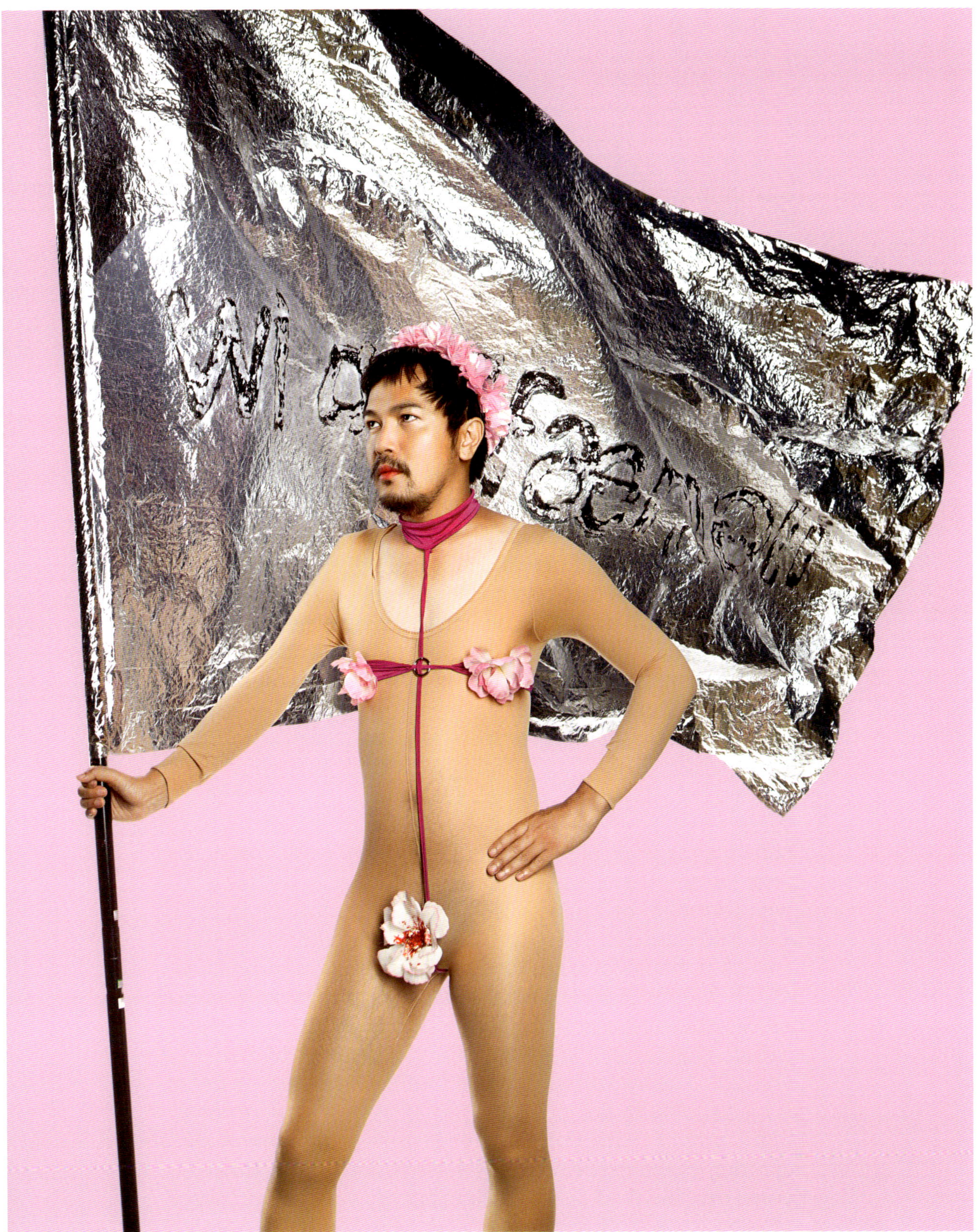

Thinh Nguyen. Photo: Austin Young.

Unidentified
The Uhuruverse

Regarding gender specifically, I identify as nonbinary. I identify as gender nonconforming. I identify as a gender-neutral person, a genderless person. A gender-fluid person. A two-spirited person. I always have just BEEN nonbinary. However, this planet is not. People place gender on children in the womb (those poor babies), and they immediately form all sorts of gender (role) expectations for them. For example, because my family already had a daughter (my big sister), they hoped I was a boy. I was still named after my father (though he was disappointed). His name is Kenneth, and my (dead) name is Kenisha. I never attached to the "isha" part, which in Black culture is how to "effeminate" a name. As a child, I didn't have the ability to articulate that I didn't connect to this name because it was femme—I just knew it didn't feel right. So I requested that my family, friends, and peers call me Ken/Kenny, which my friends and peers did, while my family called me "Nisha" or "NeNe." Here I am addressing name giving with regard to gendering (misgendering). My self-identity wasn't respected by my family. I went on to embrace the name "Uhura" to correct any misgendering coming from English/Western culture/influence because "Uhuru" is Swahili (West African), which does not gender the language. So, you see, the binary is colonial.

Following the issue of my gender identity not being respected in my name—there was the forced gender-role assignments given to "boys" or "girls" based on their genitalia (which is weird, rude, and unnecessary of cis folx and culture). Why are we clocking genitalia of humans and expecting certain cultural behaviors from them because of that?! It started with separation. Separating me from my "boy" cousins and friends, which I can say that for a child it was really violent and traumatizing to be pulled away from my closest family and friends in order for me to be "with the girls" or do what the "girls" were doing. I didn't mind SOMETIMES because I am nonbinary and thus enjoy doing whatever my energy desires as a human. But to be denied my "boy," a.k.a. masculine, energy was violent, espe-

The Uhuruverse of #SNATCHPOWER. Photo: Safi Alia Shabaik.

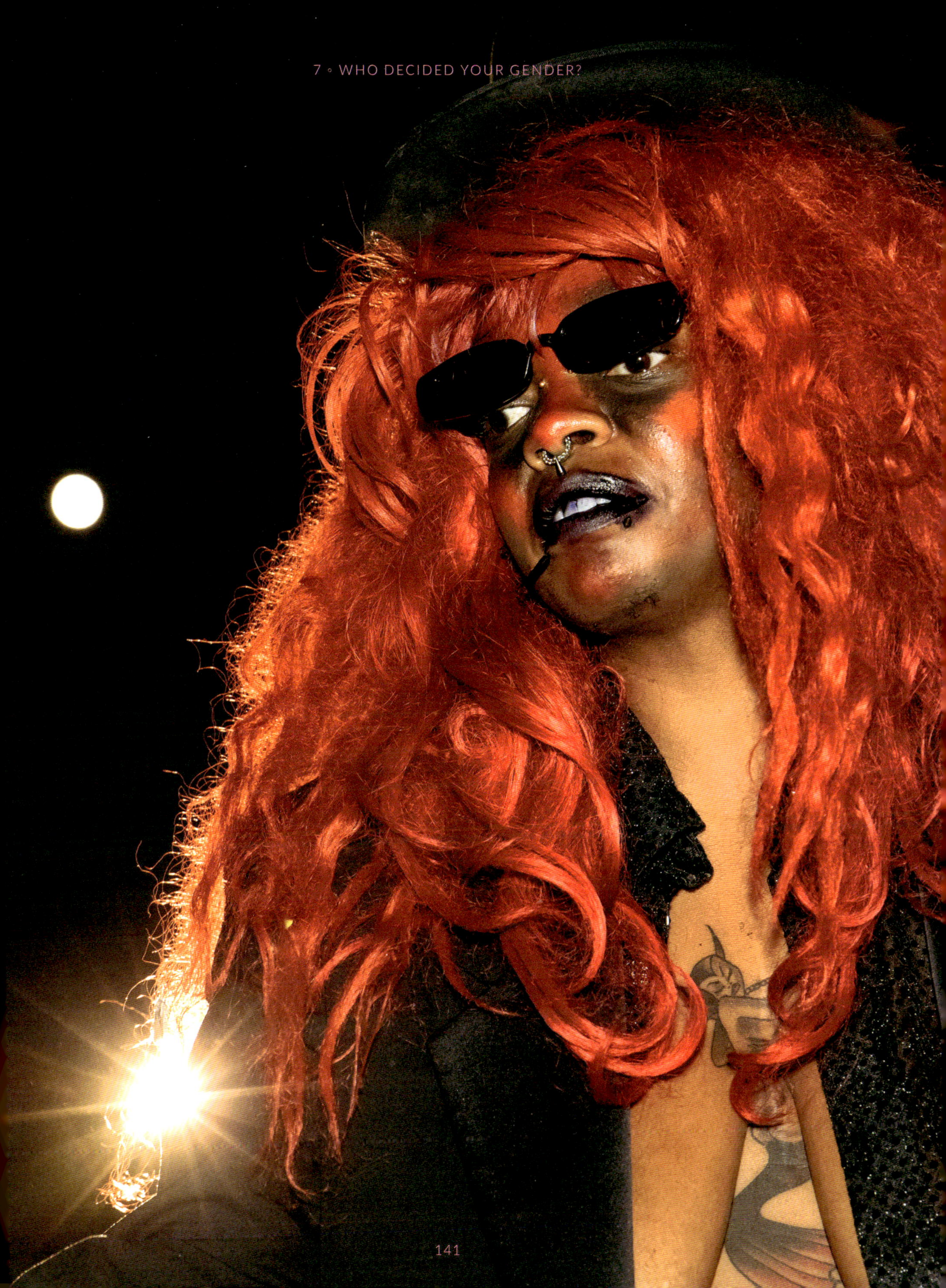

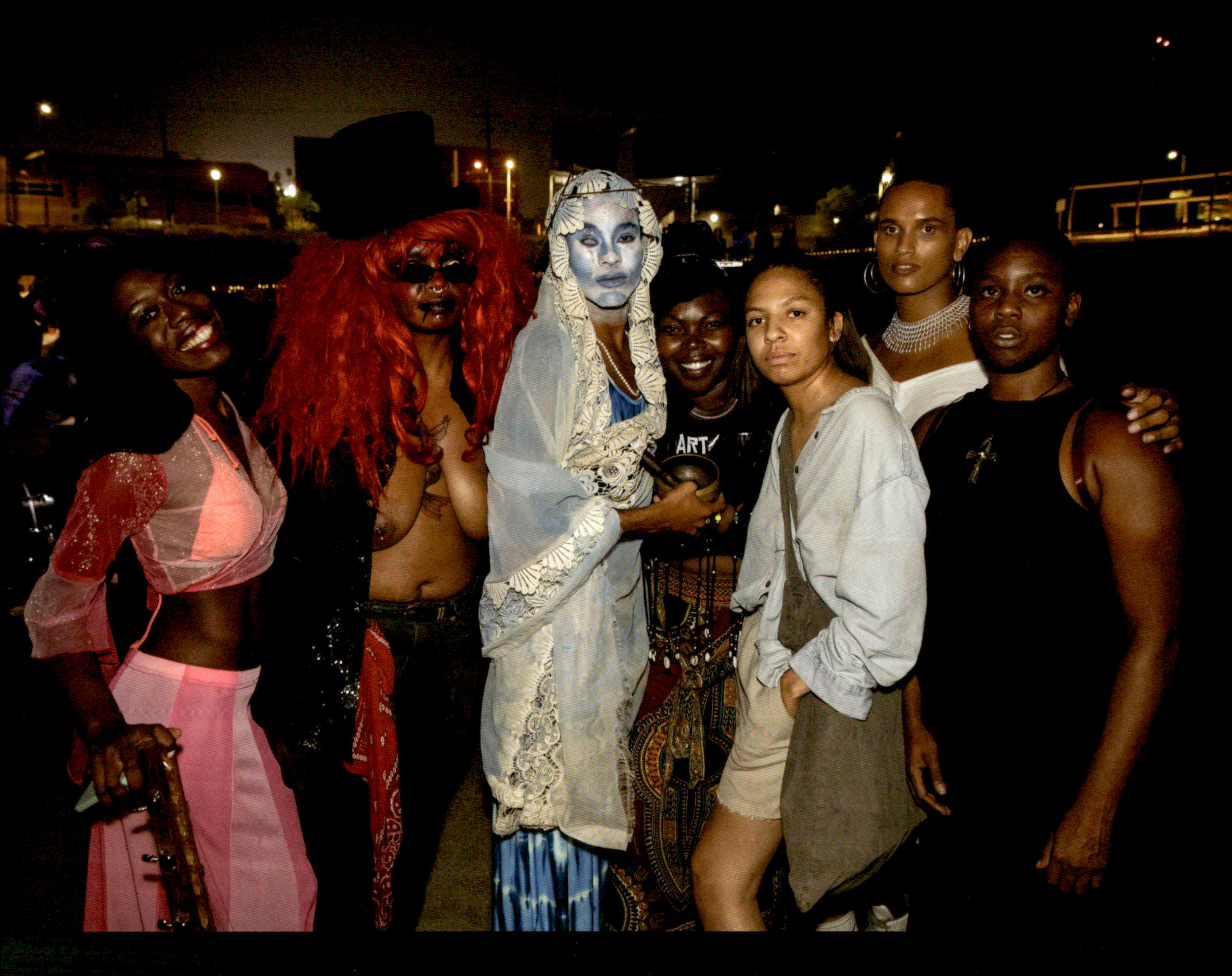

#SNATCHPOWER. Photo: Safi Alia Shabaik.

cially for a boy who could kick all those other boys butts in anything!!! But to be denied the opportunity because one day I would have breasts that can produce nutrients for a baby or a body that can birth a child was absurd! Especially when I hadn't even developed enough to decide if I'd utilize my body to do either. All in all, I realized that no one acknowledged or recognized my masculine energy because I had long hair or a high-pitched voice (now they don't acknowledge it because I have DDD breasts). Not even my dad recognized my gender when I am clearly the first son he hoped for all along and his second daughter. Not sure he ever will.

I remember hitting late adolescence/early teens and being labeled as a feminist by my mother and the women of my family because I began to refuse the femme teachings and indoctrination they passed down. They'd say, "If you don't learn to cook, you won't have a husband." My rebuttal was, "I don't need to know how to cook. How do you know my partner will not cook for me?!" They thought I was a feminist. I am now. However, at the time I was too young to cognitively articulate that my issue was one of misgendering. I didn't want to be a wife. I wanted to be a husband. I wanted to work and provide and have a wife (or wives) and take out the trash (and as a nonbinary person, I also want to wash the dishes). I now believe and know all humans need to know how to cook to eat well. But I currently don't know how to cook because I refused to be misgendered. In fact, being nonbinary provided me with the vision to have a school for humans where all humans learn human things, including "boys" learning domestic activities and "girls" learning things they're often denied, such as mechanics.

Even #SNATCHPOWER, which I founded in 2014, stemmed out of my nonbinary-gender struggle. It's amazing how interconnected womxn's rights are to nonbinary struggle. I accidentally created a gravitational pull with the most beautiful womxn when creating the moniker "#Snatchpower" as a double entendre for folx who wanted to be free from being boxed in as Black folx, as femmes at birth, as queer folx. I essentially created a space for queer femmes by seeking my own space where I could be my nonbinary self outside of cis heterosexual patriarchy.

Gender is one of those things people accept as fact. It's nothing they question or discuss. No one questions the origins of things we practice and believe as humans. When as a child or an adult you tell people you are nonbinary, THEY CANNOT EVEN FATHOM YOU or you not being what society has labeled you based on your genitalia or that you would ever expand and be anything beyond the binary—and I imagine my trans friends have gotten this same response from cis folx (people who identify as the gender they were born into). As I stated, fighting against my misgendering got me labeled a feminist (which I am! I'm honored to fight for women's equality), but that does not mean this fight isn't overlapping with my fight for nonbinary rights and visibility. I find that I was labeled a girl or woman (a cis concept). I initially refused that label, then by force accepted being labeled a girl or woman because everyone refused to see me as anything otherwise. (Then there is the mode of acceptance of the label as being what it is and fighting for equality and justice as a "girl/woman" in a patriarchy that favors "boys/men.") All this labeling to separate comes from yt western society (colonialism) and cis yt "supremacy." This is all a social construct of humanity. It's frustrating to be born, (mis) labeled something, forced to accept the label, and then have to fight for equality within the constraints of a label you never identified with. (For a disabled person, this is why socializing with humans is exhausting.)

Example of the nonbinary struggle being confused with the feminist struggle: I am a performance artist often photographed or witnessed topless. This toplessness is associated with the "Free the Nip / Free the Tits" movement (which it is, technically, for someone who is AFAB, assigned a femme at birth). However, as a nonbinary person, I protest in favor of my own nonbinaryism. I don't see my breasts as tits, but as my chest, and I most likely will not ever use them to breastfeed a human (which should not matter). And yet simultaneously, of course, I think it's absurd that misogyny and patriarchy police AFAB breasts, sexualize femme bodies, and capitalize on the sexualization.

The last thing I find ironic about being nonbinary is how my identity as a queer person is wrapped up in my (very late) coming out as a nonbinary person. In elementary and middle school, getting whooped (or as yt folx say, spanked) for being "gay" and being called "gay" by peers because I didn't like any of the "boys," because I was one and therefore wasn't gay, just nonbinary, are hilarious to me. I laugh because humans are investigating folx' sexual orientation before knowing or considering to know their gender. Had I had the mental development to understand the concepts as early as they were enforced upon me, I would not have identified as asexual to repress my (gender) queerness but instead as pansexual because I don't operate in the binary even when considering sexual partners (naturally): I'm nonbinary, and I don't understand what humans are doing trying to identify everyone and thing (lol). This is not truly funny at all; it's ridiculous that any human is sweating any other human about such ways of identifying or trying to enforce any performance of gender identity. But until the world leads with nonbinary gendering and allowing folx to choose (if they want to choose from a binary) gender and self-define their pronouns, I'll continue to laugh so I don't cry. I am an (un)identified subject.

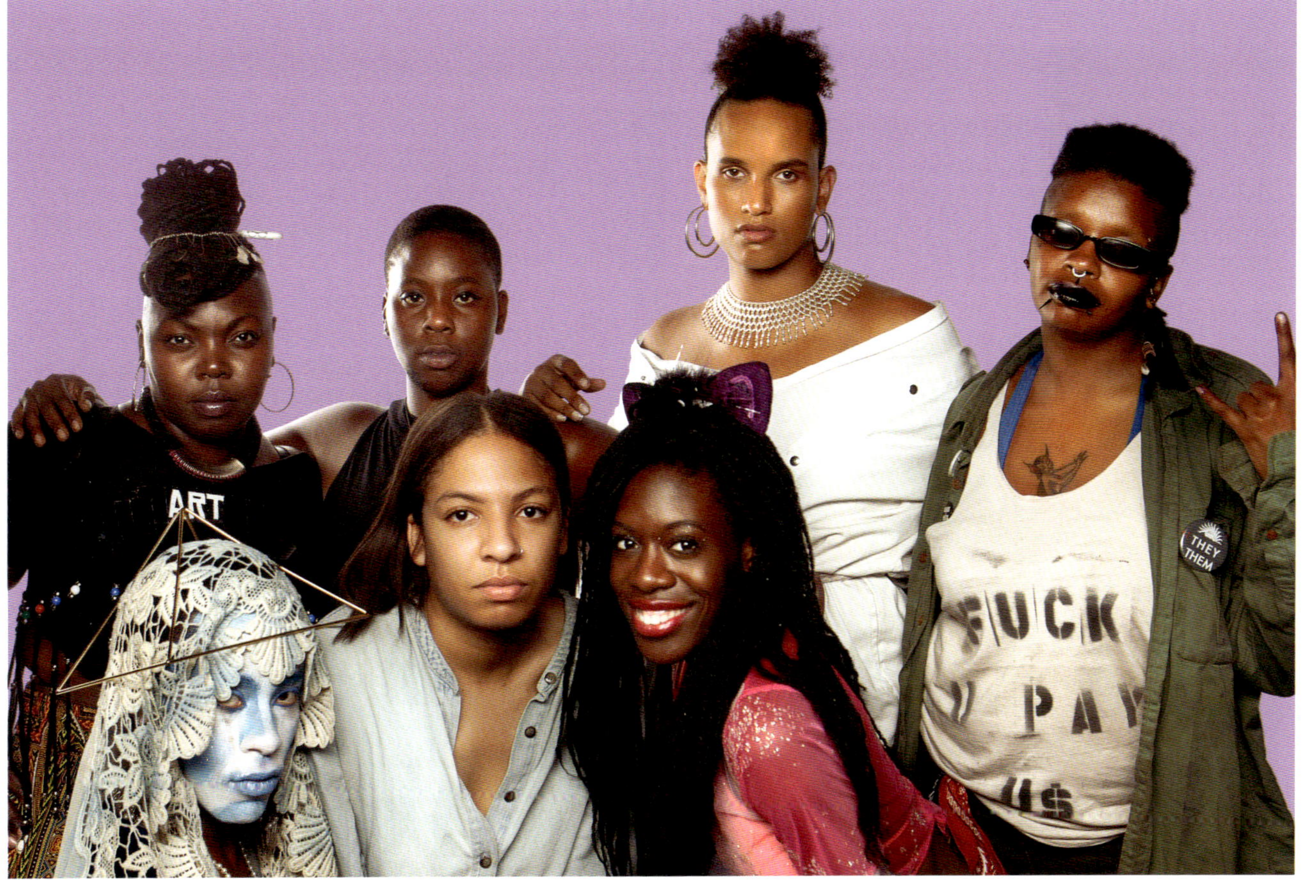

#SNATCHPOWER. Photo: Austin Young.

SOLIDARITY IS (*STILL*) FOR WHITE WOMEN

INTERSECTIONALITY NOW

8 WHITE IDENTITIES
BY BARNOR HESSE

1. White Supremacist — Clearly marked white society that preserves, names, and values white superiority.

2. White Voyeurism — Wouldn't challenge a white supremacist; desires non-whiteness because it's interesting, pleasurable; seeks to control the consumption and appropriation of non-whiteness; fascination with culture (ex: consuming Black culture without the burden of Blackness)

3. White Privilege — May critique supremacy, but a deep investment in questions of fairness/equality under the normalization of whiteness and the white rule; sworn goal of diversity.

4. White Benefit — Sympathetic to a set of issues but only privately; won't speak/act in solidarity publicly because benefitting through whiteness in public (some POC are in this category as well).

5. White Confessional — Some exposure of whiteness takes place, but as a way of being accountable to POC after; seek validation from POC.

6. White Critical — Take on board critiques of whiteness and invest exposing/marking the white regime; refuses to be complicit with the regime; whiteness speaking back to whiteness.

7. White Traitor — Actively refuses complicity; names what's going on; intention is to subvert white authority and tell the truth at whatever cost; need them to dismantle institutions.

8. White Abolitionist — Changing institutions, dismantling whiteness, and not allowing whiteness to reassert itself.

"We need you defecting from White supremacy and changing the narrative of White supremacy by breaking White silence." – Alicia Garza, co-founder, Black Lives Matter

"An ally should be personally gaining NOTHING through their activism. In fact, if you are an ally, you should be losing things through your activism; space, voice, recognition, validation, identity and ego." – Laura LeMoon, sex workers' rights activist

5 BOOKS BY WOMEN OF COLOR REFORMING WHITE FEMINISTS™ SHOULD READ *(BY THE FEMINIST LIBRARY ON WHEELS)*

This Bridge Called My Back: Writings by Radical Women of Color, edited by Cherríe Moraga and Gloria E. Anzaldúa (1981, 2016). A pioneering anthology of important writing, from women of many backgrounds and in many genres, edited and published by women of color on their own terms.

Solidarity — Despite our various cultures, identities, communities, histories, and contexts, we choose to work together — starting with ending the ways we marginalize and inadvertently oppress each other.

Unity — An insistence on an impossible sameness, the expectation that 1.2 million women march on Washington with a universal agenda, or that we all fall in line behind a pre-determined nominee. Unity flattens differences into quiet compliance.

White Feminism™ — White feminism says we're all in this together, white feminism loves to insist on unity, white feminism thinks you just need to lean in, white feminism has a pantsuit for every day of the week, white feminism congratulates itself for no arrests. White feminism believes there is a universal Womanhood, and that sexism is Woman's primary oppression, and that there is only one ceiling between marginalization and white male power. See also: Amy Schumer, Lena Dunham, Hillary Clinton, Ivanka Trump.

BEFORE WE CAN TOPPLE THE PATRIARCHY WE HAVE TO TOPPLE WHITE FEMINISM™

Accomplice — Use your body, your voice, your privilege, your access, your time, your energy & your money to undermine white supremacy while amplifying the voices of the most vulnerable women.

Colorblind — You aren't, and pretending you are does nothing to lesson the incidental and systemic racism that people of color experience.

Divisive — Racism is divisive. Homophobia and heteronormativity are divisive.

Emotional labor — (1) When white women expect women of color to teach them what they could easily google. (2) When white women want women of color to help them process their white guilt.

White supremacy culture — Relies on hierarchies, competition, individualism, perfectionism, and a fictitious "objectivity," rather than cooperation, transparency, learning, or non-linear thinking. Must be pointed out in order to be undermined.

White tears — You just realized you experience racial privilege, now you're making it about you and your feelings. However uncomfortable you might feel in this moment, it probably doesn't compare to the racism and racialized violence that people of color regularly experience.

White fragility — When learning about the ways you may be a little bit racist or are benefitting from white privilege makes you defensive, angry, anxious, or too guilty to function.

Women, Race, & Class, by Angela Davis (1983). Excellent history of women's movements in the US, revealing the links between racism, misogyny, and class-based discrimination within feminist history.

bell hooks. Maybe start with *Feminism Is for Everybody: Passionate Politics* (2000), but you might also want to read *Feminist Theory: From Margin to Center* (1984), *Ain't I A Woman: Black Women and Feminism* (1981) and *Talking Back: Thinking Feminist, Thinking Black* (1989).

Decolonize This! Young Women of Color on Today's Feminism (2002), edited by Daisy Hernández and Bushra Rehman. This anthology is helpful because it expands on the diversity of voices and experiences represented by *This Bridge*.

Sister Outsider: Essays and Speeches, by Audre Lorde (1984). Her dynamic, vibrant, strong voice still resonates for good reason, and you should read the source, carefully and closely.

Bonus titles: Gloria E. Anzaldúa *Borderlands/La Frontera: The New Mestiza* (1987); Sonia Shah, ed. *Dragon Ladies: Asian American Feminists Breathe Fire* (1997); Barbara Smith, ed. *Home Girls: A Black Feminist Anthology* (1983); *Color of Violence: The INCITE! Anthology* (2006); Maythee Rojas *Women of Color and Feminism* (2009); Mia McKenzie *Black Girl Dangerous: On Race, Queerness, Class, and Gender* (2014); Alma M. García, ed. *Chicana Feminist Thought: The Basic Historical Writings* (1997); Brittney C. Cooper, Susana M. Morris, and Robin M. Boylorn, eds. *The Crunk Feminist Collection* (2017)

We believe FEMINISM NOW must be intersectional (we reject hierarchies based on race, class, gender, ability, sexuality, or age) & that it must work to AMPLIFY the most marginalized women & that it must learn to listen and to check its privilege. We want our feminism more queer, more brown, more radical, more insistent. We want our feminism to be fun but also make us uncomfortable. We want our feminism decolonized, inclusive, and international. With better slogans & cooler signs.

CONTACT US: hey@feministpizza.org
WWW.FEMINISTPIZZA.ORG

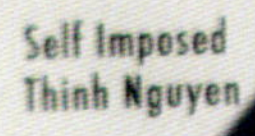

Self Imposed
Thinh Nguyen

WHO DECIDED YOUR GENDER?

Society decides the name
of your gender, but you
should be able to live in the
way that you feel

Tell us or a friend. #dismiss
@lafreewaves   @lafreewaves   freewaves.org/dismiss

FREEWAVES   DIS....MISS

who decided your gender?

RESPONSE #50

I did. I do, but that's too simple. It comes from within and the decision is constant; it doesn't happen and complete itself; it continues.

ANALYSIS

46% of respondents cited "me," often describing being assigned a gender by external forces, but then making the decision for themselves later in life. They often felt empowered in the ability to make the decision for themselves.

"DIS…MISS, Inconclusive Infographic Animation." Analyzed by Marisa Turesky. Animation designed by Catherine Bell, 2019.
Left: Postcard portrait by Alejandra Sone.

8

what makes you
bang your head?

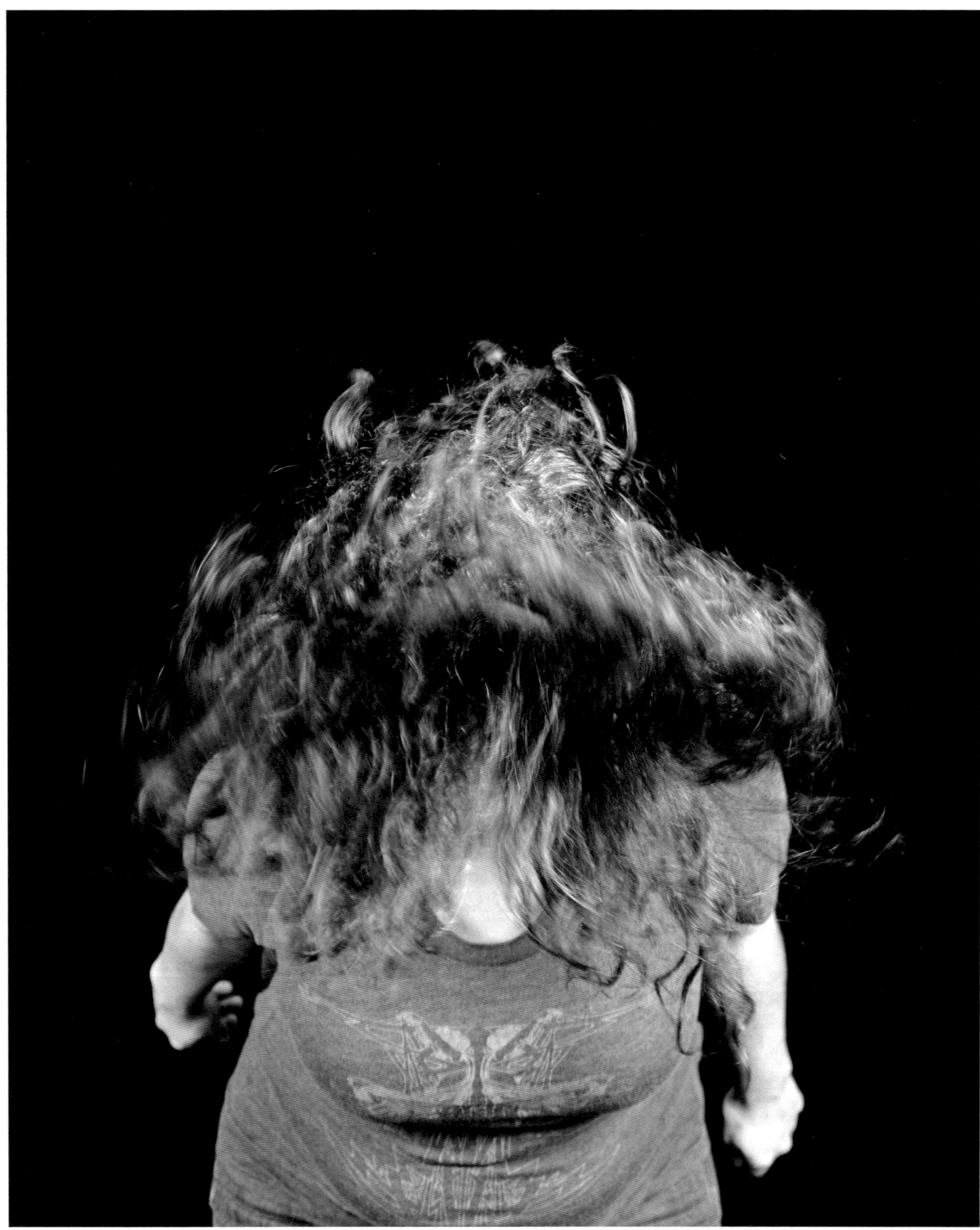

Headbang. Photo: Roya Falahi.

Headbang, Roya Falahi

Rahel Aima

I came to riot grrrl about a decade too late. Growing up in Dubai in the 1990s, I felt as if I experienced a time lag in more ways than one. I was scandalized to learn that the rare TV shows I watched had originally aired between the 1960s and 1980s and that I was interfacing with a West that didn't exist anymore and hadn't for some time. The punk and hardcore of the 1980s, which I discovered at the end of the 1990s, got me into zine culture and the intriguing landscape of North American grrrl culture, so different from anything I had ever encountered before. I learned so much about the world, about gender. I also absorbed so much orientalized nonsense about the oppression of non-Western women and would later spend years trying to develop a more nuanced understanding of the situation, helped in large part by reading Muslim feminist theorists. I bristled at the restrictions placed on women that I saw around me, both real and perceived.

I started an all-girl band and a zine distro in quick succession, impatiently waiting weeks for the issues to cross continents and badgering (haranguing, to be honest) everyone around me to make their own. At my band's first gig, we threw out tampons into the crowd of mostly Arab and South Asian metalheads, delighting in the reaction. I took the phrase "the personal is political" and ran a multiyear marathon with it, even as I failed to make the connection between other people's body positivity and my own disordered eating. I'm pretty sure that I understood myself to have *personally invented feminism*. Interviews of me from that time—nobody knew yet that the internet was forever—are as thoroughly, cringily obnoxious as you might imagine. More, even.

Roya Falahi's photograph *Headbang* (2012) takes me so sharply back to those days, to the handful of dark, smoky venues that tolerated all-ages events, to the parking lots where the crowd would pour out, to the front row of headbangers, and to all the overapplied eyeliner and all the camaraderie. In Falahi's photograph, a closely cropped figure leans forward slightly, their face hidden by a mass of hair in motion. It's a forward headbang, not one of those rotational, wildly swinging ones that I imagine must induce a sore neck. Their arms swing backward away from the body, as if they are about to do a long jump or perhaps take sudden, dramatic flight. The image is at once so dynamic and such a study in captured motion I can't help but think of that old Goethe chestnut about architecture being frozen music.

The subject is wearing the kind of band shirt that the gig-going crowd of the 2000s would probably agree is Very Kvlt. I remember resenting the dominance of extreme metal in the local scene but ending up inadvertently listening to so much of it all the same. I got really into a female-fronted Norwegian doom-metal band called Thorr's Hammer (not to be confused with the Polish NSBM, "national socialist black metal," band Thor's Hammer). I could never quite shake the feeling that despite the atmospheric, tundral beauty of the Norwegian band's music, its emphasis on Norse mythology obscured something threateningly Aryan and proud. A number of people in the scene around me were, it should be noted, white-aspirational Levantine men who overidentified with both Aryan supremacy and its inevitable antisemetism, though the latter, along with the scene's pervasive chauvinism, didn't become legible to me until after I moved to the United States.

Headbang is part of a series of self-portraits in which Falahi notably obscures her own face. They instead explore the subtle permutations and projections of identity that unspool through dress, body language, and gesture: her Iranian American background, rock, punk, and metal subcultures, and various points of intersection. One such point is the headbang, of course; another is the metallic pyramid stud. At the Vincent Price Museum of Art, the photograph was shown alongside her series *Headbang/Covert Ops* from the same year. In another image from the series, Falahi poses herself dressed in black, almost receding into the black background, and wearing a stud-encrusted hijab. Her hands are in one photo crossed on her lap, as if she is posing for a school photograph, and in a second crossed even further so that each hand, placed on an opposite knee, variously makes a peace sign or the metal horns. In a third image, she is seated cross-legged in a loose lotus position, hands holding hexagonal objects such as mudras. A recession where her face should be is also covered with studs—the cavity unsettlingly scooped out, as if waiting for a new face. Curiously, the overall effect, particularly because of the stripes created by her arrangement of the studs, suggests a man wearing a keffi-yeh. But someone else might see a pharaoh's headdress or one of those creepy pin-art sculptures.

There is a picture of me that I love, taken at Lux in Lisbon in the summer of 2013. I'm wearing an iridescent velvet-and-mesh-checkered dress sewn with pompoms and am captured mid movement, body interrupted by a strobe, dyed hair thrown up and forward as if I am skanking or headbanging. I love it as a memory of that summer, as a memento of the person I once was. But I can't remember the name of the club, only that it was a night organized by the musician Four Tet. The lineup included the Syrian wedding singer turned techno-dabke DJ Omar Souleyman and the duo Acid Arab, two white Frenchmen (they've since added some more white compatriots) melding, as their name suggests, acid house with the musical languages of the places France once colonized. I remember having fun and feeling uncomfortable at the crowd—represented in this image by a pair of orange-paisleyed baggy pants to my left— and their eager, wrist-swirling embrace of the music. I used to get so angry about such things. When I looked up the club on Tripadvisor, I saw that it was universally panned as having a racist door policy.

A number of other photographs in Falahi's series consider headbanging as a collective expression of emotion, of solidarity, of rage. One image of a funerary red-lit altar with a tilted-back mannequin's head at the center, *Layers of Unrest (2009)/Roya as Neda*, pays tribute to a student assassinated during Iran's election protests and the broader Green Revolution they birthed in 2009. Thinking back to that Norwegian doom-metal band, I wonder if there's even any possible expression of collective identity, especially a dominant one, that's not always already violent or suspect. As for me, what made me headbang back then? Not metal, certainly, but, all the same, I loved seeing people lose themselves in music like that, whether by head-banging in a club or by whirling in a devotional Sufi ghazal. And now? The same indignities and injustices—though I have trouble identifying with feminism anymore—are mostly just transposed to the art world, particularly the marginalization of Black, Indigenous, and people of color within it. I was so heartened to see the #MeToo movement and, later, Instagram accounts such as @sceneandherd in India that highlighted predatory, racist, and exploitative behaviors, and I was equally deflated when they amounted to little but lawsuits and intimidation. At the point where you're updating feminism so much to be less cis-normative, less white, why call it feminism at all?

Perhaps there's something to be said for the contrast between the exuberance of the figure's headbang, tendrils flying gloriously, and the hair-covering function of the hijab, but the contrast feels at once so expected as to be trite. I remember, with some shame, visiting Tehran a few years ago in spring's full bloom. It was a beautiful time to be in a beautiful city, especially one with such a flower-loving culture, but I found myself feeling so secretly resentful at having to cover my head, of feeling uncomfortably suffocated in my borrowed headscarf and too-heavy abaya in the blazing heat. I was certainly over-dressed—others wore chiffons and light, floaty materials. But where were all my beliefs about autonomy and the right to choose to cover or not when it interfered with my own bodily comfort on this short trip?

But there's a flip side to being covered as well, which Falahi gestures to with the "covert ops" part of her series title and in a trio of photographs in which she acts out sitcom-y tropes of camouflage, such as hiding (eavesdropping) behind a newspaper in a cafe. Part of my discomfort also stemmed from the relief I felt when walking about, sweating so profusely that I was terrified I must smell terrible, but entirely unbothered and indeed unnoticed by anyone on the street. There was such a liberatory anonymity to it, feeling not only free of any potential stares or harassment but also a kind of Glissantian opacity—like flipping your hair over your face—and feeling the rare sense of escaping surveillance, both human and algorithmic, even if just for a little while.

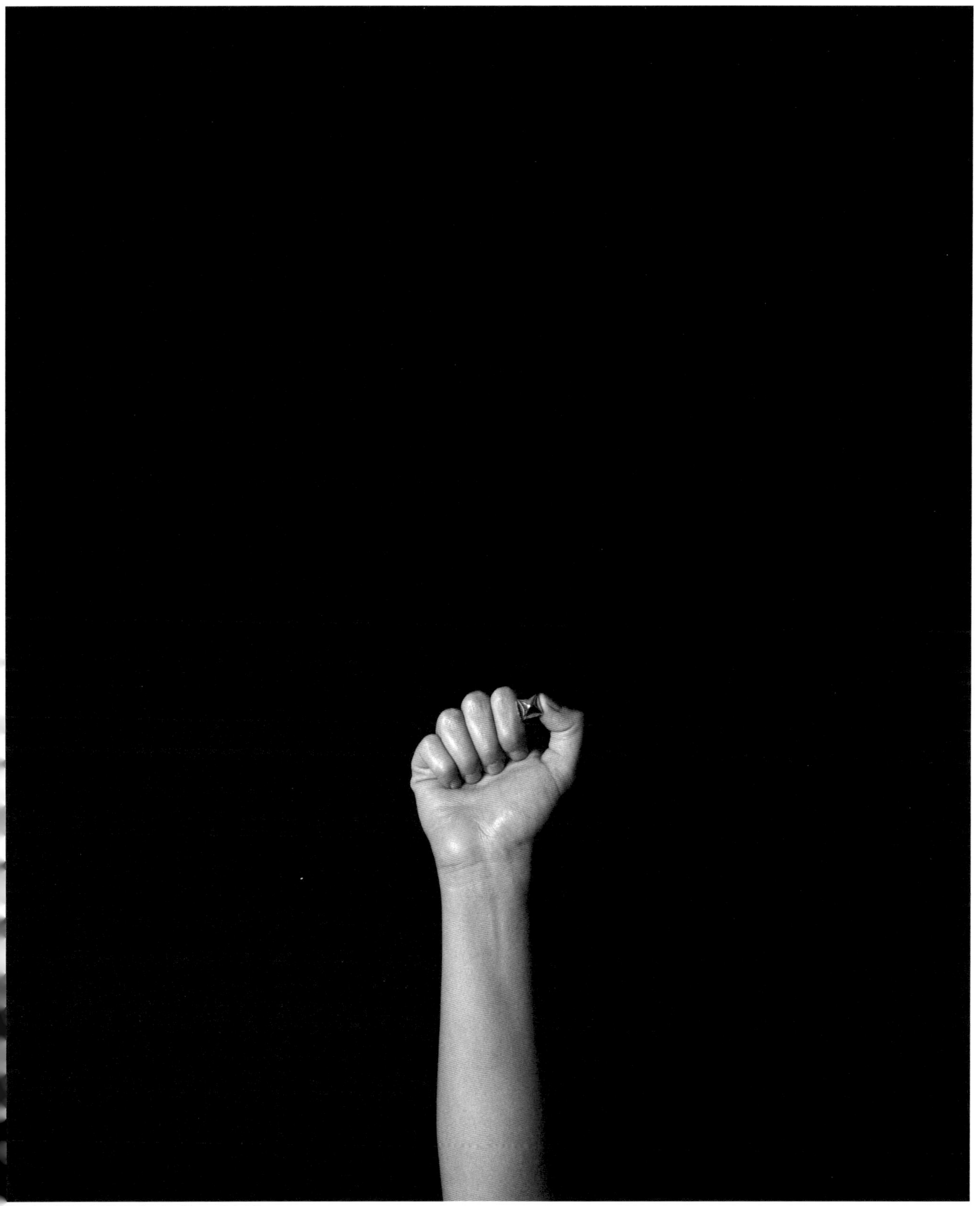

Study of Studs Fist. Photo: Roya Falahi.

Woke Black Folk
Funmilola Fagbamila

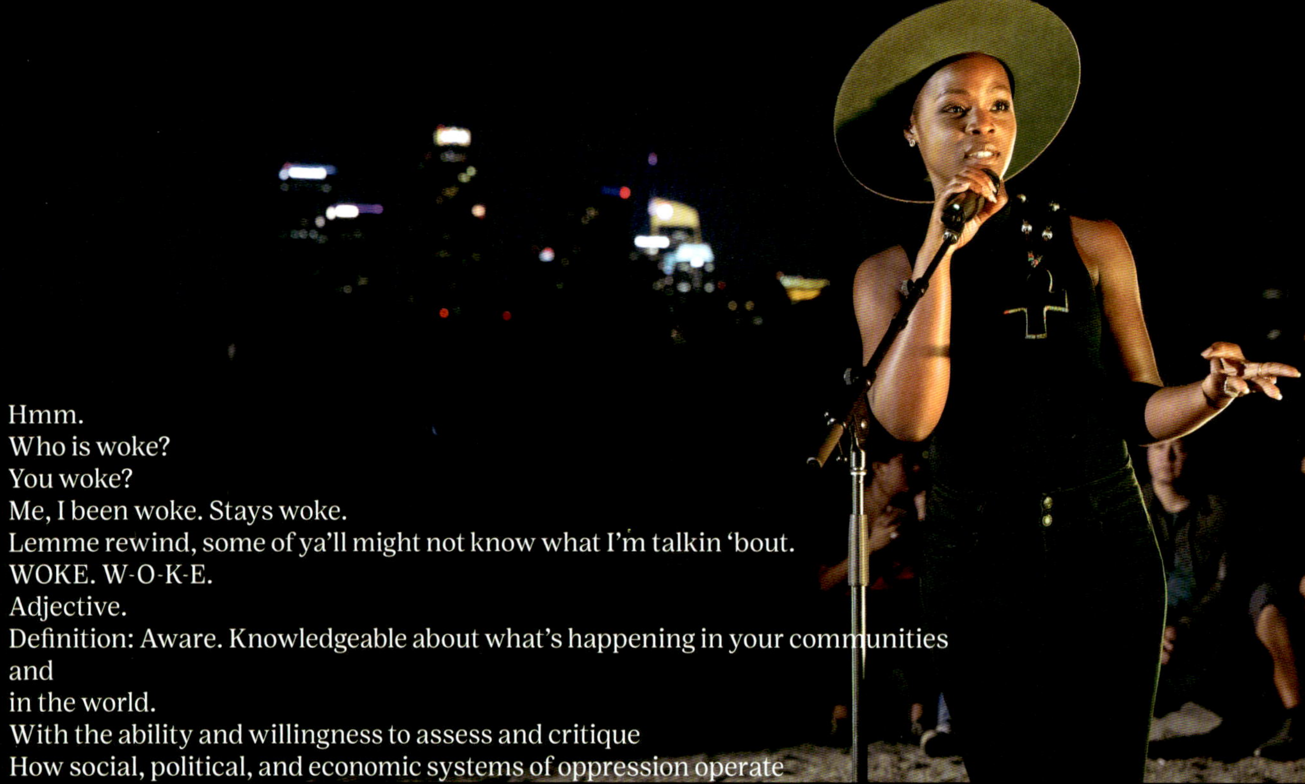

Performance by Funmilola Fagbamila. Photo: Safi Alia Shabaik.

Hmm.
Who is woke?
You woke?
Me, I been woke. Stays woke.
Lemme rewind, some of ya'll might not know what I'm talkin 'bout.
WOKE. W-O-K-E.
Adjective.
Definition: Aware. Knowledgeable about what's happening in your communities and
in the world.
With the ability and willingness to assess and critique
How social, political, and economic systems of oppression operate
At macro and micro levels.
Now that we're on the same page ...
So, I was walking one day and
I met a Black man and he seemed real woke
An ankh around his neck, a scent of nag champa smoke.
He said queen-sista-motha-of-the-earth-Black-girl
Let me treat you like goddess
Lemme come into your world
Said he's equipped with the knowledge
And he's got all the facts about the stolen history and all the good that came from Blacks.
He's talkin math and science and physical equations that THEY claimed to have created, after pillaging our nations.

Black man say if we are to win well then we have to look within
And really if we're gonna fight then first we have to reunite
And really if it's gonna work—then we gotta drop the bullshit
European influence on us no he ain't cool wit
The gays, the queers, homosexual agenda
Ploy to effeminize Black male
But no he neva will surrenda—no.
Black man. Black woman. Black child. Very simple.
See it's that white feminism, always getting in the middle.
Said he's annoyed with academics.
The obnoxious Black feminist
Well read, very angry, and probably needs a therapist
Maybe some green juice as well.
It'll clean out the system, you know that swine and that dairy is a foreign organism.
"You go to white man's school, to acquire a degree
So you can get you some prestige and earn a 'living salary'
But we don't need no recognition from the white man you see."
This man believes entirely in African divinity.
I say, "OK, Black man, but really what you tryna say?"
Said that he's woke, and he's willing, and wants freedom for Black people TODAY.
I say, "Ok," and I keep walking
And I come across Black woman reading book.
She says, "Gender binaries are an illusion and patriarchy is a crook."
Says she looks forward to the day when ALL Black lives will matter
Including queer and trans and those deemed unworthy of chatter.
No conversation about the plight of those who remain invisible
Like Black women, and girls and those for whom a gendered category is simply
inapplicable.
She's fed up.
Tired of explaining all the time about how her sexuality is not aligned
with your "feminine divine."
She tells me, "LOOK, how are Black people to prevail
when we are ideologically trapped in this damn HOTEP HELL
Reproducing the very systems that once stripped us of humanity?
Fake deeps. The epitome of anti-intellectuality."
She sighs from exhaustion, then returns to her book
Then says her dissertation looks at how Black patriarchy cooks up
The intraconflict that impedes liberation
And that if we could just deal with complexity
That'd be means for celebration.
She takes a sip from her mug
Then proceeds to explain:
That it's very important that we as Black people in academia speak and write in
ways that are accessible to Black people outside of these spaces. You know we must
fully reject any form of academic elitist exclusivity. And further, we must
acknowledge that the differentiation of radical alterities is conducive to the
conceptual logic of a truly advantageous and inclusive Black liberatory praxis.
I respond, " ... Alright.
But really, Black woman, what you tryna say?"
Said that she's woke and she's willing and wants freedom for ALL Black people
TODAY.

I say, "OK," … and I keep walkin
Then I come across a man
Who seeks to implement a plan
With a loudspeaker in his hand
He says:
It. Is. Our. Duty. To. Fight.
Like
It. Is. Our. Duty. To. Win.
Like
We. Must. Protect. One. Ano-ther
And. We. Must. Love. One. Ano-ther.
I say, "OK, Black man, what are you protesting today?"
He says, "They ALWAYS shoot us down."
And EVERY time they get away
They get away, they get away with it.
No consequence at all
But we won't take it lyin down—Na
Let's keep goin ya'll.
They said: Black. Lives. Matter.
—Then they said again
Black. Lives. Matter.
—Then the cops came
Black. Lives. Matter.
—"You're gonna have to move"
Black. Lives. Matter.
—"Now I'm warning you"
Black. Lives. Matter.
—"Sir you're under arrest"
Black. Lives. Matter.
Black. Lives. Matter.
Black. Lives. Matter.
It's now a few hours later.
He was in and out fast.
"Intimidation tactics." Says he's used to being harassed.
"You know I catch a lot of flack for all the work that I do."
Black people callin ME extreme—I'm out here fightin for you
Academics say we don't have a "thought through plan"
Sittin in that ivory tower wit a book in yo hand
Don't get me started on these "internet activists" today
Don't come to not one of the meetings—but got everything to say—on Facebook
Typin from the comfort of your seat
Black people out here DYING—You gon sit at home and tweet—Runnin yo mouth
About everything WE are not doin right
The ones that are on the ground
With our bodies in plain site
Ain't it a shame. Y'all good fa talkin.
Talk all night and day.
But y'all scared of revolution
What did the Last Poets say?
I say, "OK, Black man, but really, what you tryna say?"
He says he's woke and he's willing and wants freedom for Black people TODAY.

I say, "OK," ... and I keep walkin
And I come across Black woman on her phone.
She says she wishes these Black radicals would leave the shit alone
They're making things worse.
I mean really, how much can we complain?
We had a Black man in the white house, Look how much we have gained
And I mean YES racism's real
Ok, I get that part
But do we think you're gonna "change the world" if all you do is bark?
Just bark about every single thing that doesn't go your way
With your bullhorn and your picket sign, what really will you change?
And yes I understand—You demand—basic civility
But when are we gonna talk about Black accountability?
We have to address our part in the matter
And if we don't then we're setting ourselves up for disaster
Pull your pants up
Respect yourself and maybe then you'll get respect
We have to do better at keeping each other in check
We kill each other, then focus our attention on police
The approach is counterproductive
And quite frankly obsolete
And we MUST shift our energy—how negative can we be?
If all we think about is bad things, we manifest it ya see
I was reading like—this book like—the other day
And it literally said exactly what I always say.
You attract what you think about the most—ya know.
And if we think progressively, then it will be so.
But when I express how I feel Black people call me a coon
But I just want the best for us, and I want it soon.
I say, "OK, Black woman, really what you tryna say."
She says she's woke and willing and wants freedom for Black people today
I say ok and I keep walkin ... ...
So, I took you on a trip with me
We met 4 black folks
With 4 different ways of thinking
They ALL call themselves WOKE
Who's really woke?
Character 1? With a juice the color green
And a politic that demeans those he doesn't see as kings and queens?
Or character 2? The academic. Who speaks up for the ones most invisible.
But in a language we can't all understand. An excess of syllables.
Or character 3? The activist. Always on the front line.
But criticizes those who resist online.
Or character 4?—Respectability politicn' for sure. But still wants us to be alright.
How will THESE four people unite?
That's what it takes
No one cast away
Nobody left behind
Not even the most—problematic kind.
See ... we cannot reproduce the force that tried to kills us off
Cuz if we do—I'm tellin you

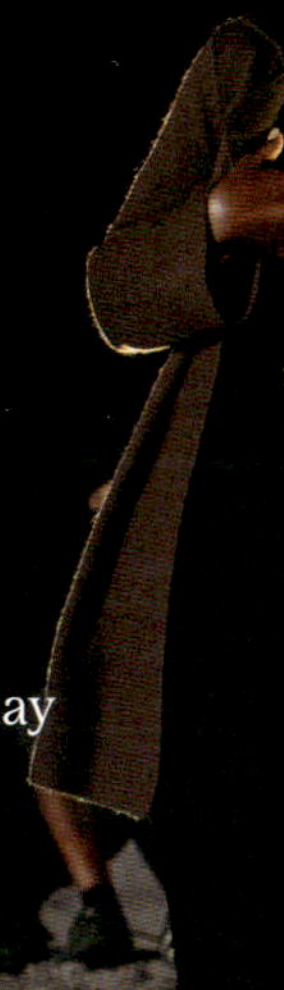

Performance by Funmilola Fagbamila. Photo: Safi Alia Shabaik.

We'll have to pay a real cost
Look what I'm sayin is quite simple
We cannot throw each other away
We are complex and conflicted
Often stuck in our ways
But regardless of all that

We're absolutely here to stay / So let's teach one another / And be open to receive / Because we really need each other

This is a fact. Guaranteed.

A place that affirms that art, creativity, and imagination have intellectual, personal, and political value. No art is neutral; it is either transforming or upholding the status quo.

We embrace a radically expansive understanding of who is an artist and what is creative practice or work.

We believe that art should not be reserved for an elite few and that culture making is a fundamental human and societal experience. Art making is much bigger and more important than the industries or institutions that frequently contain it.

At the same time, we see value in working to change contemporary creative industries. We do this by providing professional tools to trans and cis women, nonbinary people, and people of color and by encouraging them to work professionally in these fields or to create alternative ways of making and sharing work outside of these industries.

Whoever creates things, even for a small audience, is shaping culture. We consciously leverage our privilege as an art space in Los Angeles by operating as a platform for others. By elevating the perspectives and creative work of women and nonbinary artists, makers, and creative practitioners, we are challenging dominant narratives.

Art is a form of dissent.

A place that cultivates a spirit of hospitality and care, the same as we would in our own homes.

We respect the space as we would our own home, and everyone who works here, volunteers, or visits is treated like a friend.

We care for and respect the organization (board, staff, and volunteers), its capacity (our time, our energy, resources), the facility (physical space), and the community (people who are participating), and we expect the same care and respect in return.

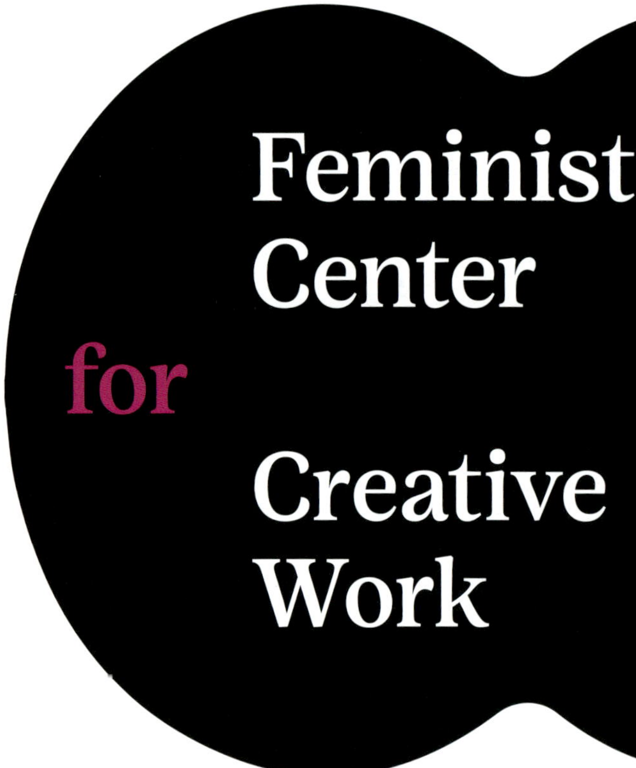

We respect and welcome those who participate in our community in accordance with our core values.

Explicitly intersectional and working toward a feminism prioritizing women of color; queer, trans, and nonbinary folx; and other marginalized communities. We have a zero-tolerance policy for transphobia, racism, anti-Blackness, homophobia, classism, ableism, and body shaming.

We acknowledge and honor that Los Angeles is located on Tongva land and that non-Indigenous Angelenos benefit from a history of settler colonialism and Indigenous erasure. We acknowledge the ongoing struggle of Indigenous folx in the face of colonialism.

We make a dedicated effort to challenge cis-heteropatriarchy,

Conceived and written by the Feminist Center for Creative Work: Sarah Williams, Kate Johnston, Nicole Kelly, Emily Walworth, Salima Allen, Hana Ward, Caitlin Abadir-Mullally, and Lea Rose Sebastianis, 2018, https://corevalues.womenscenterforcreativework.com/.

white supremacy, and exclusionary, colonial-capitalist, and ableist systems.

We are invested in opportunities for cross-cultural exchange, celebrate difference, and work to understand each other across it.

We understand and celebrate that people come from and participate in many different feminist trajectories; we welcome all of them except exclusionary feminism (white feminism and transexclusionary radical feminism, or TERF).

We acknowledge our role as an art space in Los Angeles, a city that is experiencing extreme gentrification and systemic wealth inequality. We work to organize against these forces individually and organizationally within our neighborhood and within our arts community.

We acknowledge that capitalism is the inequitable economic system under which we currently exist and work to improve the material conditions of ourselves and others through the development of collective and communal power and resources.

A space for active participation, a collective project where self-determined ownership is encouraged.

The Feminist Center is a space with many avenues for participation and engagement, including employment, event staffing, programs or workshops, volunteering, the artist-in-residence program, funding through membership and donations, and attendance at events. We view all of these avenues as valid and necessary for the center's continued existence.

We ask that everyone be responsible for their own participation and take care of themselves and that they ask for what they need from those who work here and from each other.

We understand that conflict has the potential to be generative to our evolution and aim to handle it directly and respectfully, with an emphasis on restorative justice.

We appreciate proposing solutions alongside critiques in response to any oversights, gaps, absences, or blind spots. In the words of Octavia Butler, "It's always easier to oppose than to propose."

We are invested in the idea that through experiences shared by each participant, the larger work of building communities and reframing creative conversations unfolds.

A platform for creative support and the redistribution of resources, where we consciously leverage our privilege as an art space in Los Angeles by creating, producing, circulating, and

distributing resources to our interconnected network.

We are intently invested in creating value around the cultural production of trans and cis women and nonbinary folx through supporting their exhibitions, programming, publishing, businesses, and other artistic and creative projects.

As an organization, staff, and community with varied and intersecting privileges around race, class, education, and access, we view it as our duty to consciously leverage that privilege and access to share and provide resources, especially in the form of space, information, money, tools, education, skill-shares, connections/relationships, and opportunities.

We actively engage in the creation, production, distribution, and circulation of tools to take down the white-supremacist-capitalist cis-heteropatriarchy within ourselves, our community, our city, and beyond.

An organization that values experimentation, failure, and process. The Feminist Center is a thoughtful evolution: we are collectively and collaboratively working toward. We are a process, not the product.

As individuals, a community, and an organization, we support nonlinear learning and development.

We understand feminism and creative production as processes that embrace learning through experimentation, failure, and iteration.

We accept that living a feminist life and deconstructing oppressions is a lifelong process and that we all are learning together.

We challenge the notions of success and perfectionism (by-products of capitalism and white supremacy).

A place that cultivates a spirit of abundance, generosity, and joy, with generative collaboration and radical transparency.

We believe in the generative process of collaboration and are excited by the idea of various tendrils of feminism weaving throughout the land.

We embrace collaboration and reject competition by connecting, amplifying, promoting, sharing, and helping individuals, organizations, and projects that share our values.

We endeavor to germinate and grow collectively, through mutual support.

We operate with a mindset of abundance rather than of scarcity, being as generous as possible with money, resources, and time. There is plenty—more is more.

Modeling a world we wish to see by creating space for radical imagining, visioning, and manifesting.

Through our work at the Feminist Center, we are reclaiming our labor, contesting for power, and transforming the dominant narrative.

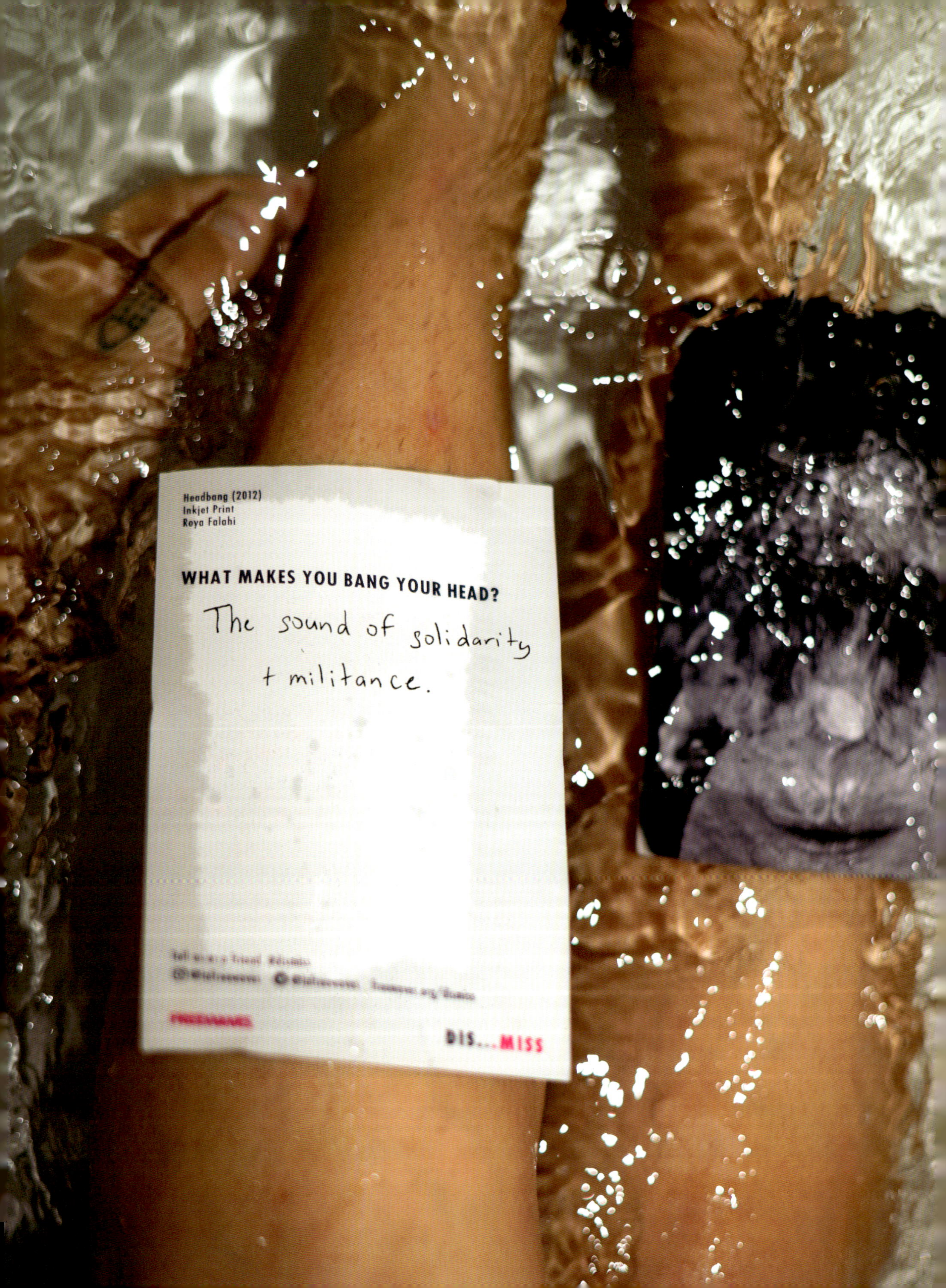

Headbang (2012)
Inkjet Print
Roya Falahi

WHAT MAKES YOU BANG YOUR HEAD?

The sound of solidarity + militance.

DIS...MISS

what makes you bang your head?

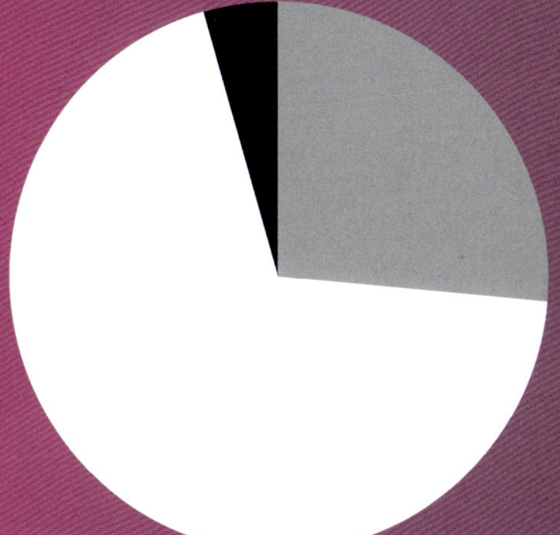

94% **Irritations**

37% **Bliss from music**

6% **Overlap**

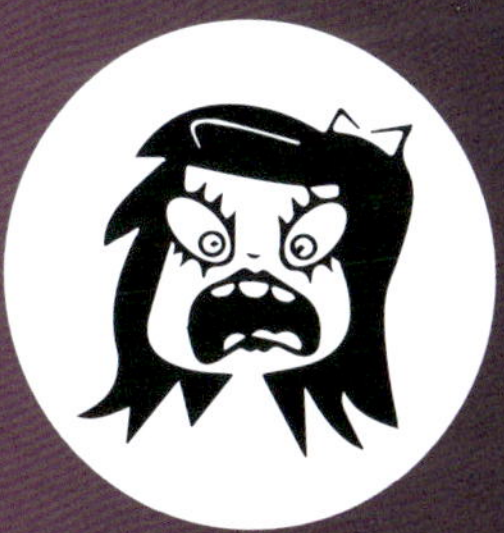

ANALYSIS

Most of people's triggers for banging their heads are external forces that are out of their control, while only a small number feel the need to bang their head due to internal cognitive experiences.

'DIS…MISS, Inconclusive Infographic Animation." Analyzed by Marisa Turesky. Animation designed by Catherine Bell, 2019. Left: Postcard purtrait by Alejandra Sone.

9

who do you worship?

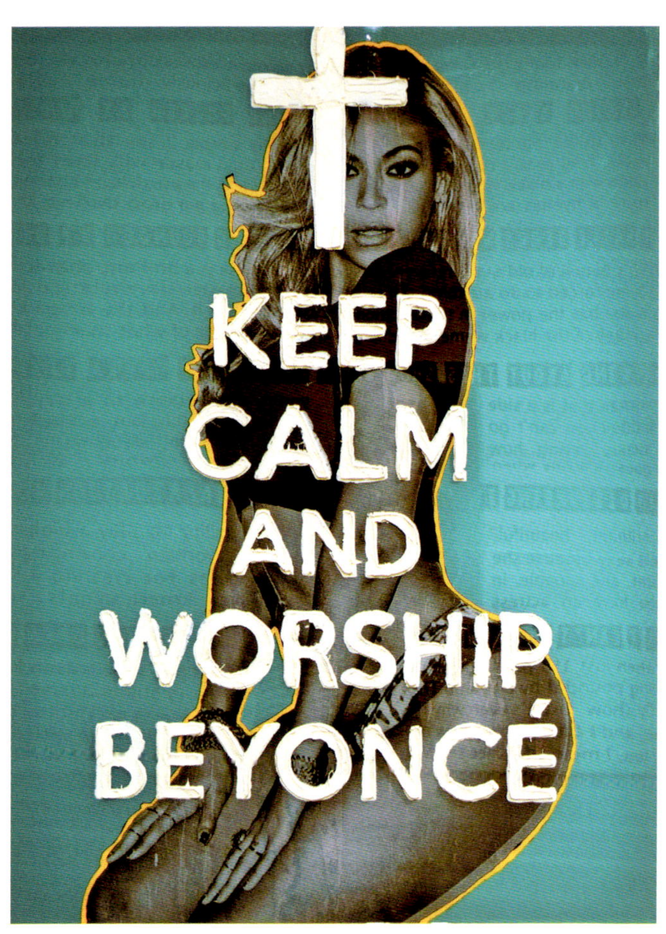

Beyoncé the Feminist (2014), oil on epoxy resin, by April Bey.

#Memesis #whodoyouworship? #BeyoncétheFeminist #AprilBey

Valorie Thomas

April Bey's mixed-media meme painting *Beyoncé the Feminist* (2014) takes an Afrxfuturist stance that deploys strategic speculative moves to subvert the dissective white ethnographic gaze, the anti-Black visual regimes, and the misogynoir saturating the social media "meme pool,"[1] while interrogating the mechanisms through which the public engages Black feminist portraiture and iconographies in the digital age. I initially thought this painting was about liking or not liking Beyoncé and whether what she's doing is actually feminism or just marketing, but Bey's work is not that naive. The painting is a subversive remix of elements that by giving us a freeze frame within a larger movement exposes how mainstreaming puts a faux patina on everything and asks us if, given this situation, we can get past our addiction to liking/not liking and instead get down to strategizing ways of critically focusing more on the feminism than on the fauxness because the faux is not going away anytime soon. Since we can't control the sheer chaotic randomness of the information we see, the painting asks if we can reopen spaces of agency for reclaiming our vision, controlling how we see, compose, and make meaning. It is also a precise example of how to seize space and agency.

Bey initially incorporated the painting into the decoupage laser print series *#whodoyouworship* (2014), which assigns a representative symbol and the message "Keep Calm and … " to each of four women celebrities (Kerry Washington, Miley Cyrus, Lena Dunham, and Beyoncé).[2] The *#whodoyouworship* series suggests that celebrity fulfills an audience's need to identify while contending with uncontainable tensions and indeterminate meanings. *Beyoncé the Feminist* features a photo of Beyoncé in a pinup pose, her face overlaid by a drippily hand-painted white crucifix and, underneath it, the words "KEEP CALM AND WORSHIP BEYONCÉ," proceeding down her torso in white block-lettered caps. Bey's image echoes at least one image circa 2012–2013 generated on the "THE KEEP CALM-O-MATIC" app.[3] It also refers to the profusion of Beyoncé-as-deity memes that emerged following her Video Music Awards performance in 2014. Alongside the other pop goddesses included in Bey's installation,[4] *Beyoncé the Feminist* riffs on the contradictions of feminism in the age of neoliberalism, neocolonialism, globalization, and digital tech; it targets and begins to dissect the compounded problems of anti-Blackness, mixed messages, misinformation, the distortions of corporate marketing, as well as social media deification and its flipside, cancel culture. Bey's work targets the dissonances among definition, the appearance of definition, indeterminacy, and obfuscation; in Bey's iteration of the meme, the layered, thickly painted words "KEEP CALM AND WORSHIP BEYONCÉ" both obscure and reveal the star's iconic image. Her meme portrait works in the context of womanist Afrxfuturism,[5] pushing past superficialities to get at contexts and meanings embedded under surface glamor and a white ethnographic gaze that has historically tended toward framing Black bodies through the pornographic and as sites of inherent violence. The lens it takes on "#Faux-feminism," a term Bey uses in her work,[6] is informed by the interplay among capitalism, cultism, misogyny, media messaging, branding, gender policing, racialized sexual politics, and anti-Blackness. This lens also holds the chaotic refractions of memes in momentary stasis and in doing so challenges viewers to contend with confusing, possibly irresolvable questions. Is Beyoncé a feminist? She says she is, but how do we know? Who gets to

---

1   Madeline Hurren, "The Meme Theory," March 30, 2019, Medium.com, citing Richard Dawkins, *The Selfish Gene* (Oxford: Oxford University Press, 1989), https://medium.com/the-public-ear/the-meme-theory-85c961654e14.

2   Kiara Kensie, "IAMKKKENSIE," blog post, August 29, 2014, https://iamkkkensie.wordpress.com/2014/08/29/wk-1-conversation-with-artist-april-bey/.

3   Tanisha, "Keep Calm and Worship Beyoncé" poster, 2012–2013, https://keepcalms.com/p/keep-calm-and-worship-beyonce/#.

4   April Bey, "Beyoncé's 10 Steps for Becoming a Feminist," *PJ Media*, August 27, 2014, https://pjmedia.com/culture/april-bey/2014/08/27/beyonces-10-steps-for-becoming-a-beyonce-feminist-n155161.

5   Amanda Quinn Olivar, "April Bey: Interview," *Curator*, September 9, 2018, http://curator.site/incarnadine/2018/9/9/april-bey.

6   April Bey, "#Faux-feminism, Womanism and Global Feminism," lecture at the Feminism4D symposium, Main Museum, Los Angeles, May 13, 2017, https://themainmuseum.org/program/feminism4d-symposium/.

say? Is Beyoncé making resistance art, or is her status as a corporate empire simply evidence of late capitalism's ability to absorb and resell resistance? How do consumers navigate the apparent dissonances between Beyoncé and her "feminist" message? In the digital hall of mirrors epitomized by meme culture, can we look to uncertainty, distortion, and indeterminacy as routes to dismantling oppression? Can the fungibility of Blackness in this neoliberal moment of hypercommodification be redeployed to implement liberatory art and social possibilities?[7]

To consider further, Bey's image parodies the viral "Keep Calm and Worship Beyoncé" meme, which parodies the contemporary "Keep Calm and ..." meme, which itself parodies a poster from 1939 invoking British stoicism under wartime duress. Bey's series suggests that celebrity icons help audiences with duress, such as the duress of patriarchy, popular culture, capitalism, race, gender, class, sexuality, mediatization, celebrity, technology, and the crisis of meaning that has proliferated through digital technologies and the internet. The parody becomes an instrument that interrogates social media with questions such as those Bey posed in a panel titled "#Faux-feminism, Womanism and Global Feminism," which Bey hosted for the Feminism4D Symposium organized by students at the Otis College of Art and Design in September 2019: "How has social media perpetuated stagnant 'movements' and the false sense of accomplishment by the privileged and elite via sharable and relatable memes? Will the concept of intersectionality within the feminist movement actually be practiced? How are figures like Chimamanda Ngozi Adichie and Beyoncé relevant and essential in the movement? Are Western feminists doing enough for global issues affecting women internationally?"[8] Following the mode of digital memes, Bey's *Beyoncé the Feminist* collides images, text, traces, allusions, inferences, and visceral responses, evoking endless trajectories of meaning. In fact, Bey's work demands intersectional and Black feminist interrogation, historicization, and theorizing of memes. The painting recalls the war poster as an analog precursor of memes, while underscoring the Christian crucifix as an earlier religious proto-meme; this mashup deploys

counternarratives and counterpolitics meant to subvert faux feminism and regimes of faux knowledge in the neoliberal status quo.

While refusing to dictate conclusive meaning, Bey tasks viewers with reading the painting in relationship to intersectionality, womanism, anti-Blackness theory, and Afrxfuturism. Bey did this portrait around the same time she wrote "Beyoncé's 10 Steps for Becoming a Beyoncé Feminist" (2014),[9] a speculative blog post juxtaposing visuals and comments on "Beyoncé, Inc." alongside branding advice such as "If you have a daughter use her in all of your feminist themed marketing." Both projects pivot on the slippage of memes to ponder the politics of consuming a feminism tethered to tensions among race, gender, class, colorism, grassroots activism, superficiality, and profit. *Beyoncé as Feminist* confronts viewers through our addiction to endorphin-driven "likes" and concomitant vulnerabilities, forcing us to grapple with the reification of feminism and to the issue of whether it is empowering to display Black femme bodies for the sake of pop-culture content in service to corporate wealth. About Beyoncé's song "Formation" (2016), one article stated, "As the Crunk Feminist Collective would say, Beyoncé is here to embrace 'disrespectability politics' in a bid to reclaim black female sexuality *for us, by us.* ... When our very bodies were enslaved and continue to be criminalized, our mastery of the body and the styling of that body is how we reclaimed our sense of liberation."[10] Such performances are possible because of commodification and can at the same time challenge the status quo, sustain liberatory agency, and build community by way of code switching, disidentifications, resignifications, and recontextualizing. Consumers who, like Bey, disrupt and redeploy meaning through editorial alteration further contest the faux effect through intensification, amplification, and managing distortion.

In relation to an Afrxfuturist distortion as ground for harmed but nonetheless potentially powerful ontological formations, *Beyoncé as Feminist* centers "misogynoir[,] ... the intersection of racism, anti-Blackness, and misogyny that Black women experience. The term is specific to Black womanhood, as Misogynoir cannot

---

7   Shannon Winnubst, "TheMany Lives of Fungibility: Anti-Blackness in Neoliberal Times," *Journal of Gender Studies* 29, no. 1 (2020): 102–112, doi:10.1080/09589236.2019.1692193.

8   Bey, "#Faux-feminism."

9   Bey, "Beyoncé's 10 Steps."

10   Janell Hobson, "Beyoncé as Conjure Woman: Reclaiming the Magic of Black Lives (That) Matter," *Ms. Magazine*, February 8, 2016, https://msmagazine.com/2016/02/08/beyonce-as-conjure-woman-reclaiming-the-magic-of-black-lives-that-matter/.

be experienced by women of any other race, but can be perpetuated by people of any gender or race."[11] Bringing misogynoir to bear places Bey's image in relationship to questions of structural violence, in particular normalized violence toward Black girls, women, and femmes. Bey's strategy in framing the Beyoncé portrait the way that she does elicits a counternarrative that underscores resistance. I would describe Bey's strategy as evoking an Afrxfuturist womanism that uses the canvas to contemplate how to dismantle the structural and everyday violence of racialized sexism, colonialism, gender binaries, and anti-Blackness.

While sharply critical of Beyoncé's faux feminism, Bey's work pivots on the simultaneity of multiple readings and foregrounds the mandate to analyze Beyoncé and feminism through race, gender, sex, and class, through what we know of the present moment and context, and in terms of the futures we want given the materials we have to work with in the here and now.[12] The work considers the possibilities of encryption and ambiguity as strategies of resistance, responding to Beyoncé's embodiment of a complex femme persona who "troubles and engages both aggressive and submissive femininity."[13] By challenging assumptions about feminism, the painting serves as a decolonizing counternarrative that deploys indeterminacy to subvert white cis-heteropatriarchal constructs of virtue, respectability, and the game of assigning moral judgment. It demands an intersectional assessment of Beyoncé's performances of normativity, contradiction, speculation, and double consciousness. Bey's work mobilizes intersectionality in its process, materials, and compositional elements, as she notes in stating, "I'm rule-based and thus process-based so my work requires ruthless strategizing and execution. My materials matter and technique is specific to the process."[14] The image performs and frames what happens when feminist principles and normative femininities collide in the same space, in the same Black body, in the same Black femme performance, in spaces defined by the dehumanization and disposability of Black women. Bey's framing calls attention to the fact that Beyoncé's hypersexualized body can be judged antifeminist because she allows herself to be objectified in ways that play to a patriarchal white

consumer gaze at the same time that it can be read as unfettered Black femme eroticism that affirms Black presence and sexuality and as Black body affirmation that endorses agency for the subject and viewer. Everything in the latter reading hinges on literacies related to race and intersectionality as well as to understandings of second- and third-wave Western feminism, decolonial politics, and a transnational Black, Indigenous, people-of-color feminist critique. Similarly, the white cross painted heavily over the performer speaks to Christian ideals of virtue, purity, and femininity that reject female sexual liberation, values that were historically attached to a respect reserved only for white Christian women. From that perspective, the performer's unapologetic sexuality breaking through the visual coverup of the white cross creates a radical tension and rejection of racist suppression of Black women's bodies and sexuality, affirms Black femme vitality, mobility, and agency, and rejects the historical idea that Black women could not claim moral virtue because they were assumed to be the subhuman embodiment of filth, sin, lasciviousness, vulgarity, profanity, and animalistic, savage, hypersexual excess. The futurist turn of the piece resides in Bey's insistence on imagining the possibilities of a disaggregated and expansive literacy of decolonial feminist possibilities, aesthetics, and technological enhancements unconstrained by a white-supremacist gaze or by horizons defined and flattened by misogynoir.

The image and the phrase "Keep calm and worship Beyoncé" together evoke interwoven, dissonant narratives of Black femme performance, embodiment, space, and time travel through lineages of Black performance, and, as such, the work is a speculative expression of womanist Afrxfuturism that opposes misogynoir. It signifies the interlocking systems of oppression that bind and incarcerate Black women in the African diaspora under colonialism and social death—religion, militarism, capitalism, patriarchy, gender, white supremacy, ethnography—and that perpetuate genocide, rape culture, settler colonialism, and social displacement. The image of the Black woman's body bisected and portioned by white lines and the language of war echoes the entertainment-ethnographic display

11 I'Nasah Crockett, "'Raving Amazons': Antiblackness and Misogynoir in Social Media," *Msodel View Culture*, June 30, 2014, https://modelviewculture.com/pieces/raving-amazons-antiblackness-and-misogynoir-in-social-media.

12 Janell Hobson, "Celebrity Feminism: More Than a Gateway," *Signs*, 2016, http://signsjournal.org/currents-celebrity-feminism/hobson/.

13 Anne M. Mitchell, "Beyoncé as Aggressive Black Femme and Informed Black Female Subject," in *The Beyoncé Effect: Essays on Sexuality, Race and Feminism*, ed. Adrienne Trier-Bieniek (Jefferson, NC: McFarland, 2016), 40.

14 Olivar, "April Bey."

and scientific dissection of Sarah Baartman, a Khoisan woman known as the Venus Hottentot, in a "freak show." The bisected Black femme body portraiture is therein both an archive of cultural memory and time travel; questions about what happened in the past and to whom unfold into questions about what is happening now when a Black woman "succeeds" onstage or in any venue controlled by white capitalist market forces. Bey's composition delves further by investigating what results when the roles of pop artist and cultural activist mesh with that of corporate entity and commodity and by asking how we make sense of these fusions. The portrait reminds viewers that intersectionality is often just an abstraction locked inside theoretical discussions rather than practiced as a living structural and organizational principle; it's a reminder that everyone is an intersection on the spectrum of race, class, gender, age, ability, and myriad structural forces as well as in the imagining of existence beyond those constraints. One argument that bears discussion here is that part of the phenomenon of Beyoncé is inseparable from attention to, appreciation of, cultivation of, and ongoing intimate dialogue with audience, in particular the core audience known as the "Beyhive"; in this compositional relationship, the Black audience past-present-future is critical to making meaning and making sense, and the artist depends on this crucial call-and-response interaction as a critical instrument in the process of the work. The audience holds and participates in constructing the integrity of the aesthetic and minds its authenticity, integrity, and well-being as a Black diasporic community.

The complexity of recursive meme processes and of Bey's portrait of the portrait additionally invite us to reach beyond intersectionality by pushing further into complexity rather than retreating. "Keep calm and…" comments ironically on Victorian ideals of controlling women through enforced chastity, repressing emotion, and worshiping the assumed intellectual and moral rectitude and inevitability of an ever-expanding empire of whiteness. In this eugenicist narrative of white superiority and nonwhite failure to deserve the future, the subjugation and killing of people regarded as subhuman heathens had the moral association of good triumphing over evil. The visual layout of Bey's graphic encodes this racialized morbidity; Beyoncé is effectively hanging from the white cross.

Beneath the spectacle of the white crucifix that dominates the top of the image and the command "KEEP CALM AND WORSHIP BEYONCÉ" in block lettering, Beyoncé's pose is seductive. The image works by exposing and simultaneously obscuring Beyoncé's body beneath whiteness and Christian morality, by provoking hyperscrutiny of that body. Beyoncé's face is immediately recognizable, though her right eye, jaw, and hair are partially hidden under the cross. She stares at the viewer, lips parted, neck high, chin flexed into her shoulder, wearing a short-sleeve crop top, bikini briefs, rings, bangles, and a thin chain hanging down between her breasts to hug her bare waistline, spine, arched hips, and bottom. The pose can be read as simply using sex to sell. But at the same time, in an Afrxdiasporic context the pose incorporates sacred postural and choreographic elements that convey vitality, intention, and a performance continuum in which, "in the Americas today, the dancing body still functions within ritual communities as a source of spiritual communication, aesthetic expression, and the site of extraordinary transformations."[15] In an Afrxdiasporic view that recognizes sacred postures, the pose is anything but shameful or a sign of selling out; it is a deliberate kinesthetic connection to an African movement vocabulary, charged by ancestral presence and the ability to transcend suffering.[16]

The image maps the body with the cross and white letters, relying on the cultural habit of hyperscrutinizing Black women's bodies as spectacle to prompt viewers to think about looking as an act of dissection. Bey's vivid yellow outline of the star's body mimics crime-scene tape and a police chalk outline, but in the context of the image's womanist Afrxfuturist underpinnings from a Yoruba-Kongo-derived diasporic spiritual perspective, the yellow alludes to Oshun, the *orisha* (divinity) who reigns over love, eroticism, fertility, and art, whose colors are yellow, pumpkin, and gold, and whose sacred element is freshwater. Bey's palette in *Beyoncé the Feminist* offers a trace allusion to womanist cosmologies that precedes Beyoncé's structuring of her video album *Lemonade* (2016) around the Oshun archetype.

The imposition of the white cross and lettering signify the structural dominance of whiteness and the white-supremacist origins and bars of the

---

15 Yvonne Daniel, *Dancing Wisdom: Embodied Knowledge in Haitian Vodou, Cuban Yuroba, and Bahain Candomblé* (Champaign: University of Illinois Press, 2005), 61.

16 Daniel, *Dancing Wisdom*, 61.

prison-industrial complex. The gold chains accent the cross and lettering, alluding to shackles and encircling Beyoncé's body. Beyoncé's persona is tagged, framed by, and marketed under the terms of whiteness. The primary impression is one of commodification. In one sense, the star's image aligns with white heteropatriarchal standards of submissive feminine beauty insofar as she displays long, blond hair, a small waist, and scant clothing. However, in this portrait Beyoncé's pose visually competes against the enclosure and commodification of the white lettering. Her eyes, even slightly blocked, are bold, balanced, and confrontational as her gaze focuses on a point beyond the white bars, breaking the barrier to convey presence and agency.

The image is a vortex of ambivalences that pivot on the cultural contexts through which we read and play with encoded cues. Not only because of Beyoncé's Blackness but also because of the hybridity of her aesthetic and pop-culture references, her performance and iconography play to Afrxdiaspora aesthetics while engaging mainstream white aesthetics. Multiple cultural literacies bear on this image: the history of the British Empire, British and American colonialism, Western heteropatriarchy, and African and African-derived diasporic knowledges. There are archives in the artist's visual rhetorics and in Beyoncé's performance of Black femme embodiment.

Most particularly, Bey chooses a Beyoncé pose that strategically memes a choreographic stance associated with sacred Kongo Songye Nkisi, Yoruba, and Bambara male and female figures: arching backs, hands often on their thighs, and flexed or kneeling legs embodying ancestral wisdom, presence, and power.[17] The pose emphasizes "sculptural multimetricity ... legs flexing one beat, the shoulders thrusting a second, the head asserting a third."[18] Although occurring in different contexts, African and African-derived aesthetic and spiritual traditions are related across cultures.[19] Beyoncé's pose in this meme bridges the sacred and secular to rearticulate[20] the body through African-derived spiritual thought, dance, and music filtered through Middle Passage memories, gaps, dissonances, and digitally amplified double consciousness. In dialogue with Afri-

can diaspora expression across time and place, the pose insists that viewers acknowledge the critical importance of choreographic gesture and flexion[21] and that these elements are imbued with a sense of self-conviction asserted across time. The pose is not ethnography so much as narration of a self excavating itself from layers of structural violence and amnesia to move into a precarious future. Performing it forces a womanist Afrxfuturist aesthetic into the midst of mainstream popular culture.

Despite the inescapable taint of commodification, the pose embodies a Black femme consciousness that rejects both a world of conclusions defined by anti-Blackness and a dissecting white ethnographic gaze. By reclaiming the erotic, it also resists the shaming of Black bodies and rejects the pornographic fantasies that underpin colonialist ethnography. The pose evokes Kongo-derived sacred art as performance to occupy and recode the space of mainstream pop culture. Beyoncé's mediatized body serves capitalism, but at the same time she counters the aesthetic logics of the dominant culture by challenging viewers to recode Black femme power through ancient knowledge about music and dance. The performer's investment in dance that conveys ancestral principles is more than entertainment because it embodies Afrxdiasporic cosmological, spatial, kinesic, vernacular, and womanist literacies; it actively resists the annihilating dissections of an anti-Black gaze.

Bey's Beyoncé is stationed in ambivalence toward aesthetics, humanism, gender, race, performance, and desire. Using the problem of celebrity as impetus, Bey addresses the duality of a Black female body that is organized by capitalist whiteness. This is also a subversively resistant and self-reorganized body and reclaims the story of Sarah Baartman. She was a South African Khoisan woman taken to Europe in 1810 by handlers and forced to perform as "The Venus Hottentot." Baartman was displayed as the antithesis of femininity and beauty. She was dehumanized, fetishized, and marketed for her perceived excessive buttocks, genitals, and ugliness (insofar as beauty was defined as whiteness), all of which were equated with savagery,

---

17 Daniels, *Dancing Wisdom*, 57–64.
18 Robert Plant Armstrong, "Thompson: African Art in Motion: Icon and Act in the Collection of Katherine Coryton White," *Studies in Visual Communication* 6, no. 2 (1980): 79, https://repository.upenn.edu/cgi/viewcontent.cgi?article=1104&context=svc.
19 Daniels, *Dancing Wisdom*, 2–3, 56.
20 Daniels, *Dancing Wisdom*, 74–78.
21 Daniels, *Dancing Wisdom*; Armstrong, "Thompson," 78.

subhumanity, immorality, and proof of white superiority.[22] Early eugenicists used her to rationalize slavery and planned extinction. *Beyoncé as Feminist* alludes to and reclaims the humanity of Baartman's life as a sentient being, while also alluding both to the history of Black performance and portraiture that is still present in the resonance of every Black femme performance and portrait as well as to the heinous treatment Baartman received in the process of her exploitation, commodification, and dissection.

Bey's meme centers Beyoncé's buttocks; the Black femme body in performance of the commercial brand known as "Beyoncé" is thoroughly fetishized in the star's branding and commodification. If we are in any way sickened by this, it may be that the dehumanization is all too familiar—we may react to the possibility that we, as spectators, are implicated as its instruments. Bey is unafraid in using her own ambivalence to draw out these questions and possibilities and to let viewers experience discomfort and shock. In the context of the history of the mediatizing and study of Black women's bodies in the West and of the work's framing of sexualization, Bey places Beyoncé in direct art historical lineage and political relationship to Baartman. Sarah, or Saartje, Baartman was the first Black superstar, yet her real name is unknown (something like "Ssehura"?).[23] She was famous throughout Europe and the West. She was turned into a meme, maybe the first Black meme. The repatriation of her remains and their final internment in her homeland represented the reclaiming of both her humanity and Black humanity. Baartman was not the only Black person who was exploited as a specimen and scientific oddity, but she was the most widely advertised and heavily mediatized.[24] Historically and aesthetically, Baartman is Beyoncé's ancestor, and the resonance raises the possibility that she is ancestor to every Black person who has to perform on any level on a stage controlled by a dissecting white ethnographic or popular gaze and to try to survive an anti-Black economic system built on commodifying Blackness. Baartman became emblematic of the racialized gender economy of colonialism; she is an indelible presence who continues to resonate in the collective racial imagination. Baartman was made to exist as the essence of nonexistence, the absence of the human as defined by Enlightenment philosophy and scientific racism, the malformed inverse of idealized whiteness and proof of "natural" racial inferiority.

When Baartman died at age twenty-six, she was dissected for medical research. Her genitals, brain, and skeleton were displayed at the Musee de l'homme for 160 years and were not repatriated until the Khoisan and the South African government under Nelson Mandela litigated to have Baartman's remains interred in the Western Cape in 2002. Many contemporary womanist Afrxfuturist artists allude to Baartman as an individual tragedy and as fundamental Black femme history; she was one among millions destroyed in the trade of Black body parts during slavery.[25] Baartman emblematizes the long history of Africans being dehumanized by a pornographic, white, pseudoethnographic gaze while performing on white stages; the white audience's role is one of performing both disinterested objectivity and offering judgments of moral and cultural fitness, mapping, partitioning, and consuming Black bodies in the process. This cultural script continues to normalize centuries of fetishizing and dissecting Black women's bodies while perpetuating stereotypes of hypersexuality, insanity, and the classification of Black bodies as excessive, animalistic, chaotic, and grotesque.

Baartman was the first Black woman superstar. The gruesome character of her captivity and dehumanization haunts every performance in which Black women must negotiate structural violence and the dissections of a controlling white ethnographic gaze. *Beyoncé as Feminist* is an unflinching critique of faux feminism yet foregrounds Beyoncé's body in a lineage of ancient African and Afrxdiasporic expression that disseminates Black femme spiritual literacies and performance, turning the question "Who do you worship?" especially toward all feminists who could do better on incorporating intersectionality, confronting anti-Blackness, and resisting misogynoir.

---

22 Deborah Willis, "Introduction: The Notion of Venus," in *Black Venus 2010: They Called Her Hottentot*, ed. Deborah Willis (Philadelphia: Temple University Press, 2010), 3–12.

23 Willis, "Introduction."

24 Willis, "Introduction."

25 Harriet A. Washington, *Medical Apartheid: The Dark History of Medical Experimentation on Black Americans from Colonial Times to the Present* (New York: Doubleday, 2006).

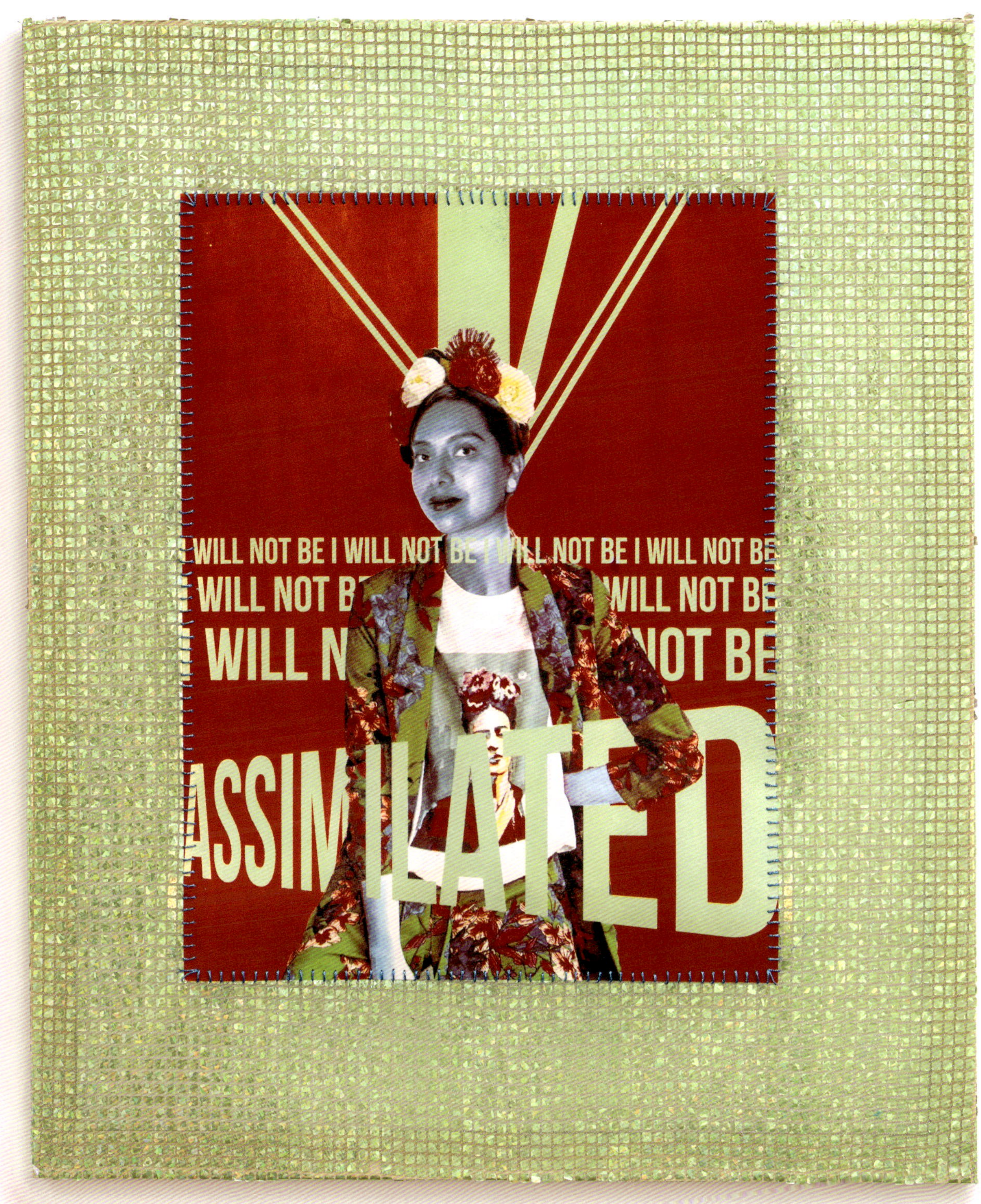

AntiAssimilation Line (Green Chunky Sequins) III (January 2022), CMYK screen print with screen-printed glitter hand-sewn into faux fur, 38 × 32 in., by April Bey.

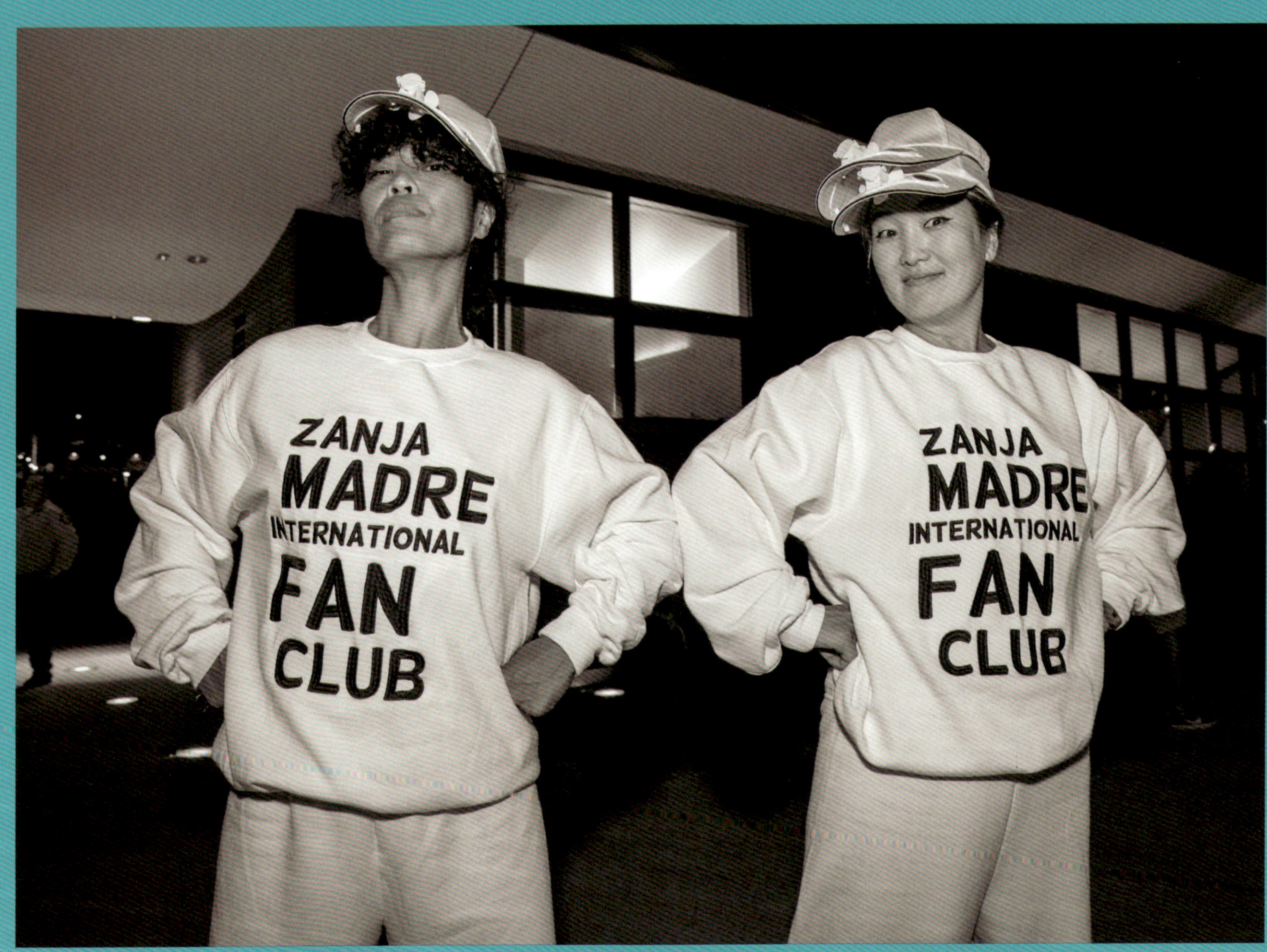

Reanne Estrada and C. Ree. Photo: Monica Orozco.

Zanja Madre International Fan Club 2.0
Reanne Estrada and C. Ree

Essential to the expansion of a then new Los Angeles, the Zanja Madre, or "Mother Ditch," was LA's original aqueduct, from its beginnings in 1781 until its abandonment in 1904. It was constructed largely by "unfree" Indian labor produced through a system of indentured servitude and racialized criminalization, which continues today (i.e., in freeway construction and road maintenance). In 2001, a piece of the Zanja was accidentally uncovered by city workers in what is now the Los Angeles State Historic Park. The physical presence of the artifact enabled the site's official "historic" designation. It remains exposed today.

Through the lens of fandom, Ree + Estrada developed a "club" of fans swarming on this exposed remnant, with a large electric fan silhouette rotating on the retaining wall behind the LA Metro Gold Line tracks. These fans made their pilgrimage from as far away as Oakland and San Diego. Along with fan portraits, a star-naming campaign, and a "walking agenda," two performances took place throughout the evening: (1) Fanatic Fan Distribution of Zanja Madre Fan Club 2.0 hand fans; and (2) Free Water Special Pour (water poured into white cups for passers-by). In the latter performance, structured as a call-and-response, Estrada + Ree bat back and forth the romance of LA's origin myth, the colonial and queering discourses used to exploit Native people, and notions of "free" resources, including labor and the very water we consume today. Faced with the turmoil within the Zanja Madre historical record, Ree + Estrada portray a fan club 2.0—a revised, conflicted, yet still heartfelt fandom in the midst of grappling with a fractured reverence for its idol.

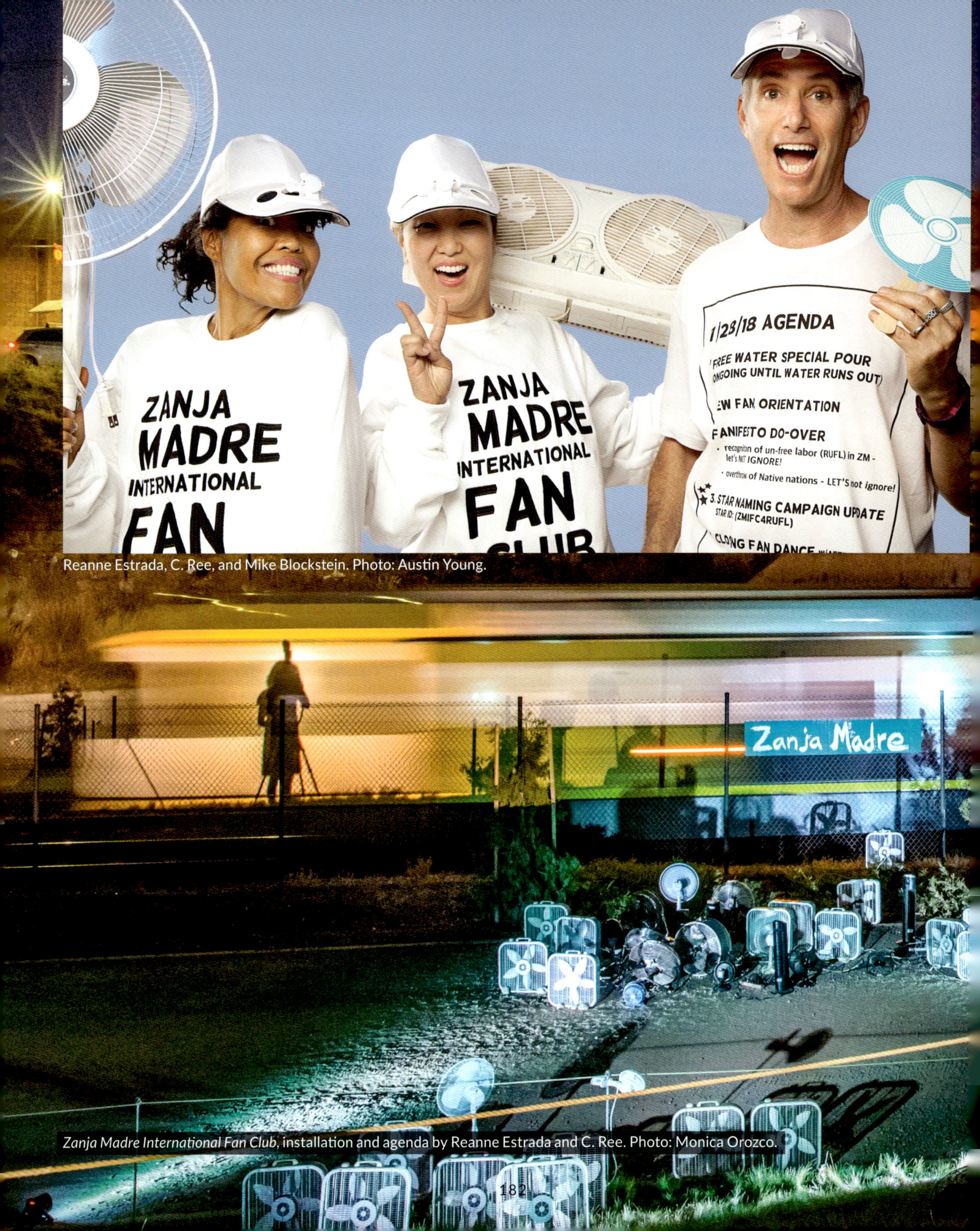

Reanne Estrada, C. Ree, and Mike Blockstein. Photo: Austin Young.

Zanja Madre International Fan Club, installation and agenda by Reanne Estrada and C. Ree. Photo: Monica Orozco.

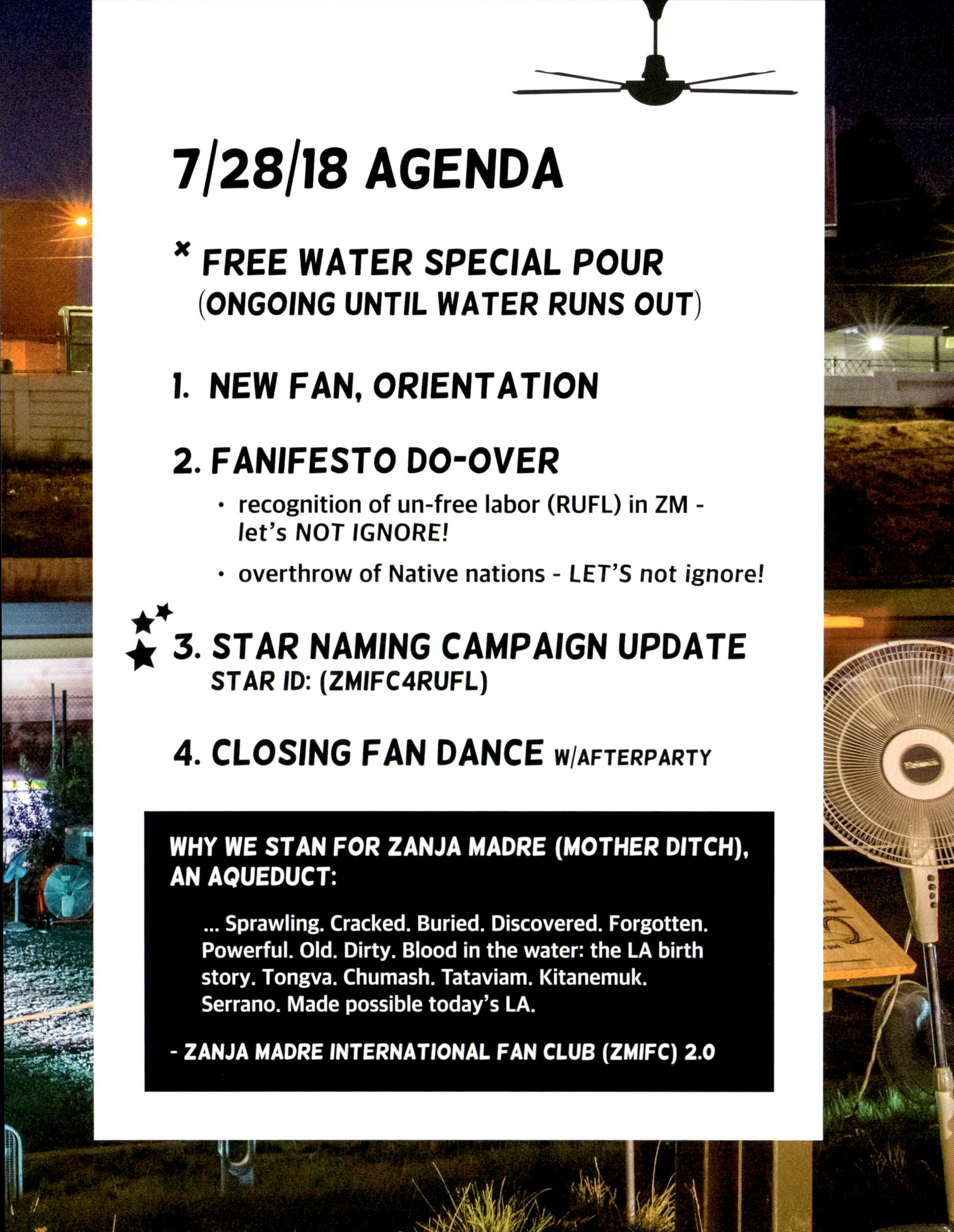

7/28/18 AGENDA

* FREE WATER SPECIAL POUR
(ONGOING UNTIL WATER RUNS OUT)

1. NEW FAN, ORIENTATION

2. FANIFESTO DO-OVER
- recognition of un-free labor (RUFL) in ZM - let's NOT IGNORE!
- overthrow of Native nations - LET'S not ignore!

3. STAR NAMING CAMPAIGN UPDATE
STAR ID: (ZMIFC4RUFL)

4. CLOSING FAN DANCE W/AFTERPARTY

WHY WE STAN FOR ZANJA MADRE (MOTHER DITCH), AN AQUEDUCT:

... Sprawling. Cracked. Buried. Discovered. Forgotten. Powerful. Old. Dirty. Blood in the water: the LA birth story. Tongva. Chumash. Tataviam. Kitanemuk. Serrano. Made possible today's LA.

- ZANJA MADRE INTERNATIONAL FAN CLUB (ZMIFC) 2.0

BLACK LIVES MATTER

These are the results of our collective efforts.

The Black Lives Matter Global Network is as powerful as it is because of our membership, our partners, our supporters, our staff, and you. Our continued commitment to liberation for all Black people means we are continuing the work of our ancestors and fighting for our collective freedom because it is our duty.

Every day we recommit to healing ourselves and each other and to cocreating alongside comrades, allies, and family a culture where each person feels seen, heard, and supported.

We acknowledge, respect, and celebrate differences, and commonalities.

We intentionally build and nurture a beloved community that is bonded together through a beautiful struggle that is restorative, not depleting.

We are unapologetically Black in our positioning. In affirming that Black Lives Matter, we need not qualify our position. To love and desire freedom and justice for ourselves are prerequisites for wanting the same for others.

We see ourselves as part of the global Black family, and we are aware of the different ways we are impacted or privileged as Black people who exist in different parts of the world.

We are guided by the fact that all Black lives matter, regardless of actual or perceived sexual identity, gender identity, gender expression, economic status, ability, disability, religious beliefs or disbeliefs, immigration status, or location.

We make space for transgender brothers and sisters to participate and lead. We are self-reflexive and do the work required to dismantle cisgender privilege and uplift Black trans folk, especially Black trans women who continue to be disproportionately impacted by trans-antagonistic violence.

We build a space that affirms Black women and is free from sexism, misogyny, and environments in which men are centered.

We practice empathy. We engage comrades with the intent to learn about and connect with their contexts. We make our spaces family-friendly and enable parents to fully participate with their children. We dismantle the patriarchal practice that requires mothers to work "double shifts" so that they can mother in private even as they participate in public-justice work.

We disrupt the Western-prescribed nuclear-family structure requirement by supporting each other as extended families and "villages" that collectively care for one another, especially our children, to the degree that mothers, parents, and children are comfortable. We foster a queer-affirming network. When we gather, we do so with the intention of freeing ourselves from the tight grip of heteronormative thinking or, rather, from the belief that all in the world are heterosexual (unless s/he or they disclose otherwise).

We cultivate an intergenerational and communal network free from ageism. We believe that all people, regardless of age, show up with the capacity to lead and learn.

We embody and practice justice, liberation, and peace in our engagements with one another.

We work vigorously for freedom and justice for Black people and, by extension, all people.

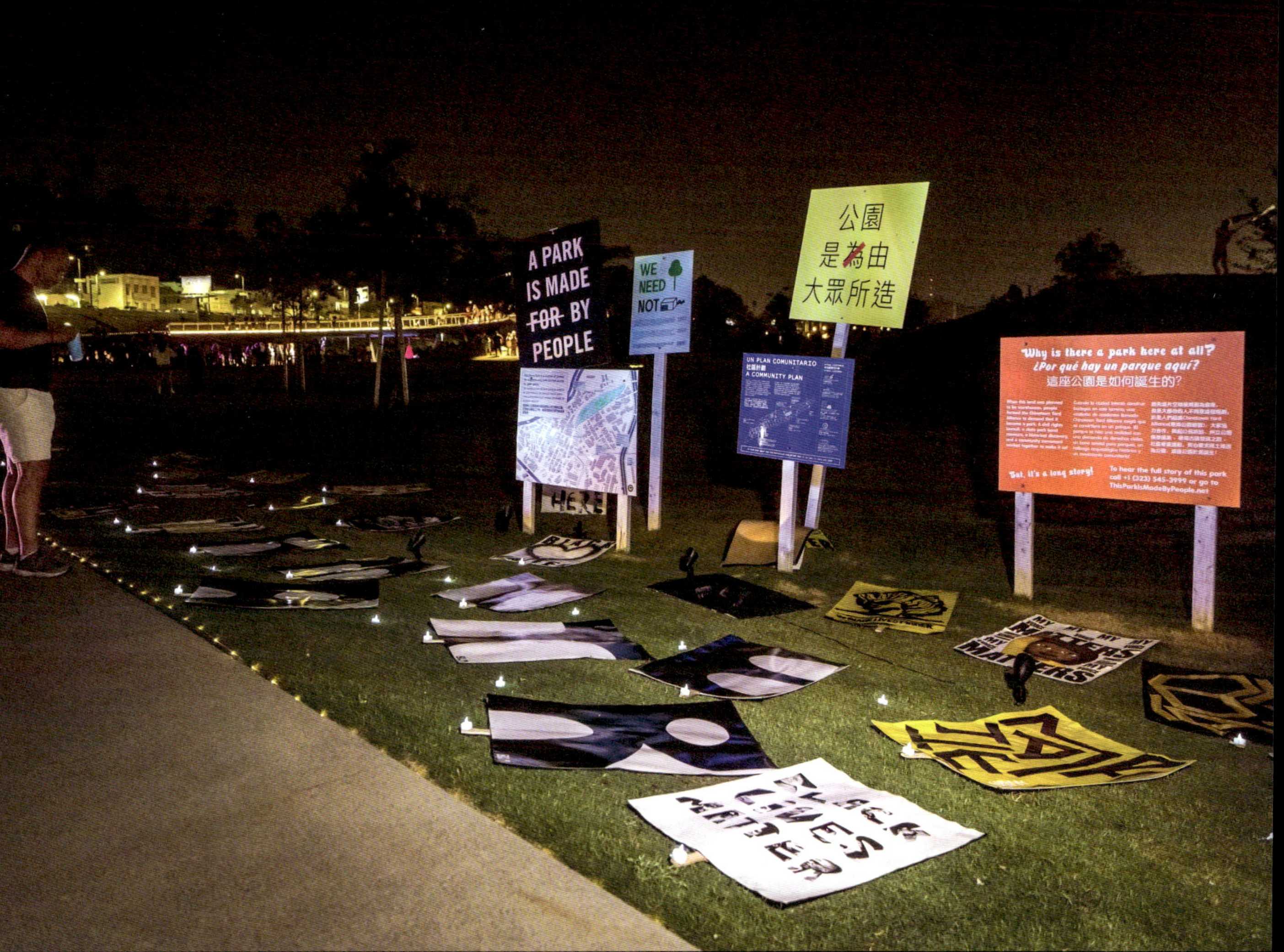

Black Lives Matter mission. Photo: Monica Orozco.

We work vigorously for **freedom and justice for Black people** and, by extension, **all people**.

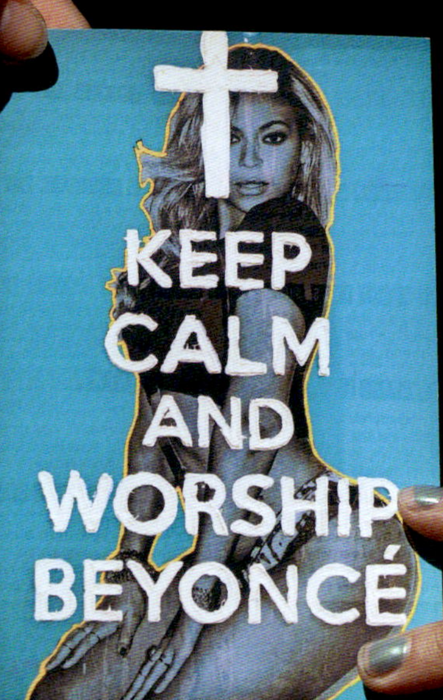

KEEP
CALM
AND
WORSHIP
BEYONCÉ

Who do you worship?

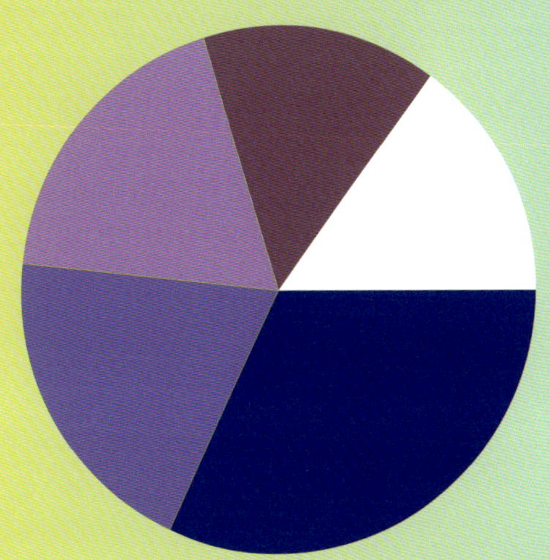

I used to worship god, but as I get older, I started to worship the universe and what it offers.

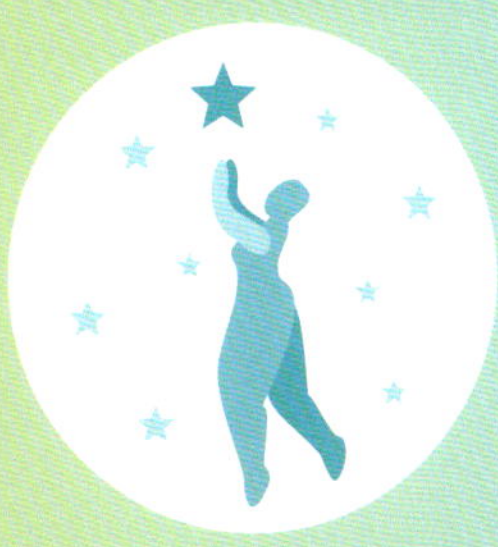

ANALYSIS

People worship **women** (**26%**) more than anything or anyone else. About one-third of the women worshipped were celebrities, another third was family (e.g. grandmother, mother, daughter). And the final third was women as a general concept.

"DIS...MISS, Inconclusive Infographic Animation." Analyzed by Marisa Turesky. Animation designed by Catherine Bell, 2019. Left: Postcard portrait by Alejandra Sone.

10

what are they
singing?

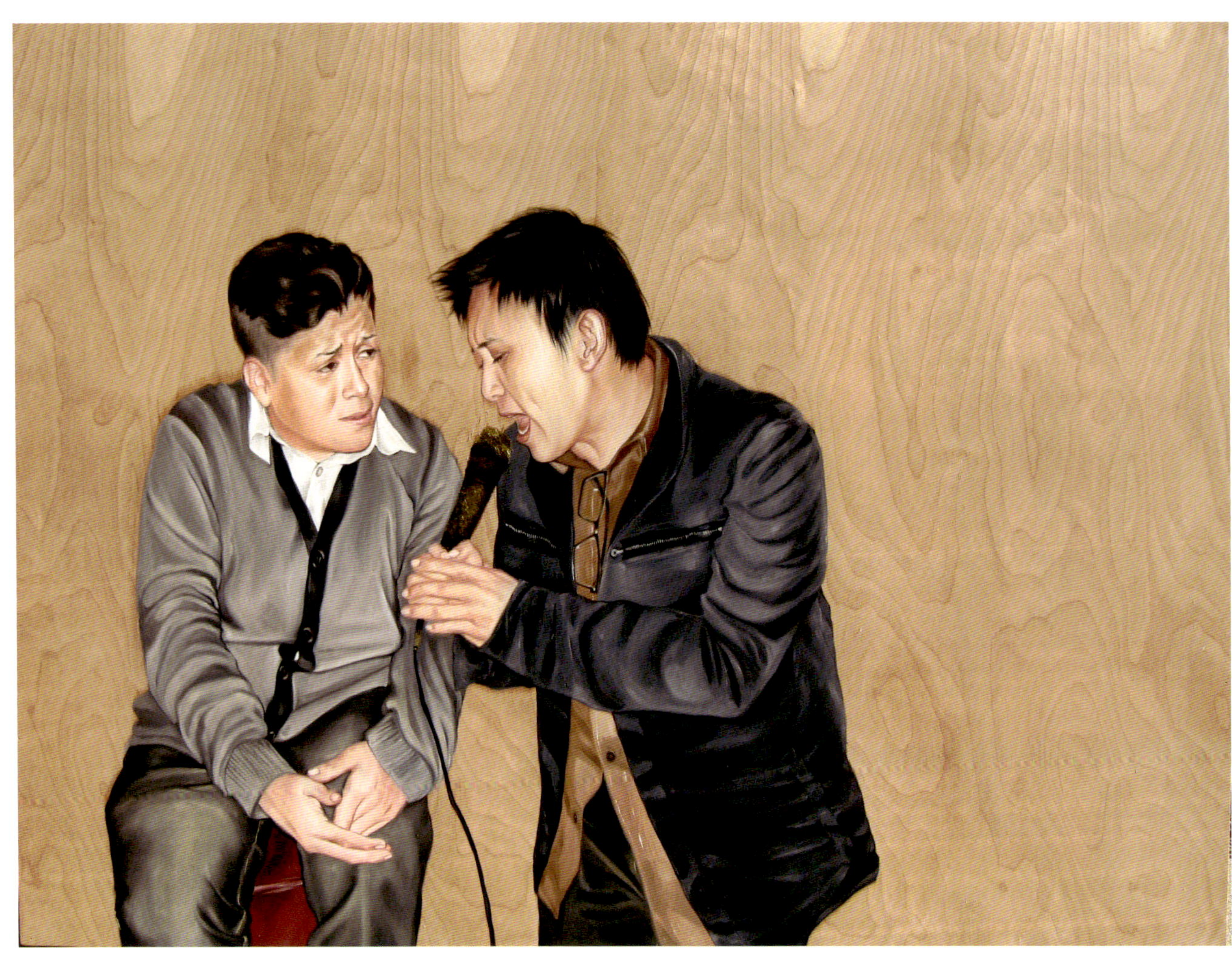

Raqui and Tongson, Smogcutter Karaoke (2013), oil, gold leaf on wood panel, by Shizu Saldamando.

Butch Love at the Smog Cutter
Karen Tongson

What are the choices we make when we perform our gender? What do other people see, and, perhaps more to the question in Shizu Saldamando's painting *Raqui and Tongson, Smogcutter Karaoke* (2013), set at a karaoke bar, what gender(s) do you hear?

I am one of the subjects of Saldamando's painting, which was sourced from a photograph taken during a night out with the artist at the legendary Los Angeles watering hole the Smog Cutter, which has since shut down. I remember the gender I inhabited then in that image. It isn't the same gender I inhabit now, though to most eyes it may appear relatively unaltered, with the exception of some minor modifications to my haircut.

At the time, I was in many respects broken: struggling with my own destructive experiments with a certain kind of emotional and erotic power I associated with masculinity, with being "a player." I was trying to find power in a space of feeling powerless in other arenas of life, such as my professional life. Now I've settled into myself, into my relationship with others, and into my presentation of masculinity as if it were a favorite pair of well-worn, broken-in jeans.

The expressions of both figures in the painting, Brown, masculine-presenting butches in the throes of an exchange, impart some clues to the gender performance I was leaning into at that juncture in my life. The singer, open-mawed, brow-furrowed, is reaching for something—maybe a note beyond her range. Her listener is poised on a stool right next to her and shares a similar expression, albeit with her mouth closed, but knowing instead of searching. Sympathetic to the search and along for the ride but not as unmoored as the singer trying to find the right note.

Any observer of this painting can fantasize about the repertoires, the kinds of music that might score this exchange and scene of striving. Asked to produce responses to this image at an LA Freewaves event about gender at the University of Southern California (USC)

Annenberg in 2018, some viewers who focused on this painting assumed we were singing love ballads and songs of heartbreak. Others speculated upon a repertoire based on how we look, in one instance assuming we were singing the Smiths, who are known to be beloved by Latinx and queer people of color, especially in Los Angeles. Most respondents to the image guessed that we were luxuriating in songbooks from the 1980s. The '80s, after all, bear a powerful association with karaoke itself, not only for its capacity to trigger nostalgia but also for its stylistic suitability to hamming it up with power ballads, rock falsettos, and big feelings.

Pop-music repertoires, the kind we animate in scenes of karaoke like this one, are our own archives of feeling, to invoke the concept introduced by Ann Cvetkovich.[1] They touch upon the intimate not only as it unfolds in relationships between individuals but also in our commitment to our politics, which are bound up with our attachment to certain places. The popular is too often considered inconsequential, not serious enough to be worthy of art or representation. But the intimacies that popular music inspires can sometimes become the source of our deepest commitments beyond ourselves: to the others around us and to our communities. Popular music is how we find each other. And, depending on what we like to listen to, it helps us find others who share the same passions, not only for the music itself but also for what it opens us up to, how it shapes us, and how it defines our roles in the world.

The third figure in this painting, the one represented by a polished wood background without any other distinguishing features, is the Smog Cutter itself—the karaoke bar in Virgil Village/East Hollywood where this scene was first captured. Its blankness—indeed, its unrepresentability—seems all too apt. Long an anchor of sociability, the space, which shut down in November 2017, became just as ephemeral as the assignations, negotiations, and aspirations nurtured there. As with so many of the spaces where queers and people of color gather, the Smog was eventually lost to the economic ascendancy of the neighborhood and the inflated property values that followed.

It is right that we cannot see the space itself in this painting because the Smog Cutter's significance resides beyond its actual walls, lights, or tattered Naugahyde

---

1   In her book *An Archive of Feelings: Trauma, Sexuality, and Lesbian Public Cultures* (Durham, NC: Duke University Press, 2003), the scholar Ann Cvetkovich explains how the eclectic archives of lesbian public cultures, including performance, literature, and activism, help queers work in and through both individual and collective traumas.

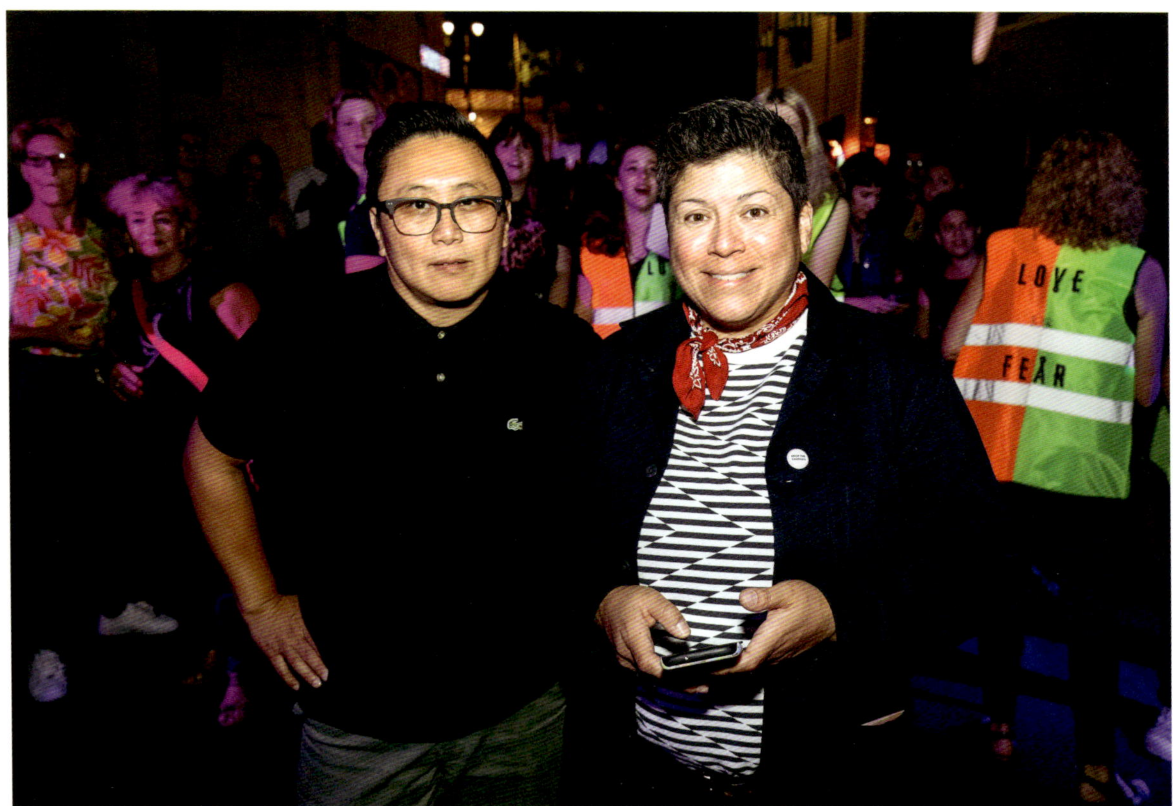

Karen Tongson and Raquel Gutiérrez, public karaoke at *LOVE &/OR FEAR*.

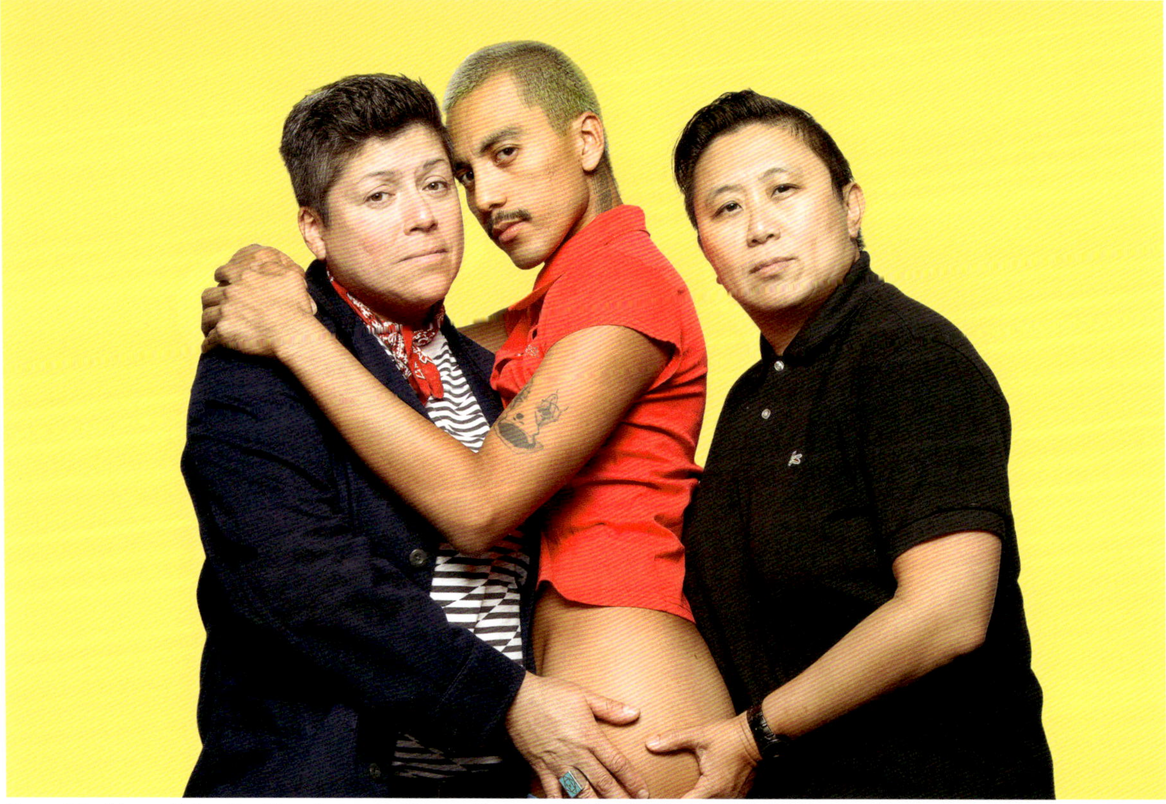

Raquel Gutiérrez, Sebastian Hernández, and Karen Tongson. Photo: Austin Young.

stools. What remains and what endures are the intimacies that were crafted there through the seemingly debased activity of karaoke shared between queers, immigrants, dreamers, the broken, and the self-possessed. Karaoke is not a dignified pastime in US culture but is often depicted as a scene of excess and shamelessness fueled by the imbibing of a few too many substances. Its association with "foreign" cultures, in particular Asians and Asian Americans, further alienates the respectable mainstream from the mere concept of karaoke. The Smog Cutter harbored and nurtured all manner of intoxicated "strangers" and others. Who are the people who surround the subjects of the image? Whom do we see there—did we see there? Who are these two at the focal point of a painting with a title that belies how important this particular place is, which would otherwise go unnamed?

Some viewers might assume the two are queer lovers. Many eyes are trained to see "homosexuality" through the lens of sameness: a mirroring desire for the same sex, the same gender, even though generations of LGBTQ+ studies scholars have tried desperately to break us of this way of seeing. Responding to the postcard version of this painting, an audience member at the Freewaves event at USC Annenberg noted, "They look like a couple. This is one of the few opportunities they could be themselves and feel comfortable in public." If this were the case, the fact that this scene transpires at the Smog Cutter would carry even greater meaning. It would, in effect, queer the space, even though the space is already queered by virtue of this pair's presence, lovers or not.

A viewer with a deeper sense of the artist Shizu Saldamando's body of work, which focuses on scenes and subcultures that often remain unnoticed, found this image resonant with the other scenes of intimacy the artist has rendered: "I am intrigued by what they are feeling and their relationship. ... Now that I see it is Shizu's work, perhaps I understand why I am attached to it. I love the pathos and intimacy of her work."

To be sure, there is love between the two. There is pathos. And there is intimacy. There is a resonance between them that negotiates the dramas of the erotic—not (as some viewers assume) as it might exist between them as individuals but as they see each other negotiating their desires for the things that are not them, that are beyond them. It is a love beyond the couple and toward the communal. It is a vision of the commu-

nal as politics amid a scene that feels personal and intimate. What makes itself apparent in the painting, in other words, bleeds beyond what it captures into the practices of queer, everyday life, which is to say a queer, everyday politics. It is a politics of solidarity and endurance sustained by friendship, not simply by romantic relationships.

"Raqui" sees "Tongson's" pain. She witnesses her efforts at exorcism through balladry, her reaching for something in that moment beyond the high note, that might fail or succeed spectacularly. She is there for the inevitable failure even after the high note is achieved, and the other patrons erupt in cheers. She is there for the come down after "Tongson" wields the mic and peacocks around the bar but ends up shattering her life outside of that magical space. She is also there when it becomes her turn at the mic, when it's her turn to reach, to succeed, and to fail spectacularly, while "Tongson" watches and listens.

One of the best responses to this image was probably meant to be flippant but ended up ringing truest: "I don't know what they're singing, but probably something about butch love." Indeed, butch love is what Shizu Saldamando has captured in this image. Butch love models a form of politics forged from the intimate, from the "safety" these figures insist upon in a space we can ostensibly know nothing about just from looking at the image. Butch love is about the safety—and risk—we create through our emotional labors and about the modes of survival we improvise through repertoires and activities that are popular and thus are sometimes construed as debased. Saldamando's painting offers a scene of friendship, filiality, support, and even the skepticism that is absolutely necessary between intimates. Which song is inevitably irrelevant, or, rather, there are too many songs to choose from that would be apt and that were actually sung not only in this scene but also in others like it. I honestly can't remember what I was singing when the photograph was taken. Whatever the song was, it most likely captured the damaged, wounded, and destructive masculinity I inhabited then, which was kind of like Don Draper's before he went to Esalen to dry out and meditate. (I'm definitely Don post-Esalen and enlightenment now.) But what was said before, what the feelings were during, and what healing there was after will never be forgotten.

COVEN
Zackary Drucker

We had a date with the moon. all blank surface and blinding endless light. we were opening a portal to an illuminated sphere. which is everything that ever happened. and everything that will ever be.

We were opening a part of our mind. which could only be opened once, and right now. In the shape of the only moon we've ever known. In the presence of this moon, we are looking at our phones and it is epic. It is an epic fucking nightmare, and not at all boring.

This is everything you ever wanted and it's something you'll never touch.

We are fools in love, stumbling through darkness. we are gasping and breathless. split open and splitting open. We are working. crouched forward, seated or standing. Heads bent, faces illuminated.

We are connecting and not connecting. We are stretched thin and disembodied. We are asking questions we cannot retain the answers to. We are seeking truth. or an emotional high. or attention. or affirmation. We are assholes, but we are yearning. We are yearning to create something new, and yet we are ancient. We are ancient survivors.

We are illuminated by our phones photographing the moon. We are transmitting the image to our followers who are also on their phones. We are both doing it and telling them that we are doing it. We are fucking them into oblivion and they love it. It is their definition of joy.

We are touching them with our hands and with skin stretched across our bodies. We are skin-stretched bodies and we are touching you with our words. We are moving along you like a landscape, positioning you as a horizon. We are dwelling on you as a picture that we find to escape.

The percentage of this that you can absorb is diminishing. We will never be back to where we were. Even if we return for the rest of our lives.

We are time travelers. We will die feeling like things are worse than when we were born. Our descendants will colonize space and produce garbage that will remain suspended and preserved forever. That timeless garbage is the definition of forever.

We are holy because we are alive. We are chosen for and we are choosing you. We are coded and monumental. Every human who has ever existed has perceived the moon. Imagine the scope of everything that has seen this moon.
We look in love or nothing at all. Sadness, maybe, but we never look in shame. We are shameless. We are prideless. We are constantly replacing everything. We are taking our home. We are being taken home.
We are shameless because we are free.
We are covered in neutral feelings, cowering over our phones to quell and stoke the anxiety of being on the edge of extinction. We are making films about it. Every single day. So much money spent visualizing our extinction.

E
X
T
I
N
C
T
I
O
N

We were hellbent on creating magic and loving each other. We hijacked you into our dreams to save you from your darkness. But there's no saving you from yourself. As if the love you pulled out of us wasn't enough, would never end, would never run out.

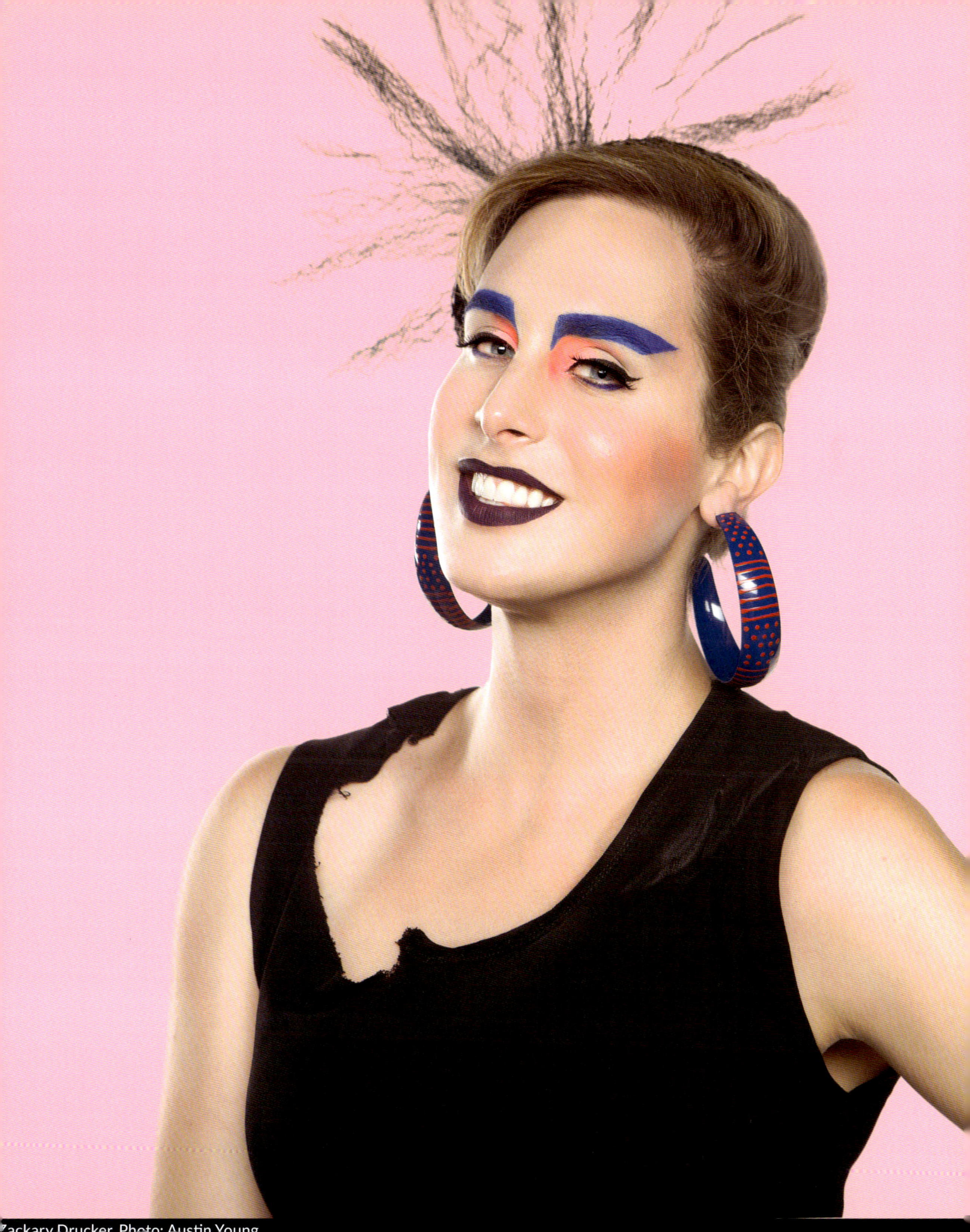

Zackary Drucker. Photo: Austin Young

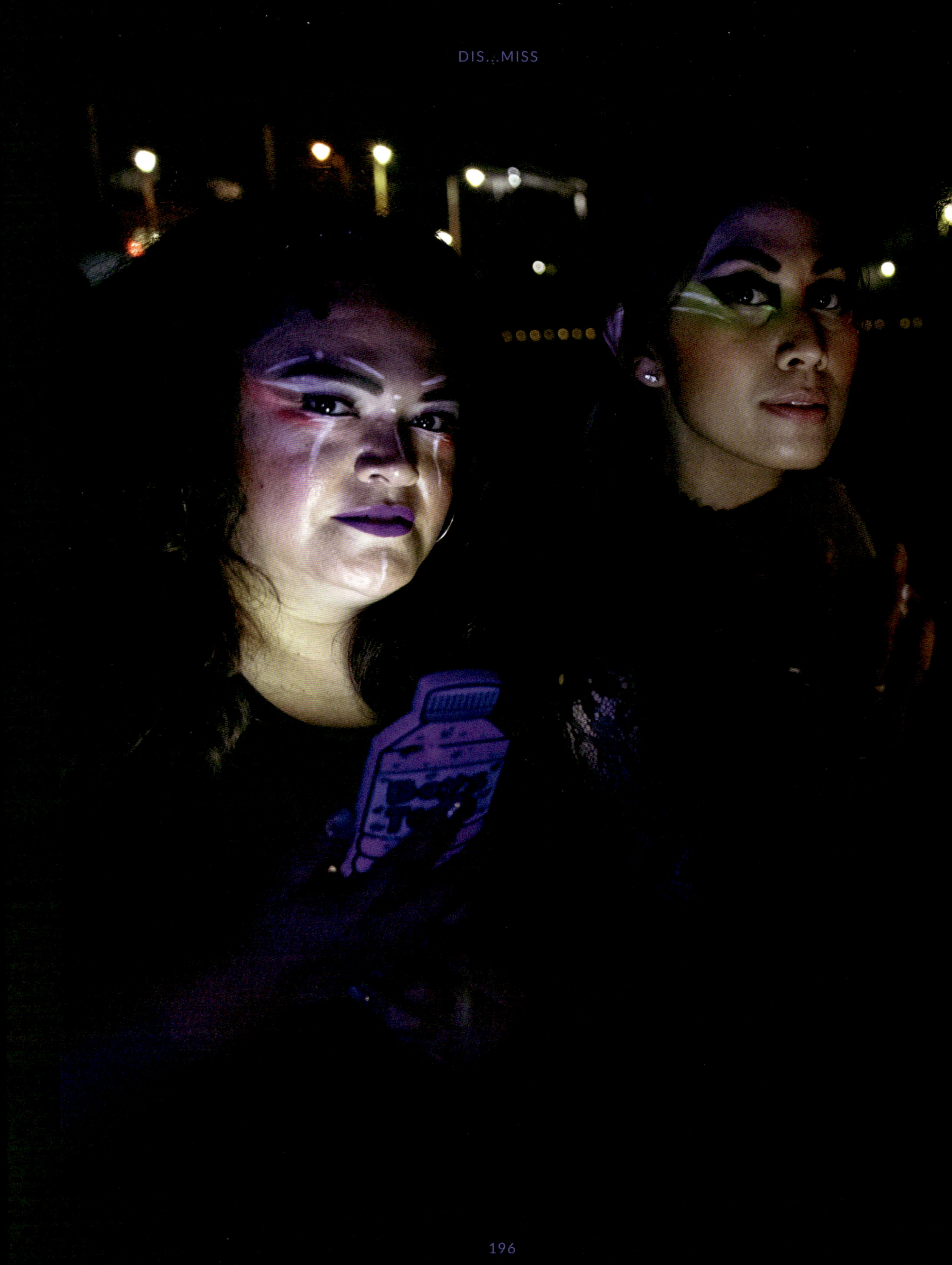

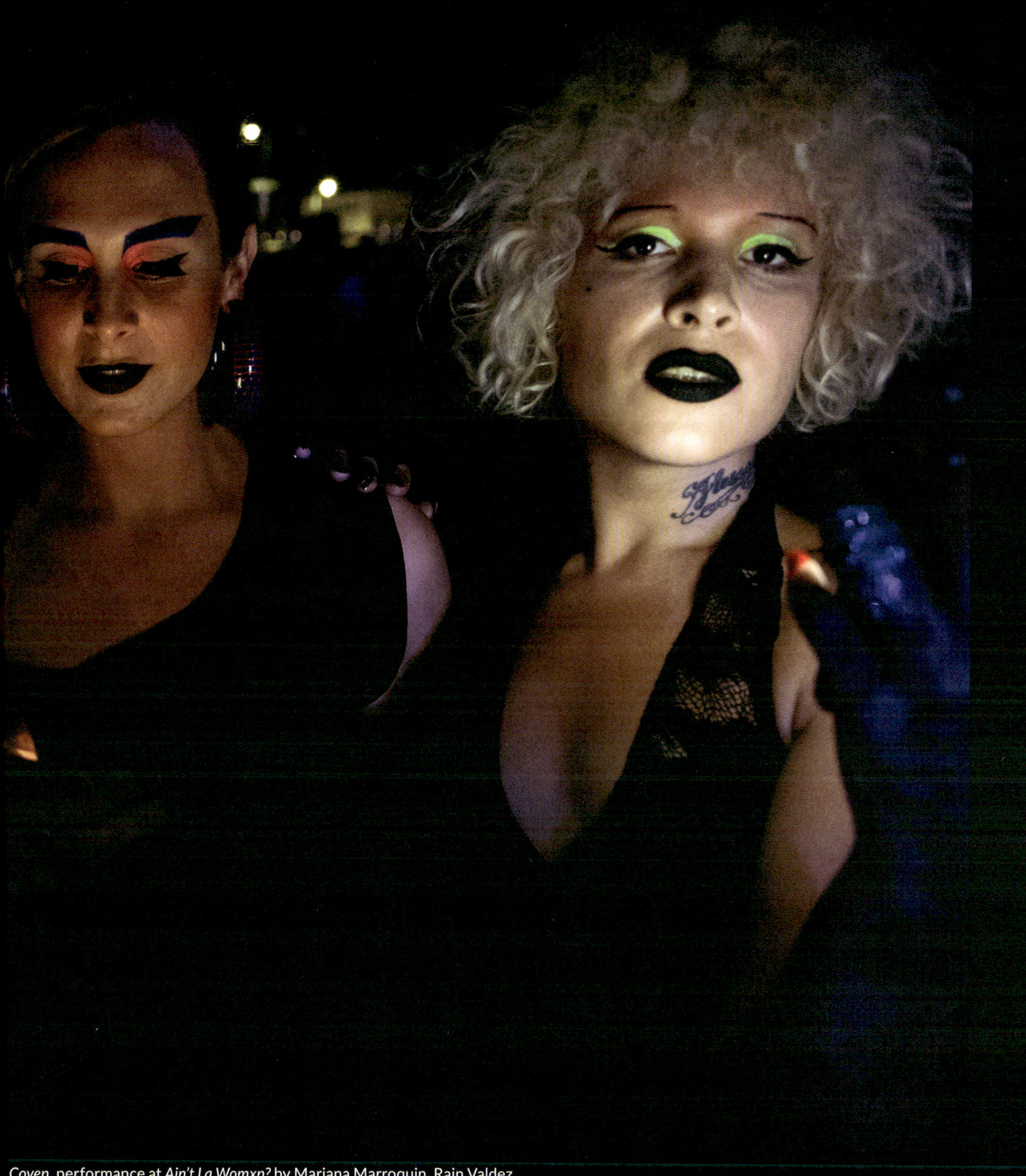

Coven, performance at *Ain't I a Womxn?* by Mariana Marroquin, Rain Valdez,
Zackary Drucker, and Mz Neon. Photos: Safi Alia Shabaik.

We are carcass people running on the hope that we will evade our eventual decay.

We love in order to understand the unknown. We are all of our previous selves accumulated. We are all of our future selves possible. We are corpses for a moment before we are vaporized, or burned, or buried, or released to sea.

We are alive. We are finally over you, and we are not afraid of death.

When our heart stops, you will still be there, dormant. Safe within the universe of our eternal soul. We can walk away from the wreckage for now and unpack it in therapy later.

Some hurts never disappear, but they haunt us longer than they affect us.

We are shell humans during the day so we can fall apart every night.

We fall apart in pieces of various sizes. Larger parts first, entire limbs, one arm, and then the other, piece by piece. Hands, fingernails, knuckles, wrists, tendons, veins, muscle membranes, fingerprints. Every part of the body we memorized living in, all of our skin memories gone.

We represent the earth under our feet. The air in our lungs. The fire in our heart. The water in our body. We represent a ghost town. We represent the beginning and the end.

We represent a tidal wave moving toward you in slow motion. A wall of water crashing away everything you know. We represent the survival of our predecessors and the survival of our descendants. We represent a people that will exist, will persist, despite knowing that no human will make it out of life alive.

We represent living. We represent the living. We represent our lives until we don't. We represent ourselves as spirits in the future. We represent our words, bodies, thoughts. We represent hearts that have been obliterated but are still beating. We represent all of the feelings we produce and hope that they do not destroy us.

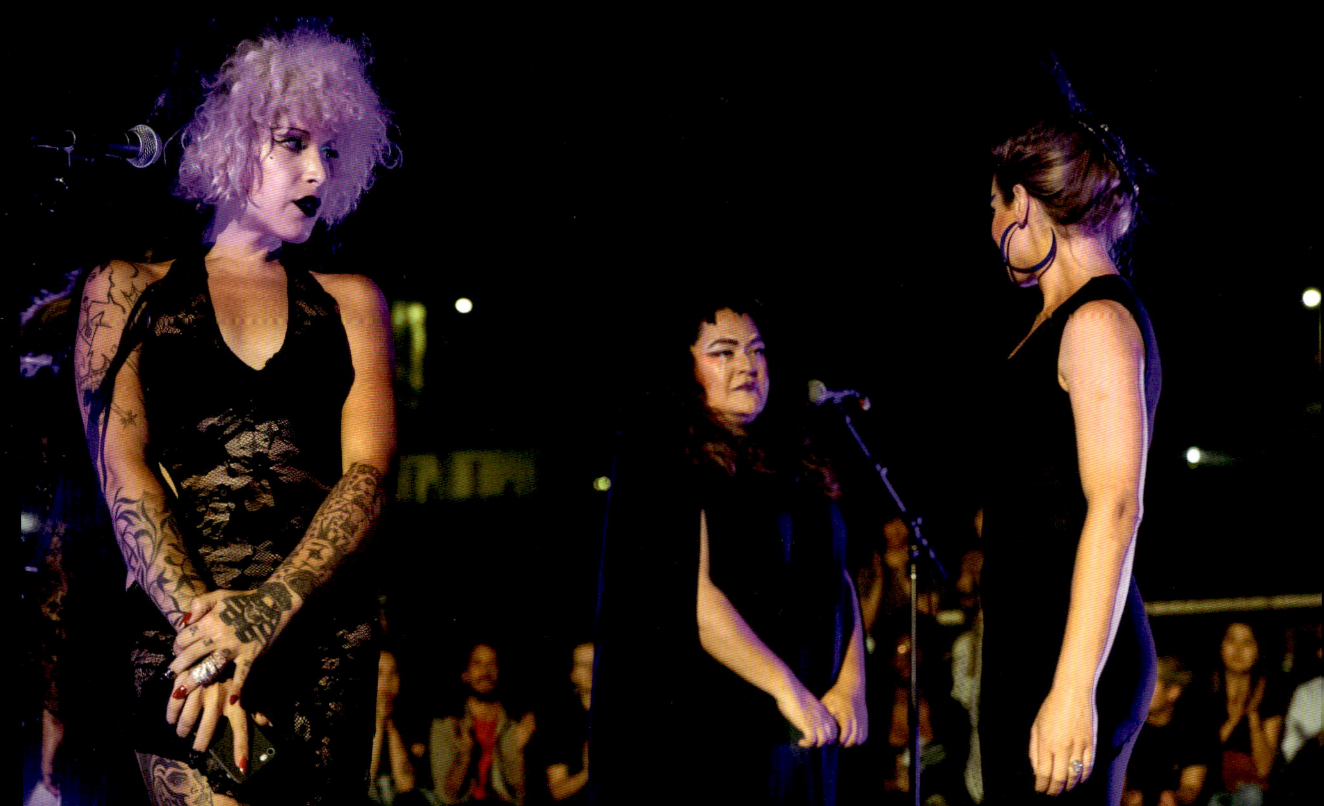

Coven, performance at *Ain't I a Womxn?* by Mariana Marroquin, Rain Valdez, Zackary Drucker, and Mz Neon. Photos: Safi Alia Shabaik.

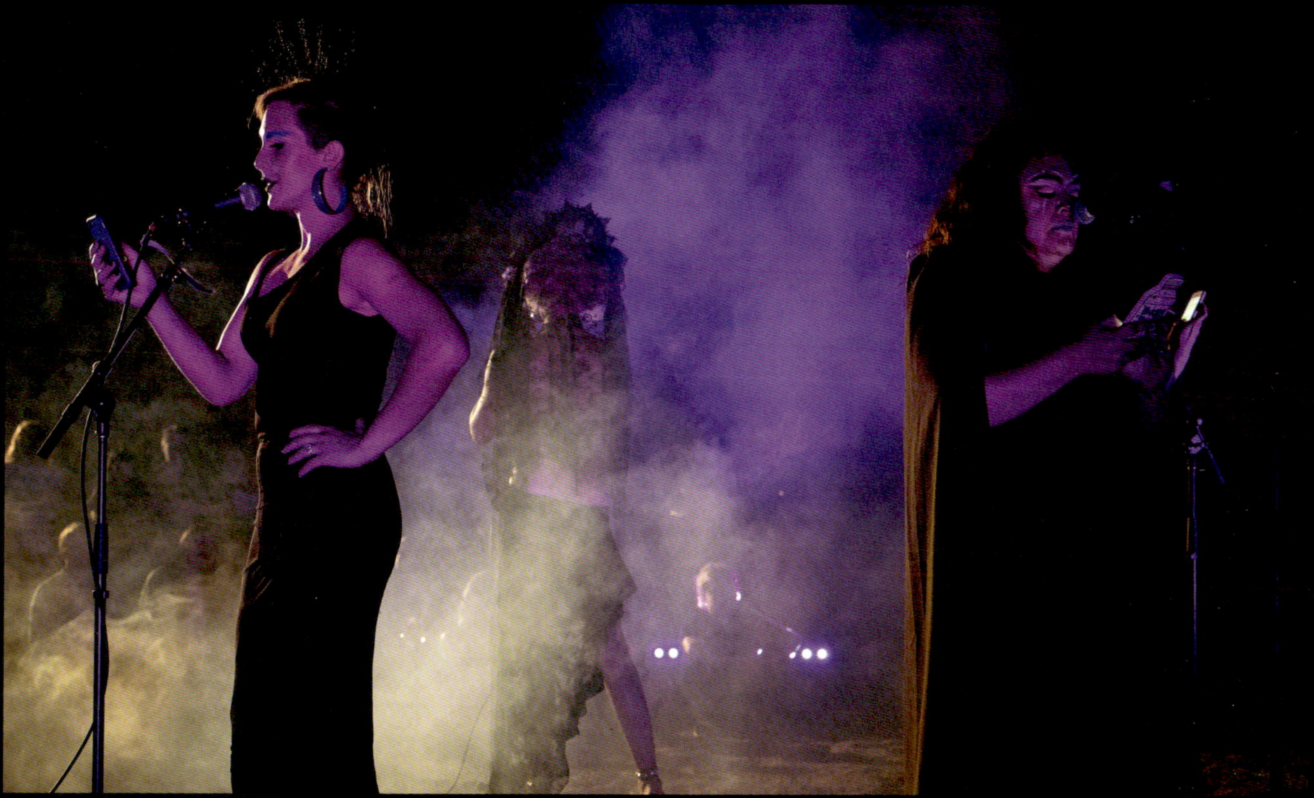

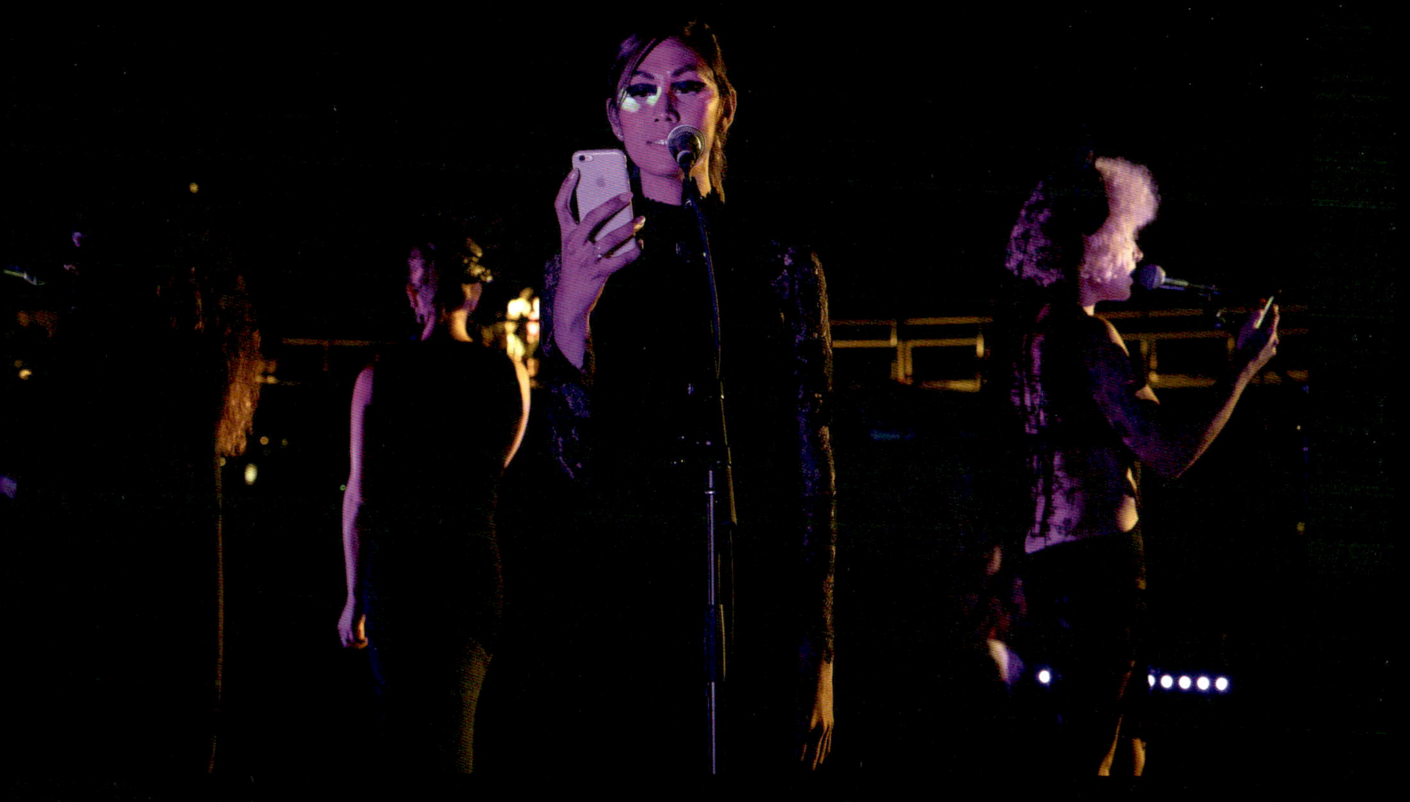

A Windo[w]

Between

To empower individuals and communities impacted by violence and trauma through a transformative healing-arts program.

VISION

Window Between Worlds views art as a catalyst to release trauma, build resilience, and ignite social change. When individuals create art in a safe community, they can be heard and respected— replacing violence and shame with safety and hope.

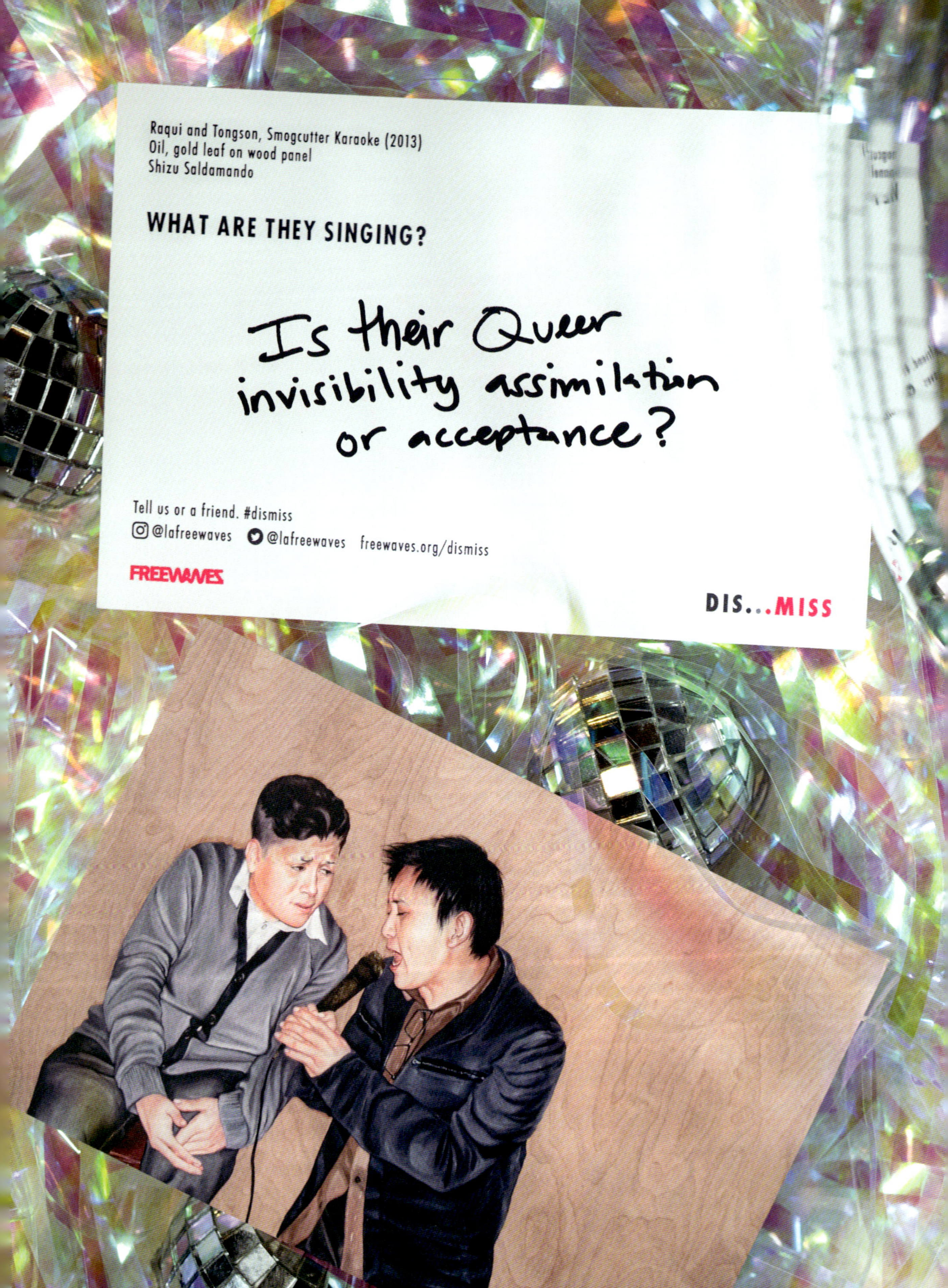
Raqui and Tongson, Smogcutter Karaoke (2013)
Oil, gold leaf on wood panel
Shizu Saldamando

WHAT ARE THEY SINGING?

Is their Queer invisibility assimilation or acceptance?

Tell us or a friend. #dismiss
@lafreewaves   @lafreewaves   freewaves.org/dismiss

FREEWAVES

DIS...MISS

what are they singing?

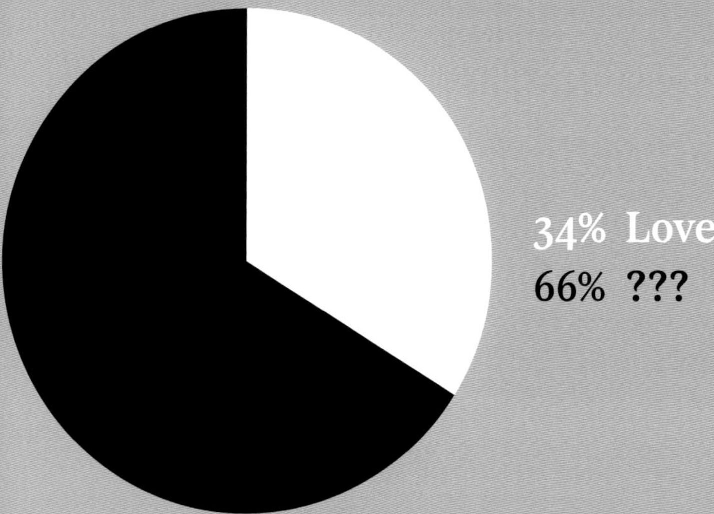

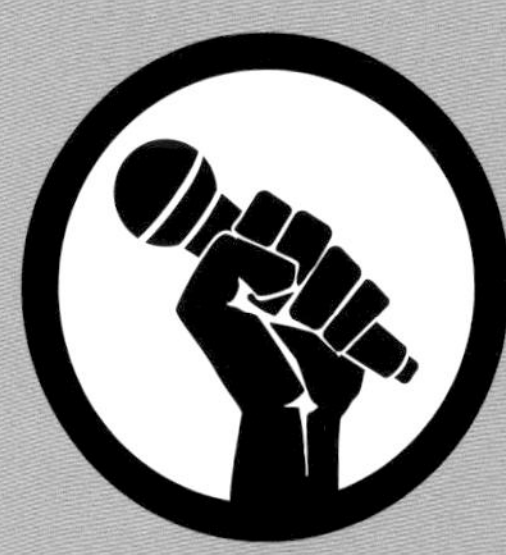

ANALYSIS

Most responded with specific songs, some being love songs. Of the love songs about half are related to heart-ache. A few answers (11%) point out there might be a **heartache or pain** in their expressions.

"DIS...MISS, Inconclusive Infographic Animation." Analyzed by Marisa Turesky. Animation designed by Catherine Bell, 2019.
Left: Postcard portrait by Alejandra Sone.

11

what were you
born for?

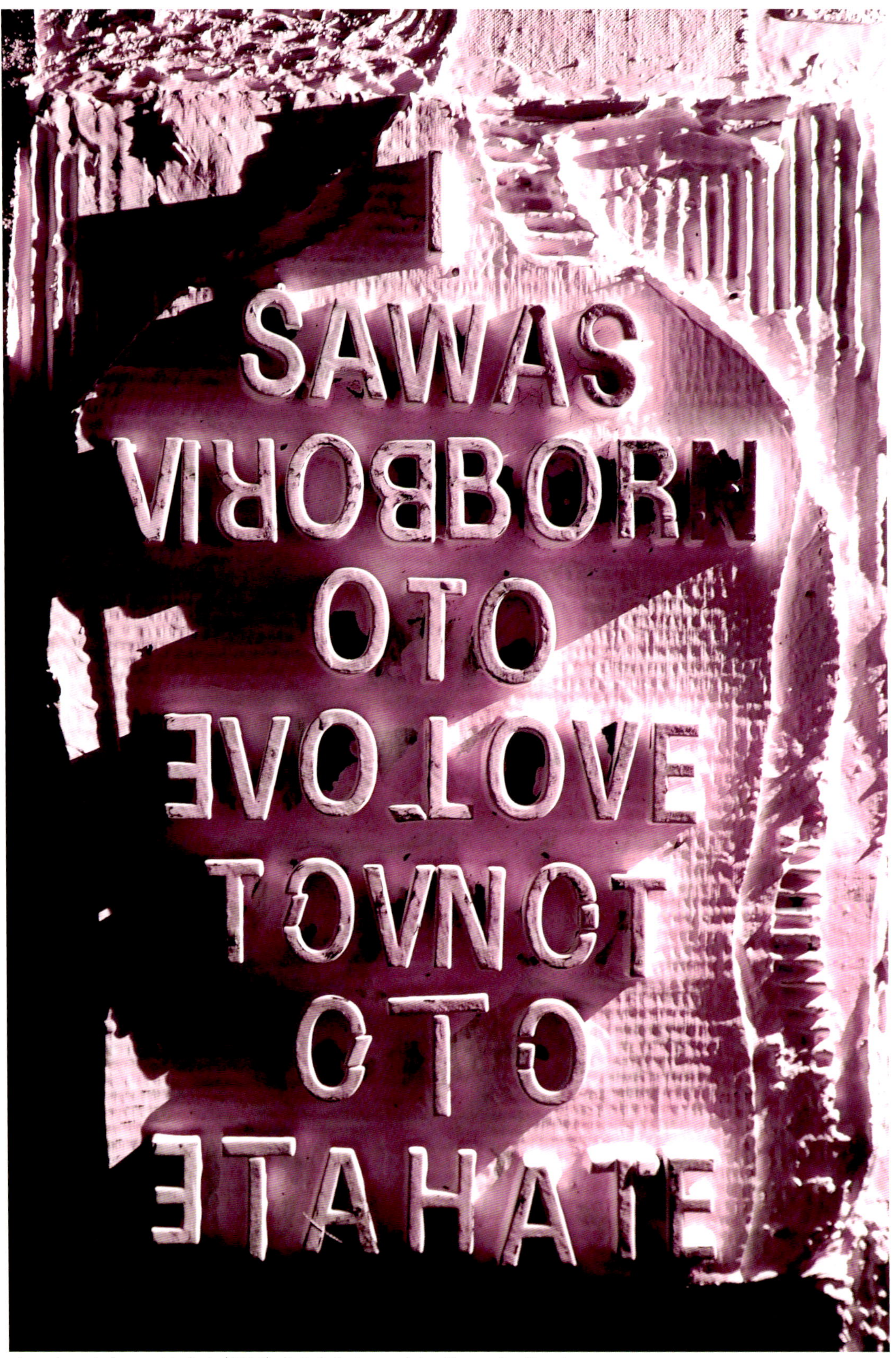

I was born to love not to hate (2016), digital photograph by Alexandra Grant.

I Was Born to Love Not to Hate
Alma Ruiz

The phrase attributed to Dante Alighieri was for a while repeatedly quoted on television, online, and in print: "The hottest places in Hell are reserved for those who in time of moral crisis preserve their neutrality." It implies that in difficult times, such as the ones we are experiencing now, amid a raging pandemic and a polarized political landscape, we have to choose sides by reorienting our values and ethics toward what we have learned to be just and honorable. Despite its uncertain attribution, this oft-quoted, Dante-inspired maxim, with its call to "do the right thing," is meant to rally us into rejecting neutrality under the premise that not doing so shows a lack of compassion, negating aspirations for a fair society—one that benefits all and not just a few.

The phrase "I was born to love not to hate" appears for the first time in a series of text-based works that Alexandra Grant began around 2011. Referencing literary sources—Sophocles's tragic play *Antigone*, the writings of Audre Lorde, seminal psychological texts by Sigmund Freud, and cultural movements that probe the unconscious mind, such as feminism and surrealism—Grant's explorations of philosophical concepts of identity (who we are, who the OTHER is, and the voices in our unconscious that shape us)[1] were first collected in the series Grant titled *Century of Self*.[2] Works from this series that bore Antigone's pronouncement were included in Grant's piece *Drawn to Language* at the USC University of Southern California Fisher Museum in Los Angeles in 2013 and in *Century of Self* at the Lora Reynolds Gallery in Austin, Texas, the following year. While working on the paintings, works on paper, and a floor installation that eventually constituted the series *Century of Self*, Grant considered several expressions—Shakespeare's "To thine own self be true" and the French symbolist poet Rimbaud's "I am an Other," but "I was born to love not to hate"

---

1   Alexandra Grant's website, referencing *Drawn to Language*, exhibition at the USC Fisher Museum, September 3–December 7, 2013, https://alexandragrant.com/portfolio/century of the self at uscs fisher museum 2013/.

2   Grant borrowed this title from Adam Curtis's BBC Four documentary of the same name.

had made an impression, and she came back to it frequently. To Grant, it seemed right and worthy of further investigation.[3]

In Sophocles's play, Antigone expresses her choice of love over hatred as she tells her uncle Creon, king of Thebes, about her determination to give her brother Polynices—who has been labeled a traitor—a proper burial. Antigone is aware of the risks in defying Creon, yet her resolve to accord her brother a hero's funeral is stronger than her fears. Adhering to civic order, Creon refuses to concede. Antigone insists, knowing that she cannot do otherwise. "I cannot side with hatred," she says. "My nature sides with love."[4] Her filial love comes naturally to her; it is as deep as the roots of a tree. In the end, Antigone chooses to "do the right thing," knowing that her intention will anger her uncle and that she may pay for this choice with her life.

After the exhibition at Lora Reynolds, Grant began to focus solely on Antigone. Since then, the line "I was born to love not to hate," which had burrowed its way deep into Grant's subconscious, began to reappear with insistence in her paintings and drawings, becoming a frequent, mantralike recurrence. After almost a decade, Antigone's words have become synonymous with Grant's work, recognizable by anyone familiar with her artistic practice. Depicted columnlike, each word on a separate line, or imitating a Rorschach test with the sentence reading from left to right on one side and from right to left on the other, Antigone's simple but profound words direct power and inspiration in Grant's work. For Grant, repeating the line has become a way of understanding the "perennial Antigone question of what it means to choose love over hate or to be called upon to "do the right thing" and of hoping that every generation may reinvent it for their moment.

Grant's use of words to represent visual ideas has been the foundation of her work since the early 2000s. She combines mostly abstract imagery with text that often derives from her collaborations with international writers and poets. In 2013, Grant began to look for a relationship with a living writer who "would write me an Antigone of the future." The following year,

---

3   Author's conversation with the artist, 2018.
4   Sophocles, *Antigone*, trans. and with introduction and notes by Paul Woodruff (Indianapolis, IN: Hackett, 2001), 22.

Grant created *Antigone 3000* (2014),[5] a series of large paintings on linen. Purely abstract, the works did not contain text because they were "an announcement of a change in style that was still awaiting first a writer and then the text, to arrive."[6] The writers she approached did not work out, and the lack of a partner led her instead to make a series of smaller works on paper between 2014 and 2015, again using that line from Antigone: "I was born to love not to hate."

As Grant's interest in Antigone persisted, she became intrigued by the idea that a young girl is the one to stand up to power in Sophocles's play. She proposed a participatory project at the all-girls Archer School in Los Angeles. Like the *Forêt intérieure/ Interior Forest* project, organized in 2013 in collaboration with the French writer and philosopher Hélène Cixous and involving neighborhood communities in Santa Monica, California, and Saint-Ouen, France, the Archer School project would encourage the students and faculty, including those without artistic experience or skills, to participate in the making of an enormous mural-like drawing Grant called *Antigone is you is me*. Grant enlisted her sister Florence to write the text setting the Greek myth in a contemporary milieu by imagining Antigone and her sister, Ismene, as two teenagers in Los Angeles. Grant and Florence presented Archer students and faculty with this text and a collection of sticky notes containing prompts from the text to help them begin to make drawings. The exercise would lead the participants to explore their own identities through art and mythology—and to consider how anyone can be an Antigone given the right circumstances. The Archer School project, completed in 2017, successfully conveyed messages about love, forgiveness, and trust.

While doing research for *Dis...Miss* (2018), Anne Bray conducted a studio visit with Grant. During their encounter, Bray described *Dis...Miss* as a "public visual art experience with short videos, postcards, and audience engagement,"[7] all meant to invite

---

5   Grant wanted to imagine an Antigone for the year 3000. She was also influenced by Dr. Octagon's hip-hop song "3000." The rapper used the number to reimagine power relations and rap in the year 3000. *Antigone 3000* was exhibited in 2015 as part of the Los Angeles Municipal Art Gallery's individual artist fellowships, COLA (City of Los Angeles) exhibition

6   Author's conversation with the artist, 2018.

7   Anne Bray, "*Dis...Miss*," n.d., retrieved December 12, 2020, http://www.annebrayart. com/projects/dis-miss/#1.

dialogue about gender and intersectional feminism. Looking at Grant's work, Bray seemed to connect to the message in "I was born to love not to hate" and suggested creating a postcard with it. Grant saw this as an opportunity to develop new work and to consider the important ways in which Antigone's statement fits in the context of the work of the other artists included in *Dis… Miss*. The resulting postcard image is a photograph showing plaster letters on the surface of another painting from which Grant created a rubbing of the text for her *Antigone 3000 works* on paper. Grant, who thought of this photograph as documenting her process, tinted the postcard pink to reference Antigone's young age and gender.

The enduring power of Antigone's words in Grant's work is a testament to their universal appeal and psychological richness. They resonate today more than ever, an echo of Dante's maxim. Would life be any different if we took sides at a time of polarizing political beliefs, climate-change upheaval, and a pandemic whose enormity we can't yet fully grasp? It is perhaps too early to know, but as Grant notes, "For a myth to have lasted over 2,000 years, it had to be meaningful to each new and subsequent generation."[8]

I agree and am hopeful for our generation and future generations. Each or all of us could be an Antigone for our time.

---

8   Author's conversation with the artist, 2018.

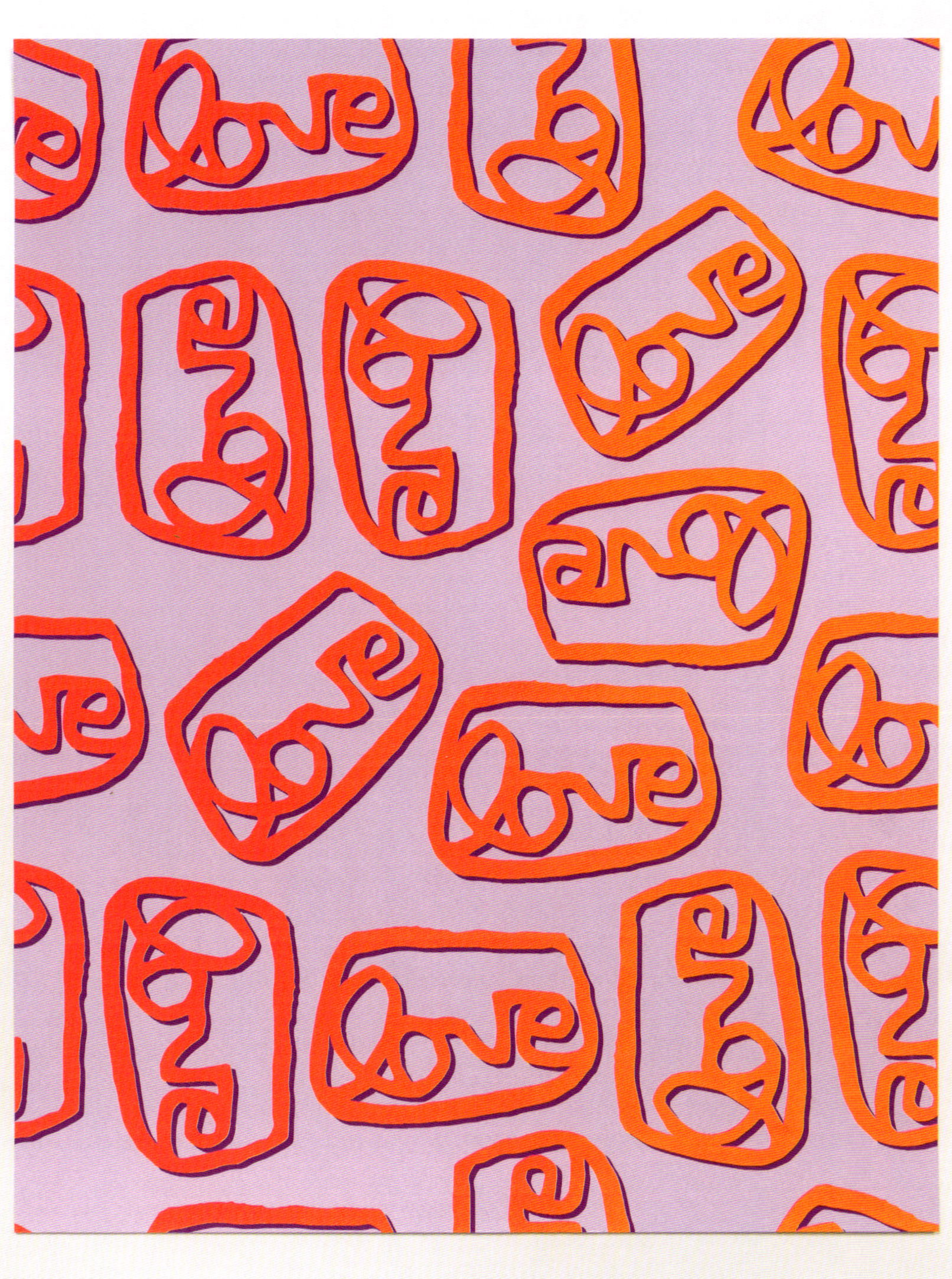

LOVE, 2019 (lavender), screen print on 100c French's paper, 20 × 16 inches, edition of 100 in 4 colorways, 15 APs, and 5 PPs, by Alexandra Grant, with designer Kimberly Varella. Printed by Maggie Lomeli in collaboration with andSons Chocolatiers. Photo: Ruben Diaz.

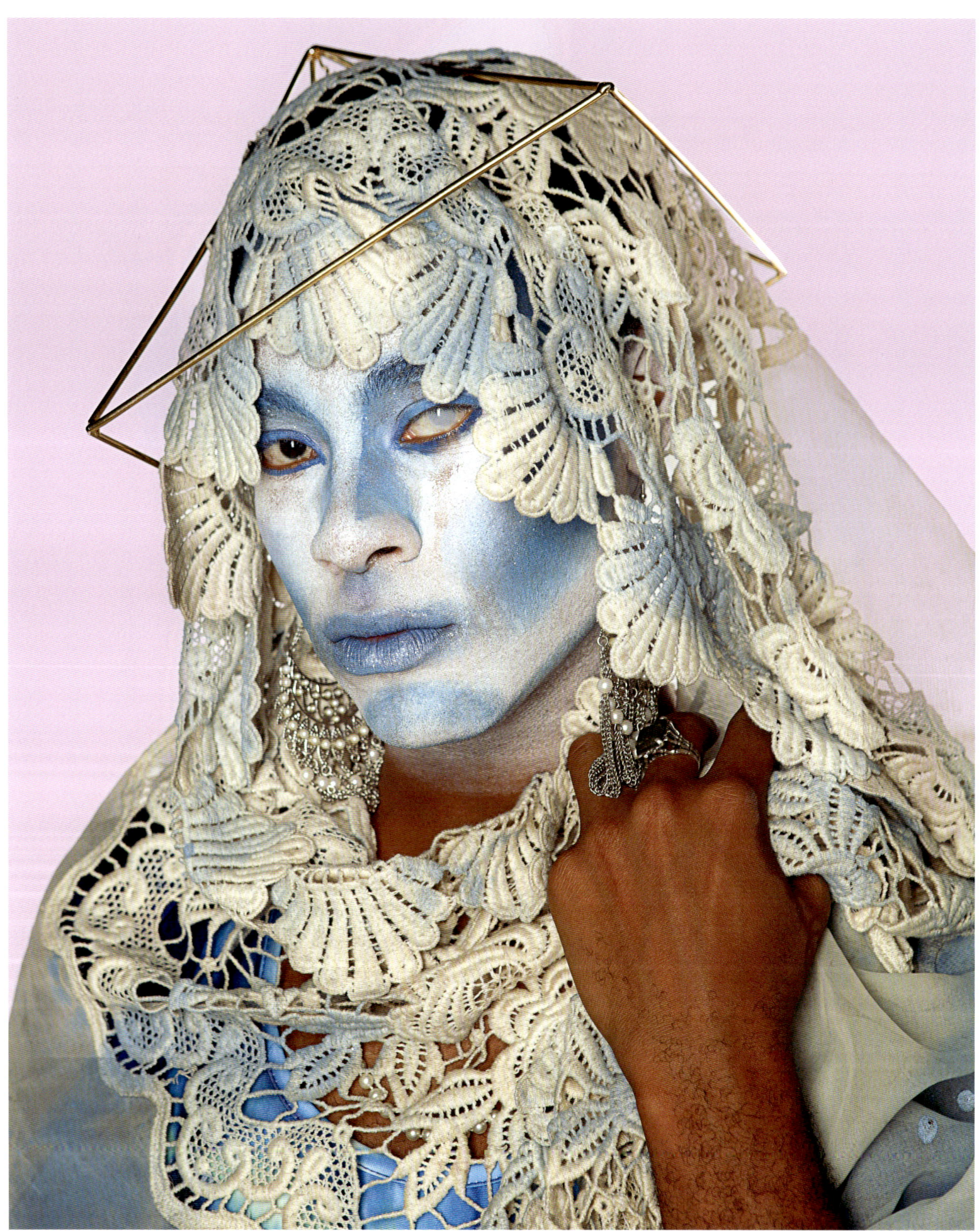

Earth to Jordi at *Ain't I a Womxn?* Photo: Austin Young.

Decolonize Gender Excerpts
Earth to Jordi

First Snippet:

I'm not a woman. I'm not a man. I am something that I'm trying to understand. The gender binary has got us fucked up. I'm beginning to find my footing now, but this dance between masculine and feminine has been a deep source of trauma, confusion, and invisibility for me from a young age in a world where it seemed people "saw" me before I even did. My earliest memory of imbalance was Halloween. I was five years old. I wanted to be Esmeralda. We remember feeling my mother's hesitance to let me walk out when I told her who I was. I was prepared with my "skirt" that we made with a blanket and my hair fashioned in the same way. I had done this routine before and did it many times after, more recently with brightly colored wigs and makeup LAID! I remember her changing my outfit; I think we took the hair off. I remember that day slamming our finger in the car door as I was dropped off at kindergarten; it was our right hand. ... Maybe we're blending memories, but I'd like to think our memory is impeccable. That night as we went trick-or-treating, I remember the family we were going out with asked who I was, and my mother answered for me, "A gypsy." I remember thinking she was lying, and I didn't know why. ... I had told her who I was.

The next years were filled with aggressions (mostly by masculine figures) toward my identity that I'm thankful I survived. I also owe it to my Marine Corps-trained grandfather for instilling a mentally tough attitude in me at a young age. The aggressions came in overt and covert waves. So many were unintentionally guilty. McDonald's employees giving me the "boy" toy when I wanted the one with hair; my bestie letting me play with hers when we were in the back seat of the car. I was able to play with my cousin's Barbies and Easy Bake Oven without judgment; I developed a skill for cooking that allowed me to create in many ways. I remember getting punished for painting my nails with my cousins, both of whom were safe from this scrutiny simply because of our genital difference. I didn't understand why I was being molded into this box labeled "MAN." This box whose walls were made up of "don't bend your wrist," "don't pop your hip," "put some bass in your voice," "don't step like that," "don't dance like that," "that's girlie," "MEN don't do that," "be a MAN," "MAN up." These rules were taxing on my psyche—mostly because I knew MEN. I knew what they did quite intimately in relation to what they did to my family. They cheated, they lied, they abandoned you, they beat you, they looked at your body like something to be consumed, they were rough, they wanted you to be rough, they didn't feel, they didn't hug, they were dirty, they had no fashion sense at all! But mostly it seemed they were walking around with amnesia in disgust and so distant from the feminine within themselves, trying to get me to drink the Kool-Aid. I'd smile, take the pills, hide them in my cheek, spit them out, and then hang with the girls.

Second Snippet:

In this world of abuses, I was embraced by the feminine. My grandmother's kitchen was where I mostly found myself. On football days, I would go upstairs and watch cartoons in her bed. Once my mother and I were free of a toxically masculine household, she allowed me breathing room to pursue my passions. I was able to escape in the world of art and find freedom within a world of dance, usually surrounded by femmes. I had no male friends. Most of them bullied me or just weren't interested in the energy I emitted. This I was fine with. I was able to express myself quite freely but was often met with attacks on my sexuality. This was not new. The first time I was called "gay" was when we were seven. It was during this time that I started to grow disdain toward labels—how you had to be one thing and how that thing defined the rest of your interactions in society. And *gay* mostly had negative connotations. The church we were regularly attending would invite multiple male speakers who had converted from their sinful ways and settled down into a heterosexual christian relationship only to have two kids that they "couldn't be happier to have." It seemed I was forced to choose, and *straight* was the label that seemed most safe. It wasn't necessarily a lie. I was attracted to girls, but as I started to explore and expand my desire, I began to realize how fluid things were. This was a wild roller coaster winding around self-hate, confusion, denial, therapy, church camps, lies, sexual promiscuity, sex behind closed doors, and it seemed the ride didn't end.

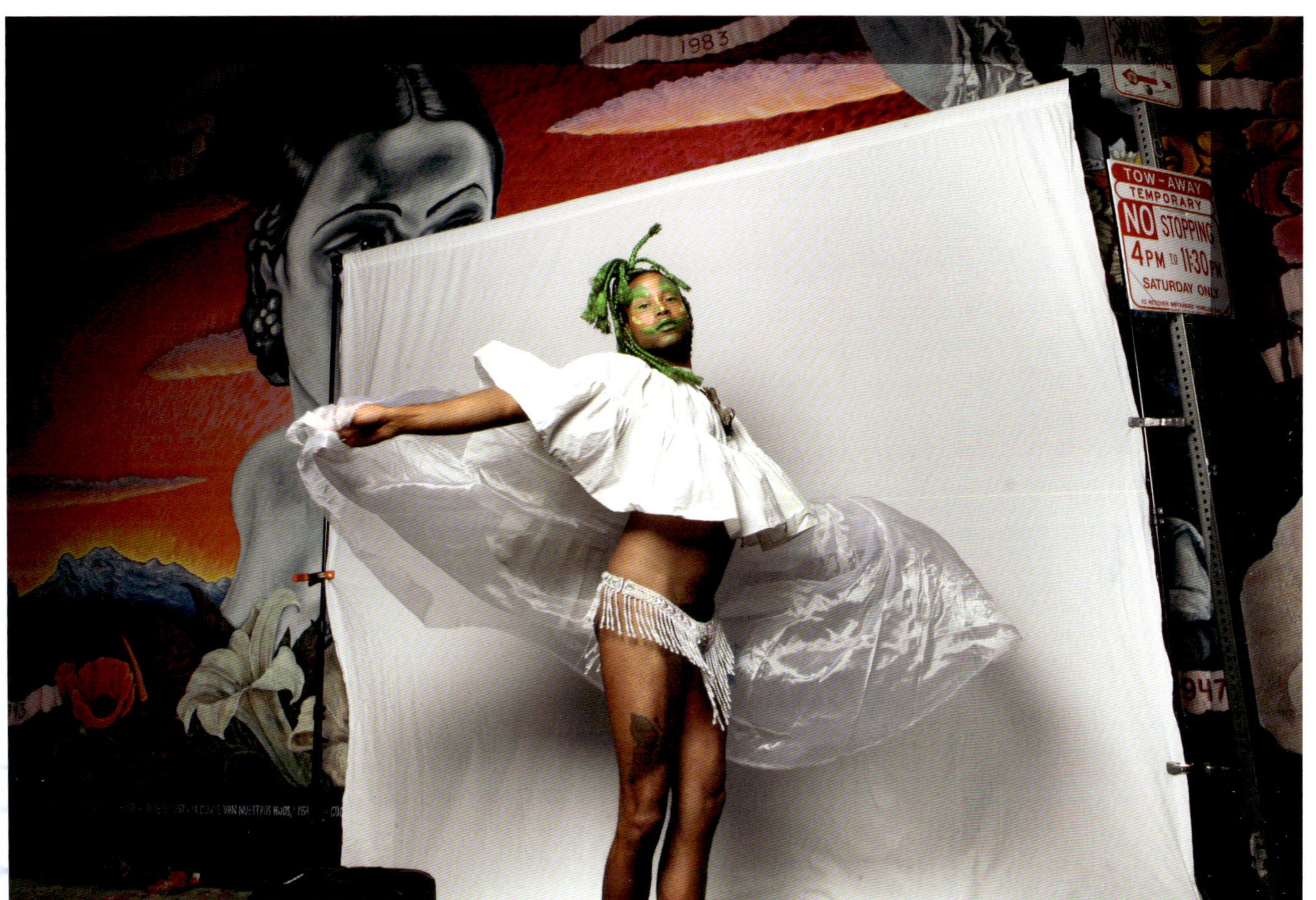

Earth to Jordi at *LOVE &/OR FEAR*. Photo: Austin Young.

GENDER JUSTICE LA

Gender Justice LA (GJLA)
is a grassroots social justice
organization led by and for gender
nonconforming, two-spirit, Black,
Indigenous, trans people of color
in Los Angeles.

Gender Justice LA organizes,
holds space, provides resources,
and collaborates with others so
that our communities can **resist**
oppression, **develop** community
responses to violence, **heal** from
present and historical trauma,
and **come together** in ways that
feel brave and affirming.

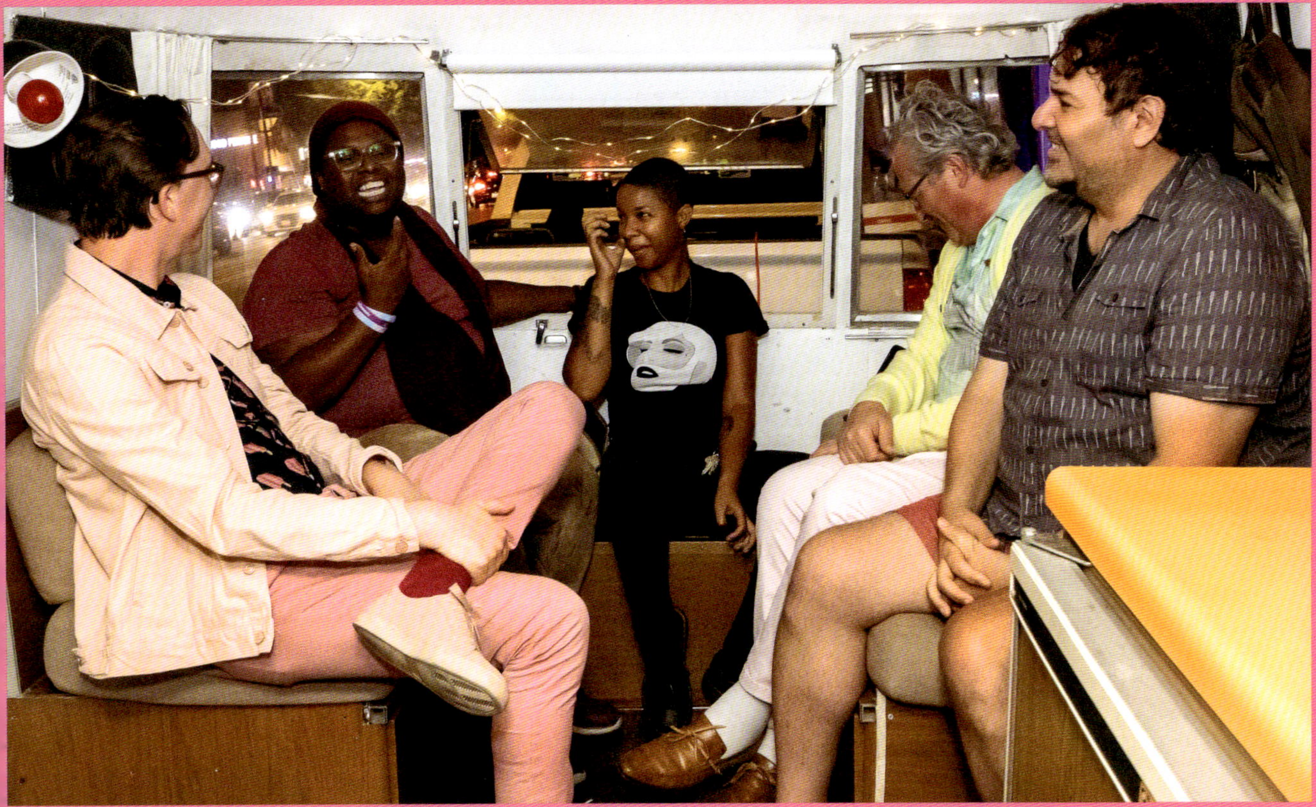

Gender Justice LA at *LOVE &/OR FEAR*. Photos: Monica Orozco.

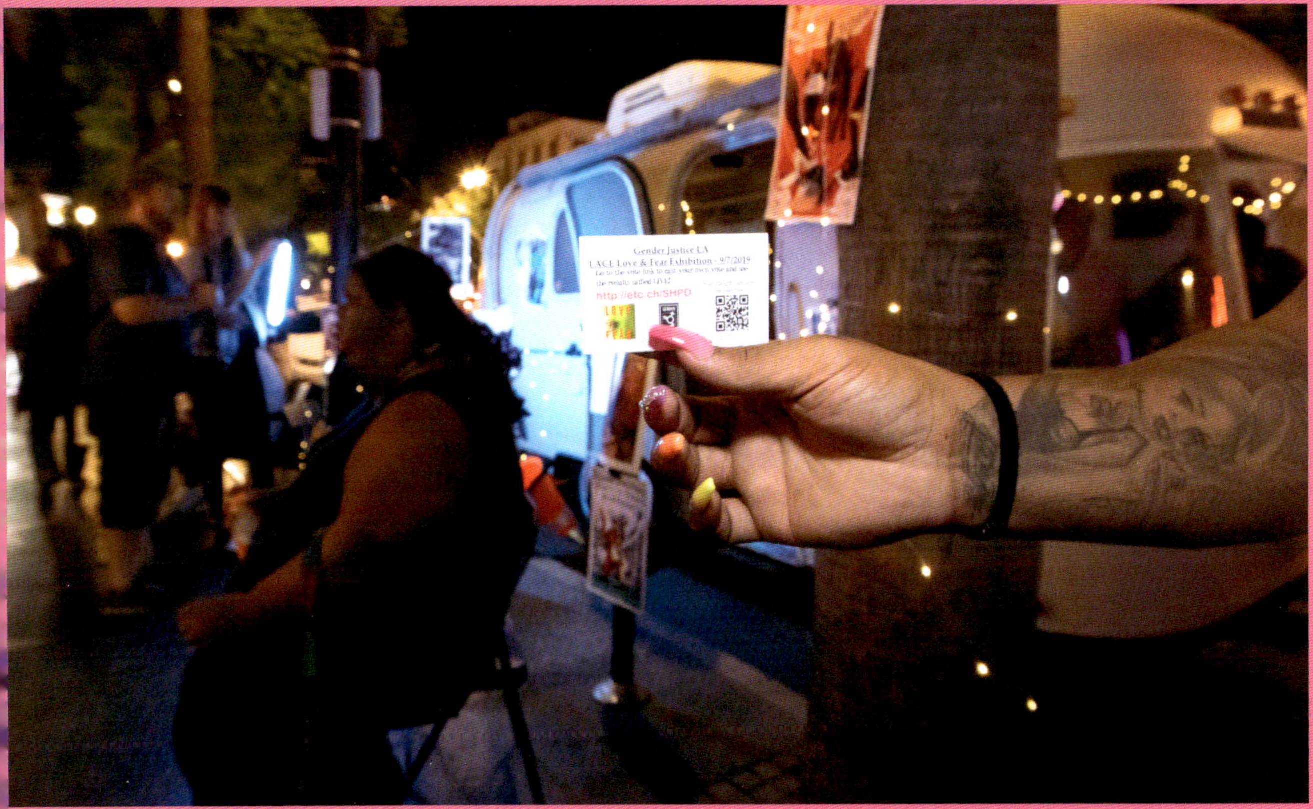

Sydney Rogers, Yozmit, and féi hernandez in Conversation

In the two-hour conversation on June 20, 2021, necessary questions about the future of/for trans, gender-noncomforming, and intersex folx "post"-COVID[1] were posed. A thrilling and inciting conversation took place by three powerful speakers.

Sydney Rogers is a Black trans nonbinary artist, writer, and organizer. Yozmit is a trans Korean immigrant designer and artist. féi hernandez is a formerly undocumented Mexican trans and nonbinary writer, artist, healer, and organizer. All speakers are within the Black, Indigenous, and people of color (BIPOC) bracket; they therefore are not white adjacent and therefore have a particularly keen lens through which they view power structures, the nature of surviving/thriving, art making as a tool for revolution, and the power of community.

The questions posed weren't questions the folx in conversation hadn't already thought about. Their focus, from the time they were a very young age, was to question the world around them, to seek justice, to question authority/"normalcy" and lack of inclusion. These folks have always been hyper aware of their presence, their visibility (or "I visibilization"), their lack of resources, society's disdain and questioning looks, and so on. Through this conversation, the high priestesses shed light on the karmic shift of our time. They articulate a powerful vision of a future with trans BIPOC at the center of this reimagining. The following manifesto is the result of their combined prowess.

---

1   "Post" is in quotation marks because as this statement is being written, a new strain of COVID has already begun to plague Planet Earth. Therefore, we aren't fully past a point of recovery.

TGIFESTO
féi hernandez

Bring the hard-to-reach depths of the ocean into every conversation. Don't hold back, showing up with your purse filled with sketches, crumpled journal entries, and one of the 100 best looks in your closet when you arrive at the table. Don't make your intricate narrative lose weight; it's beautiful in its joy and angry fat beauty. Be the axis shift, the reason the world cocks its head in awe every time you do something as insignificant as your given extravagant prowess. We are the retrograde: the high priestess reborn, the unmassacreable trans, gender nonconfirming, intersex Black, Indigenous walking deities. Be your being in all its glory and render it enough of an art piece to rest, to be your primary partner in the polyamorous relationship with the world. Getcha coin, no free labor unless you got liquid gold to spare. This time you greet anything outside of yourself at the door; this time you CHOOSE who and what stays and for how long. In our immigrant bodies, always in migration and translation, we resist dimming our light for humility. Pack all of your guilt and doubt into a metal trash can, drizzle it in gasoline, strike a match, and see the fireworks of possibility go off in the sky. There is no going back to normal; the new world has always begun with us. Strut with permission and approval. We demand safety in every part of the planet. Choose your people wisely; don't excuse violent behavior because you're "understanding." We are not brave, we're hardworking and magically regular; it's not our fault the ancient world is slow to come back to stasis to see our glory just as we are. Dream our people fed.[1] Dream ourselves eternally thriving. "Knife to the soul"[2] when your own community is the first to strike you; bird to the sky when you make it home to your chosen family, always alive. "Enlightenment is going beyond the binary thinking"[3] because any "absolute power corrupts absolutely," so pick your role in the revolution and be the best at it; we need you. Be a gift for yourself before being a gift for someone else. Let your art be a home for yourself before it can be for everyone else. Make a fashion revolution and call it regular (as in extravagant, but it's our daily so). We are the new world. We are the new world. We are the new world.

---

1 féi says.
2 Sydney says.
3 Yozmit says.

I was born to love not to hate (2016)
Digital Photography
Alexandra Grant

WHAT WERE YOU BORN FOR?

Living in A society
that profits from my
self-doubt, louins
myself is A RADICAL
Act of self-care

Tell us or a friend. #dismiss
@lafreewaves @lnfreewaves freewaves.org/dismiss
FREEWAVES
DIS...MISS

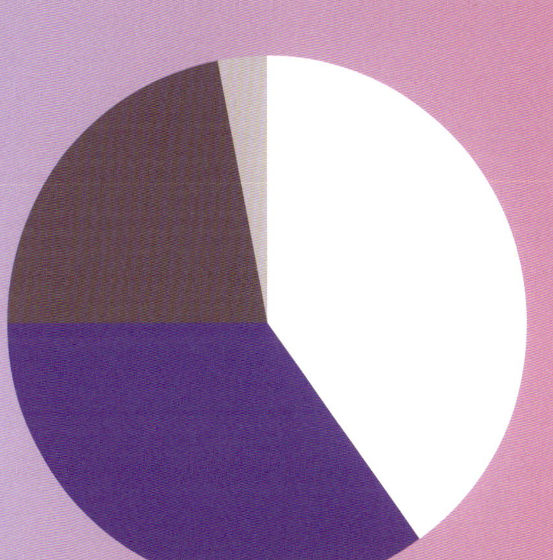

RESPONSE THEME

40% Love
35% Head
22% Hands
3% Existing

ANALYSIS

Most respondents (56%) responded by using words related to love or the heart. **Love was one of the most used words**, appearing in 40% of responses.

"DIS…MISS, Inconclusive Infographic Animation." Analyzed by Marisa Turesky. Animation designed by Catherine Bell, 2019. Left: Postcard portrait by Alejandra Sone.

12

love &/or fear

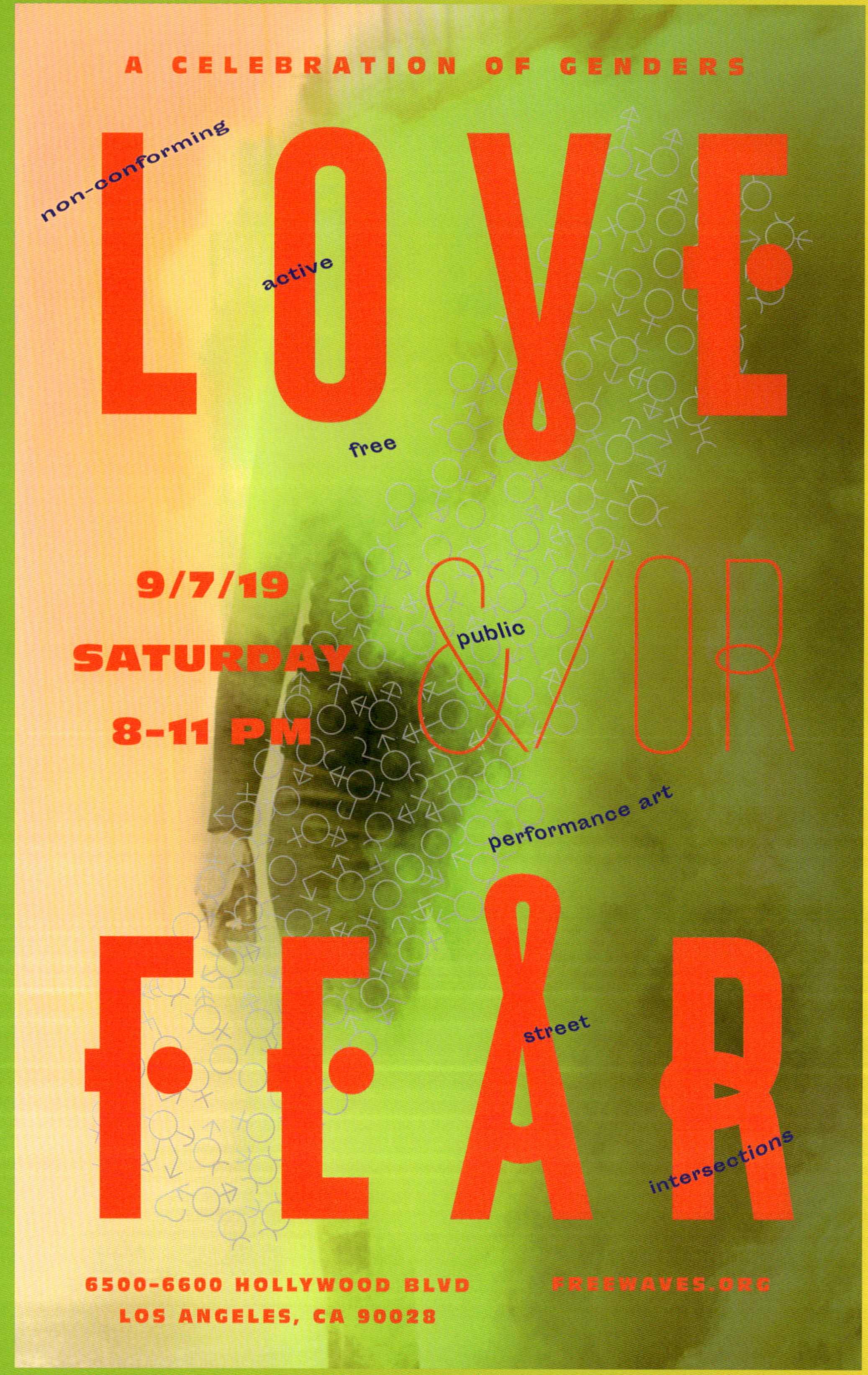

LOVE &/OR FEAR flyer by Soyun Cho.

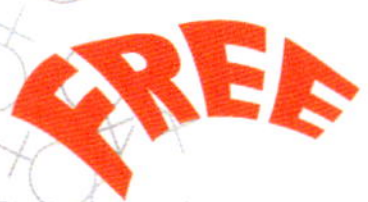

PRESENTING ART IN A SEXUAL HARASSMENT FREE ZONE
WITH PEACE OVER VIOLENCE AND LACE

OPENING PERFORMANCE
AT LACE
8PM ONLY
Sebastian Hernández

DURATIONAL PERFORMANCES
8:30–10:30PM
Martha Carrillo
Reanne Estrada
Raquel Gutiérrez & Karen Tongson
Marcus Kuiland-Nazario
Young Joon Kwak
Jennifer Moon
Thinh Nguyen
Ni Santas
Reach LA
Christy Roberts Berkowitz
The Fingerjoint
Kristina Wong
Austin Young
Yozmit

FINAL PERFORMANCE
#SNATCHPOWER
AT HUDSON ST. STAGE
AT 10:30PM ONLY
(The Uhuruverse, Davia Spain, SondriaWRITES, Jordi Phi)

INSTALLATIONS
bauhaus.photo
Marsian De Lellis
Arshia Haq in collaboration with Cassils
Pato Hebert
Amitis Motevalli
Dakota Noot
Julio Salgado

Saturday September 7, 2019 8-11 pm

FREE

near LACE

6500-6600 Hollywood Blvd, Los Angeles, CA 90028

freewaves.org

INCONCLUSIVE INFOGRAPHICS
AT LACE
Catherine Bell

POSTCARDS
April Bey
boychild
Cassils
Chan and Mann
Roya Falahi
Alexandra Grant
Micol Hebron
Thinh Nguyen
Shizu Saldamando

VIDEOS
Adebukola Bodunrin
Mail Order Brides
Gloria Morán
Meena Nanji
Caress Reeves

PARTNERS
Black Lives Matter LA
Foxhole Creative
Gender Justice LA
LACP – Los Angeles Center of Photography
LACE – Los Angeles Contemporary Exhibitions
LA LGBT Center
Otis College of Art and Design: Creative Action
Peace Over Violence
Women's Center for Creative Work
WUHO – Woodbury University Hollywood Outpost

SUPPORT
National Endowment for the Arts
City of Los Angeles Department of Cultural Affairs
Los Angeles County Department of Arts & Culture
Pasadena Art Alliance

FREEWAVES
30th anniversary

DIRECTOR & PRODUCERS
Anne Bray, Jackie Castillo, Gina Valona

DESIGN
Soyun Cho

CURATORIAL ADVISORS
Evonne Gallardo
David Orozco & YBLA: Yarn Bombing Los Angeles

#dismiss **#lafreewaves** **#loveandorfear**   

LOVE &/OR FEAR flyer by Soyun Cho.

FEAR, or….
Badly Licked Bear

At 2:15 a.m. on the night of August 17, 2020, while waiting for a rideshare, three trans women, **Eden the Doll**, **Jaslene Whiterose**, and **Joslyn Flawless** were robbed and assaulted. During the assault, they were subjected to a battery of transphobic slurs and mockery by both the assailants and onlookers. One of their assailants was armed with a crowbar. The arena for this violence was the exact same stretch of Hollywood Boulevard where the artists and audiences of *LOVE &/OR FEAR* had gathered and roamed hundreds of nights— almost a year of nights—earlier.

This kind of violence takes place every day in the United States. You may have experienced it. You may bear the scars of it or the small, invisible pains that never quite heal. You may have been a witness to it. Many people experience this kind of violence as a permanent fixture in their lives. It is the daily fear felt by bodies that refuse to carve away parts of themselves to fit into either the round hole or the square hole of gender. Bodies that don't emerge into the world whole, fully formed from a puff of pink or blue smoke. Bodies whose gender reveals itself to itself like the shimmer of heat haze on the far horizon, moving from birth, through being, and into nonbeing. Nonbeing comes far too early for far too many bodies.

It is perhaps helpful to think of each night—even under the weight of the terrifying pandemic that grips our nation at the time of this writing—where any of us do not experience similar violence and to consider how peacefully some of us sleep, while others cannot. Perhaps you, too, have never slept easily or peacefully.

Violence against gender is on the rise in the United States. Gender-based hate crimes rose 20 percent in 2019. We know that statistic includes only the crimes that are reported. Rights barely established are being eroded. Simultaneous to this assault, a community of and across genders is emergent, normalized in blood and chosen family, present in media, increasingly represented in legislatures, employed in the arts, protected in the workplace, and gaining expanded access to medical care and basic legal rights. Genders within and without genders, genders bound to race, ethnicity, religion, and migration are all blooming, coming into—or back into—the light of the sun. Push, pull.

This community of emergent and reemergent genders survives, balanced on a razor, walking a slow and narrow path toward the promise of a future.

There are no life-expectancy data on trans women in the United States. It is often said that the average life expectancy of a trans woman is 35 years. This statistic is apocryphal. But it feels true enough, so it's passed along from mouth to ear, weighty as a curse. It reflects the lived experience of the most vulnerable gendered communities. The essential truth is this: it is in the interests of our oppressors that gender remains confined to a narrow path. To stray from that path is to risk terrible and increasing danger to one's body. To stay on that path is to risk terrible danger to one's soul.

One does not have to have the lived experience of a trans woman to be familiar with these dangers. It is only a matter of degree and a question: What does it say about us when we cannot or will not protect the most vulnerable among us?

The experiences of Eden the Doll, Jaslene Whiterose, and Joslyn Flawless, three trans women of color, on Hollywood Boulevard are not unique, atypical, or surprising to any of the artists who participated in *LOVE &/OR FEAR*, even if statistically these women represent the most vulnerable population within our community of genders. Your own experiences may and will vary. It was just one night on Hollywood Boulevard—one night like and not like many others. Every night that follows must be survived as well. The dice never really stop rolling. ...

Any Saturday night on Hollywood Boulevard is another sort of arena, a hippodrome of sorts, where heteronormativity prances up and down the streets. Proud and muscular ponies, fast and wild ponies, graceful, long-legged ponies shod in tall, tiny shoes. The spectacle on display mirrors the idea of glamour, the idea of celebrity, the idea of sexuality, and the idea of gender as a rigid binary. Each weekend, these ideas are exercised in ritual fashion, with ritual garments (tracksuits and bodycon dresses), ritual meals (bacon-wrapped hot dog or overpriced sushi), and the all-too-familiar rituals of mating. It's just like on TV, only more crowded, and you watch where you step. It's still Hollywood, after all.

LOVE &/OR FEAR's participants—artists, activists, and audience—represent a broad swath of genders. They are also the bearers of a broad swath of embodied histories. Those histories propose a rival force to the rote heteropatriarchy of any Saturday night on Hollywood Boulevard. The histories these participants bear include immigrant histories, women's histories, closet histories, histories of historic violence and the violence of right now. These histories are equally present in the bodies that cruise the ad hoc arena of gender on any given Saturday night—only they are usually subsumed and bound by fear, not love. Love and fear always coexist, but love can truly thrive only once fear has been cast aside, held at bay, seen, acted in spite of, and disregarded. Love is, of course, always a risk.

Acting out of love, artists make their own risks. Artists risk embarrassment, ridicule, and challenge to say what must be said. It is love that pushes a Chinese American woman to run for the neighborhood council and bring the debate stage to the street in order to challenge a belligerent puppet, a proxy for our opportunistic oppressors. It is love that pushes an artist to play the part of her own immigrant Jewish ancestors, bearing a weighty, transparent reminder that while her body and being are the marker of their flights from danger, the same dangerous journeys are being made all around us today. Our relative safety demands risk. And it takes risk and love to storm up and down the street as part of artist-led protests, demanding that attentions be shifted from routine pleasures to the weighty matters of racial and sexual violence or to the contradictory truths of our relationships to those issues. And there is the risk of even existing, of putting one's gender on display, of demanding to be spectacular and a member of society at the same time. There is a fine line between creating awareness and eliciting a reactionary, violent response. This is the narrow path that artists

> (Pirates aren't always either male or female)
> — Kathy Acker, *Pussy, King of the Pirates*, 1996

must walk so that they might speak for themselves, for others, and reach the ears of still yet others.

All of this love is fueled by rage and righteous anger at the injustices of the past and the present. The noise of rage chases away the demons of fear. The noise of Black and Indigenous bodies, baring souls and bodies on asphalt, casting an ever-widening circle that invites the demons of fear to be challenged, cast aside, stared down. A limousine hugs a curb, waiting; inside, a magician (of sorts) draws a circle of rented luxury. In the circle, spirits of rage are called down, spat out, and cried out in hidden mystery. Down the street, kicks and punches are thrown as an audience trains for violence that is all too real, which forms in hasty circles of dust and concrete with the channeled anger of the no-longer-victimized. Rage takes its place alongside our love.

These and the other artists of *LOVE &/OR FEAR* celebrate the other in themselves and find themselves in others, all marching together, with no boundary between artists and audiences. All this so that we might, like pirates, live our intentions in community rather than live out expectations for community's sake. That is the dream, isn't it? The dream serves a purpose: to make this night and the next and the next unlike the others that have preceded, to change the rituals, to break the spell that allows for nights and bones and beings to be shattered. To march toward a world where we wander and grow into the fullness of being, where challenges and confrontations shape us but do not break us, that we might move beyond living in and building/rebuilding ourselves from our own ruins time and time again.

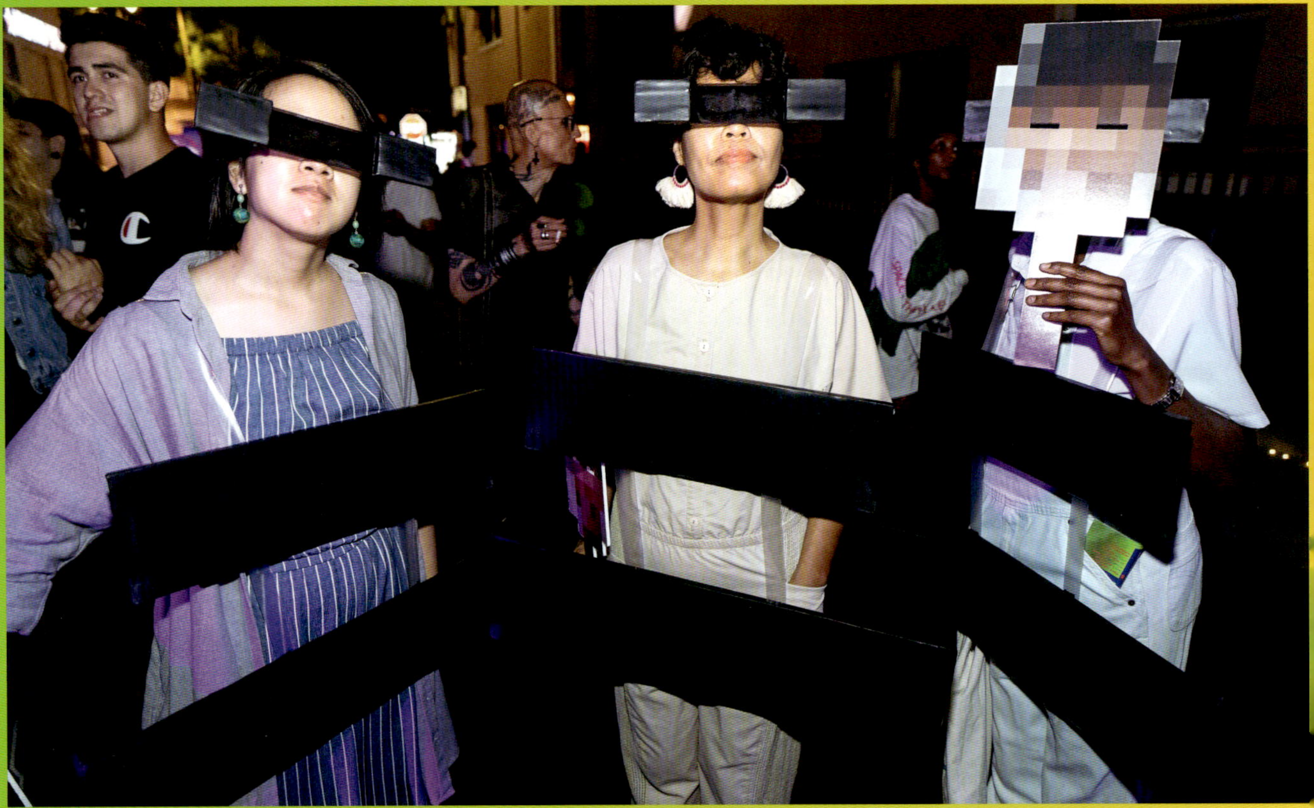

Performance by Reanne Estrada. Photo: Safi Alia Shabaik.

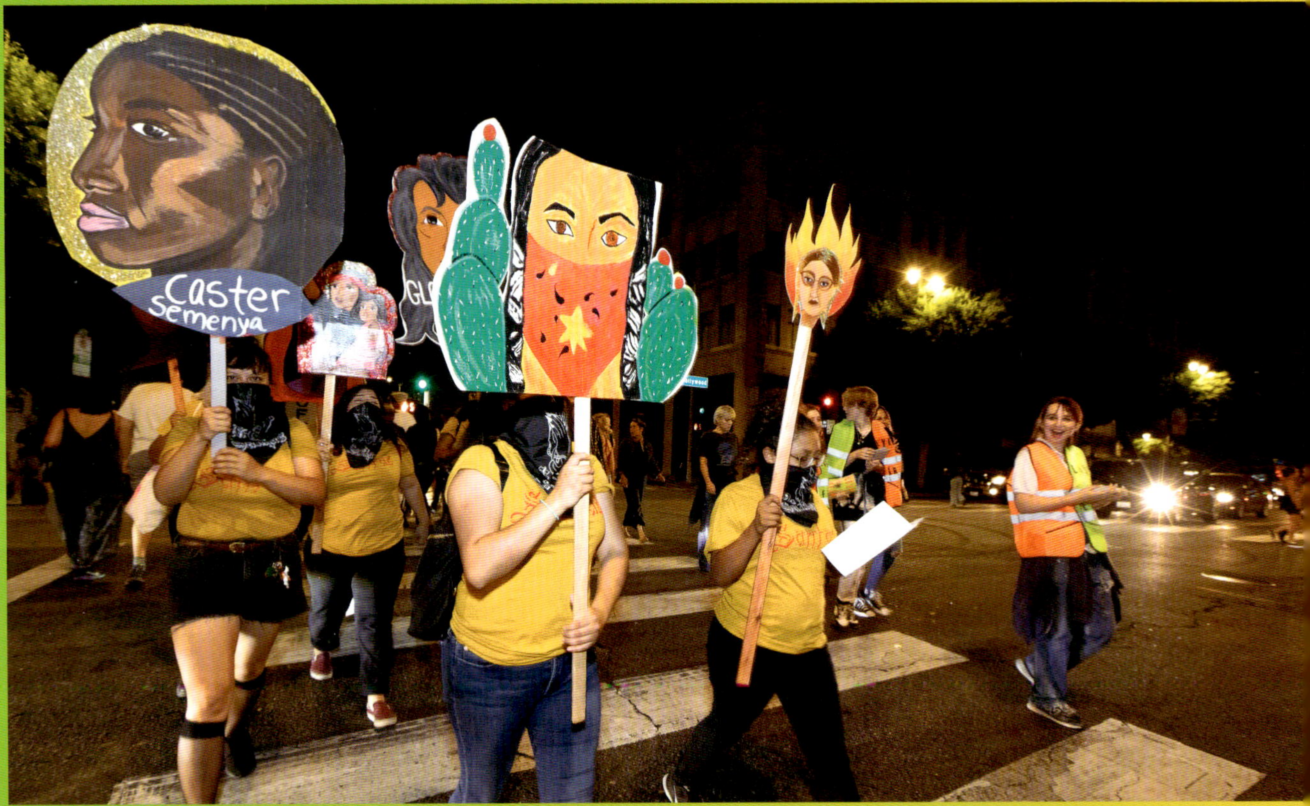

Protest parade by Ni Santas. Photo: Monica Orozco.

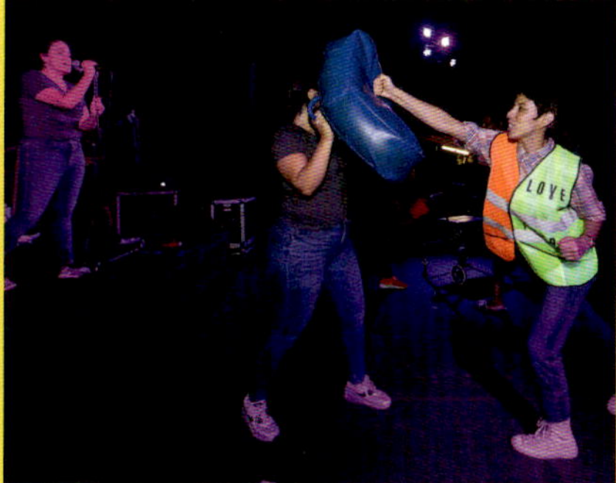

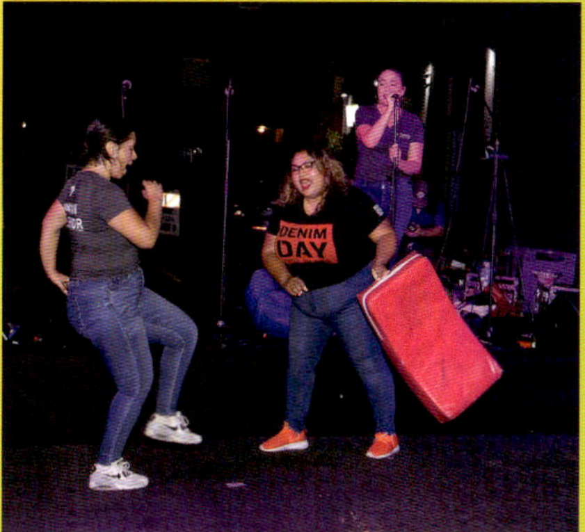

Peace Over Violence self-defense workshop.
Photos: Monica Orozco.

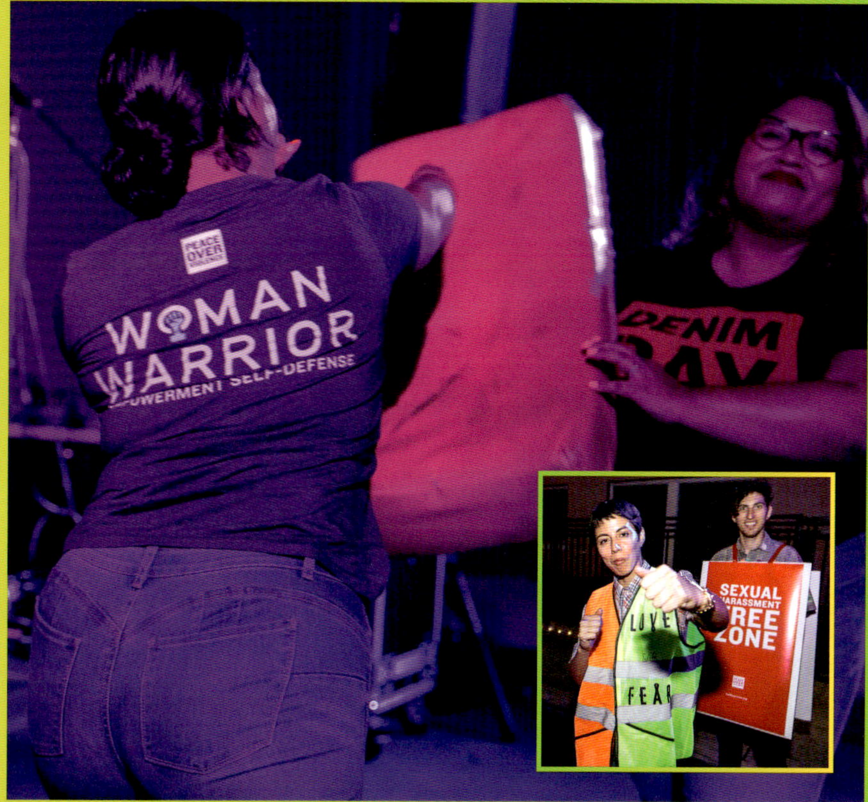

Peace Over Violence self-defense workshop. Photos: Safi Alia Shabaik.

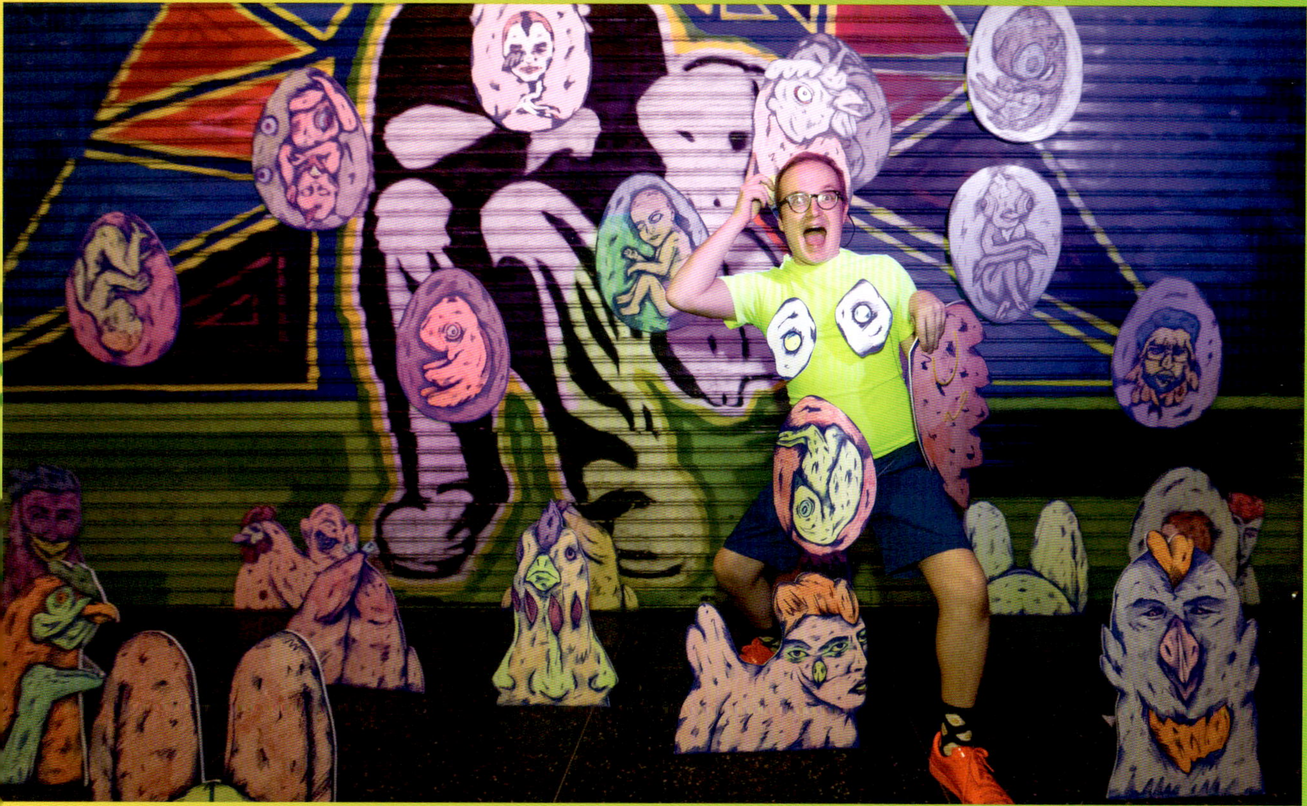

Installation by Dakota Noot. Photo: Monica Orozco.

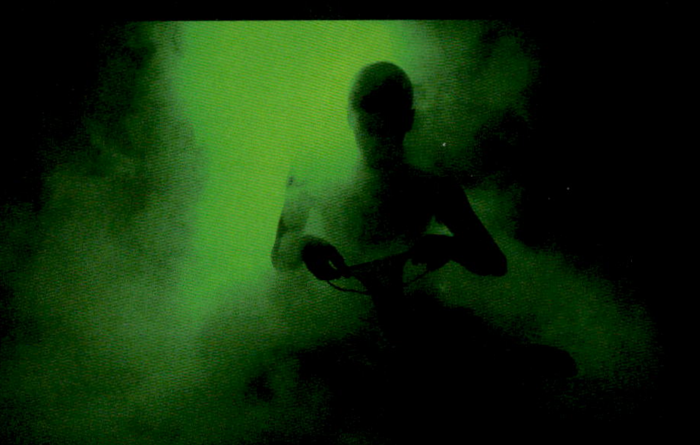

Performance by Sebastian Hernández. Photo: Safi Alia Shabaik.

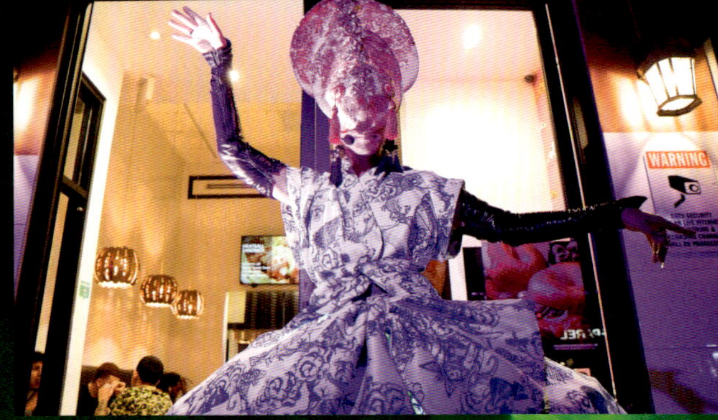

Performance by Yozmit. Photo: Monica Orozco.

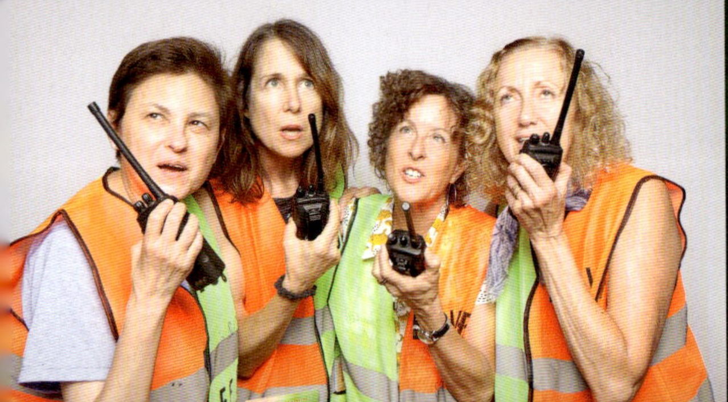

Security by the moms: Ginger Holguin, Cathy Gudis, Cynthia Brophy, Deborah Oliver. Photo: Austin Young.

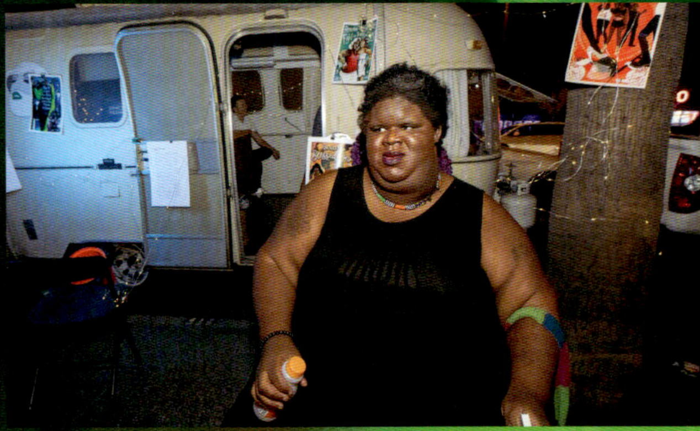

Gender Justice LA, installation. Photo: Monica Orozco.

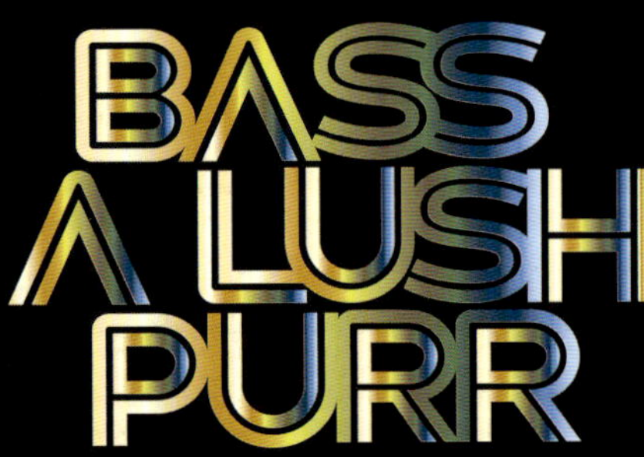

Text art by Pato Hebert.

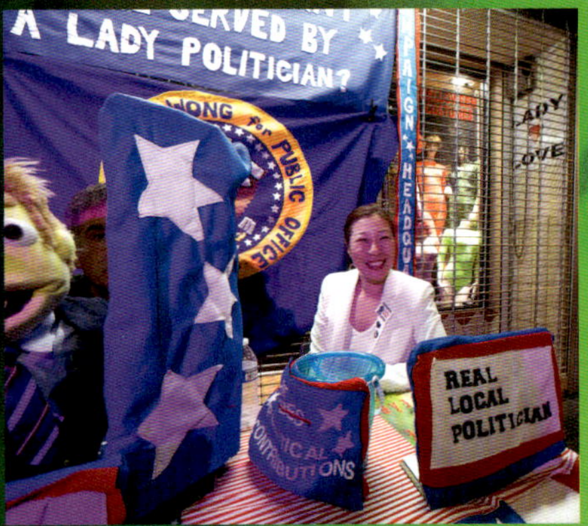

Political candidacy by Kristina Wong, with puppeteer Walter Santucci. Photo: Monica Orozco.

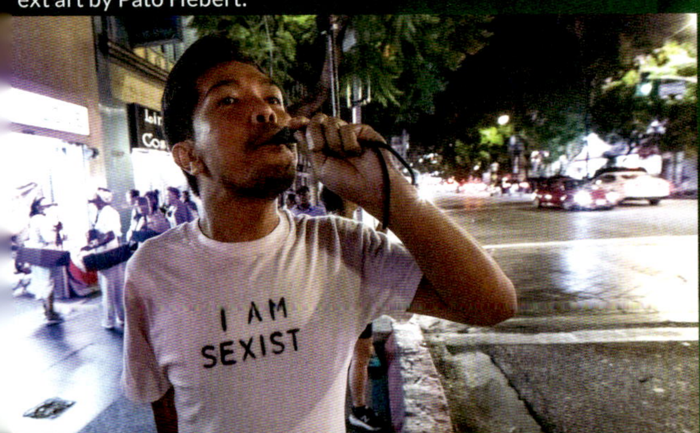

Performance by Thinh Nguyen and friends. Photo: Monica Orozco.

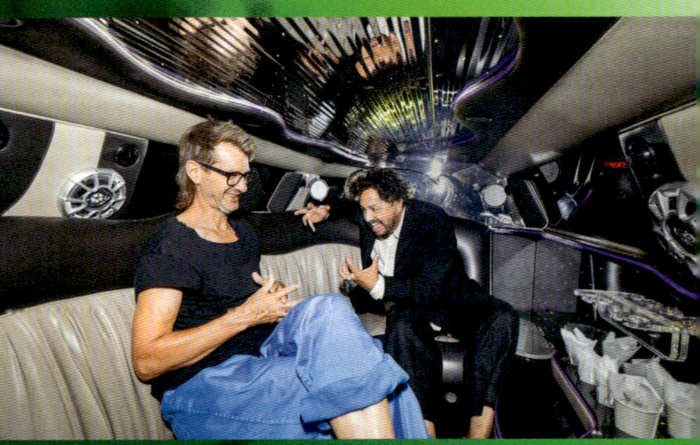

Rage room in limo by Marcus Kuiland-Nazario, with participant Paul Donald. Photo: Hiroshi Clark.

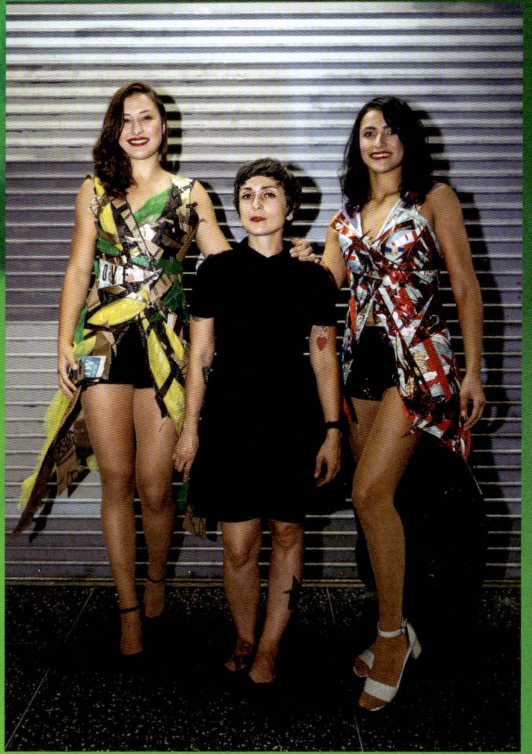

Models in paper dresses by Martha Carrillo, catwalk at crosswalks. Photo: Safi Alia Shabaik.

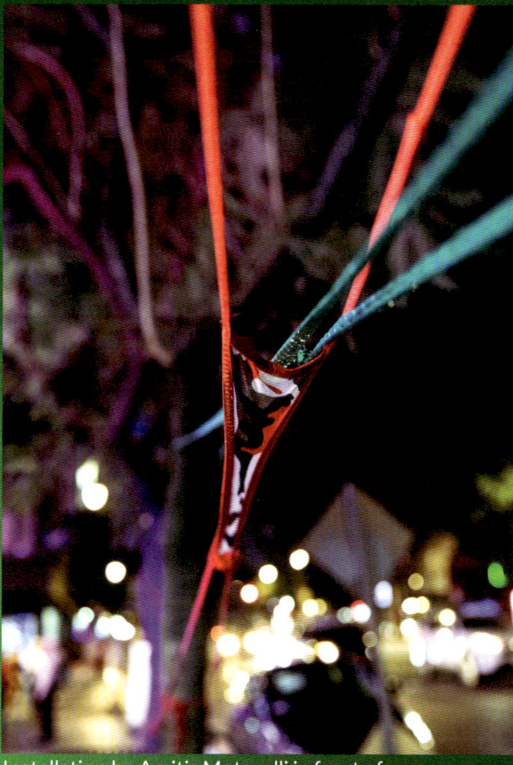

Installation by Amitis Motevalli in front of Hustler. Photo: Safi Alia Shabaik.

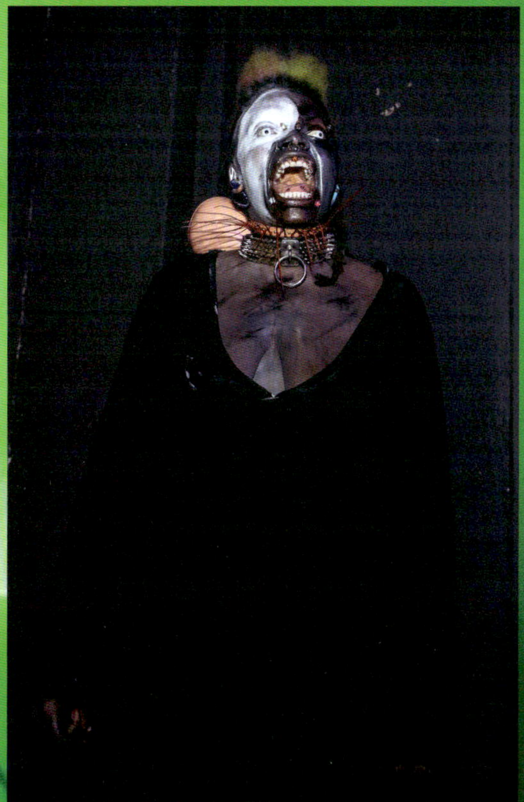

#SNATCHPOWER: The Uhuruverse. Photo: Monica Orozco.

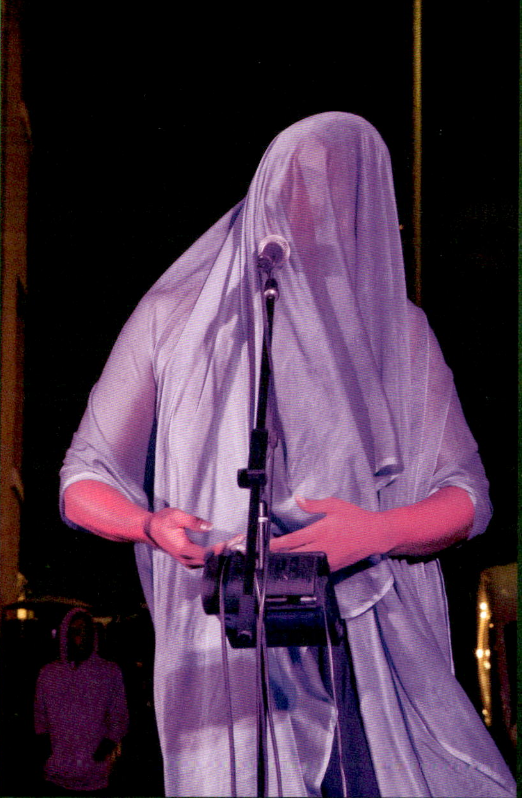

#SNATCHPOWER: Davia Spain. Photo: Monica Orozco.

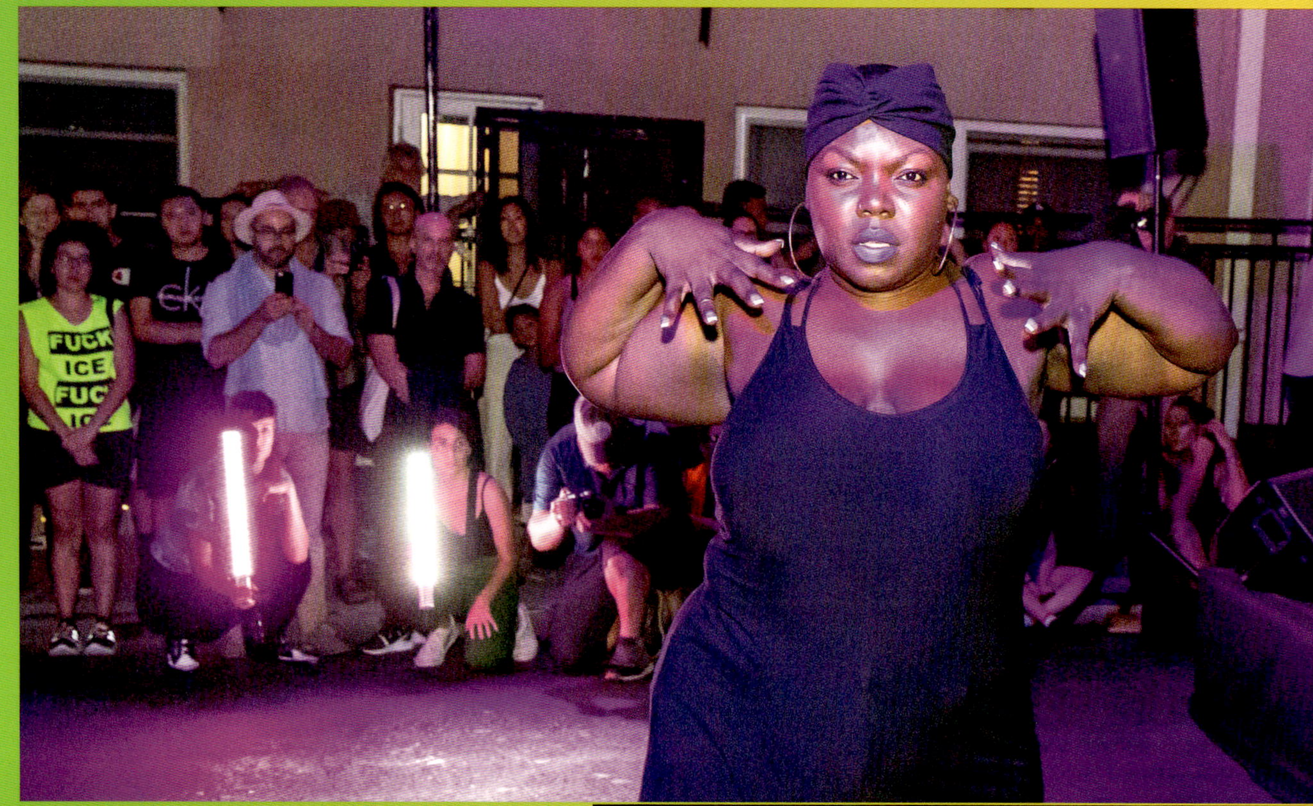

sondriaWRITES. Photo: Monica Orozco.

#SNATCHPOWER: The Uhuruverse, sondriaWRITES, Earth to Jordi, Davia Spain, and Mx. Matias. Photo: Monica Orozco.

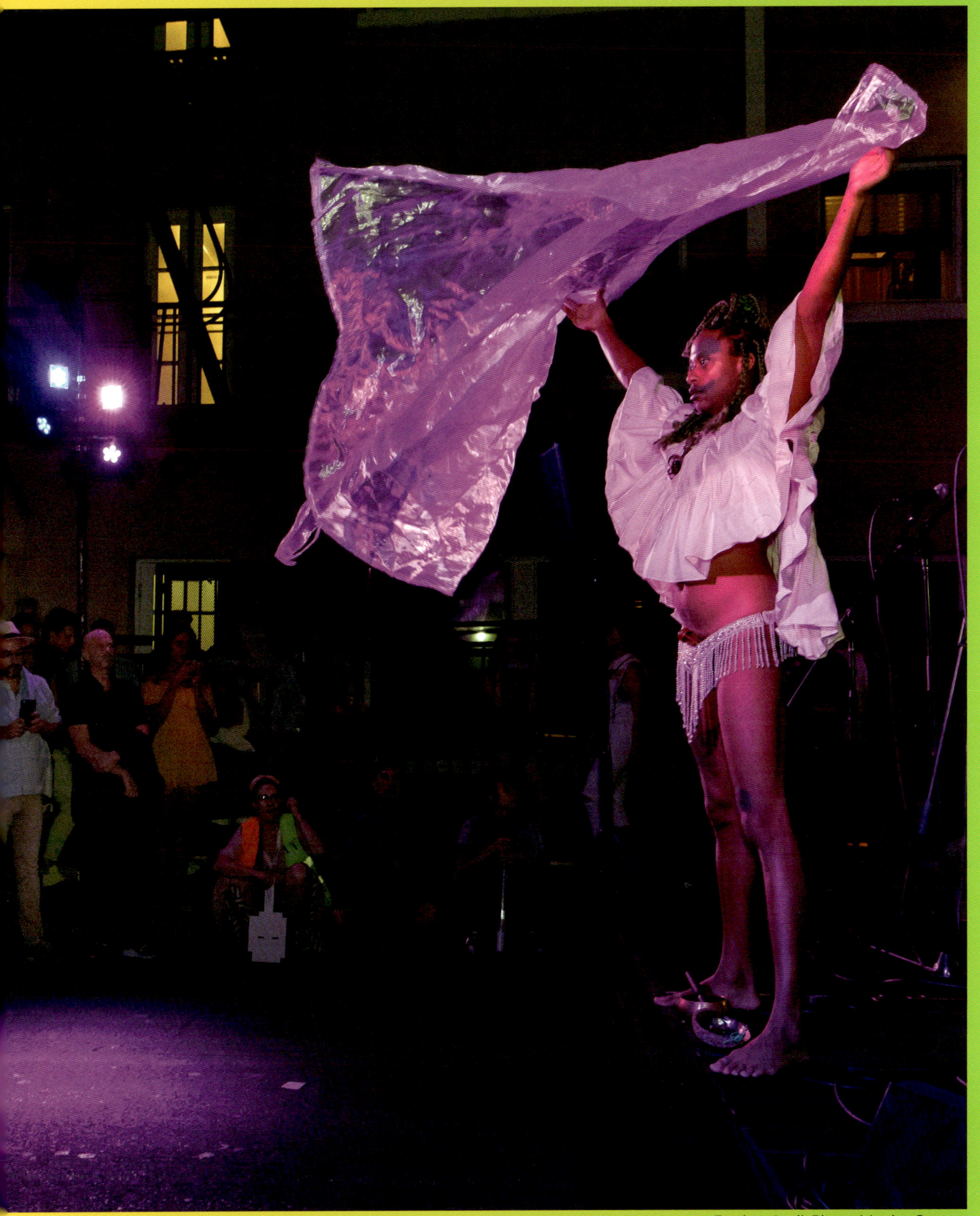

Earth to Jordi. Photo: Monica Orozco.

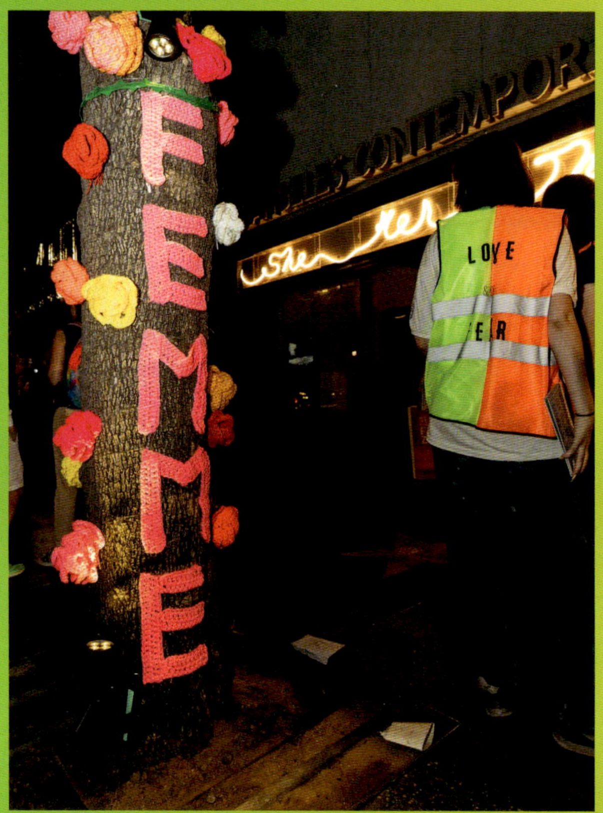

Yarn Bombing Los Angeles. Photo: Safi Alia Shabaik.

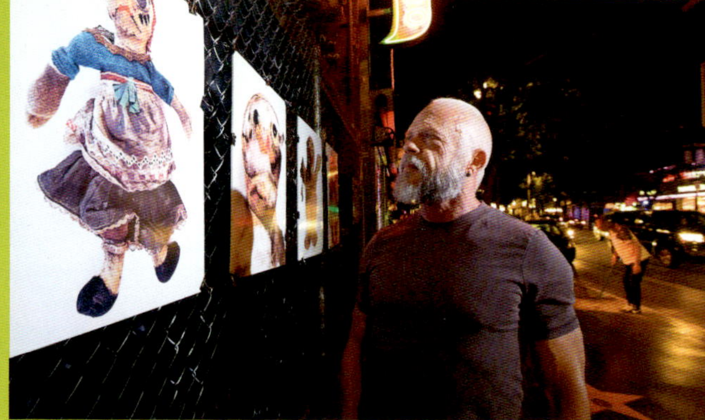

Photos of dolls hand sewn by Marsian de Lellis. Photo: Monica Orozco

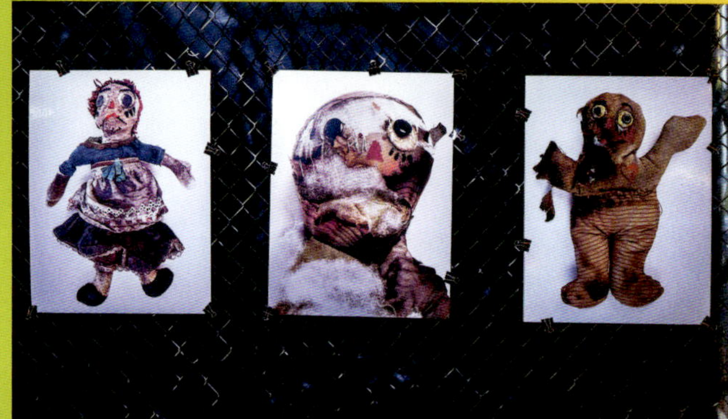

Photos of dolls hand sewn by Marsian de Lellis. Photo: Safi Alia Shabaik.

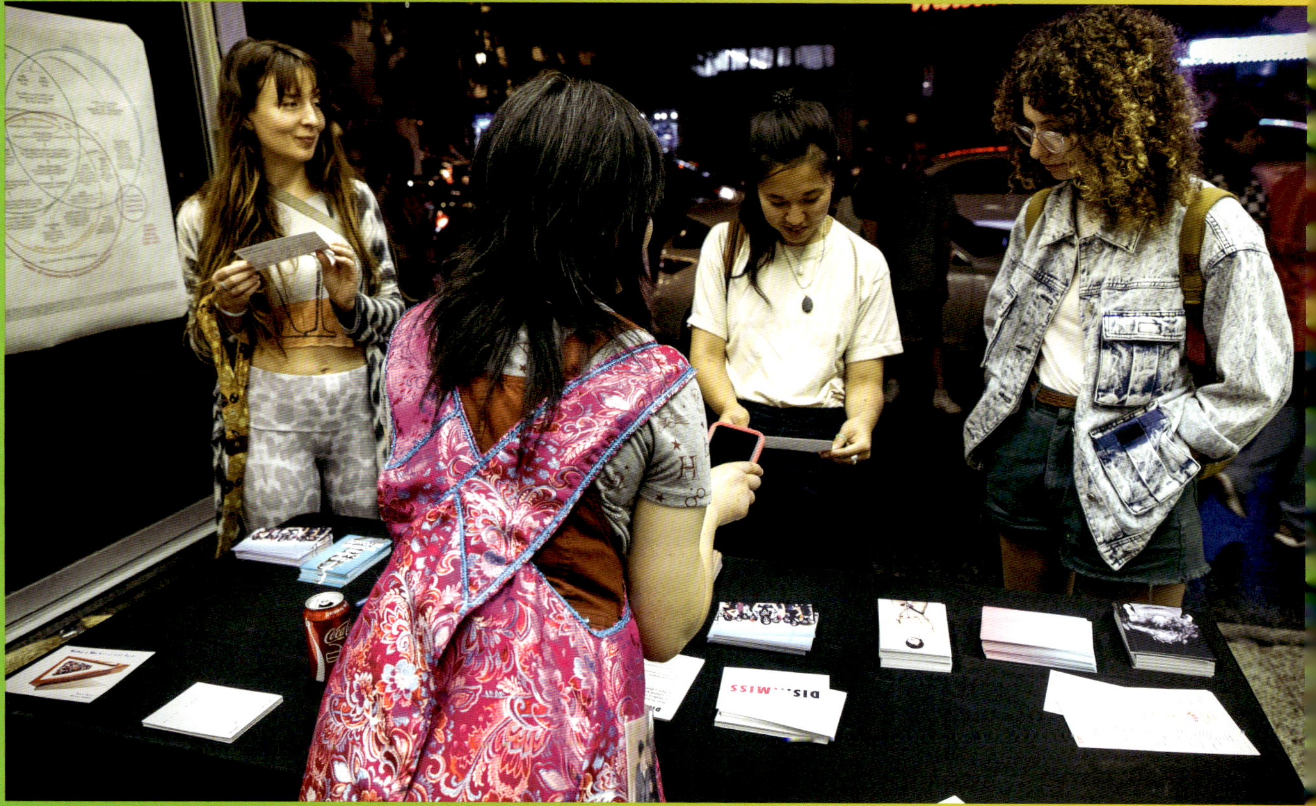

Jennifer Moon distributing *Dis...Miss* postcards. Photo: Safi Alia Shabaik.

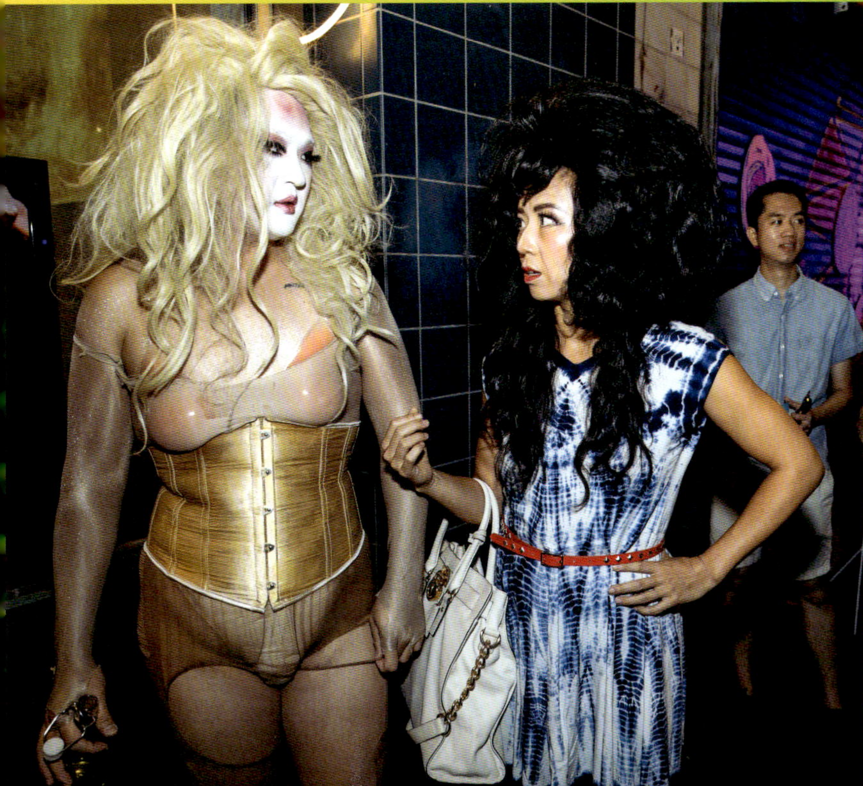

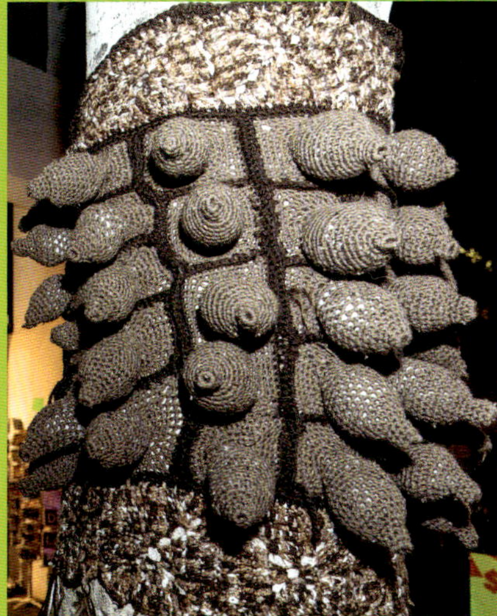

Yarn Bombing Los Angeles.
Photos: Safi Alia Shabaik.

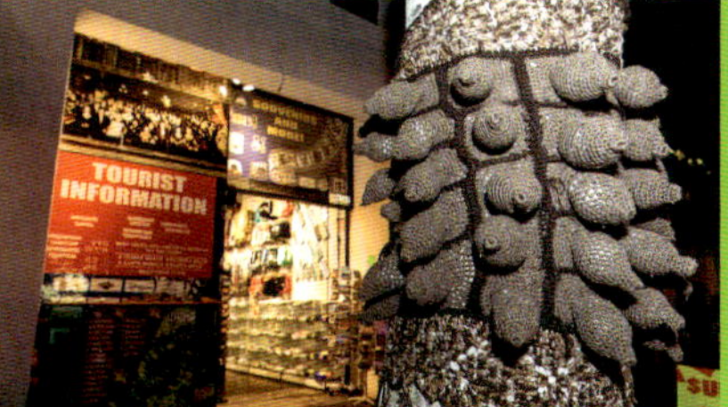

Sign and performance by Young Joon Kwak and Kim Ye at Los Angeles Contemporary Exhibitions (LACE). Photos: Safi Alia Shabaik.

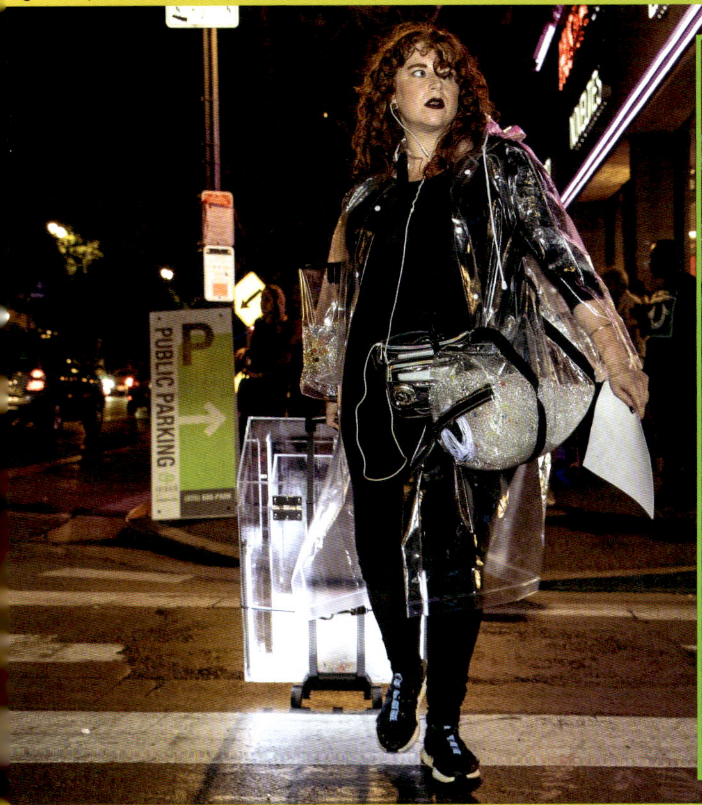

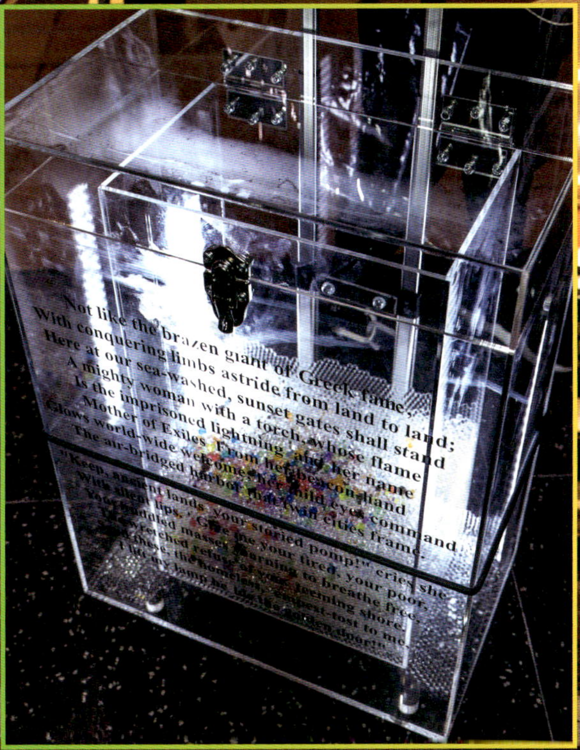

Performance by Christy Roberts Berkowitz. Photos: Safi Alia Shabaik.

The institution of religious capitalism *transformed* the body into one
that could be disciplined and tamed, so as to extract work

The witch's body is

The witch's body

In the moments *I own my*self the most

I am a witch

In the moments I *dance* around naked to Fleetwood Mac, my cat wandering through my feet,
the smell of incense, taste of wine, eyes closed, all senses feeling what it feels like to be free,
although we are never *free* unless we are white, unless we are men, unless we are able to be a
body that work can be extracted from

I am a witch

I don't want to be a worker

I am a witch

I don't want to be a vessel

I am a witch

I don't want to be *yours*

I am a witch

I don't want to behave

I am a witch

I don't want christianity

I am a witch

I don't want a king

I am a witch

I don't want borders

I am a *witch*

I don't want punishment

I am a witch

239

I don't want oil

I don't want plastic

I don't want meat

I don't *want* war

I want mutual aid

I want collectively owned resources

I want *bodily* autonomy

I want freedom from gender

I want anarcho-syndicalism

I want decolonization

I want reparations for the atlantic slave trade and Indigenous genocide

I want a *cultural* revolution against white supremacy

I want to hang the last king with the entrails of the last priest

I want an end to speciesism

I want to *restore* the nonhuman natural world

This is a witch hunt and

I am a witch

I am a witch

I am a witch

I am a witch
I am a witch

I am a witch

I am a witch

I am a witch

I am a witch

I am a witch

I am a witch

I am a witch

I am a witch

I am a witch

I am a witch

I am a witch

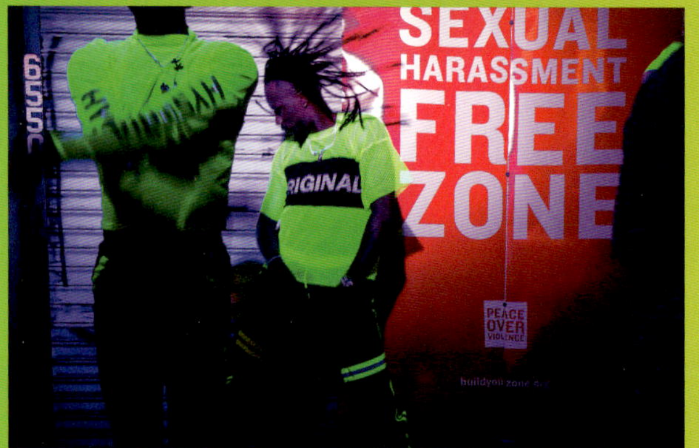

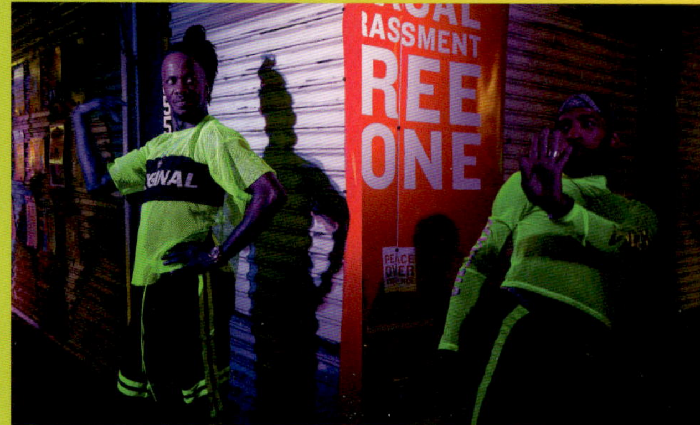

Street voguing by Reach LA, poster by Peace Over Violence. Photos: Safi Alia Shabaik.

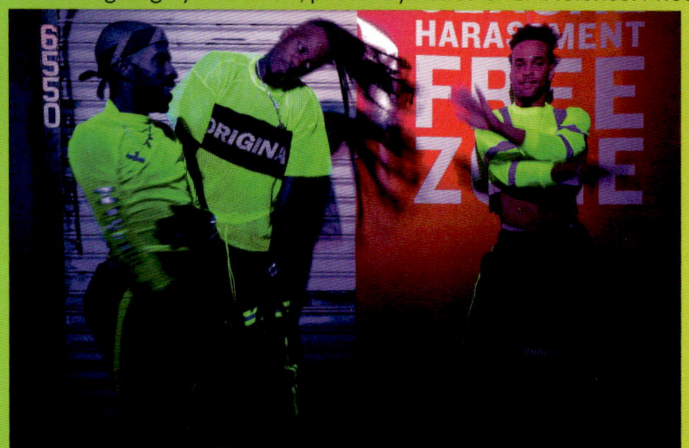

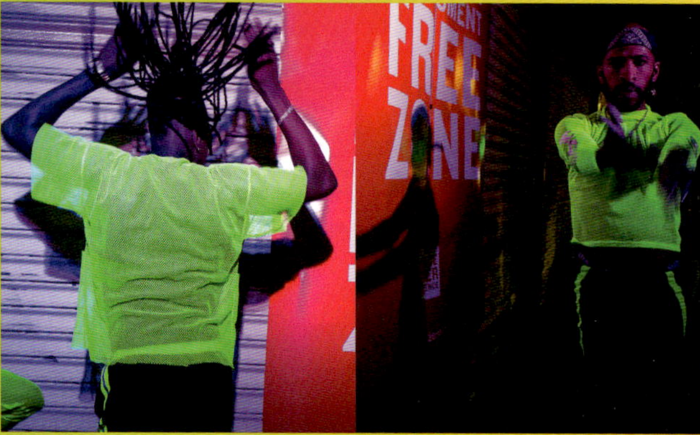

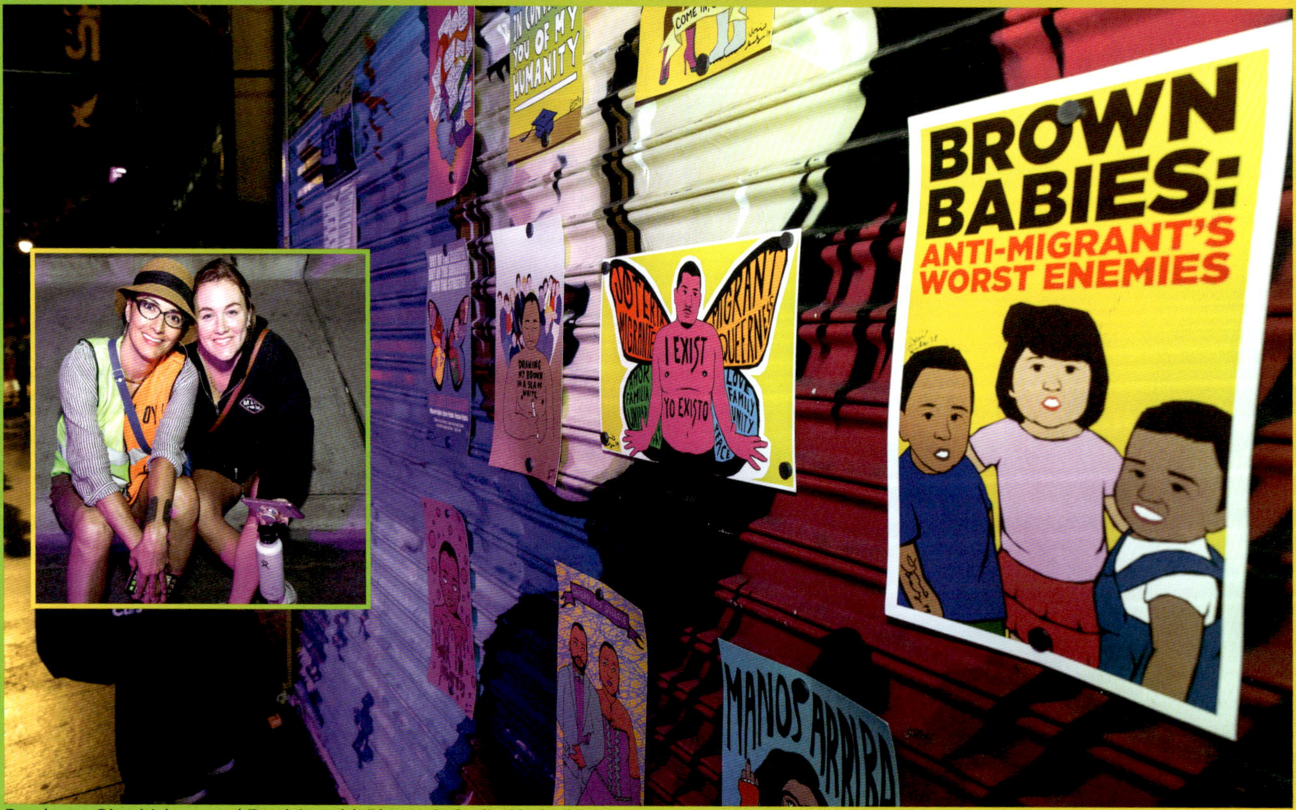

Producer Gina Valona and Dani Arnold. Photo: Safi Alia Shabaik.   Posters by Julio Salgado. Photo: Safi Alia Shabaik.

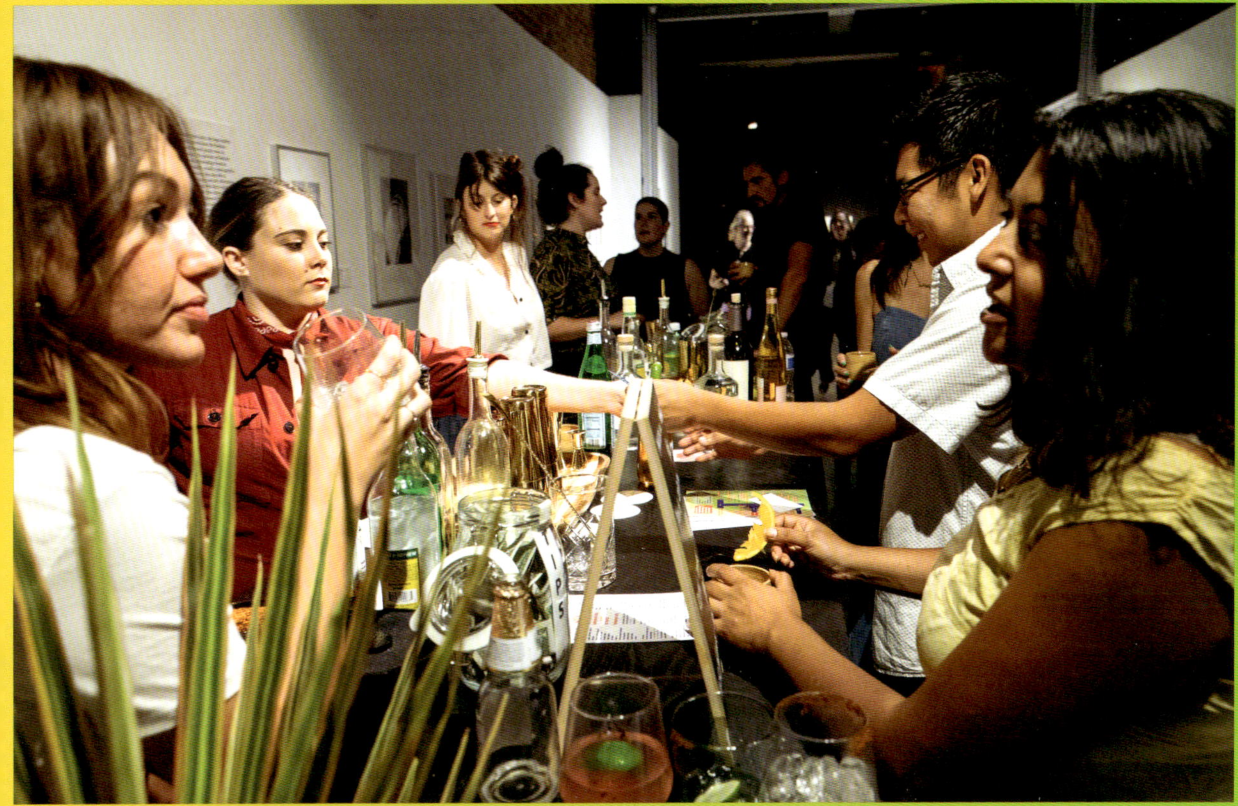

The Fingerjoint, a lesbian pop-up bar at Woodbury University Hollywood Outpost (WUHO). Photo: Safi Alia Shabaik.

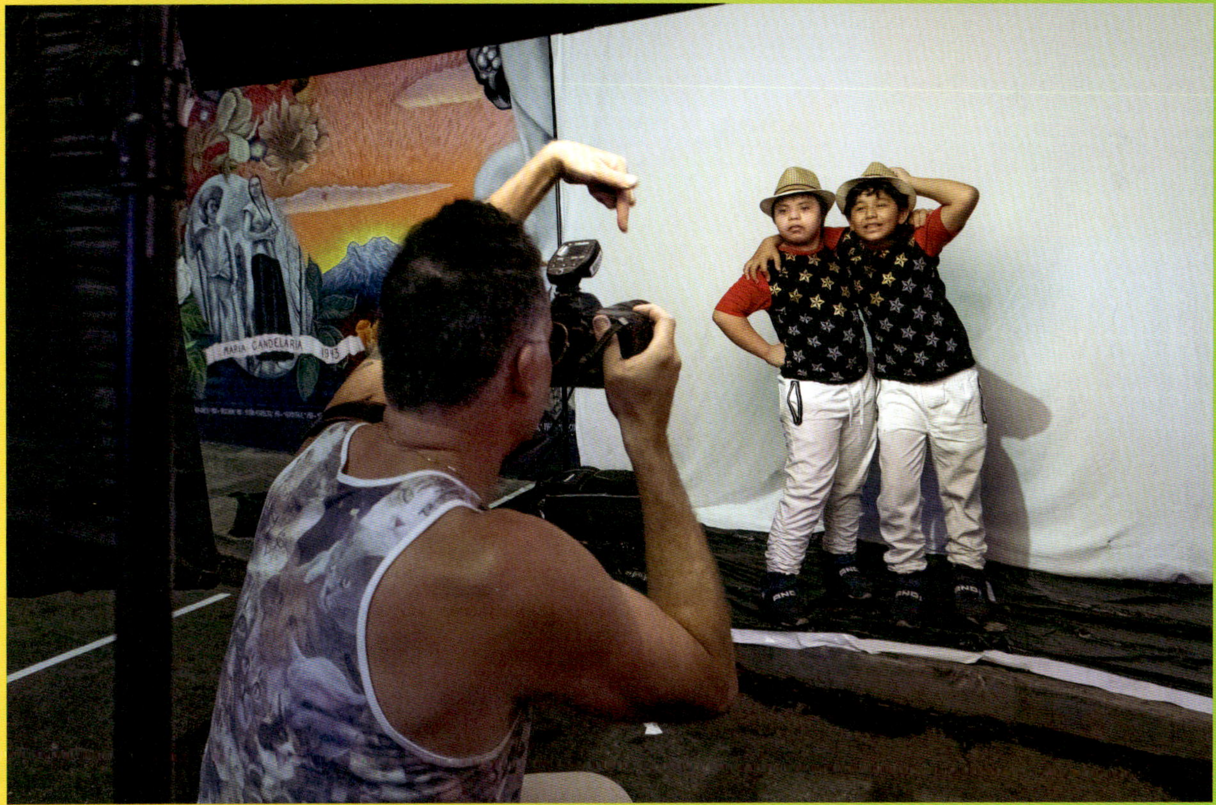

Austin Young photographing attendees of *LOVE &/OR FEAR* in his outdoor studio. Photo: Monica Orozco.

Reach LA

MISSION

Engage and empower young LGBTQ people of color and their communities.

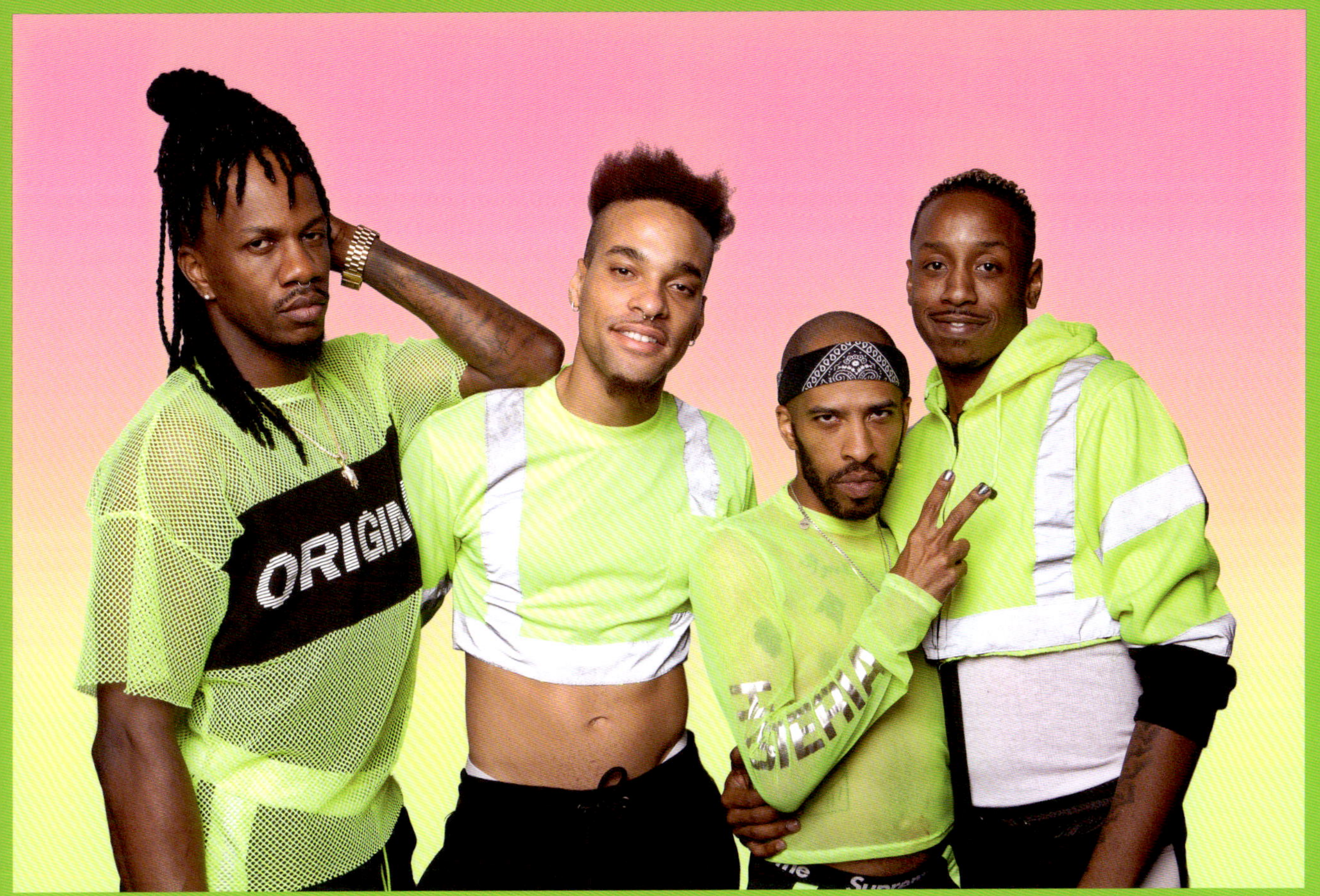

Reach LA. Photo: Austin Young.

VISION

Increase self-sustainability by encouraging creative expression, supporting safe spaces, and promoting health and wellness, one person at a time.

13

change the narrative

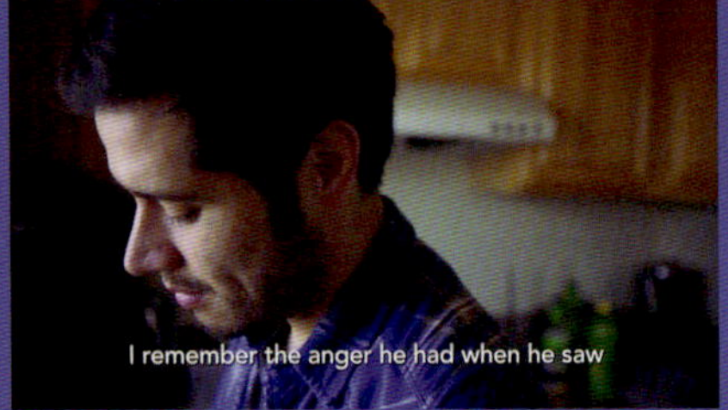

Gloria Morán.

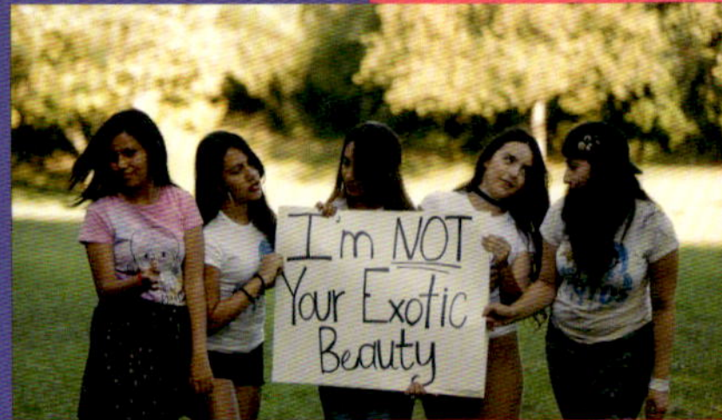

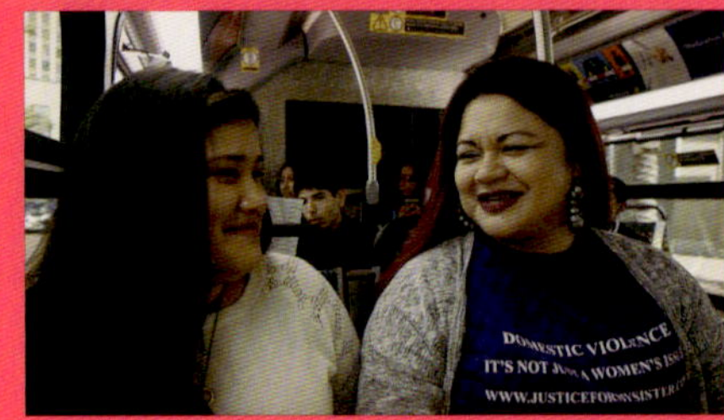

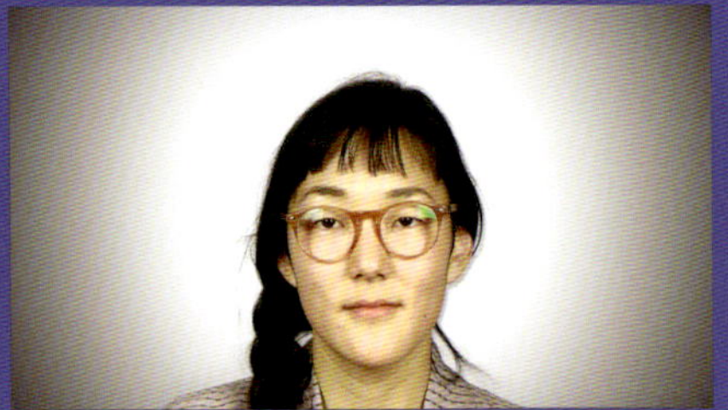
Adebukola (Buki) Bodunrin.

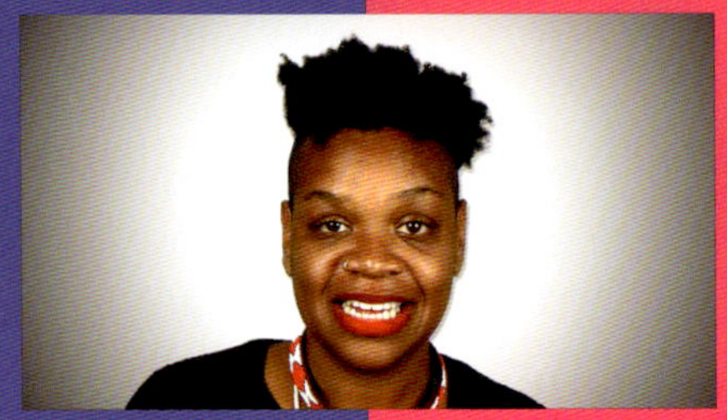

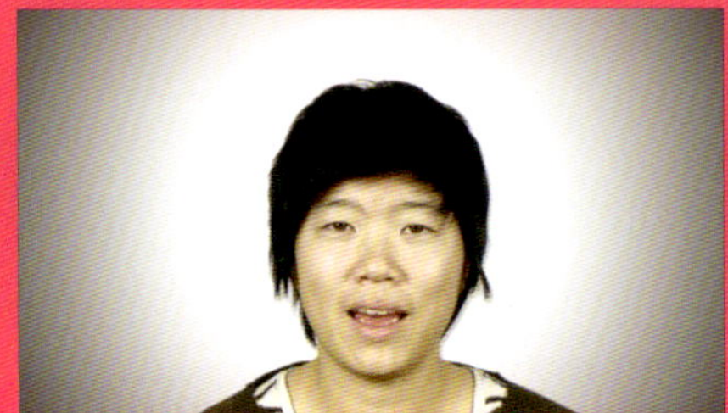

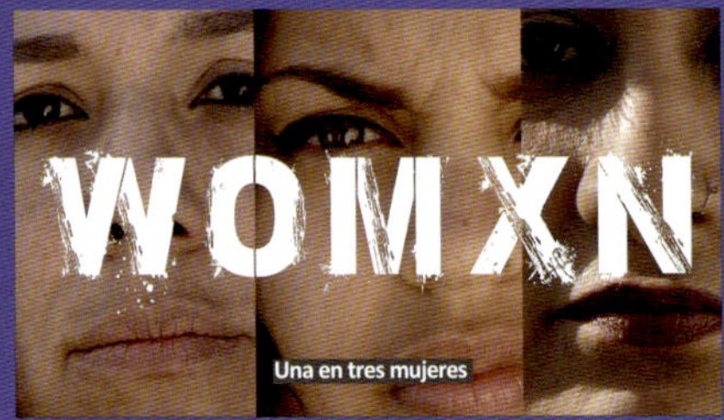

Meena Nanji.

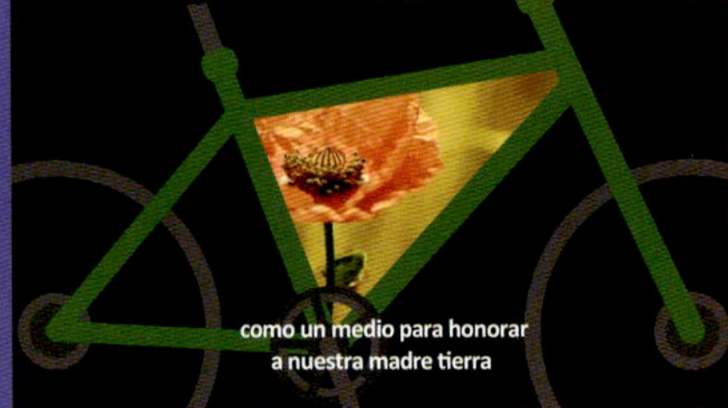

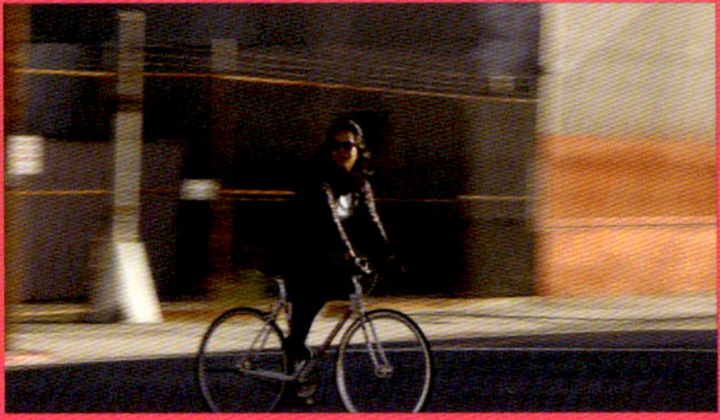

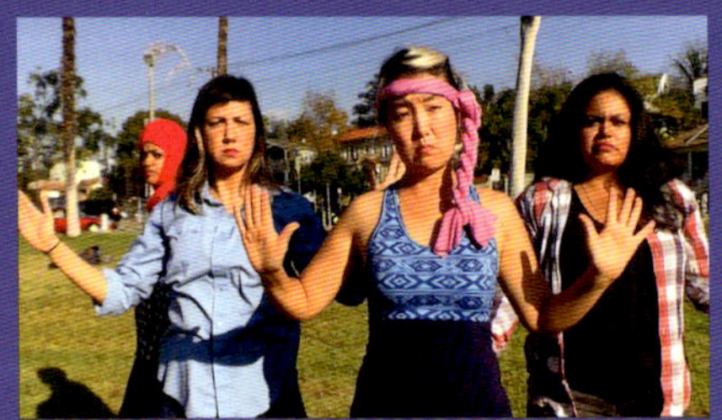
Mail Order Brides/M.O.B..

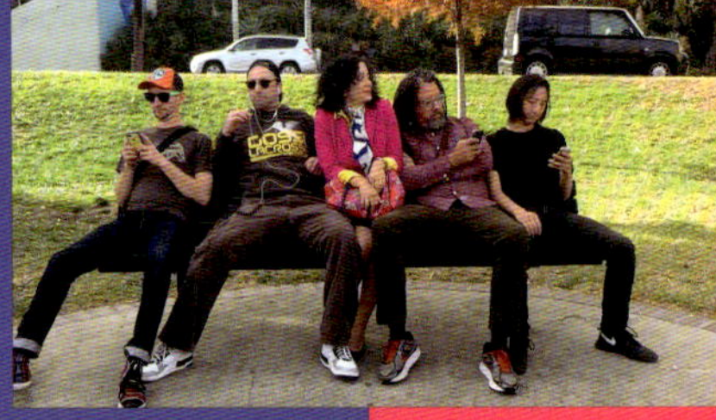

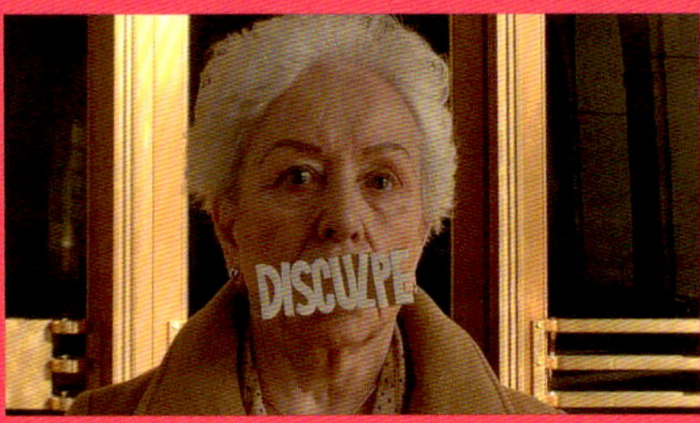

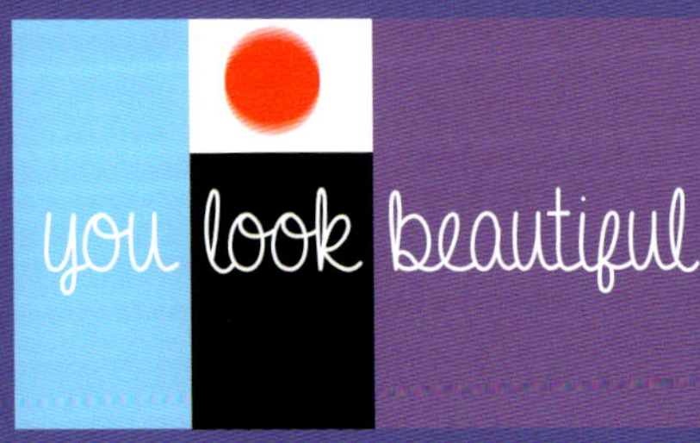

Caress Reeves.

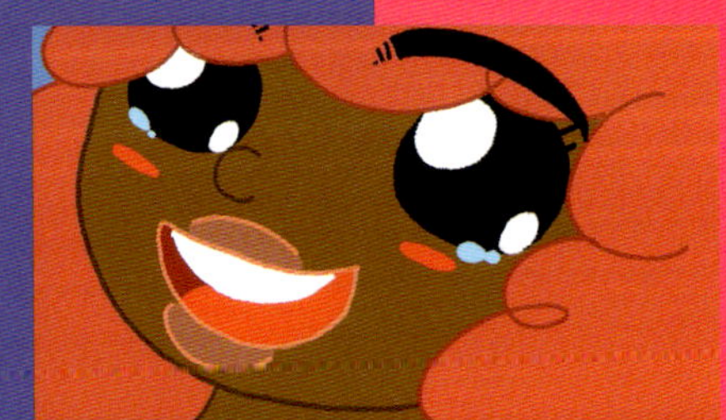

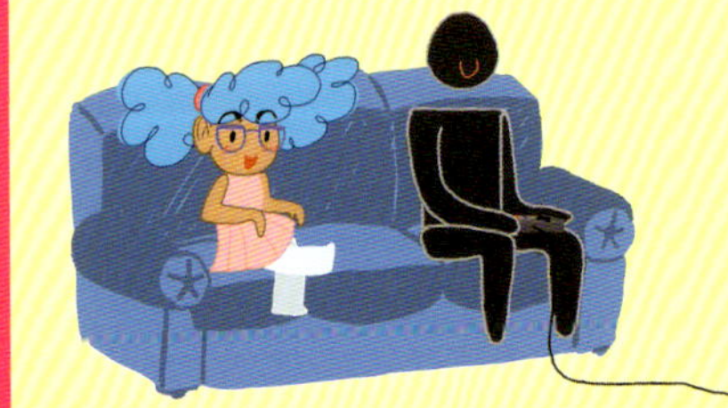

Change the Narrative: Dis…Miss Videos

Holly Willis

Audacious, funny, and in your face: the 25 videos commissioned by LA Freewaves for the *Dis…Miss* public-art experience augur a poetics of social engagement, aspiring not to beauty or formal achievement but to connection, disruption, and change. Although very brief—often 30 seconds or a minute or two—they are not tidy narrative videos with cause-and-effect plotlines. Made by Gloria Maria Guadalupe Morán, Meena Nanji, Caress Reeves, Mail Order Brides/M.O.B. (Reanne Estrada, Eliza Barrios, and Jenifer Wofford), and Adebukola (Buki) Bodunrin, they have been showcased both online and at numerous events designed to encourage dialogue about gendered stereotypes. The videos are not documentaries, commercials, or PSAs, with clever calls to action or clearly articulated points of resistance. Although they are cognizant of this newest era of moving-image storytelling, they definitely do not resemble the self-congratulatory social media "stories" we scroll past on Instagram or Facebook. The most frequently invoked imperative—explicitly or implicitly—in these short-form wake-up calls is *change the narrative*. These videos question who gets to tell the story, how the story gets told, and who hears and sees the story. And, finally, they ask, What will we all do with what we've heard and seen? Taken together, the videos suggest that *changing the narrative* requires a radical act of the imagination.

The destabilizing of normalized storytelling in the *Dis… Miss* videos occurs perhaps most overtly through the layering of word and image. Video after video invites us to pair reading and viewing, thereby undermining the assumed transparency of the cinematographic image, so long the hallmark of on-screen realism. For example, in filmmaker Gloria Maria Guadalupe Morán's video *I'm Not Her I'm Me*, five young women standing outside in a park deliver a series of statements on hand-written posters. "I'm not one ethnicity," reads one. "I am diverse," reads the next. "I am not your translator" is followed by "I am your linguistic competition." The camera pans slowly back and forth across the line of women, holding them in their entirety from a slight distance while we as viewers slip between reading and

viewing. We cannot sustain a single perspective. We cannot isolate, identify with, or fetishize. We are kept in continuous motion. Further, at the video's beginning and conclusion, we see the women's faces divided and recombined, suggesting a relationality that allows them to be together without obliterating differences.

Although the history of poetry is very different from that of film and video, we see a call for a similar redefinition of terms and values in poet and writer Cathy Park Hong's essay for *New Republic* in 2015, "There's a New Movement in American Poetry and It's Not Kenneth Goldsmith." In her alternately humorous and caustic piece, Hong queries how the historical elision of poets of color from the history of avant-garde experimental writing undermines the genre's very definition as political and adamantly resistant. Hong claims that in place of a moribund poetic practice we are currently witnessing "a new movement in American poetry, a movement galvanized by the activism of Black Lives Matter, spearheaded by writers of color who are at home in social media activism and print magazines." She goes on to note, "Some poets are redefining the avant-garde while others are fueling a raw politics into the personal lyric. Their aesthetic may be divergent, but they share a common belief that as poets, they must engage in social practice."[1] Hong's essay had an immediate impact, which was both to name and to catalyze a national movement, and, indeed, we are witnessing a cultural moment in which women and artists of color, fueled by activism and the drive for social justice, refuse to remain silenced. They are instead leading the effort to redefine the terms and values not only of particular art forms but of political debate and social practice as well. The insistent use of the written word on-screen in so many of the *Dis…Miss* videos participates in this "raw politics" that becomes "personal lyric," reimagining the role of language by pushing its limits.

Further, while the *Dis…Miss* videos echo long-standing histories and practices of tactical political video—including feminist media making and the work of racially diverse and queer film- and video makers from

---

1   Cathy Park Hong, "There's a New Movement in American Poetry and It's Not Kenneth Goldsmith," *New Republic*, October 1, 2015, https://newrepublic.com/article/122985/new-movement-american-poetry-not-kenneth-goldsmith.

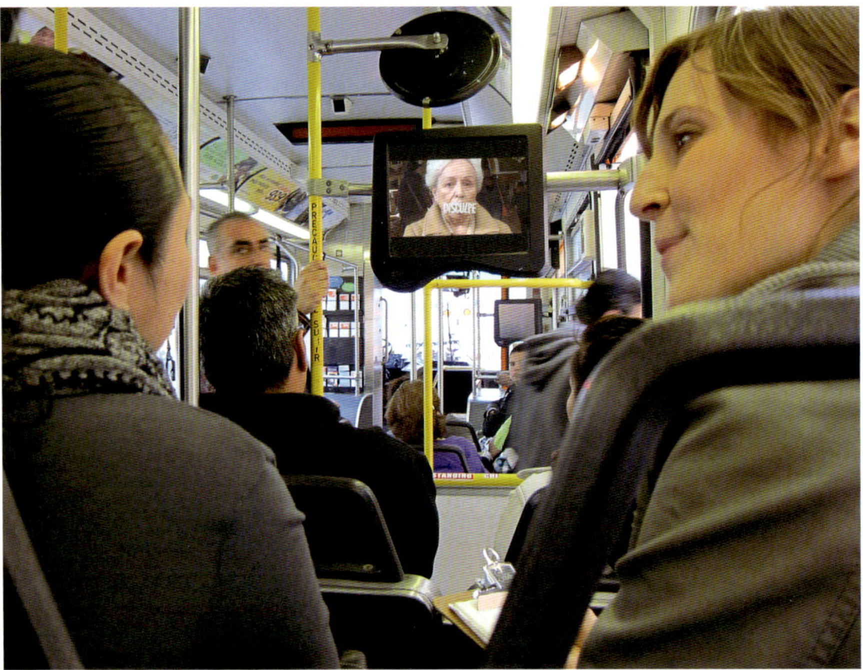

Diss…Miss video *No Apologies*, from the series *Out the Window*, shown in an LA Metro bus. Photo: Anne Bray.

a demand and then into downright insult. "You look beautiful" transforms into "You look at me," and while the words are at first written in wispy, appealing handwriting, they quickly shift into white all-caps on a black background: "Stop being a bitch." The woman in this piece is never heard or seen, but she is there, the target of misogyny and the recipient of this 33-second escalation of spoken violence. Despite the absence of any visible figure, these words conjure an experience of verbal abuse familiar to many female-identified people, who have heard their partners or relatives swiftly move from compliments to misogynistic outbursts in their efforts to control and manipulate women.

the 1980s and 1990s (such as Sadie Benning, Cauleen Smith, and Valerie Soe)—these pieces also assert a raw urgency and insistent form of address. They want action now! As an emergent poetics, the work is often explicitly collective in point of view and address, and it is avowedly political, demanding attention to the choices we make and the actions we take.

We see this collectivity in the video *We Are All Women* by filmmaker Meena Nanji about the feminist collective Ovarian Psyco-Cycles (OPC). In the video, a series of statistics about violence against women appears in brightly colored type over the faces of angry women looking directly at the camera, sometimes in close-up and other times from a distance. The video asks viewers to look women in the face and meet their eyes while reading that "1 in 3 womxn experience physical or sexual violence." From close-ups on faces, the footage transitions to members of the Ovarian Psycos on their bikes riding together in the city, and the force of the piece moves from the pathos of acknowledging outrageous violence to the empowering force of collective resistance.

Similarly, the animator Caress Reeves's video *SlutWalk* also uses text as well as graphics. The video stages a one-sided conversation as a compliment morphs into

The question of who actually gets to speak is a key element of the emergent video poetics evident in the videos commissioned for *Dis…Miss*. All five videos by Mail Order Brides/M.O.B., a collective composed of Filipina American artists Reanne Estrada, Eliza Barrios, and Jenifer Wofford, tackle this topic, staging scenes of silencing, shame, refusal, and more. In *No Apologies*, an older woman, trying simply to walk at her own pace in public space, is jostled and pushed relentlessly. Considered too slow for the world's youth-oriented momentum and too old to be particularly visible, she just gets in the way. She silently holds the word "Disculpe" (Sorry) written on cardboard in her mouth, literally labeling her body as an apology. Simply being older and female and moving out of pace with the rest of the world require an act of remorse. But it is a delight when the woman finally turns and slugs a guy with her suitcase out of pure frustration. She drops the label and moves from begging for forgiveness to taking her own place in the world.

In another piece by Mail Order Brides, *No Is Ok*, we see a series of quick scenarios in which a woman feels pressured to just say yes. She is presented with sexual advances, offers of marriage, the opportunity to procreate, and, a bit more benignly, to eat foods she does not want to eat or to accept pets that make her sneeze. Near the end, after the woman has been presented with a baby, she shakes her head as her formerly composed face breaks out into laughter, and the countermessage becomes clear—you can just say no. A title card appears: "No is OK."

If written text recurs frequently, so, too, is voice emphasized. This is seen in the five videos that the artist Adebukola (Buki) Bodunrin made for the *Hear My Voice* series, which focuses specifically on voice and the right to speak. Starting with five audio recordings of derogatory statements about the quality and tenor of women's voices, Bodunrin uses these declarations as a voice-over, paired with a fast-paced sequence of women's faces as they are speaking. The result is a kind of silencing: we cannot hear what each woman might actually be saying; all we hear is the dismissive voice that drowns out the women. By extension, dismissing the *way* women speak dismisses what they are saying.

If anger and empathy fuel some of the work, humor catalyzes much of the rest of it. In two other videos by Reeves, *Gaming While Girl* and *Dating While Femme*, the artist wields humor like a ninja, sketching the boundaries of appropriate female behavior. Using flat 2D animation and brash colors that feel quick and spontaneous, she sketches scenes of despair—sexual comments and images sent through a dating app, for example—that are at the same time funny. Mistreated? Mansplained? We see the animated protagonist scream and grimace in disgust! The power of Reeves's work lies in the invitation into each character's perspective—the combined attitude, horror, and humor of these 2-D characters pull us into a shared sense of communal outrage.

The 25 *Dis...Miss* videos demonstrate a powerful new form of activism that is visual, funny, outrageous, and in your face. They also insist that it's time for a new poetics and a new narrative, and they revel in the sense of disruption that change produces. Changing the narrative stirs up the sedimentation of the everyday sexism, gendered violence, and rampant racism that constitute normative American existence. Changing the narrative means changing how we speak, look, and listen. Changing the narrative conjures potential futures based on a profound reimagining of how we relate to each other in the world. In short, different stories require different structures, different paradigms, and different voices. Ultimately, the *Dis...Miss* videos ask: What narrative is yours to tell, and how will you tell it? How will you answer?

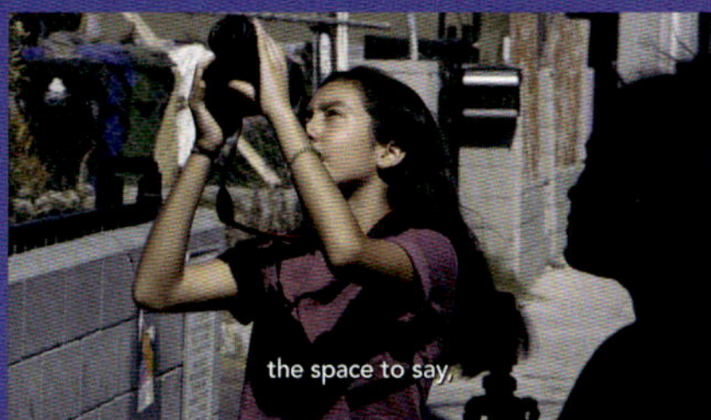

Gloria Morán.

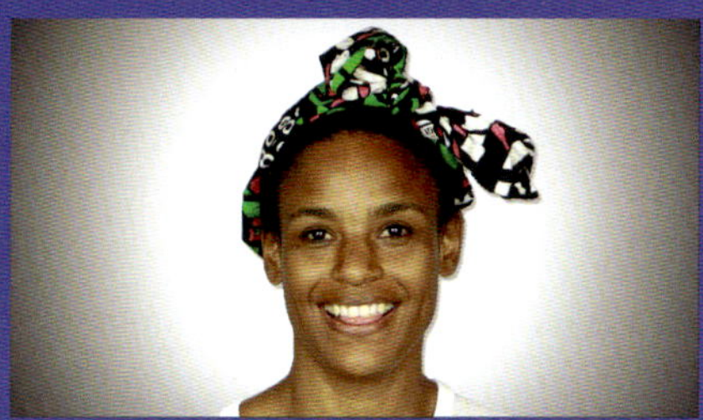
Adebukola (Buki) Bodunrin.

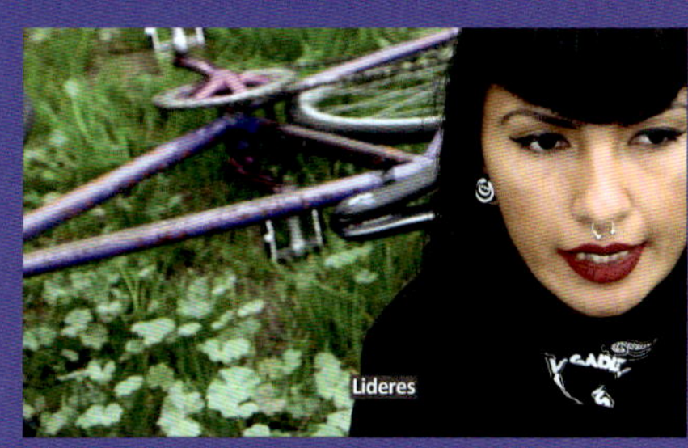

Meena Nanji.

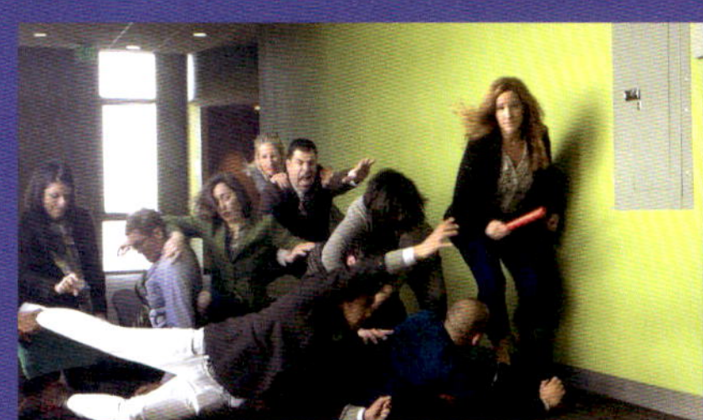
Mail Order Brides/M.O.B.

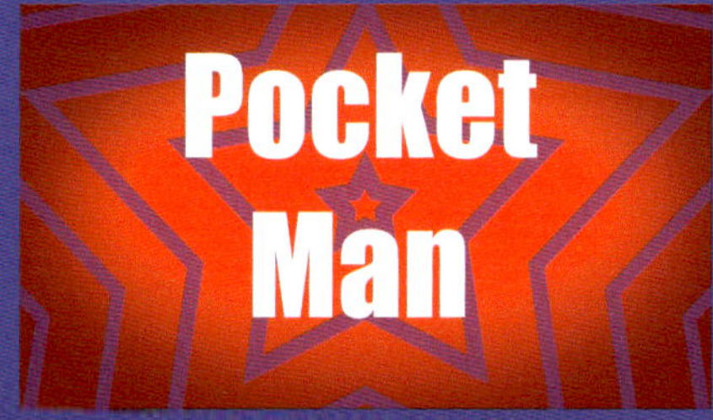

Caress Reeves.

acknowledgments & contributors

Conceived by Anne Bray, artist and executive director of LA Freewaves

Edited by Catherine G. Wagley

Designed by Carolina Ibarra-Mendoza

Video infographics by Catherine Bell

Online engagement by Abriel Gardner

Photography by Monica Orozco and Safi Alia Shabaik

Studio photographs by Austin Young

Postcard portraits by Alejandra Sone

Front cover image: performance by Sebastian Hernández, photo by Monica Orozco.

Back cover image: Performance by Sebastian Hernández. Photo: Safi Alia Shabaik.

Dis...Miss has been made possible through the generous support of

Andy Warhol Foundation for the Visual Arts

Mike Kelley Foundation for the Arts

Robert Rauschenberg Foundation

Metabolic Studio

National Endowment for the Arts

Pasadena Art Alliance

Los Angeles County Arts Commission, City of Los Angeles Department of Cultural Affairs

University of Southern California (USC) Visions and Voices

Cypress College Art Gallery

Crossroads School

Members of LA Freewaves

Dis...Miss includes:

Postcards by artists: April Bey, boychild, Cassils, Chan & Mann, Roya Falahi, Alexandra Grant, Micol Hebron, Michael Raines, Thinh Nguyen, Ovarian Psycos, and Shizu Saldamando.

Performance artists: Nao Bustamante, Marcus Kuiland-Nazario, Zackary Drucker, rafa esparza, Exposure Drag, Funmilola Fagbamila, Rudy "Bleu" Garcia, Janice Gomez and Fatima Hoang, Raquel Gutiérrez with Karen Tongson, Reach LA, Jennifer Moon, Amitis Motevalli, Thinh Nguyen, Patty Schemel and Object as Subject, #SNATCHPOWER (The Uhuruverse, Jordi Phi [Earth to Jordi], Davia Spain, sondria WRITES), Christy Roberts Berkowitz, Yozmit, Kristina Wong, Kiki Xtravaganza, and Xina Xurner (Marvin Astorga and Young Joon Kwak).

Installation artists: bitchface, Martha Carrillo, C. Ree and Reanne Estrada, The Fingerjoint, Elana Mann, Ni Santas Collective, Austin Young, and Yarn Bombing Los Angeles.

Visual artists: Pato Hebert, Marsian de Lellis, Dakota Noot, and Julio Salgado.

Video PSA artists: Adebukola (Buki) Bodunrin, Mail Order Brides/M.O.B. (Eliza Barrios, Reanne Estrada, and Jenifer Wofford), Gloria Morán, Meena Nanji, and Caress Reeves.

Video-screening artists: Arshia Fatima Haq in collaboration with Cassils, Johanna Breiding, Deanna Erdman, Andre Keichian, and T. M. Felderstein.

Art organizations: ArtworxLA, Dirty Looks, Feminist Library on Wheels, KCHUNG, Los Angeles Contemporary Exhibitions (LACE), Las Fotos Project, Otis College of Art and Design, Self Help Graphics, and Feminist Center for Creative Work.

Activist organizations: AF3IRM, Black Lives Matter, Gender Justice LA, Peace Over Violence, and People for Mobility Justice, with La Mikia Castillo as emcee.

Producers: Anne Bray, Jackie Castillo, Soyun Cho, Sara Daleiden, Nateene Diu, Fefifolios, Ginger Holguin, Marcus Kuiland-Nazario, Vera Makianich, and Gina Valona.

Curatorial advisers: Evonne Gallardo, David Orozco, Daisy Noemi, and Dirty Looks.

Moderators: Evonne Gallardo, Nicole Kelly, Marcus Kuiland-Nazario, Elana Mann, and Kristina Wong.

Rahel Aima is an art critic, writer, editor, and associate editor at Momus. Her writing has appeared in or at *4 Columns*, *Artforum*, *Art in America*, *Artnews*, *ArtReview*, *Atlantic*, *Bidoun*, *Bookforum*, *e-flux architecture*, *Frieze*, *Garage*, *Harper's Bazaar*, *Art Arabia*, *Mousse*, *New Republic*, *Real Life*, *Rest of World*, *Tank*, *Vogue Arabia*, and *World Policy Journal*, among many other publications. Based in Dubai, she regularly contributes exhibition texts, catalogue essays, and book chapters.

Tiffany E. Barber is a scholar, curator, and critic whose writing and commentary has appeared in academic journals, popular media, and documentaries. Her work spans abstraction, dance, fashion, feminism, and ethics of representation and focuses on artists of the Black diaspora in the United States and beyond. Barber is assistant professor of Africana studies and art history at the University of Delaware. During 2021–2022, she was completing her first book as a postdoctoral fellow at the Getty Research Institute.

Badly Licked Bear is or has been an arts administrator, community leader, writer, curator, student, artist, and educator. Their artistic work stands in two circles— one a performance practice of embodied discipline and the other a subject-making practice concerned with survival. Their work has been exhibited or performed at venues MOCA Los Angeles, the Hammer Museum, REDCAT, Human Resources LA, and others, including less institutional locales. Their work is in the library collections of MoMA , the Met, and Otis College.

Catherine Bell is a user-experience/user-interface designer who specializes in working with art museums and fine artists. She designs tech to spark a human connection with artifacts of the past and present. Her clients have included Barbara Kruger, David Byrne and Brian Eno, Sam Durant, Cassils, the Robert Mapplethorpe Foundation, and the Getty Museum. She teaches at USC and holds an MFA in photography and integrated media from CalArts.

Christy Roberts Berkowitz, an artist, educator, agitator, and emotional laborer, composes experiences, images, and objects to reconcile the intersections of resistance and escapism, community and individualism. A third-generation Southern Californian, Berkowitz holds an MFA from Claremont Graduate University. She is an associate professor at Riverside City College and the University of La Verne. She has exhibited at the American Jewish University, CURRENT LA, KCHUNG, MOCA Los Angeles, Getty, Telfair, Chrysler, REDCAT, the Hammer, and the Los Angeles County Museum of Art, among other places.

April Bey grew up in the Bahamas and now resides in Los Angeles, where she is a visual artist and art educator. Her interdisciplinary artwork is an introspective and social critique of constructs of race within supremacist systems. Her work has been included in several solo shows and collected by

the California African American Museum, the National Art Gallery of the Bahamas, and other venues. She has exhibited internationally, including in biennials in the Bahamas. Bey is currently a tenured professor at Glendale College.

bitchface is hosted and produced by Nicole Kelly and Phoebe Unter. Kelly and Unter have also collaborated on parties, a collection of zines, and live events with KCRW and the One Archives. They also initially worked in a collective called Intersectionality NOW with Hyunjee Nicole Kim, a writer and editor residing and working in Los Angeles.

Adebukola (Buki) Bodunrin is a Nigerian Canadian film and video artist who explores language, culture, and media. In her collage animations, she manipulates film using unorthodox manual and digital techniques to produce unexpected experiences. Her animation has been featured on the TV series *Transparent* and KCET's program *Lost LA*, for which she won a Los Angeles Area Emmy. Her work has been collected by the Whitney Museum and screened by the Rotterdam Film Festival, Images, Anthology Film Archives, BFI, Redcat, and MOCA Chicago.

boychild, a.k.a. Tosh Basco, is a movement-based performance artist now in Zurich. Her practice employs improvisation as a mode of survival and world building at the thresholds of becoming and representation. Her performances have been presented in museums, dance houses, and nightclubs, including at the Venice Biennale, MoMA PS1, MOCA Los Angeles, Stedelijk Museum, ICA London, and Berghain. Tosh Basco has toured with Mykki Blanco and collaborated with Korakrit Arunanondchai, Wu Tsang, and the streetwear label Hood By Air.

Anne Bray has been working at the intersection of public space and media art as a hybrid artist and director of the nonprofit arts organization LA Freewaves. Engagement with edgy, demanding, clarifying art by a broad public is Bray's mission. Questions are often the format. Her educational experience includes photography history at the Bibliotheque Nationale in Paris, new technology art with MIT artists, and new genres at UCLA (MFA, 1985), creating the conceptual framework to posit media arts as public art. She directed eleven biennial festivals presenting more than 3,000 artists with the partnership of 125 curators and 100-plus organizations, held at MOCA Los Angeles, Getty Center, Hammer Museum, on Hollywood and Chinatown streets, supported repeatedly by the National Endowment for the Arts as well as by the MacArthur, Rockefeller, Rauschenberg, and Warhol Foundations. As an artist, she has produced public-art projects and mixed-media installations at the Armory Center for the Arts, Side Street Projects, Highways, NewTown, Civitella Ranieri, Santa Barbara Contemporary Arts Forum, Public Art Fund, First Night, SkyArt Festival, New York Avant Garde Festival, Sixth International Triennial of Art at Umetostna Gallery, Cité des arts et nouvelles technologies de Montreal,

Banff Center, Pacific Film Archive, Artist Space, Hayden Gallery at MIT, and other venues. As a lecturer, she taught graduate seminars for 25 years in the new genre arts at Claremont Graduate University as well as in digital art and public art at USC. She has given and participated in 150 lectures, juries, and panels in Los Angeles and throughout the world.

Nao Bustamante's precarious work encompasses performance art, video, virtual reality, visual art, film, and writing. According to the *New York Times*, "She has a knack for using her body" (July 5, 2009). Bustamante has presented in high-end and underground sites worldwide. In 2021, Bustamante showed at REDCAT and ArtPace San Antonio, and in 2022 she performed at Park Avenue Armory. An alum of the San Francisco Art Institute, she is currently associate professor and vice dean of Art at USC.

Martha Carrillo is a visual and theatrical artist with expertise in prop making, set decoration, printmaking, and large-scale papier-mâché objects. Martha curates a recurring series of live arts and music events as Heart On Productions and is a teaching artist with the Self Help Graphics & Art's Barrio Mobile Art Studio team. She has also worked with the Music Center, Center Theater Group, and other organizations.

Cassils, raised in Montreal and living in Los Angeles, is a transgender artist who makes their own body the material and protagonist of their performances. Cassils's art contemplates the histories of LGBTQI+ violence, representation, struggle, and survival to examine the present moment, drawing from the idea that bodies are formed in relation to forces of power and social expectations. They have had solo exhibitions at Human Measure, Phillips Gallery One, MOCA Perth, Station Museum, Ronald Feldman Fine Arts, and National Gallery of the Republic of Macedonia, among other venues.

La Mikia Castillo is a consultant at Castillo Consulting Partners and is dedicated to empowering diverse leaders to use their voices for systemic change. She is also a community organizer, urban planner, policy analyst, and adjunct professor at USC, where she received her master's in public policy and urban planning. She focuses on health, foster care, and Latinx-Black relations.

Chan & Mann was a collaborative LA-based duo comprising Audrey Chan and Elana Mann from 2005 to 2018. Both artists are dedicated to liberating, motivating, and gyrating through feminist and ethnic roleplay within live, painted, and animated realities. Their projects occurred at Otis College of Art & Design and the LA Art Fair as well as on postcards and a bus tour. Elana Mann has received numerous awards and presented her work in museums, galleries, and public spaces internationally. She has had recent solo exhibitions at the 18th Street Art Center, Artpace, Pitzer College Art Galleries, and Commonwealth & Council. Audrey Chan is an artist, illustrator, and educator. Her researched projects use drawing, painting, public art, and video to challenge dominant historical narratives. She created public art for the Little Tokyo Metro Station and was artist-in-residence at the ACLU of Southern California.

Olivia Chumacero is a First Nation being of the Americas. An artist and author living in California, she speaks of our responsibility to the flora and the fauna of our home planet. Drawing from blood memory she teaches Indigenous ways of reciprocity and reiterates that we are integral in nature. Founder of Everything is Medicine (e.i.m.), Chumacero says that it is a class, a community, a vision, a way of life, where modern scientific and traditional Indigenous knowledge are woven together.

Allison Noelle Conner is an interdisciplinary writer, performer, and zine-maker. She holds an MFA in creative writing from CalArts. She is currently at work on her first book, a prose project exploring institutionalization, Black woman geographies, and possessions. She lives in Los Angeles. Her writing has appeared in *Bitch*, *Full Stop*, *Triangle House Review*, *Contemporary Art Review Los Angeles*, *Hyperallergic*, and elsewhere. She writes about movies at loosepleasures.substack.com.

Marsian de Lellis is an LA-based artist who investigates animism, desire, and neurodivergence. They employ artificial figures, cutouts, pop-ups, performing objects, and wearable architecture. They construct installations and tactile spectacles that memorialize obsessional lives. They hold an MFA from CalArts and have received numerous grants and appeared in many group exhibitions. Their work as a puppeteer informs their visual work. De Lellis is now developing an installation-performance hybrid, a morbid comedy centered on a disgruntled dollhouse maker turned investigator.

Zackary Drucker is an independent artist, cultural producer, and trans woman who breaks down the way we think about gender, sexuality, and seeing. She has performed and exhibited her work internationally in museums, galleries, and film festivals, including the Whitney Biennial 2014, MoMA PS1, the Hammer Museum, the Art Gallery of Ontario, MOCA San Diego, and MoMA San Francisco, among others. Drucker is an Emmy-nominated producer for the docuseries *This Is Me* as well as a producer on the Golden Globe and Emmy-winning series *Transparent*.

Earth to Jordi is a gender-expanding, multidimensional artist, facilitator, and guide, weaving healing energy into all of their practices. Their performance artwork has been welcomed at the Getty Center and the Banff Centre. They have guided group-care workshops centered around meditation, ritual, herbology, and decolonial organizing for the liberation of marginalized people. Most recently, they spoke at UCLA and the Hammer and guided workshops at Vimeo, Headspace, and Navel LA.

rafa esparza is a multidisciplinary LA artist whose work reveals his own relationship to colonization and its disrupted genealogies. Grounded in labor with land and adobe making, esparza employs site specificity, materiality, and memory to expose ideologies, power structures, and binary forms of identity. He invites Brown and queer cultural producers to realize large-scale collective projects, gathering people together to build networks. His work has been recognized by multiple national awards and featured in numerous solo shows, performances, and group shows.

Reanne Estrada is an LA-based visual artist whose practice includes drawing, sculpture, and installation. She collaborates on performance, video, and photography with Mail Order Brides/M.O.B. and on socially engaged art with the social enterprise Public Matters, where she is creative director. Her work has been shown in exhibitions and film/video festivals in the United States and abroad. Since 2015, she has collaborated with *C. Ree* on work about alternate systems of knowledge and everyday worldmaking. Ree's new genres practice focuses on the quotidian, monstrous, and the fantastic. Ree launched Drive-By Cinema and publishes articles on art, colonialism, dispossession, and haunting. She is one-third of the artist group Super Futures Haunt Collective, a film programmer for the San Diego Asian Film Festival, and associate professor of art at Mira Costa College.

Exposure Drag is a weekly drag show and dance party on Monday nights at 8:00 p.m. at the Offbeat on York Boulevard in Highland Park, Los Angeles.

Funmilola Fagbamila is a Nigerian American playwright, artist, and scholar. Her internationally touring play *The Intersection: Woke Black Folk* was met with critical acclaim. Funmilola teaches Pan African studies at Cal State LA. As an original organizer of Black Lives Matter, Funmilola contributed to its inception in 2013 and served as its arts and culture director in Los Angeles for years. Funmilola has delivered keynote addresses and performances at UCLA, Oxford, Stanford, and Harvard.

Roya Falahi, an artist born in Washington, DC, now lives and works in Pasadena, California. Using the realism of large-format photography, Falahi captures surreal narrative tableaux that explore disguise and veiling. Informed by the global political context, Iranian American culture, hard-rock music, and pop-culture/fashion imagery, Falahi's work investigates issues of identity and culture. Falahi received her BA from the University of California at Irvine and her MFA from UCLA . Falahi had solo shows at the Vincent Price Art Museum and Cal Poly Pomona.

Rudy "Bleu" Garcia is a first-generation, LA-born Chicano, queer, mover, shaker, organizer, curator, and zine maker. Rudy began organizing in the late 1990s while writing his seminal queer zine *Scutter*. For World of Wonder, he produced RuPaul's DragCon LA in 2015 and the first New York edition in 2017. He has curated group shows at Charlie James Gallery and other spaces and manages the rising vocal priestess San Cha.

Janice Gomez and Fatima Hoang are multidisciplinary artists and educators living and sometimes collaborating in Los Angeles. Together they accept challenges and redefine rules, sometimes even winning national air-guitar competitions. They are cofounders and codirectors of Summercamp's ProjectProject, an artist-run exhibition space in El Sereno, California. They have exhibited in New York, Washington, DC, Milwaukee, Honolulu, and Southern California.

Alexandra Grant is an LA-based artist who uses text in various media to probe notions of translation, identity, dis/location, and social responsibility. She has collaborated with the author Michael Joyce, the actor Keanu Reeves, the artist Channing Hansen, the philosopher Hélène Cixous, and others. She asks how languages and images form how we think and exchange ideas. Grant has exhibited widely at international galleries, and her work is included in the collections of MOCA Los Angeles and the Los Angeles County Museum of Art, among other venues.

Raquel Gutiérrez is an arts critic/writer, poet, and educator in Tucson. Born and raised in Los Angeles, Gutiérrez is a recipient of the Rabkin Prize in Arts Journalism and the Andy Warhol Foundation Arts Writers Grant. Their writing has appeared in *Art in America*, NPR Music, *Places Journal*, and the *Georgia Review*. Their first book of prose, *Brown Neon* (2022), an ekphrastic memoir, considers what it means to be a Latinx artist during the Trump era.

Pato Hebert is an artist, educator, and cultural worker based in New York City and Los Angeles. His work explores the aesthetics, ethics, and poetics of interconnectedness. He has developed innovative approaches to advocacy and HIV prevention in queer communities of color since 1994. He has presented recent projects at Beton7 in Athens, MOCA Zagreb, and the Chrysler Museum. Hebert's work has been supported by the Rockefeller Foundation, Creative Work Fund, and other organizations. He teaches at New York University.

Micol Hebron is an interdisciplinary artist who has engaged in individual and collaborative projects since 1992. Her practice includes studio work, curation, writing, social media, crowdsourcing, teaching, and public speaking. Hebron is an associate professor at Chapman University. She has also founded/directed multiple projects for the larger creative community, including the Situation Room, the Gallery Tally Poster Project about gender equity in contemporary galleries, and the online Digital Pasty/Gender Equity initiative.

féi hernandez is a trans, immigrant artist, writer, and healer raised in Ingelwood, California. They have been published in *POETRY*, *Pank Magazine*, *Oxford Review of Books*, *Frontier Poetry*, and *The Breakbeat Poets*, vol. 4: *LatiNext*, among other publications. They are a Define American Fellow for 2021, the board president of Gender Justice LA, and the author of the full-length poetry collection *Hood Criatura* (2020), which NPR included in its Best Books of 2020 list.

Sebastian Hernández is a Los Angeles native and multidisciplinary trans femme artist who received a BA in both art practice and dance and performance studies from the University of California at Berkeley in 2016. They make art that ranges from sculptures to performance art to photography. They have presented works at REDCAT, Human Resources, Los Angeles Contemporary Exhibitions (LACE), Commonwealth & Council, the Geffen Contemporary at MOCA Los Angeles, Institute of Contemporary Arts Los Angeles, MUSTACHE Mondays, Performance Space New York, Club Scum, NAVEL LA, and other venues.

Carolina Ibarra-Mendoza is a graphic designer, visual artist, and Xicana feminist from East Los Angeles. She has a double bachelor's degree from the University of California Davis in gender studies and design and an MFA in graphic design from Otis College of Art and Design. She notably worked with Suzanne Lacy and Leslie Labowitz-Starus as the creative strategist and web designer for the feminist archive website AgainstViolence.Art, which was featured in a MoMA San Francisco exhibition in 2019.

Amelia Jones is the Robert A. Day Professor and vice dean of academics and research at USC. Jones's retrospective *Ron Athey Queer Communion: Ron Athey* took place at Participant Inc and the Institute of Contemporary Arts Los Angeles in 2021 and was accompanied by an edited catalogue by the same title. Her book *In Between Subjects: A Critical Genealogy of Queer Performance* (2021) presents 60 years of theory and practice around the ideas of "queer," "gender performance," and "performativity." Her newest book will address the structural racism of the art world and its institutions.

Nicole Kelly (NK) is a writer and independent audio producer whose work moves toward discomfort and hidden feeling. Based in Los Angeles, she is the senior producer for *Black Mountain Radio Hour* and holds an MFA in writing from the University of California at Irvine. Her audio work has aired on the Heart, VICE's Source Material, and Afropunk's Solutions Sessions, and she was a co-creator and host of bitchface. NK was the first programming director of the Feminist Center for Creative Work, where she edited the workbook *Decolonizing Nonviolent Communication*.

Olga Koumoundouros received an MFA from CalArts in 2001. In her artwork, she currently examines the economics and flow of energy and resources within the dynamics of labor that provide sustenance for all humans. Koumoundouros has had solo exhibitions at Commonwealth & Council, Los Angeles Nomadic Division, Clockshop, Vielmetter Los Angeles, the Hammer Museum, Project Row Houses in Houston, and L.A. Louver.

Marcus Kuiland-Nazario, a Los Angeles native, is an interdisciplinary artist, performance curator, and producer. His works are long-term, research-based, cross-genre projects exploring extreme states of emotion, such as grief and anger, and influenced by cultural and spiritual traditions. His performance works have been included in national and international festivals. He is a founding artist of 18th Street Arts Center, Oficina de Proyectos Culturales, and the LA Community Health Project. He recently received the Santa Monica Artist Fellowship.

Las Fotos Project's mission is to elevate the voices of teenage girls and gender-expansive youth from communities of color through photography and mentoring, empowering them to channel their creativity for the benefit of themselves, their community, and future careers. It was launched to provide opportunities for those who are both systemically and socially silenced to make themselves heard, advocate for social change, and create their own pathways to successful, creative futures.

Melissa Lo is a feminist historian of early-modern science, medicine, and visual culture. Her current interests lie in intersectional histories of medicine, paradoxes of visual representation, and critical history. She is a freelance researcher and writer and currently serves as development producer with Mash-Up Americans. She has taught in the Department of History at UCLA, has contributed to SCI-Arc's Liberal Arts curriculum, and was founding faculty at Cedars-Sinai's Program in the History of Medicine.

Mail Order Brides/M.O.B. (Eliza Barrios, Reanne Estrada, and Jenifer Wofford) work collaboratively as M.O.B., a trio of Filipina American artists engaged in an ongoing conversation about culture and gender. Enforced enlightenment has arrived in the form of karaoke videos and museum makeovers, photographic psychodramas and parade performances, bridesmaid entrepreneurships and corporate dominations. M.O.B. has exhibited at de Young Museum, Yerba Buena Center for the Art, Southern Exposure, and San Jose Museum of Art, and their videos have screened widely.

Jennifer Moon, a conceptual artist, began in 2009 to create the Revolution, a movement that envisions a worldwide shift in thinking through principles of abundance and continuous expansion. Blending political theory, self-help, and fantasy, Moon uses the Revolution in performances, videos, writing, and sculpture. Moon also leads "death of self" workshops, publishes writing, and hosts a radio show on KCHUNG. She has collaborated with laub on shows at the Getty Center, Commonwealth & Council, and the Armory Center for the Arts.

Gloria Morán, a postmodern chola filmmaker-writer born and bred in the Bay Area. Morán directed the short documentary *The Unique Ladies* (2011), about San Diego's only all-women lowrider club. She has worked in partnership with ITVS (Independent Television Service), the *American Experience* series for PBS, WORLD Channel, and the Corporation for Public Broadcasting. Her self-produced videos and her video work with mitú, attn: media, and All Def Digital have garnered more than 20 million views.

Amitis Motevalli, an artist born in Iran, explores the cultural resistance and survival of people living in poverty, conflict, and/or war. Through sculpture, video, performance, and collaborative public art, her work juxtaposes iconography with iconoclasm. She asks about violence, occupation, and decolonization and invokes the significance of a secular grassroots struggle. She lives in Los Angeles, exhibits her art internationally, and creates an active and resistant cultural discourse through information exchange in art, pedagogy, and activism.

Meena Nanji is an award-winning filmmaker who has produced, written, and directed independent documentaries and experimental videos. *View from a Grain of Sand* (2006), about women's rights in Afghanistan, won several awards at film festivals and was broadcast on international TV. She cofounded Global Girl Media and has produced short films for Channel 4 UK and RAI TV Italy. Her work has been supported by grants from the Rockefeller Foundation, the National Endowment for the Arts, and the Paul Robeson Fund.

Thinh Nguyen is an artist, educator, curator, and cultural critic whose works investigate the intersections of cultural values. Utilizing various media, they explore and expose oppressive sociopolitical power structures. Nguyen has performed and exhibited nationally and internationally, most recently at the Mistake Room, the Hammer Museum, REDCAT, Los Angeles Contemporary Exhibitions (LACE), and the Contemporary Irish Art Center Los Angeles. Their work has been written about in *Artforum*, the *LA Times*, *Los Angeles Magazine*, *LA Weekly*, *Hyperallergic*, *Artillery Magazine*, and numerous online forums.

Ni Santas is a women-of-color collective with a shared attraction to graffiti whose mission is to write their history through art and to create socially conscious visual narratives. Ni Santas envisions creating a safe space by cultivating a community of women, free of judgment, to nourish emerging artists. The collective is currently composed of Andi Xoch, former Ovarian Psyco-Cycles (OPC) member Joan Zeta, and the Clover Signs, who has also joined OPC bicycle rides.

Dakota Noot, an LA-based artist, uses drawings, paintings, and installations to create animal–human hybrids that explore rural yet fantastical queer identities. Originally from Bismarck, North Dakota, he continues to show in both North Dakota and Los Angeles, including in solo and two-person shows at Highways Performance Space, MuzeuMM, and PØST. His cutout-drawing installations have been shown at Cerritos College Art Gallery and Otis College. He holds an MFA from Claremont Graduate University and is an adjunct professor at Oxnard College and Orange Coast College.

Eve Oishi is an associate professor in Claremont Graduate University's Cultural Studies Department. Her primary research interests include Asian American cultural studies, independent and experimental film and video, transnational media, and gender and queer theory. With a PhD in English literature from Rutgers University, Oishi is the recipient of several postdoctoral fellowships, including a Mellon Postdoctoral Fellowship and Fellow-in-Residence at the Humanities Research Institute at the University of California at Irvine. She is also an independent film and video curator.

Monica Orozco creates photographic images that are dark, quirky, and sexy, with a touch of the vintage. Her work has been published in magazines and online, including in *Anthem*, *Spin*, *Time Out London*, *Interview*, *Swindle*, *Whitehot*, *Westside*, *JPG*, *ARTINFO*, and *ForYourArt*, and has been shown in Berlin, London, New York, San Francisco, and Los Angeles.

Ovarian Psyco-Cycles (OPC) is a bicycle brigade established in Boyle Heights, Los Angeles, in 2010. The group was formed to foster a sisterhood in which its members could feel comfortable taking up space as well confronting the harassment of women. Public rides have been organized monthly on the full moon. A documentary about the group by Joanna Sokolowski and Kate Trumbull-LaValle premiered in 2016 and was screened on PBS in 2017.

Reach LA, a nonprofit organization, showcases vogue dancing, heels class, visual art, poetry, drag, and video, highlighting emerging performance and visual arts talent. It provides inclusive sexual health services, such as a safe space to discuss the social determinants of health faced by marginalized communities impacted by HIV. It hosts socializing groups for LGBTQ people and their allies to deliberate on social justice, sexual health, and more. Gaymer Nights focus on social interaction through group games and community building.

Eva Recinos is an arts and culture journalist and creative nonfiction writer who tells stories left out of mainstream media. She focuses primarily on visual art and design, often in Los Angeles, where she was born and raised. In her creative nonfiction writing, she explores Latinx identity, education, and mental health. She was a recent finalist for awards from the LA Press Club, Center for Women Writers International Literary Awards, and Pen America Emerging Voices Fellowship, among others.

Caress Reeves is an animator in 2D, director, designer, and special-effects artist. She uses animation to tell psychological stories and display physically impossible feats. Her personal work has screened in animation and film festivals such as the International Black Film Festival, and she works as a compositor at Stoopid Buddy Stoodios. She holds an MFA in animation from USC.

Alma Ruiz is former senior curator at MOCA Los Angeles, where she curated numerous exhibitions of emerging artists and art in the postwar United States, Italy, and Latin America. She also served as the curator of 20 Bienal de Arte Paiz, Guatemala City, and has curated exhibitions at Fundación Jumex, Mexico City; the Center for Contemporary Art, Tel Aviv; Fundación Telefónica, Buenos Aires; and the Fowler Museum at UCLA . Ruiz is advising Self Help Graphics for the Getty's initiative Pacific Standard Time: Art x Science x LA.

Shizu Saldamando uses portraiture to assert agency and reclaim representation for her subjects, who are her friends and fellow members of the Chicanx creative community. Shizu was born and raised in San Francisco's Mission District, received her BA from UCLA and her MFA from CalArts, and currently lives in Los Angeles. She has exhibited widely, including at the Smithsonian American Art Museum, the National Museum of Mexican Art, Occidental College, and the Charlie James Gallery. Her work is collected by the Los Angeles County Museum of Art, the Crystal Bridges Museum, Cheech Marin, and others.

Julio Salgado is the cofounder of Dreamers Adrift and the Migrant Storytelling Manager for the Center for Cultural Power. His status as an undocumented, queer artivist fuels his visual art, which depicts key moments of the DREAM Act and the migrant rights movement. Undocumented students, organizers, and allies across the country have used Salgado's artwork to call attention to migrant rights. He has exhibited at the Oakland Museum, the MoMA San Francisco, and the Smithsonian.

Patty Schemel is a songwriter and musician who rose to prominence as the drummer of the platinum-selling band Hole from 1992 until 1998. In 2010, Schemel cocreated *Hit so Hard*, a documentary and book chronicling her time in Hole. She continues to perform, teach, and tour with various bands, including Object as Subject, a witchy, feminist, art punk project led by Paris Hurley and fueled by raw keening vocals, explicit gestural iterations, and relentless phrases of wild abandon.

Safi Alia Shabaik, a.k.a. flashbulbfloozy, is a founding member of the Los Angeles Street Collective and an artist working in photography, collage, sculpture, and experimental video. Her photographs have been featured in several magazines and in Grace Jones's book *I'll Never Write My Memoirs* (2015). In partnership with the Parkinson's Foundation, Shabaik is now nationally exhibiting Personality Crash, about her father's experience with Parkinson's, courtesy of an National Endowment for the Arts grant.

#SNATCHPOWER is a postapocalyptic, Black Indigenous, futuristic, queer liberationist artist collective of humans who are deliberate and fearless. They are diverse in how they define themselves in terms of race, class, gender, sexual orientation, political affiliation, and religion but are united in their commitment to self-definition, self-expression, self-governance, and nonhierarchical collaboration. They subvert the hegemonic mainstream through radical Queer artistic expression. *The Uhuruverse*, a.k.a. Uhuru Ali Moor, is their electric guitarist and singer, a transgender nonconforming Los Angeles- and New Orleans-based artist. They also cofounded the band FUCK U PAY US (FUPU).

sondriaWRITES is a writer, performer, and media-content provider based in the Inland Empire. She is also a contributing member of #SNATCHPOWER. She has released short-story collections such as *Boxes & Bottles of Booze: A Series of Therapeutic Fiction and Unthinkable Acts* (2017). Sondria also teaches private writing lessons and hosts community-based writing workshops. She writes with flare about music, fur, fat, and facts for podcasts, zines, and publications.

Alejandra Sone is a Chilean photographer currently working in Los Angeles whose photography tells personal, textural stories. Sone has a BA in design from the Universidad de Valparaíso and is currently enrolled in the MFA photography program at the New York Film Academy. She does freelance work in the street and studio.

Davia Spain's art is a mélange of mediums, a stew of classical and jazz training, electronic experimentation, theater, intrepid filmmaking, and sinuous dance. Through live performances, she creates experiences that are tempestuous and capricious. Her sets use minimalist staging and instrumentation to create an experience that is as soothing as it is inspiring. Spain's artistic journey started in church at a very young age, and the music of our past girds her present-day Afrofuturistic explorations.

Valorie Thomas, the Phebe Estelle Spalding Professor of English and Africana Studies at Pomona College, originated the concept of "diasporic vertigo" as a motif of decolonization. Thomas studies film and visual art; has an ongoing interest in the healing connections among writing, art, and social justice; and is the author of academic essays, op-eds, screenplays, and creative nonfiction. She recently curated an art exhibition titled *Vertigo@Midnight*, inspired by her work on Afrofuturism, speculative art, and spirituality.

Karen Tongson is an associate professor of English, gender and sexuality studies, and American studies and ethnicity at USC. She is the recipient of the Lambda Literary Jeanne

Córdova Award for Lesbian/Queer Nonfiction, the author of *Why Karen Carpenter Matters* (2019) and *Relocations: Queer Suburban Imaginaries* (2011), and the coeditor of the Postmillennial Pop book series at New York University Press. Her commentary has appeared in NPR, the *LA Times*, and the *Washington Post*, among other media. She now cohosts the podcast *Waiting to X-hale*.

Marisa Turesky is a PhD candidate in Urban Planning and Development at the University of Southern California. She examines how identity, especially gender, race, and class, shapes peoples' housing and urban service needs across the lifespan. Her research and publications in top urban planning journals use interdisciplinary and mixed-methods approaches to advance our understanding of how cities and neighborhoods can create places and networks for historically underserved communities to navigate care and loneliness.

Phoebe Unter makes audio and visual art interrogating things people avoid talking about. She was a senior producer for the most recent season of *The Heart*, an award-winning podcast about power and intimacy. Before that, she cocreated bitchface, an experimental audio project, with Nicole Kelly. She produced the first season of *Checking In*, a health-and-wellness advice podcast from Conde Nast's *SELF Magazine*, and the debut of a companion podcast to HBO's queer teen dramedy *genera+ion*.

Anuradha Vikram is a writer, curator, critic, and educator based in Los Angeles. She works with process-based, public, and participatory art forms, with a focus on transcultural approaches to technology, social engagement, and the body. She is co-curator of *Atmosphere of Sound: Sonic Art in Times of Climate Disruption*, part of the upcoming Getty initiative Pacific Standard Time: Art x Science x LA. Her book *Decolonizing Culture* (2017), a collection of 17 essays, addresses questions of race and gender parity in contemporary art spaces. She is on the faculty at UCLA.

Catherine G. Wagley is an art critic and journalist based in Los Angeles. She is an editor at *Contemporary Art Review Los Angeles* and at *Momus*. She served as an art critic for the *LA Weekly* from 2011 to 2017 and contributes to *artnet News*, *Artnews*, *LA Times*, and the *LAnd*, among other publications. She is a recipient of the Rabkin Prize for Visual Art Journalism.

Holly Willis cochairs the Media Arts + Practice program at USC. Her research centers on handmade feminist film practices as well as postimage, postcinematic, and posthuman digital-image capture. Her writing spans arts journalism, creative nonfiction, and scholarly forms, including the books *Fast Forward: The Future(s) of the Cinematic Arts* (2016), *New Digital Cinema: Reinventing the Moving Image* (2005), and the exhibition catalog *Björk Digital* (2017. Her own image-based work explores cyanotypes, phytograms, animation, photogrammetry, and image processing.

Kristina Wong is a performance artist, comedian, writer, and elected representative whose work has been presented across North America, the United Kingdom, Hong Kong, and Africa. She has been a guest on shows on NBC, Comedy Central, and FX. She is a recipient of a residency from MacDowell and of grants from Creative Capital and the MAP Fund. *Kristina Wong for Public Office* is simultaneously a real-life stint and rally campaign show, filmed for Center Theater Group. During the pandemic, Kristina founded Auntie Sewing Squad as a mutual-aid collective, book, play, and residency.

Kiki Xtravaganza, a wardrobe stylist, designer, performance artist, and voguer, was just deemed a Ballroom Icon at the legendary House of Xtravaganza, established in 1982, and has been featured in *Paris Is Burning* and *Pose*.

Xina Xurner is an experimental music and performance collaboration between Marvin Astorga and Young Joon Kwak, whose cathartic performances combine do-it-yourself and power electronics, mutated vocals, and bad drag to expand ideas about queer and trans bodies. Xina Xurner has released two albums. They have performed at sCum, the Smell, the Hammer, Cool World, Mustache Mondays, and Los Angeles Contemporary Exhibitions (LACE) and have brought their performances to audiences in Paris, Tokyo, Seoul, and Mexico City.

Sue Bell Yank, executive director of Clockshop, is a writer, curator, and educator. She formerly served as deputy director at 18th Street Arts Center and head of Academic Programs at the Hammer Museum. Her expertise lies in art with social impact, public art, and cultural programming, and her interest in urban planning and affordable cities led to the podcast *Paved Paradise*. Yank received a BA from Harvard University and an MA in public-art studies from USC.

Austin Young is an image maker celebrated for his work in portrait photography. His numerous projects reveal the sublime qualities that make celebrated people unique. Based on a pop-culture iconography as well as through his trademark style and techniques, he has captured a broad range of musicians and artists, including Debbie Harry, Leigh Bowery, and Margaret Cho, among many others. His work has been shown internationally.

Yozmit, an LA-based performance artist, costume designer, and singer-songwriter, emphasizes the transformative body. Her ornate costumes shatter physical confines while expanding notions around identity. Her songs—a mixture of pansori, a traditional Korean genre, and electronic music—are captivating and spiritual. She was the first recipient of West Hollywood's grant for transgender artists. This "avant-garde vaudeville artist" has performed internationally